Online Teaching Tools

3 Manuscripts: Google Classroom, Google Apps, Teaching with Zoom

Emily Crawford

Table of content

Introduction to Google Classroom

The book will provide some practical tips about how to get started in google class, and why a middle school teacher will find it useful.

Most high school elective teachers are searching for tools and resources to save time and make their lives easier. Such a large part of your classroom time is taken up by the process of organizing students work and making sure your students are aware of all the upcoming assignments as a solution, several teachers have started using google classrooms to assist with classroom management. If your school provides you with a G Suite for Education (previously Google Apps for Education) account, you may want to look at setting up and maintaining google classrooms for all of your classes.

Google Classroom makes it very easy for all the teachers to provide a digital or hybrid learning classroom. Designed from the ground up with teacher feedback, the platform allows teachers to communicate with students, share innovative and technologically productive tools, and create creative projects and educational elements in their everyday lessons. Google Classroom streamlines the process of having students on the same page, connecting with others, and exchanging ideas through collaborative projects. You should continue using google classroom as a way to collect work and files that students turn in for grading. Like with every new device, the problem is: what can I do about it? You'll find practical ideas for using Google Classroom in this book, along with comprehensive guidance and screenshots to help you through the learning process. We're excited to teach you how to use this vital tool in your classroom. Once you start reading this book, you'll be able to see how far we've come to help you learn more about Google Classroom.

Before getting started with a Google Classroom summary, I’d love to share some information about me. I am a 26-year public high school American teacher. I hold a Bachelor's Degrees in History, and my passion is technology applied to teaching. I have always used Google tools since 2000, and now write books about teaching online in order to explain to other teacher how to use those tools for an effective learning.

Thank you for choosing this book, please leave a short review on Amazon, if you enjoy it. I would really love to hear your thoughts!

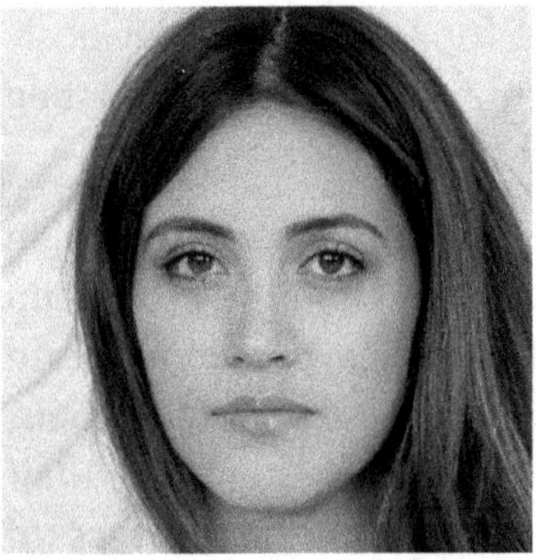

Thank you so much!
-Emily

Chapter1: Basics of Google Classroom

1.1 Getting Started with Google Classroom

What Is Google Classroom?

Google Classroom is an application that allows teachers to streamline the learning process for their students. Teachers can create a class within the Google Classroom, provide their students with an add-on code, or email them, and quickly start interacting with students about class details, assignments, and documents. As part of the Google Apps for Education series, Google Classroom incorporates the other Google Apps to provide a more seamless learning experience. Google Classroom is a free web service created by Google for Schools to simplify the creation, delivery, and grading of assignments in a paperless manner. The primary goal of Google Classroom is to streamline the process of sharing files between teachers and students. Google Classroom is an application only available for schools with Google Apps installed for Education or Google Apps for Non-Profit Accounts.

Google Classroom incorporates Google Drive for the creation and distribution of tasks, Google Docs, Sheets and Slides for writing, Gmail for correspondence, and Google Calendar for scheduling. Students can be invited to join a particular class using a secret code or automatically imported from a school domain. Each class creates a separate folder on the respective user's drive, where the student can send a job to the instructor. Mobile apps, available on iOS and Android devices, let users take images and add to assignments, share files from different apps, and access information offline. Teachers can track the progress of each pupil, and after graduation, teachers can return to work with feedback.

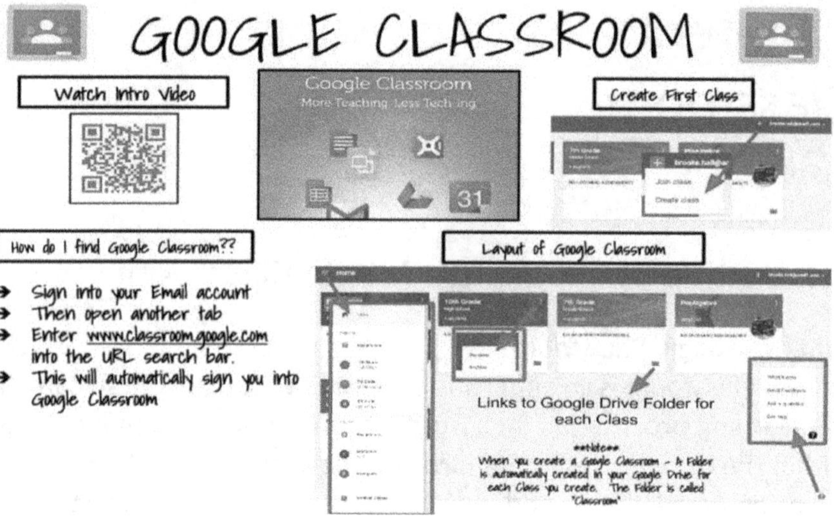

Google Software for Education (GAfE) is a free suite of Mobile resources available for schools. GAfE includes Gmail, Google Calendar, Google Drive, Google Docs, Google Pages, YouTube, Google Classroom, etc. Schools can sign up to https:/www.google.com/work/apps/education. Google Apps schools will have a Google Apps domain manager who can allocate accounts to staff and students. The Apps Manager can also allow or disable the features and products of Google Apps, depending on the needs of the school. By default, Google Classroom is available for teachers and students, so the Google Apps domain manager in the school or district does not need to be available.

History

Google Classroom was released on 6 May 2014, with a preview available to some of the participants of Google's G Suite for Education program. This was made public on 12 August 2014.

In 2015, Google introduced a Classroom API and a website sharing button to enable school administrators and developers to further connect with Google Classroom.

Google also incorporated Google Calendar into Classroom in 2015 for task dates, field trips, and class speakers.

In 2017, Google opened the classroom to allow any personal Google users to enter classes without the need to have a G Suite for Education account. In April of the same year, any private Google user was able to build and teach classes.

In 2018, Google announced the redesign of the classroom, the inclusion of a classwork area, the enhancement of the grading system, the re-use of classwork from other schools, and the introduction of teacher tools to organize material by subject.

In 2019, Google launched 78 new illustrated themes and the ability to drag and drop items and assignments in the classwork section.

What Does Google Classroom Do?

Google Classroom is situated between you and Google Drive and offers a teacher / student-friendly way to handle classroom documents. Here's what things can be done with Google Classroom:

- **Making Assignments**

The critical thing you, as a teacher, can do with Google Classroom is to make homework assignments for your students. Once you make an assignment, you will upload the documents you need for students to read or work on. Students may receive email notification of a new task. Students "turn in" assignments when they're done, and then you can list duties.

- **Make Announcements**

When you have a short report for the whole class, you can quickly type a statement that is sent to all the students in the class.

- **Store Classroom Items**

The items you apply to the assignment are not the only documents you can store. You can save any other materials you need for students on Google Drive.

- **Allow Students to Communicate With Each Other**

Students can comment on assignments and announcements, as well as to email each other through the Classroom app.

Overview of Google Drive and Docs

Google Docs (https://drive.google.com) provides users with online storage of digital documents. Google Docs for text documents, Google Slides for presentations, Google Sheets for spreadsheets, Google Drawing, and Google Forms can also be created on Google Drive. Students and teachers can use these collaboration resources to build documents from the cloud. This means that no hardware needs to be mounted on student devices; only an Internet connection is required. Students and teachers can access documents on Google Drive from any Internet-enabled computer, including mobile devices. Students are exempted from having to be on a particular network to do their work.

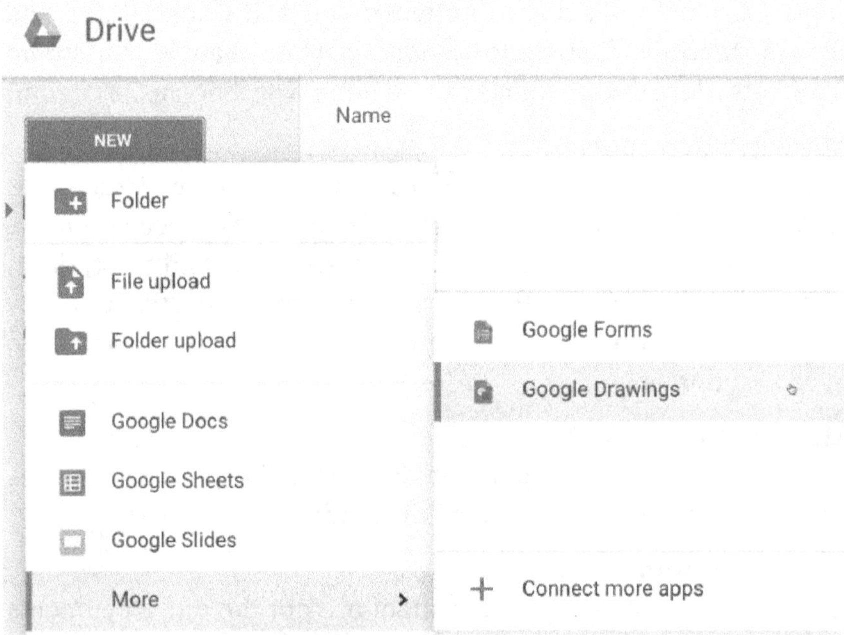

One of the most critical capabilities of Google Documents is real-time collaboration. Students and teachers can edit the text at the same time. Documents are accessed via a shared web connection or through Google Drive.

Collaborators of the same material just need to open the paper so that they can locate the new version and function side by side with other users. Since this collaboration is all cloud-based, there is no need for collaborators to be in the same space. Some classrooms have students working with students in other countries around the world. This ability eliminates confusion in the version. Collaborators on the document have the confidence to know that they are looking at the current version. Real-time collaboration has encouraged the process of peer review and input from students.

1.2 Importance and Benefits of Google Classroom

Why Is Google Classroom Important?

In today's changing world, students need to leave school with a range of technical skills that can help them succeed in the world job market. There's a great, fantastic resource for teachers that can help us give students the skills they need: Google Classroom.

Whether you've been using Google Classroom for the last few years, you're probably already "sold" why it's a good thing to use. But if it's new to you, you might want to learn why this change is a good thing for students. Here are a few things to consider:

Google Classroom Is Easy to Use

as compared to other LMS (Learning Management Systems) that have been popular over the last decade; Google Classroom is incredibly simple. It doesn't take much time or experience to set up a new classroom. Our tech team had been trained for about an hour, and all of us had a class set up and running by the end of the training.

More Efficient Means of Communication

You reach the students ' email addresses only once, and the contact in the classroom is completed. Only by joining the student at the school, the instructor immediately generates an email address, a discussion group, and a Google Calendar. And it's simple to add and remove students from the classroom as needed.

The Dominant Way of Communicating

Google Classroom allows you to communicate more effectively. Perhaps more important than being easy to use and effective, communication tools are also handy. Since it's all cloud-based, there's no more "loss" of student assignments. If the student is not present, contact is seamless. Just last month, Google Classroom introduced a parent notification feature to keep parents updated on what's going on in the "classroom."

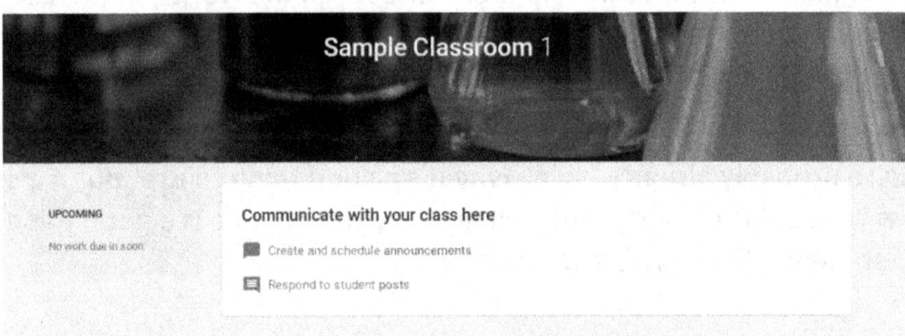

More Cost-Effective and Better for The Community

Paperless learning is not particularly satisfying for younger students. Yet a particular advantage for schools is that they are more profitable when it comes to copying and printing. If every student has a laptop that already links to the Internet, every sheet of paper that we save can just make the school more effective and environmentally friendly.

Method of Studying in The Future

This is how students can continue to study in the future, which is why we need to let our "paperless" hang-up go. University campuses no longer require undergraduates to print their five-page essays. As K-12 educators, we will take notice and train our students for the world in which they live.

Suitable for Students Who Struggle

It's better for students who struggle as long as you help them manage the system. (The computer itself can be a hassle at times, so handling it needs to be taught.) The reason why Google classroom is better is the organizational benefit it offers them. The assignments never get lost, and the instructor already coordinates every class.

However, something has to be taught to these students to handle. Even though students are digital natives, that doesn't mean they understand how adults structure their environment to help them learn.

More Straightforward Collaboration Outside of School

With Google Classroom, collaboration outside of school, is more candid (i.e., Flipped classroom). Again, it is cloud-based and available from anywhere with a connection. Students will exchange home assignments and work together to complete them. Collaboration is not limited to interacting with other peers in a group. Teachers can flip the classroom by uploading a video to go live in the evening, allowing students to watch it that night to practice for a quiz the next day. There are infinite possibilities.

Teacher Planning Is Easy

Teacher preparation is simple, and the up-front time is worth it. Some more new features in Google Classroom allow teachers to schedule assignments in the future. Designated tasks may be programmed to go live on a Monday in October, and then close on a Friday. When a teacher has a long absence, she would be able to arrange tasks and not have to rely on a sub to do all of them. Classrooms can also be used for the semester or year system. It would be horrible for a teacher to simply copy and paste a lesson for the next few groups of students, but it does save some time to have some stuff already in place (lesson curriculum, grading standards, etc.).

Instant Feedback

Through embedding elements, feedback is immediate and accessible. One of the teachers the other day had students complete a multiple-choice quiz while watching the film. It enhances interaction and transparency but still allows the instructor to see the results at the end of the lesson.

Instead, if students failed to respond with the correct answers, they may cover the material again.

Providing positive input to students is a crucial part of the learning process. Within the Classroom grading tool, teachers will give feedback on assignments to every student. The ability to create a comments bank for future use is also included in the grading method. Also, the Classroom mobile app helps users to annotate their work.

Updates Are Constant

This is, by far, one of Google Classroom's bestselling points. If something needs to be changed or corrected, Google will listen and respond (both the assignment schedule and the parent contact have come from this). It also means that teachers will have to start learning how to use it, which isn't a bad thing either!

Google Classroom Benefits

Google Classroom provides a range of opportunities for students and teachers as a free online learning site. Some of the main reasons why teachers should seek it out are discussed below.

Accessibility

The Google Classroom can be accessed from any computer through Google Chrome or from any mobile device on any platform. All files shared by teachers and students are stored in the Google Drive Classroom tab. Users can access the classroom at anytime, anywhere. Students no longer need to think about broken machines or hungry dogs.

Exposure

Today, many colleges expect students to take at least one online class before their graduation.

If you get a master's degree in education, some of your coursework may be online. Sadly, many of the students have never had any experience with online learning. That's why you want to make sure that you give your students as much exposure as possible at a young age. Google Classroom is a simple way to help students make this move because it's super user-friendly, making it a perfect intro to technology.

Paperless

teachers and students do not have too much paper to sort because the classroom is entirely paperless. When teachers upload tasks and tests to the classroom, they are saved to Drive simultaneously. Students will complete assignments and analyses directly from the school, and their research will also be collected to Drive. Students may access lost work due to absences and find other services that they may need.

Time Saver

The classroom is a huge time saver. For all the money available in one place and the freedom to access the class anytime, teachers will have more time to perform other tasks. Because the classroom can be accessed from a mobile device, teachers and students can participate in their phones or tablets.

Commitment

The majority of digital natives are confident with technology and would be more likely to take control of their learning by using technology. The classroom provides several ways to make learning immersive and collaborative. It provides teachers with the opportunity to separate assignments, to include videos and web pages in classes, and to create shared group assignments.

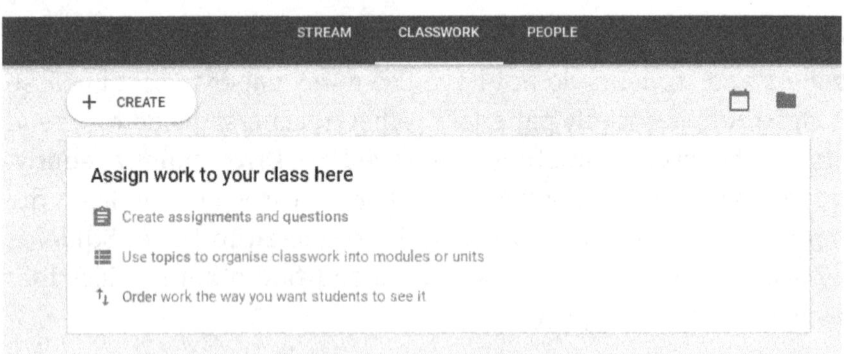

Differentiation

Teachers are quickly able to distinguish instruction for learners in the classroom. Assigning lessons to the entire class, to individual students, or groups of students takes only a few easy steps to build assignments on the Classwork board.

Data Analysis

To make learning meaningful, teachers should evaluate evaluation data to ensure that students recognize learning goals. Evaluation data can be quickly transferred to sorting and review sheets.

1.3 Features of Google Classroom

Google Classroom Google Classroom is a versatile resource for classroom management. This is a unique forum for student evaluation, assessment, and teacher-student contact. This is not as effective as LMS, maybe, but it still allows all participants in the learning process to produce better outcomes.

Google Classroom links all various Google resources to help teachers and organizations get paperless. Google Drive provides the assignments. Gmail is used for correspondence in the classroom. Students can receive updates in two ways: via an organization database and an individual file, which can then be applied to the student interface or exported from the LMS.

Some essential features of the Google Classroom can be used by both teachers and students to enhance learning and interaction.

Grading

Google Classroom grading can work with various grading schemes. Teachers should add assignments to text files that students should access, edit, and copy. Students can also build files. We will add their records to the task unless the instructor does it. Instructors can track the progress of every student working on the assignment. We can comment and edit it, too.

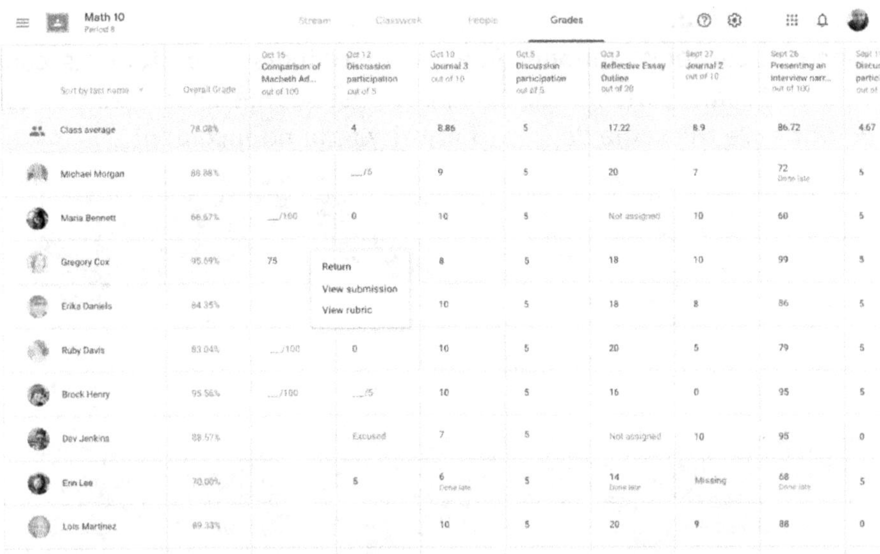

Assignments

Teachers store assignments in the Google Class and share them with students. The files are stored on the student's drive and then submitted when they are finished.

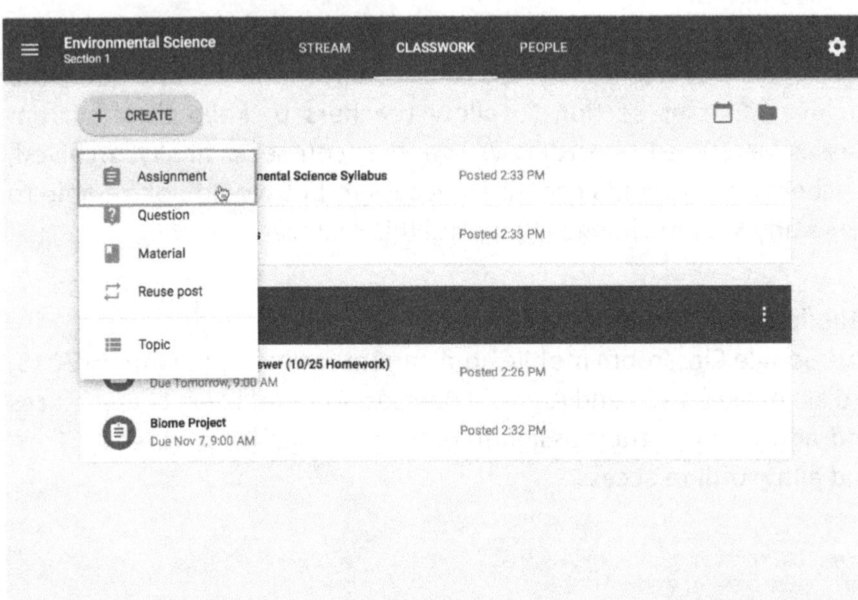

Communication

Teachers can post announcements to students, and students can vote on them. Students will also post class sources, but their places do not have the same degree of priority as announcements.

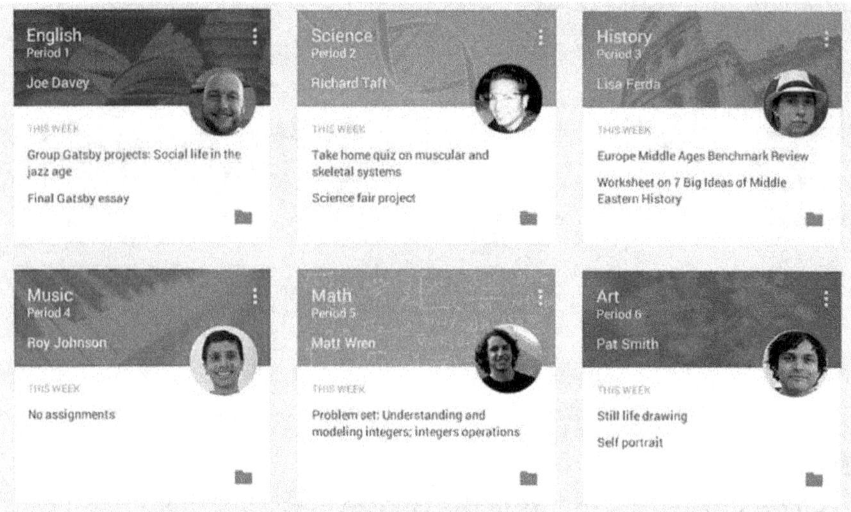

Archive Course

The classroom allows students to archive lessons at the end of the year. Once a course is filed, it is removed from the site and put in the Archived Classes section to allow teachers to keep their current classes organized accordingly. When a course is finally archived, teachers and students can easily access it, but would not be able to make any kind of changes to it until it is restored.

Mobile Applications

The Google Classroom mobile applications, released in January 2015, are available for iOS and Android devices. Apps let users take pictures and add them to their assignments, share files from other devices, and allow offline access.

Privacy

In comparison to Google's consumer services, Google Classroom, as part of G Suite for Education, does not display ads in its student, staff and instructor app, and user data is not scanned or used for advertising purposes.

New Features Added to Google Classroom

Originality Reports

Google Classroom's originality reports act as a tool to correct uncited content and potential plagiarism. Additional functionality added to Google Originality reports. This feature is no longer in beta mode-it's now available in French (French, French, and Portuguese are in beta) for those using the classroom.

Teachers must simply check the box to make this function appropriate for a mission.

Teachers are currently able to view originality reports for three tasks free of charge (if the school uses G-Suite Business, there are no constraints). All teachers and students are free to comment on the assignment at any time. The reports have expiry dates (because web content changes continuously). They will use the tool up to 3 times before students return their assignments. For each file sent, teachers can view reports.

After the completion of the originality study, the 'View Originality Report' link opens the report, highlighting any problems.

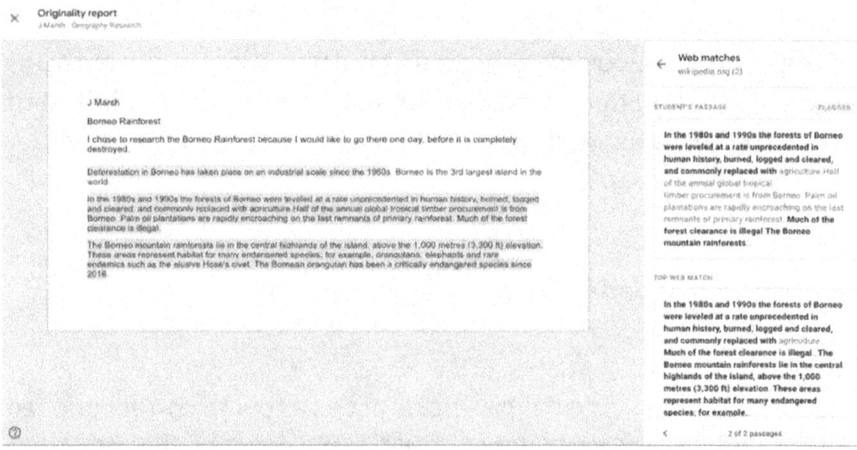

The study reveals the meaning of the flagged material, and confidently highlights the commonalities. When you click on the section, you can directly access the dubious content website. Eventually, school-owned repositories for content within each domain should be available to test student research internally. There is a difference between the overall percentage of the mission flagged and the number of flagged passages.

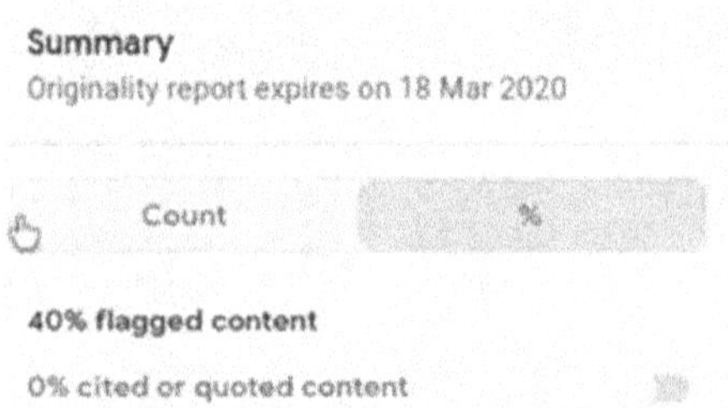

The method is less about "catching" a student in wrongdoing and more about helping them to recognize possible errors and to correct them before they finish their research.

Citations Using Explore

Students can use the Explore tool to quote sources that allow students to insert soccer notes in different quote formats. You just click on the button and explore links between the topics of documents and online content.

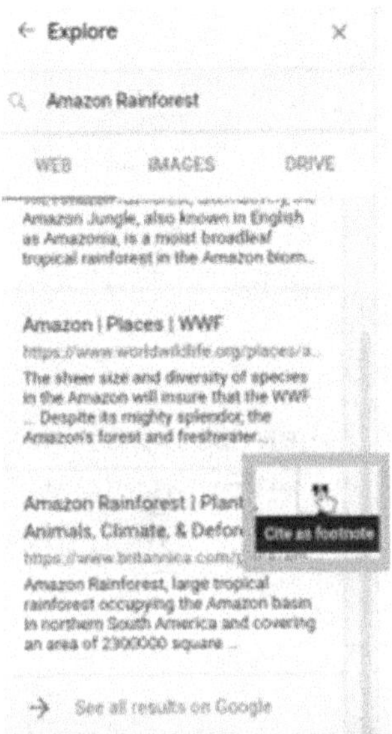

Clicking the icon next to the appropriate resource marker will cite the selected passage (e.g., APA, MLA, Chicago).

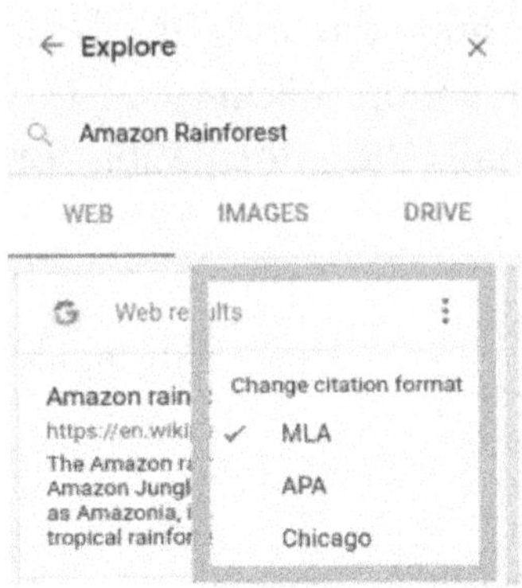

When the link is quoted, a footnote appears, like this:

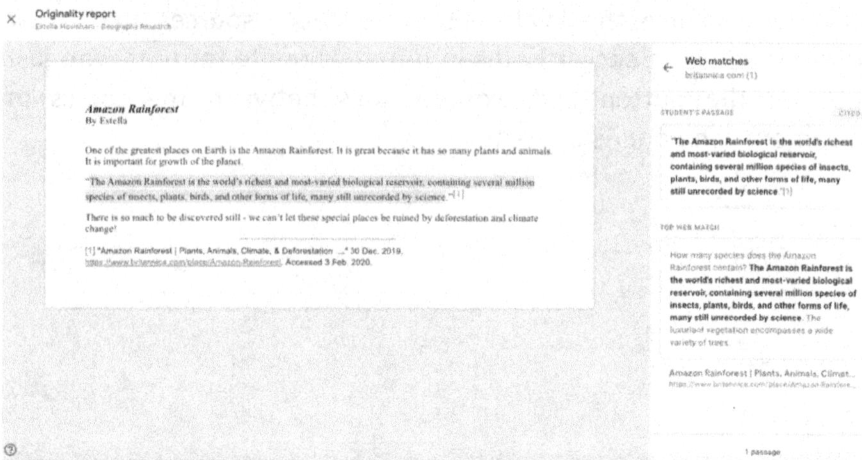

maintain a plagiarism-free document. Even when passages are quoted, when an originality report is produced, the reference(s) will show. Teachers will also use their judgment to assess if there has been plagiarism.

Rubrics

Rubrics allow students to look at the degree qualifications before applying and to help teachers graduate more efficiently.

For rubrics, there can be several parameters and points. As of now, a numeric value must be assigned to each location. Clicking on the arrows on the right (next to the points total), the information for each criterion will show or hide.

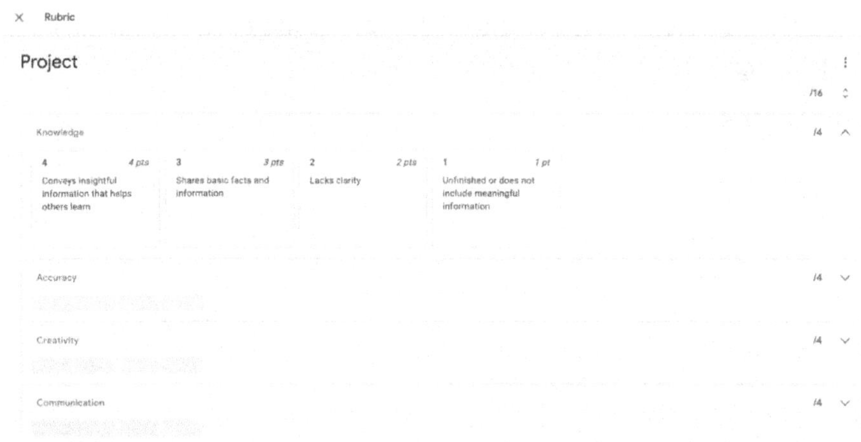

Assignment rubrics can be made from scratch, or a Google Sheets file with the requirements can be uploaded. Note time-saving tricks of duplicate criteria when building a section (click on the 3-point 'more' button, as seen here), and of course, copying and pasting!

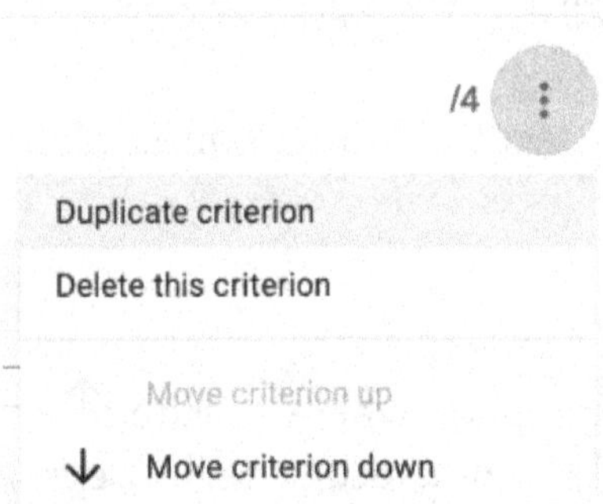

The scoring is optional; if the teachers agree to score the work of the students, the degrees are automatically added to the grade book in the 'Grades' column.

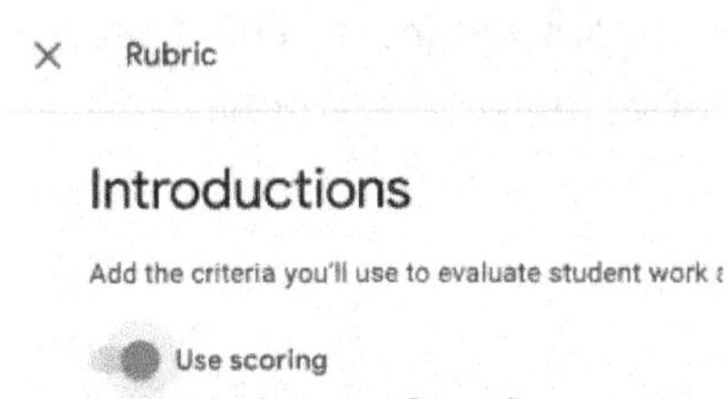

If using a grade work object, open the task to be graded and click on the grading button underneath the files.

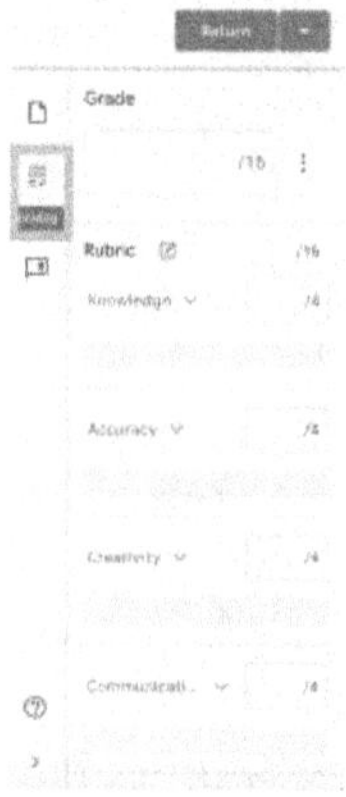

If appropriate, you can adjust the total score and input scores for various parameters here.

You may also provide private feedback for each student, as with other assignments.

Rubrics will provide timely, detailed descriptive input on student work!

Drag & Drop on The Classwork Page

"Last fall, we created the new Classwork page where teachers can stay organized and schedule their classes". They recognize, however, that teachers plan their classes differently and require additional flexibility in their school resources. You can now drag and drop entire subjects and classified objects and easily rearrange them on the list. You may transfer an entire subject to a different position on the classroom page or drag items into and from subjects. This feature was released on mobile last year, and now the web is ready.

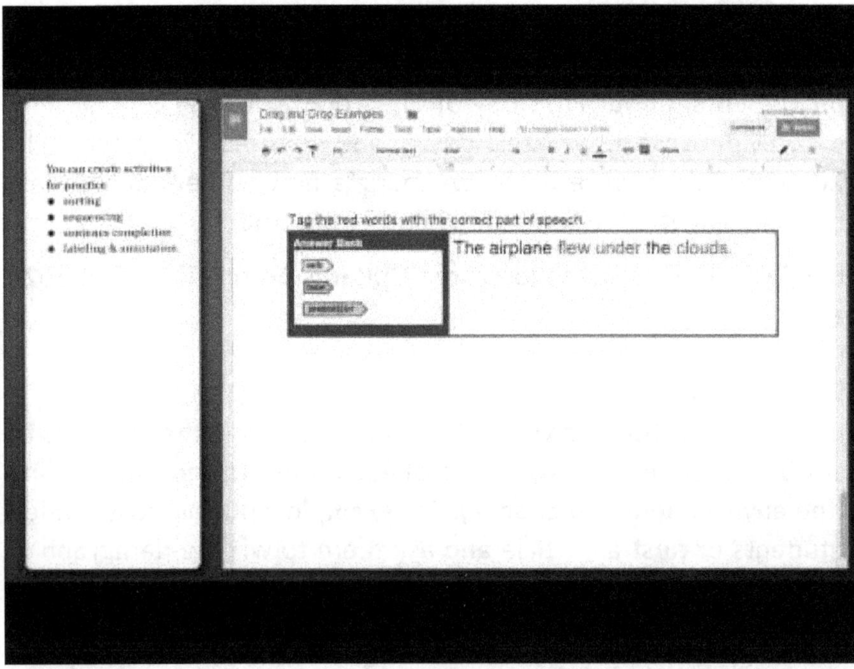

Refreshed Ux

Starting January 2019, you can also see that classroom has a fresh look, first on the website, and then on mobile devices in the school. In 2014, we launched Google's latest content style to make Google products and services more reliable. Among the improvements, there is a more natural flow of design — plus a modern approach to both the web and the mobile app for form, color, iconography, and typography. We also make the class code simpler for students to access and project. Finally, we show 78 new themes, ranging from history, mathematics, hair styling, photography, and personalized illustrations. Now, you can more than ever adapt to your classroom.
"

Improved Preparation and Help

"The need for more assistance with new resources and improvements. In our First Day of Classroom training, you can find updated videos with the latest design and features, which we built-in 2018. While we were there, we made a new and enhanced Help Centre, along with our Community and Brand Hub. "

Other / Previous Google Classroom Updates Before The 2019-2020 Year

1. Post Questions

You can ask questions to your school and encourage the students to speak by answering the responses of each other (or not, depending on the environment you choose). For example, you can post a video to students or post an article and ask them to write a paragraph in reply.

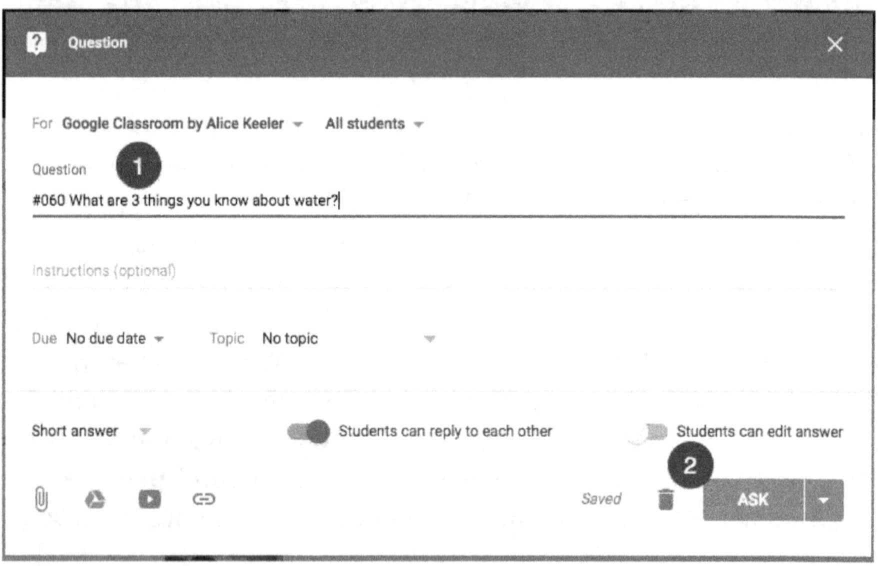

2. Reuse Assignments

If you repeat curricula year after year– or at least repeat papers, you will want an upgrade. You can repeat assignments, journals, or questions in all of your classes – or any class you co-teach from last year or last week. You will also be able to make adjustments before you post or allocate them after you have selected what you want to copy.

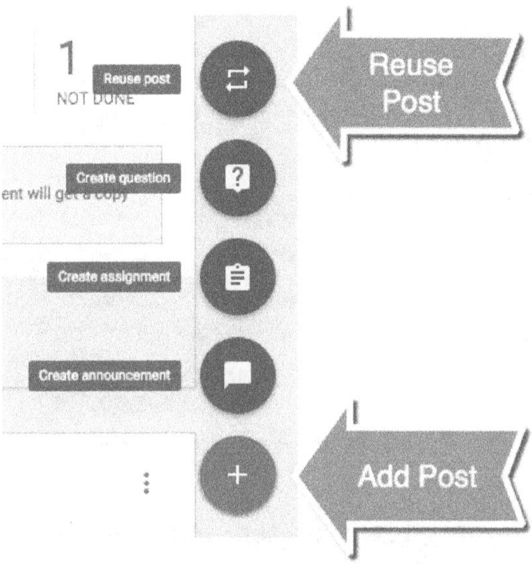

3. Bump A Post

Sticking posts on forums, tweets, or Facebook updates was a thing for a long time. You can do it now on Google Classroom by pushing every job to the top.

4. Due Dates Optional

If you use long-term assignments or other duty-free activities, you can now build jobs in Google Classroom without due dates.

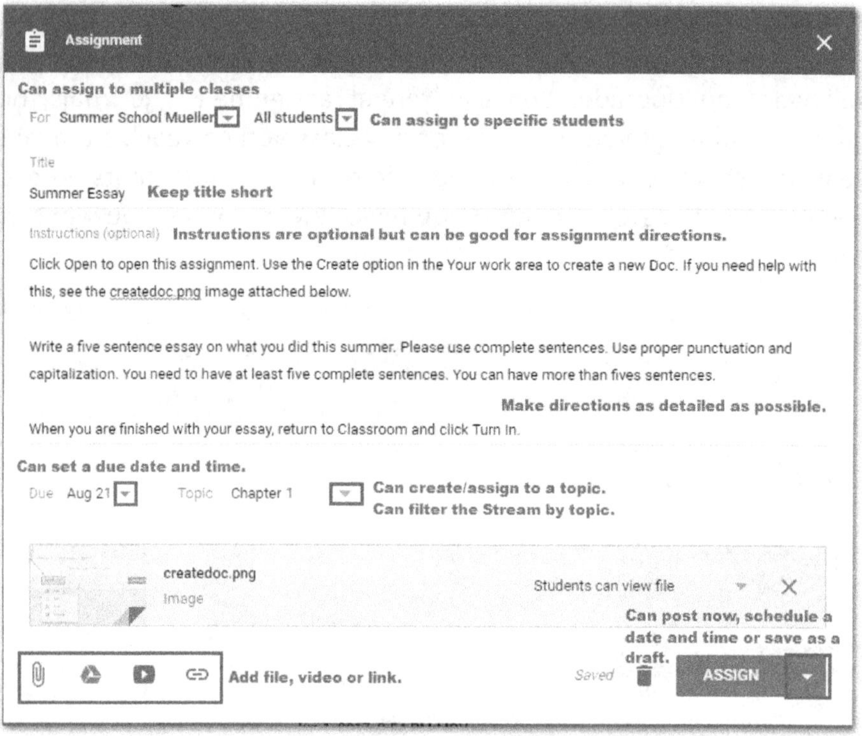

5. Attach A Google Form to A Post

If you're a fan of Google Forms, this is a step you're going to appreciate. Most teachers use Google Forms to allocate a questionnaire, or survey to the class. Teachers and students will soon be able within the next few weeks to add Google Forms from Drive to the posts and assignments and to connect them in the classroom to read the answers.

6. YouTube Functionality

YouTube Features, but with inappropriate content? Google is listening to you. "We introduced advanced YouTube settings for all Google App domains last month as an add-on feature because they often contain material that a company or school does not find suitable. Such parameters allow Apps to limit the YouTube videos viewed by signed-in users as well as signed-out users on admin-managed networks.

Google Classroom Special Features

With new generations so sensitive to interactive learning, teachers seem to have little choice but to implement innovative approaches to involve students in the process.

Google's first appearance in 2014 has been a success in K-12 schools, not because they introduced anything technological, but because they provided their software to all teachers around the world, thereby supplying them with the resources they needed to revolutionize the program. Since then, developers at G-12 and other technology firms have enhanced existing tools and developed new tools to support teachers in the classroom.

A compilation of some of the most relevant developments concerning the GBP, which will undoubtedly come in handy at the beginning of the new year, is discussed below.

Unicheck

One of the most awaited features that Google did not have: the possibility of testing submitted plagiarism papers Unicheck is the first plagiarism checker to integrate with google classroom, and what it means for teachers is that the plagiarism issue in the documents has now become more accessible to solve and avoid.

The resource is one of the favorites among teachers because it can identify parallels to the school's internal library, which means that peer-to-peer plagiarism has been left in the past. Unicheck is capable of presenting correctly formatted citations and references in the paper in almost all academic styles. Unicheck automatically conducts tests and sends a comprehensive and easy-to-follow report to Gmail teachers.

Unicheck also overcomes the financial challenge that many teachers face when searching for a quality plagiarism checker, as unicheck provides a free choice.

Quizizz

Another valuable application is Quizizz, a free app that turns content analysis and student evaluation into a fun-filled game-based experience. It operates in such a fantastic way to take away some of the excessive workloads of the teachers.

You don't need to compile quizzes manually or spend hours looking for an acceptable exam online since this quick integration of the API does it for students.

Both teachers will be delighted to hear how their quiz practices will work right now: first, choose a quiz; then, choose a class to use it. Students will be provided with a connection that will take them directly to the game. As soon as the quiz is finished, answers and scores will be submitted to the teacher. No work was expended on putting together the questionnaire, no time spent on the technical task of classifying each inquiry.

A further benefit of Quizizz is that it brings excitement to the educational process and lets students review the content and evaluate their skills in a gamified way.

Decimal Grades

Google Classroom teachers may take the following action: show assignments, rate assignments, return them, adjust grades, and show rate history. The default value of each grade is set at 100 points. It is now possible to define any assignment using decimal numbers. Teachers are free to use multiple digits after the decimal point, but the amount will be rounded to two decimal digits after the decimal point. Teachers can also use grades less than 1.

Class Calendar

Google Calendar and School, as well as other smartphone and web applications, can now be incorporated via the Calendar API.

This update is what makes it worthwhile to use Google Calendar: running on a single platform, calendar entries can appear automatically when teachers add assignments.

It is easy for students to have due dates for papers and assignments in their calendars without having to design them manually. It's one more excuse not to be late with the documents.

Other applications can also be built into Google Calendar, such as a hiking app that adds a path to the calendar entry.

Google Bar

It's now possible to conveniently juggle classroom and other G Suite Google resources, as the Google bar offers you direct access to all applications. Teachers can find it most convenient to handle alerts, configure menus, search, and do certain things they need with their Google Account.

Confirmed Teacher Recognition

All users who have been checked by Google can now be found. Not only does this enhance the visual aspect of Classroom use, such as getting people's names adequately written; the program also provides some privileges and rights to the teachers that have been checked.

Google Group Invites

Google is actively working on removing unnecessary steps and clicks while working in the classroom. Teachers will now add classes of students instead of adding each one separately. To do this, teachers need to be members of the community they are linking to and using Google Groups.

It is still possible to add pupils, or co-teachers, inviting them or giving them a code to add themselves, so it saves time and energy in the case of other members to add.

Class Cards Reorder

This may sound trivial, but it contributes significantly to productivity.

This feature offers teachers the ability to rearrange how classes are viewed in the Google Classroom. The new class order will be accordingly synced to all computers. The most recently added classes would show first, as well as unarchived ones, so if teachers need them elsewhere, they'll have to move around.

Single View

Here is another useful feature that makes school life easier for teachers. The Single View will do as it says: it provides teachers and students with a view to all the research, grades, and feedback that have been made or submitted for each class. -- student has a filter: success can be evaluated by the status of their job, as assigned, turned in, done late, or absent.

Class Ownership Transfer

Class ownership is not an issue, because the Domain Administrator can do it now in a few clicks using the Classroom API. The move would also make the new teacher owner of the Class's Drive folder, all resources, and the student's turn-in works. Deleted materials and practices would remain the property of the previous teacher, who will become a co-teacher in the classroom.

Real Presence in Classrooms

There are conflicting views on the extent of the actual presence of Google Classrooms in K-12 schools in the US and internationally, but one thing is clear: Google is developing itself as a forum for teachers to operate and manage their classrooms based on accessible apps. And although most higher education institutions still need more sophisticated resources, Google Classroom is increasingly appealing to secondary schools.

Recent research reveals that in the US, the preschool to the 8th-grade group has embraced Google Classroom as the primary platform.

Approximately 35.4 million children attend preschool to Grade 8, and 1/2 of them use Google Classroom daily. This is an astonishing number, even without counting high school students in the U.S. or any other schoolboy in the world.

The future of Google Classroom looks promising, and teachers should rest assured that further changes and integrations will take place, allowing even more excellent opportunities to be realized in classrooms.

Google Classroom Hidden Features

Over the last two years; Google Classroom has become a popular teacher's learning platform. Google Classroom provides a productive workflow for teachers and students by arranging courses and class contents in an easy-to-navigate online environment, thanks to its capabilities to seamlessly incorporate G Suite tools such as Google Documents, Google Slides, Google Papers, Gmail and Google Calendars. Although Google Classroom provides many great opportunities, three can save teachers and students a lot of time and improve workflow capacity. So, let's use these exciting apps!

The Assignment Calendar

Google Classroom Assignment Calendar automatically generates an assignment calendar to better coordinate students and teachers. Whenever a teacher inside the Google Classroom creates a job or query and adds a due date, the task will automatically be on the class calendar inside Google Classroom.

Find the three lines in the top left corner of the screen for this calendar and click date. Teachers and students can see the work assigned to the class on this computer.

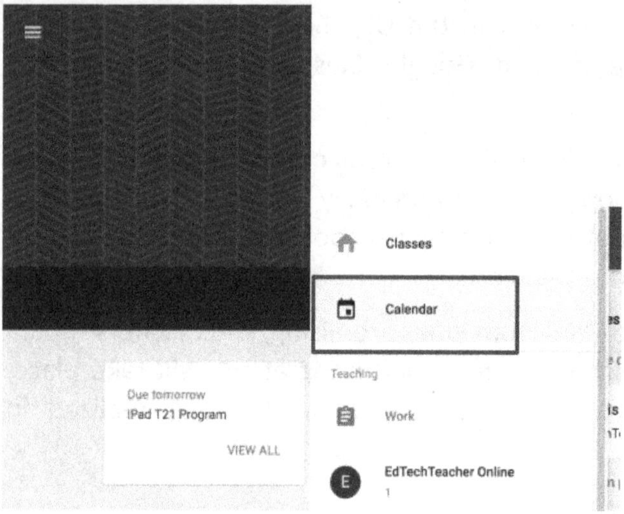

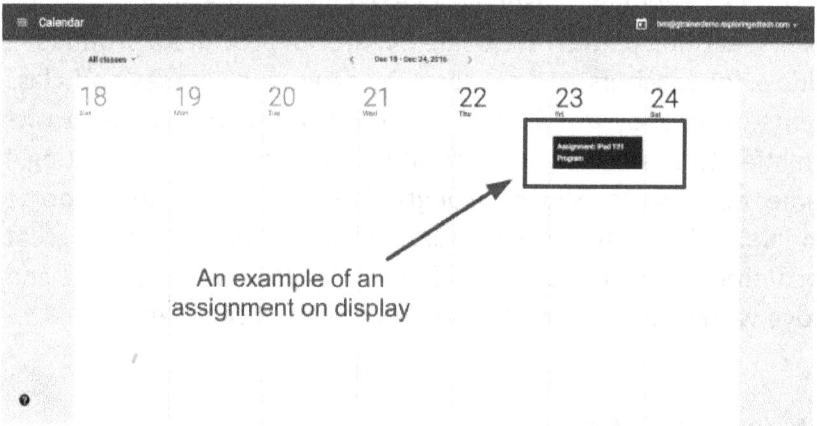

Teachers will also note that their G Suite schedule now contains a new calendar. Not only can teachers assign activities to this schedule via the classroom, but they can also access it directly through the G Suite Calendar to assign events for a class not bound to the due date. Examples of teachers who use this calendar feature include organizing field trips, providing extra tutoring time, and scheduling a post-school meeting. To make the calendar more available, make it public in the settings of the calendar, and then share the URL link with the parents.

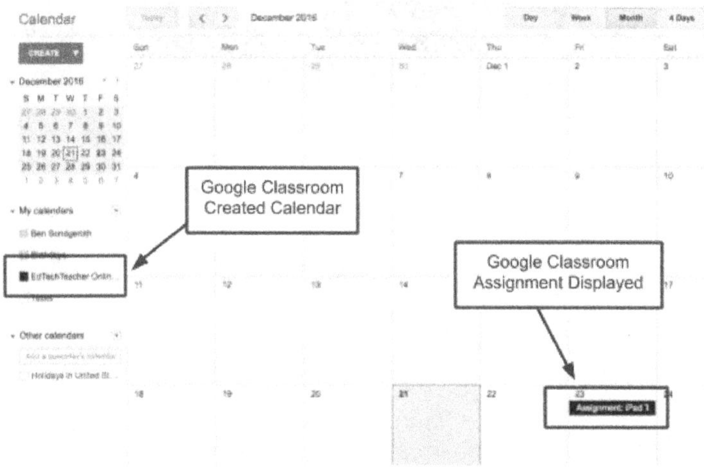

The Work Area

Teachers and students may also take advantage of the Google Classroom's workspace to gather all outstanding jobs in one place. If a teacher has still not graded a particular assignment, it will show in this field. Likewise, if a student does not enter a job, he will also be shown in his workplace. The Workaround may also serve as a default task list and allow teachers and students to define and control their workflow efficiently.

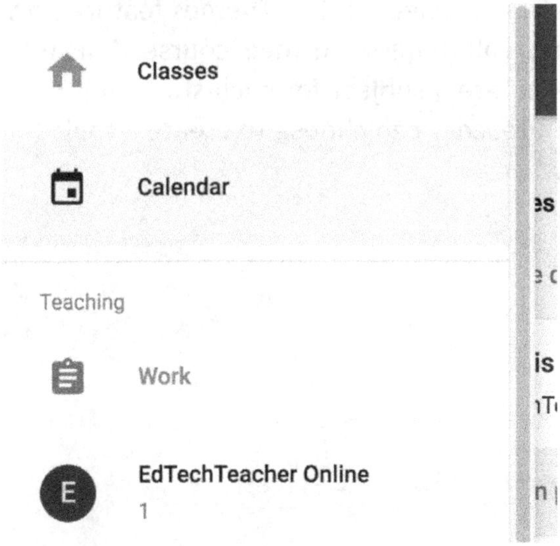

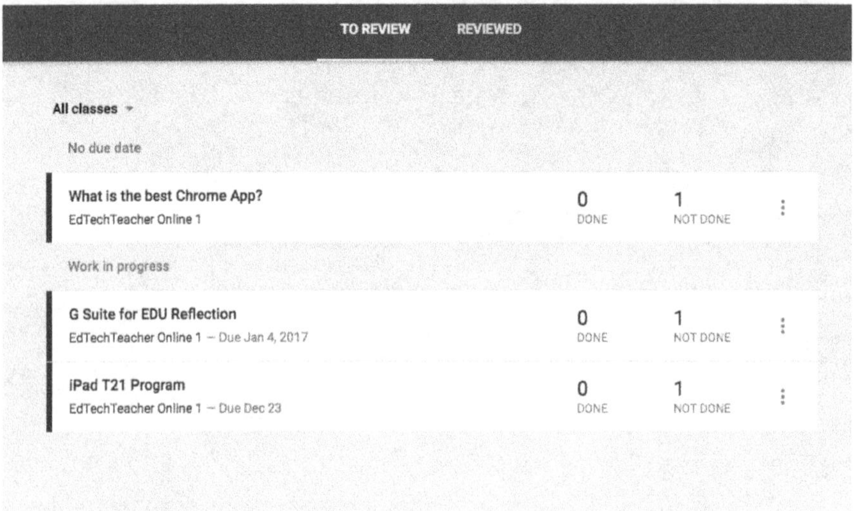

Organize A Class Stream with Topics

A new function inside Google Classroom that will enable teachers to organize the posts that they attach to the 'Path' classroom, and now teachers can allocate a subject to the announcement, assignment or query, which can be organized efficiently for each post.

When a new topic is created, the problem will be displayed on the left side of the classroom stream, and all the posts related to that topic will appear when an item is selected. The Themes feature now enables teachers to organize all material in their course. A history teacher may, for instance, create a subject for each study unit such as "Ancient Rome." A math teacher can choose to create a topic for each study unit or chapter.

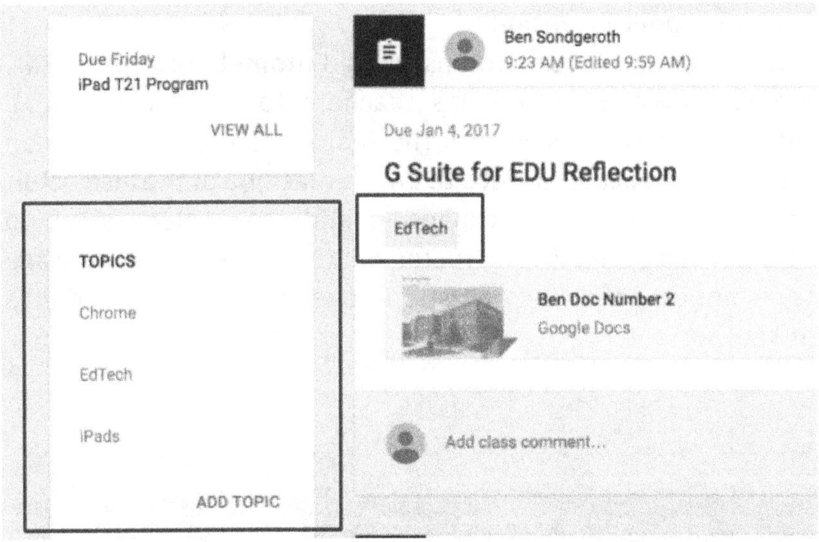
Due Friday
iPad T21 Program
VIEW ALL
TOPICS
Chrome
EdTech
iPads
ADD TOPIC
Ben Sondgeroth
9:23 AM (Edited 9:59 AM)
Due Jan 4, 2017
G Suite for EDU Reflection
EdTech
Ben Doc Number 2
Google Docs
Add class comment...

Share to Classroom Extension

For teachers in school classrooms using Chromebooks or tablets, Chrome Extension Sharing helps teachers to view and sharing student work and screens quickly. The Share to Classroom extension allows students to access a website on the machine of the instructor. Students first click on the expansion and then select Move to Instructor. When done, the instructor will receive a pop-up message on their computer that they must approve it before the student's page is shown

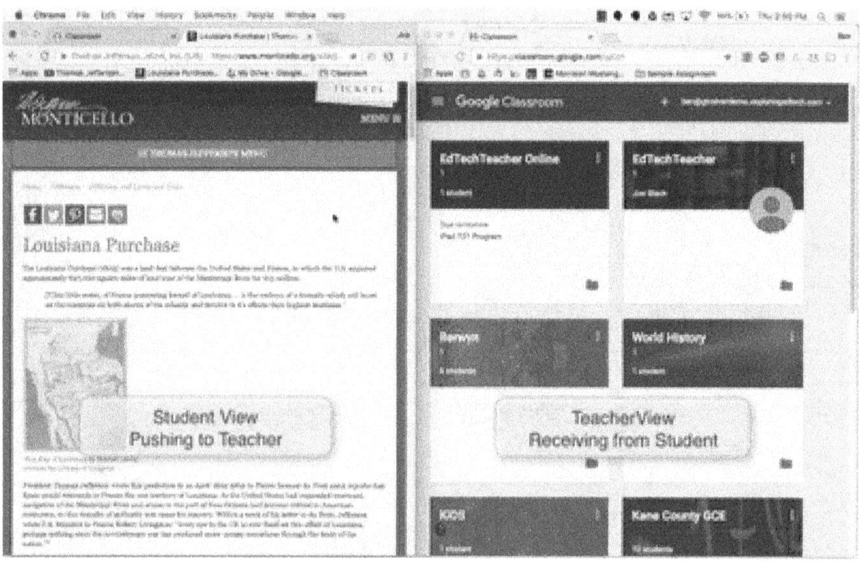

Through following the same steps, a teacher will push a website in real-time to the devices of his students!

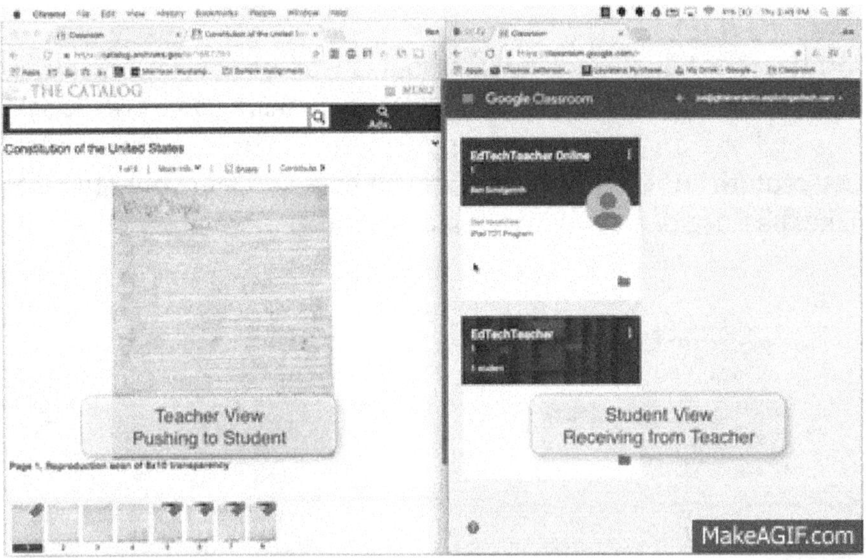

Teachers can also create Google Classroom material directly from the extension. When a professor discovers a website he or she needs to add as part of a mission, query, or announcement in Google Classroom, he or she may use the extension to build any of those choices.

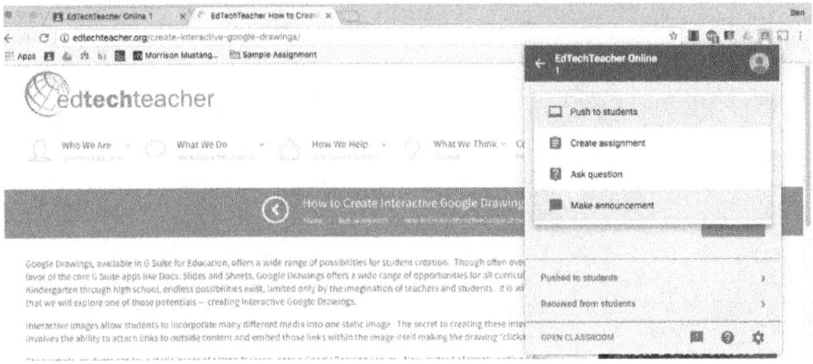

With the Share to Classroom extension, teachers and students now can quickly and efficiently share new insights and stories.

Wrapping It Up

On the other hand, Google Classroom is well known for organizing their student's research on Google Drive, making copies of Google Docs and the organization of digital materials, these three under-used features of Google Classroom will help you and your students make their use of classroom technology much more productive!

Chapter 2: Step by Step Guide to Google Classroom

2.1 Getting Started using RosterSync

The technology of step by step has become one of the main drivers of educational progress in recent years, increasing learning and teaching possibilities, by expanding the range of teacher-student resources, data, and learnings available.

Roster sync is a free Google Sheets Add-on that allows Google Apps to create and update Google Classroom teacher's courses and lists directly from its Student Information System.

This tool works together with Google's launch of the Classroom API, allowing developers to build learning apps that connect with class lists of teachers in an open, widely accepted, and stable network. Classroom, launched by Google in August 2014, has already served as a critical resource for teachers through the development of a simple, intuitive workflow to manage Google Docs and Drive assignments. Classroom enables teachers to monitor and review cloud-based student writing in real-time by allowing bulk copying and distribution of templated "starter files" in Drive.

RosterSync

The roster sync tool can be installed conveniently from the Google Sheets Add-ons tab, but it only runs for Google Apps domain managers. The domain administrator is asked for the first time when launching roster sync, to define and map the relevant student data sources (e.g., CSVs or Google Sheets) with the corresponding classroom data fields.

The Add-on begins when the user uploads the student data file (called the "Information Source Registrations"). Additional sources of data may be "joined" for the required mappings, such as course information or instructor and student emails. In different data files, where similar column headings exist, RosterSync will also automatically identify the "join" columns. Once such mappings are made, they will be stored for use with all updates after the column, so that any CSV files can be easily re-documented to allow rosters to be modified. Respond to this guide to learn how to optimize and create roster sync from the NYCDOE STARS info.

RosterSync is only in the early version of the beta. Since we don't have access to each student information system to check, we want to invite all domain administrators in the roster sync Google+ group to help evaluate and develop the tool.

Powering Personalized Learning

The purpose of building roster sync was to increase the adoption of teachers through cloud-based tools that help to streamline writing instruction both in New York City schools and across the country. We agree that Google Drive's low-cost, device-agnostic platform provides teachers critical and incomparable opportunities to enhance writing education for students who are most in need. Google has built with the Classroom API a rich framework for a simple, scalable, and interoperable platform that can use roster data to help individual students learn.

Teacher Version allows teachers to sync a course roster – including student email addresses – with Google Sheets for easy use of complements such as Doctopus, formMule, autoCrat, formRanger, and others.

Features

• Switch from a friendly sidebar app is to be done manually.

• Sync can be executed in either direction: classroom — > board — > classroom.

When Running in Classroom

Sheet mode, the Add-on inserts the First Name, Last Name, Email Address, and Classroom Status columns into the sheet and populates the sheet with all active and invited students. On subsequent syncs, new students are added, and the students removed are flagged. Formulas and formatting will typically be copied when new students are added to the Classroom board.

When Running in Sheet

Classroom mode, the Add-on can change (add/remove) the student list in the Classroom section using the email address in the Email Address column of the document. A preview is given before any other action is taken to avoid the error by the user!

• Several tabs (sheets) inside the spreadsheet may be linked to the same and different parts.

• Headers are designed to suit those used in the English version of the Doctopus Add-on to allow for reasonably simple interoperability and network synchronization.

Use Cases

• Use to quickly move a class list to a sheet for use with any number of add-ons that can use student name and email address to improve personalization and teacher workflow: Doctopus, AutoCrat, FormMule, FormRanger, etc.

• Use to create informal record-keeping sheets that are always up-to-date for your classroom segment.

• Using to circumvent the enrolment code process by producing class invites for a list of students.

Syncing Your Class with Google Classroom

With Actively Practice, Google Classroom can help organize classes and centralize where you exchange assignments with students.

To use Google Classroom with Actively Learn, both teachers and students need to build Actively Learn accounts using their Google Accounts school.

Note: Popup blockers will prevent you from importing your classes correctly. Don't forget to either disable your popup blocker or allow activelearn.com popups to ensure smooth import!

Step 1
Click "Add a new class"

Step 2
Select "Export courses from Google Classroom"

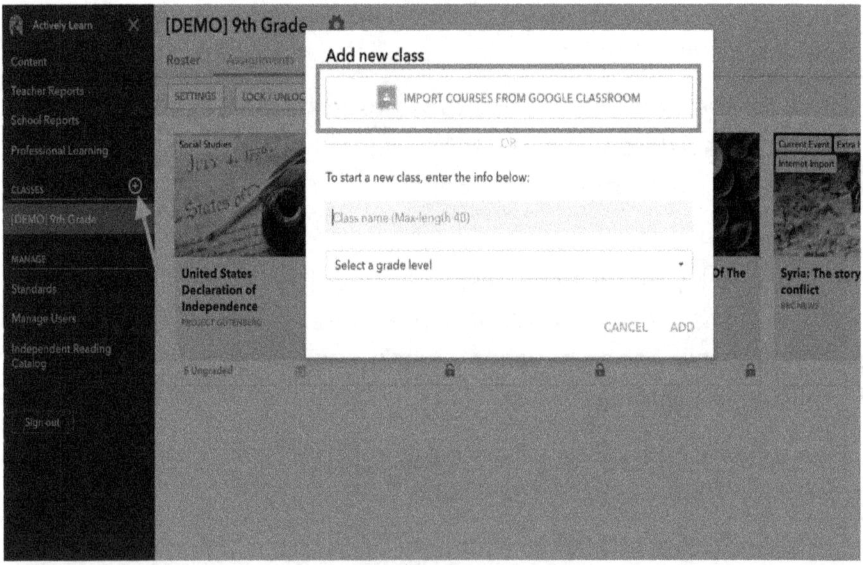

Step 3

Choose the classes you want to export from Google Classroom, then select "Import"

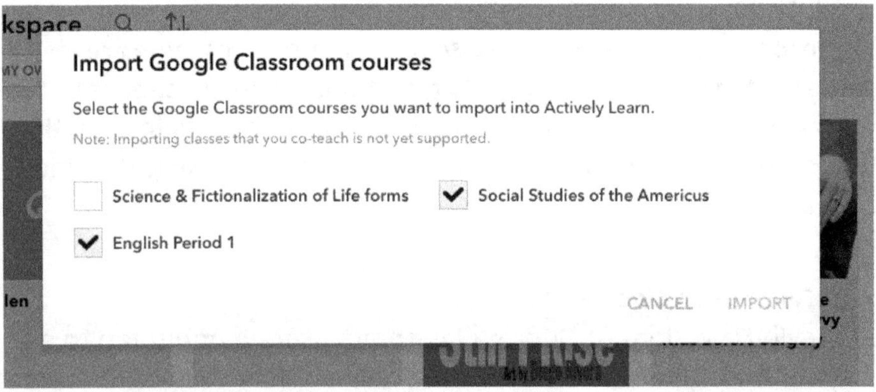

Note: If you are not the original developer of the course in Google Classroom, you cannot import the course and list to Learn Actively. Furthermore, if the original developer has imported the class into Actively Learn, you may be asked to co-teach for entry.

Advance tips to begin using Google Classroom

Google Classroom is designed to help teachers and students connect and collaborate, handle tasks on a paperless basis, and remain organized. Google Classroom is a part of the Google Apps for Education toolkit and is only accessible on Google Apps for Education accounts.

Creating a Google Classroom

The Classroom is the first step for teachers who want to set up a Google Classroom online space.

Customize the Appearance of Your Class

When you first build your course, you will be given the default header picture. This is the picture students will see when they click on your level to access assignments and announcements. You can customize this picture with a couple of fast moves.

There are several images to choose from, but most of them are about some kind of academic Subject. For starters, you might choose books for language classes, pianos for music, colored pencils for painting, and so on. You can also upload your photo by clicking the Photo Upload button.

Add Syllabus to Google Classroom

In previous versions of Google Classroom, use the About tab to add a syllabus or other class tools. In the new edition, you use a feature called Materials, which you can find on the Classwork tab. Here's how to add to your class what you like.

Remember that if appropriate, you can delegate materials to different classes, or even to individual students. Select the choice you need from the top left corner when you build a new Material for your class.

If you want your Syllabus Subject to be at the top of your Classwork tab, click the three arrows in the top right corner of the Subject and select Step Up. Repeat as often as needed. Additionally, you can drag and drop Topics or Materials by clicking and dragging them up and down on the Classwork tab.

Adding Students to Google Classroom

Once you've built all the classes you need, you can easily add students to your page. It can be achieved in one of two ways. The first is to let students sign on their own.

Remember that the teacher's class code can be changed or disabled at any time. Just click the drop-down next to the class code and choose to reset or disable it as required. Reset or disable the system does not impact a student who has already registered for your class.

The second way to add students is to assign them manually to the instructor. It is relatively simple, and maybe not as cumbersome as you would imagine.

Remember that G Suite for Education teachers can only connect students that are part of their Google domain. When your students use public Gmail accounts, they will not be able to access your online material in the Google Classroom. It is deliberate and is part of the protection and privacy that Google needs to ensure that teachers and students use this platform.

Move, Edit or Archive a Class

When you first try Google Classroom, you could end up building some test classes just to get a feel for what it has to offer. That's perfectly normal because we all want to try new products and see if they're going to work for us.

Nonetheless, you might want to change the name of your test class or simply delete it when you're done.

Renaming your class or change the section, topic, or room number is possible through the edit button. The Moving button helps you to rearrange the class order in your dashboard. The archive button will delete and archive the class from your dashboard. When a course is archived, you can still access it through Settings by clicking on the icon of the menu in the top left corner and selecting Archived Classes. From here, you can either restore or permanently remove archived classes.

Classroom Contact

There are two ways to promote interaction between students and teachers in the Google Classroom. The first is the Stream-a Facebook-like wall of messages that can be accessed by all members of the class. This functionality is open to students and teachers alike.

The second way to connect is via email. Students should press the three dots next to their teacher's name on the class homepage to open a Gmail message that is auto-filled with their instructor's email address. Students may also contact each other by clicking on the Students tab and clicking on the three dots on the very right side of the student name and choosing the Student Contact.

Teachers can do the same by clicking on the "People" tab, but they have the option of selecting several students and then clicking Actions > Email to send a message to a group of students.

Create an Assignment in Google Classroom

Assignments can be created and assigned to students from inside Google Classroom, and there are a variety of useful choices for educators. A lot of teachers using Google Classroom are likely to opt to add assignments from their Drive, as that is potentially where a lot of teacher tools are now kept. However, there's an additional value of selecting a Drive tool of Google Classroom, and that's obvious with the choices you get when you pick a file from Drive.

Grading and Returning Assignments to Student

Teachers can identify student submissions in a variety of different ways. Nonetheless, maybe the most productive approach is to join the class that you're involved in grading by clicking on the assignment name from the Stream view. If you notice that tasks are hidden between student conversations, look at the sidebar at the top left of the Stream screen, and you will see the "Upcoming Tasks" tab. Tap on and do the task you want to score.

2.2 Basics of Google Classroom

Logging in With Google Classroom

Step 1

Go to class.google.com

Step 2

Sign in with your school Google account details

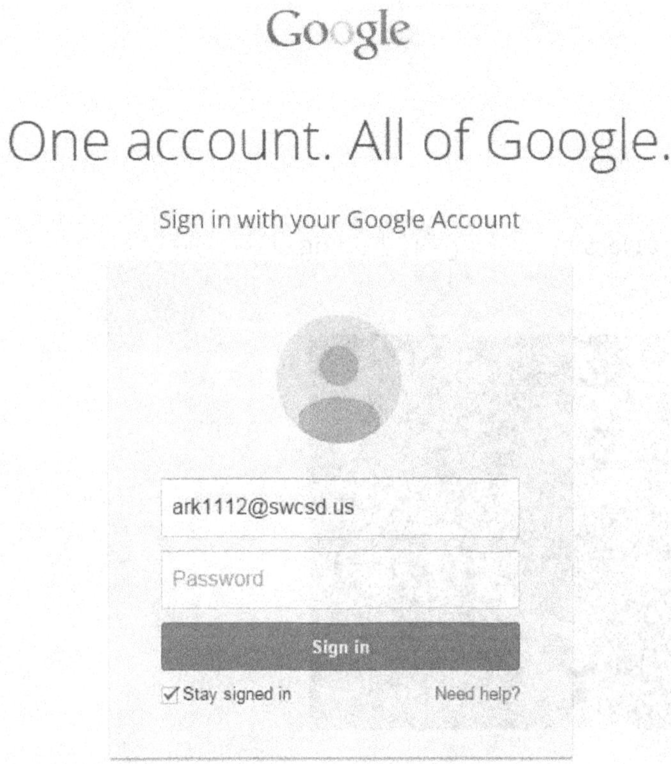

Step 3
Scroll down and select "Teacher."

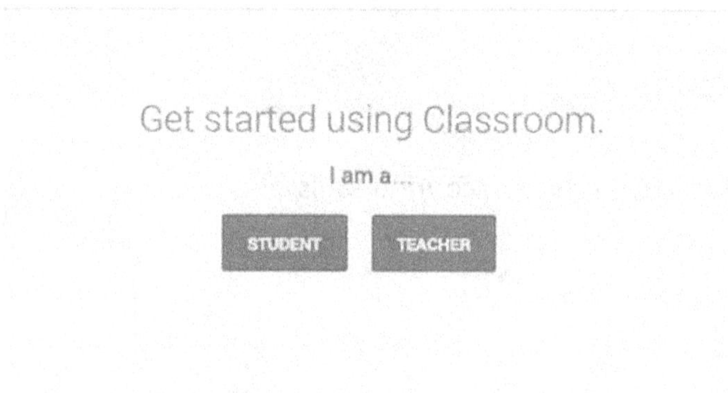

Step 4
Build your first class by clicking "+" Adding class

Adding A Class

Step 1
Sign in to Classroom using your email address

Step 2
Click at the top of the page and click create class

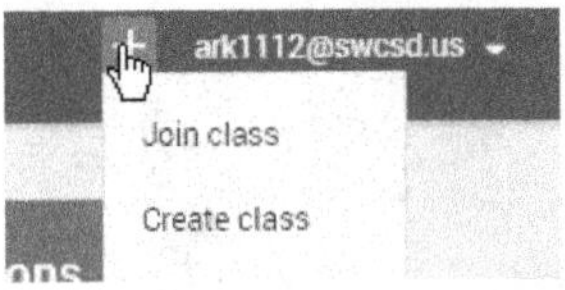

Step 3
Enter the class name in the first text box

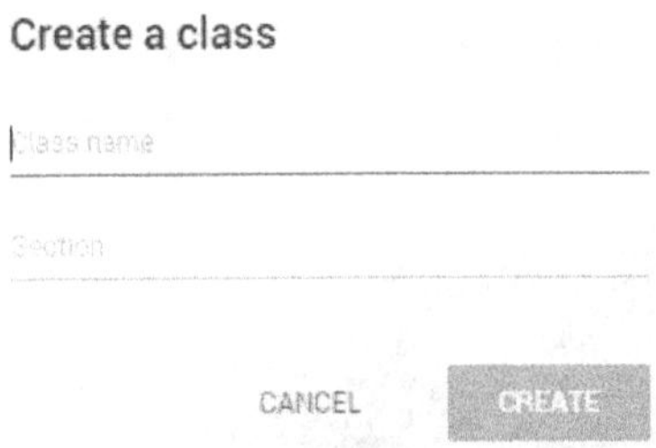

Step 4
Enter a short description in the second text box, such as section, grade level, or class time

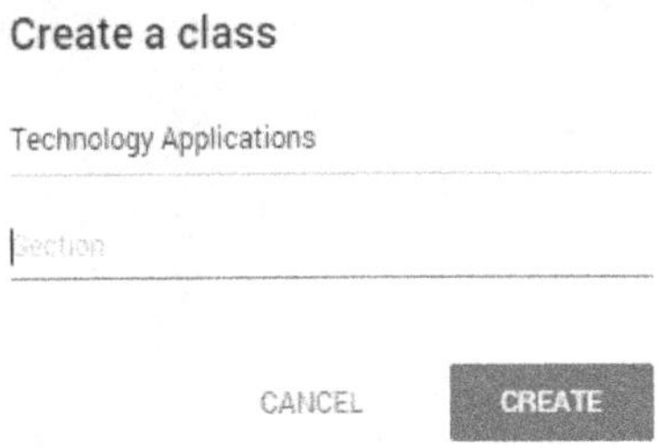

Step 5
Click "Create"

Applying A Theme

Step 1

Locate "change class theme" on the header (top right-hand corner)

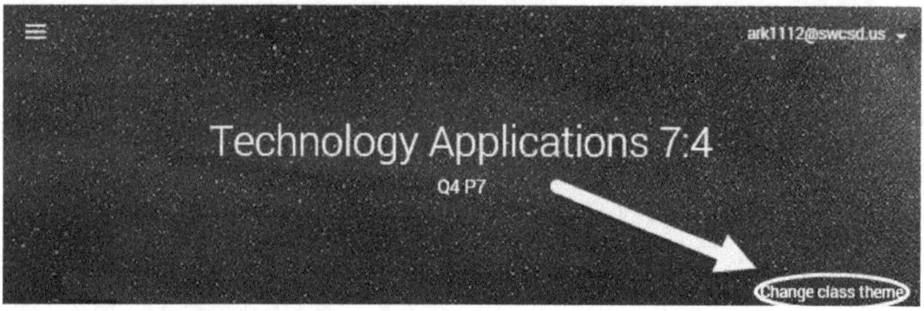

Step 2

Select a theme you like from the gallery by clicking on it.

Step 3

Click "Select class theme"

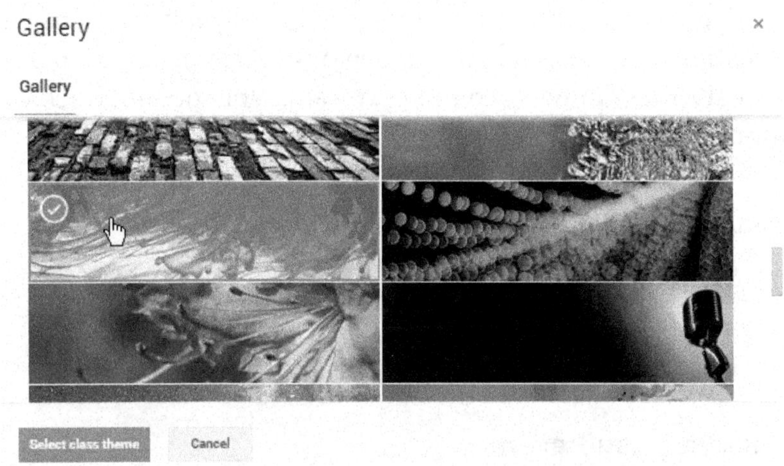

Setting Notifications

Step 1

Click the three bars in the top left-hand corner, scroll to the bottom and click "Settings"

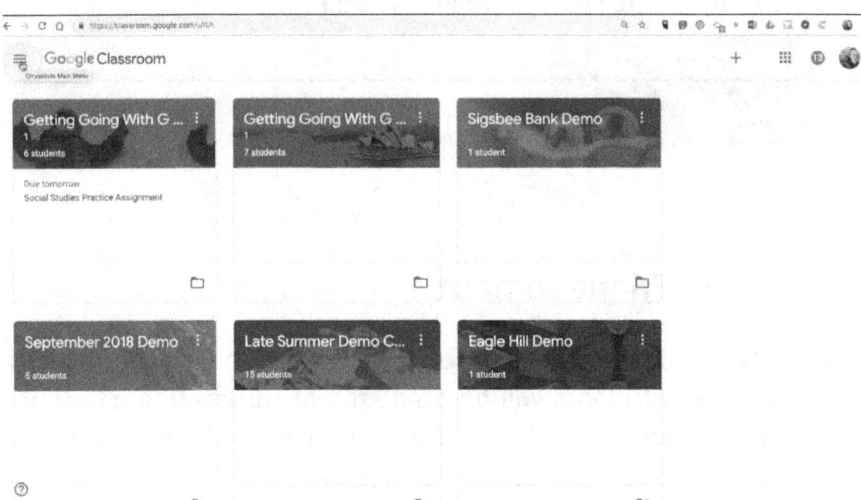

Step 2

Put a checkmark next to the "Send email notifications" if you would like to receive them or deselect if you would no longer like to receive the notifications. You will recently receive notifications any time a student posts or comments on the stream. You do not receive notifications about students turning in assignments.

Will Receive Notification

Will Not Receive Notifications

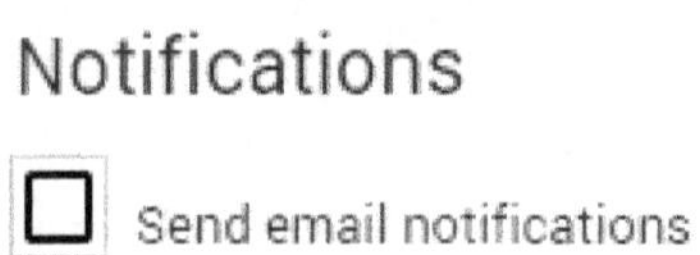

Step 3

Automatically all the changes will be solved

2.3 Student Management

how to get students enrolled in your course and change the settings that affect your students will be discussed in this section. Students are the most crucial part of the school, and having them adequately registered is vital to the success of the school.

Inviting Students to A Class

Through email, you will ask a group of students to enter your level. However, you must first build a group of students in your Gmail account

Step 1
Click the "students" button at the top of the page.

Step 2
Select "invite"

Step 3
Pick a group of students that you would like to invite.

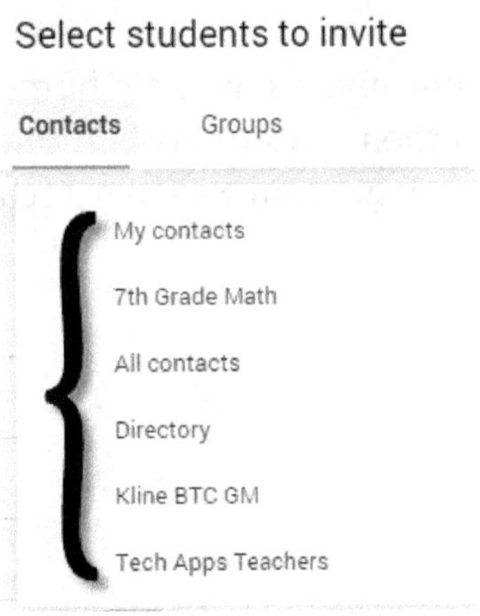

Step 4
Click "Pick All" then "Invite Students" Add Students by Code

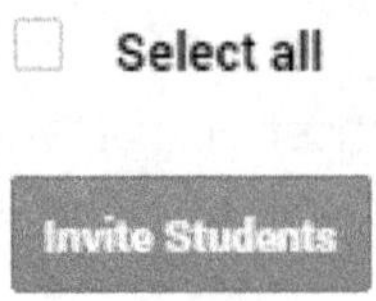

Adding Students by Code

Step 1
A "Class File" is created automatically by Google Classroom and will appear on the left side of your "path"

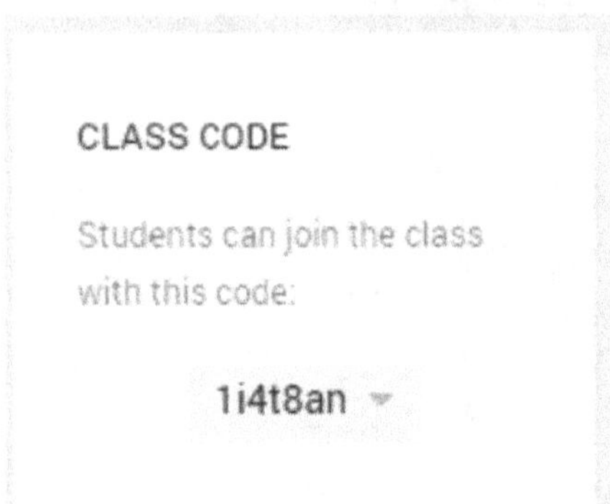

Step 2
Ask students to visit classroom.google.com and from their home page, click "+" in the top right corner, and then "Enter Class". If this is their first time to log in to classroom.google.com See the tech leader get students to enter their first class.

Step 3
Ask students to insert the code you are giving them in the box provided. Students can then pick "Enter".

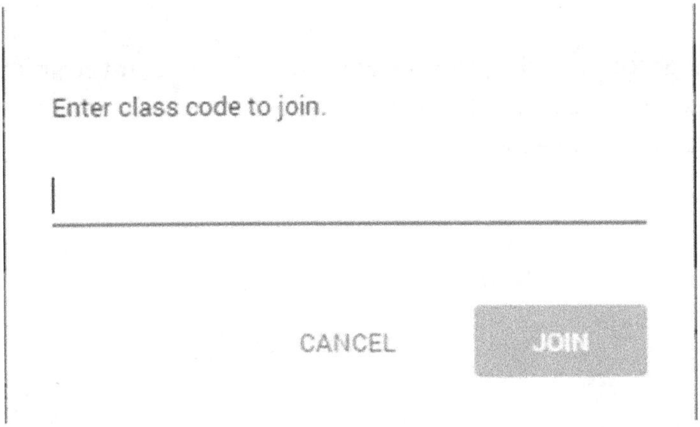

Reset or Disable Class Code

Step 1
Go to your "Source" and find the class code on the left sidebar.

Step 2
Press the drop-down arrow next to the code to update the class code and press "Delete." Google Classroom is going to create a new application for you. You are not in a position to build your system.

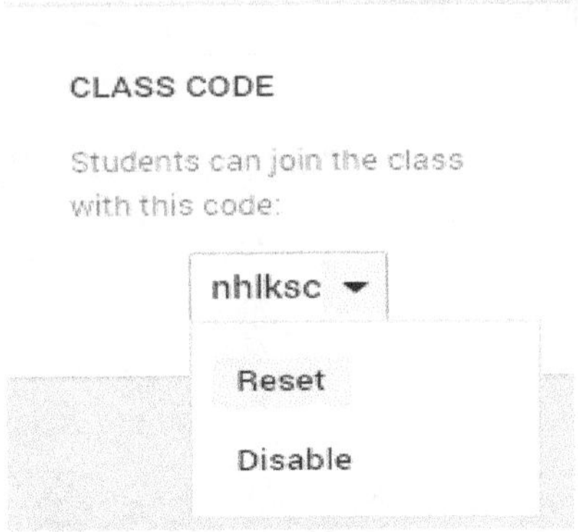

Step 3
To disable the account code (no one would be able to enter your account by default), select the drop-down arrow next to the negligence and press "Disable"

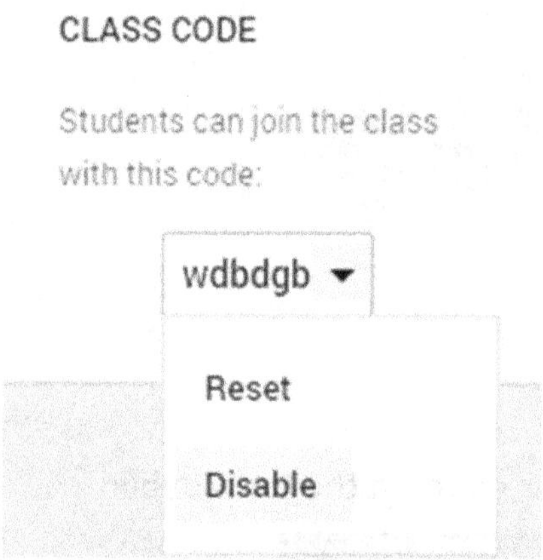

Sorting of Students

Step 1
Pick "STUDENTS" from the top menu bar.

Step 2
Choose "Students" and then select "Sort by First Name" or "Sort by Last Name"

Email Students

Step 1

Choose "STUDENTS" on the top navigation screen.

Step 2

Pick students you want to email or press "Select all" button

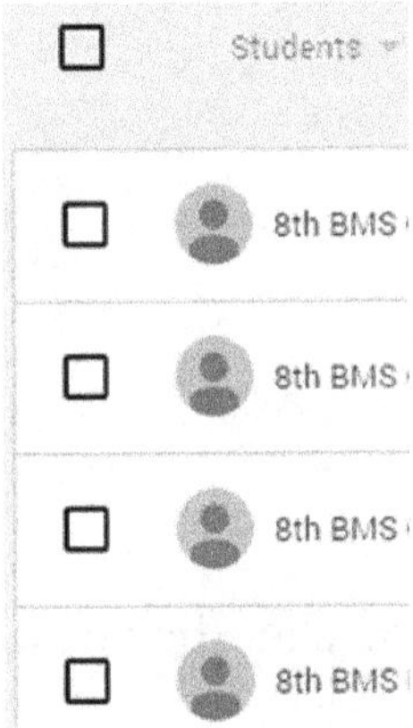

Step 3

Press "ACTIONS" at the top of the screen and then "Email."

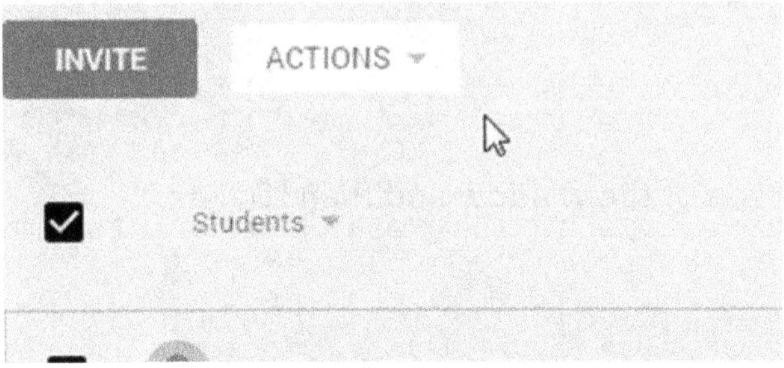

Step 4

You will be sent to your Gmail account, and all selected students will appear in the "BCC" area.

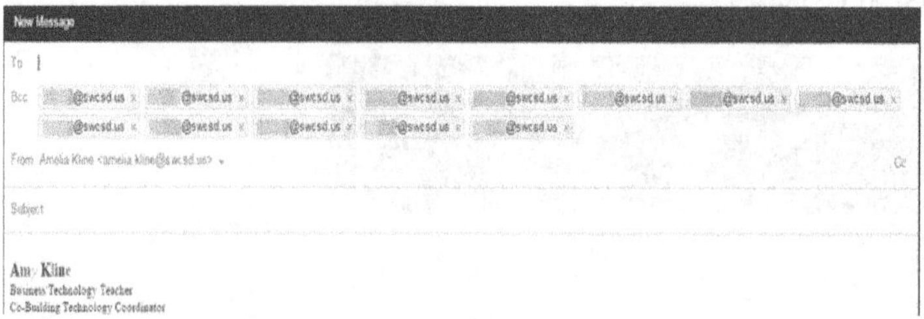

Remove Students from Class

Step 1

Click "STUDENTS" on the top navigation screen

Step 2

Select the student you want to delete by clicking the checkbox next to the student's name.

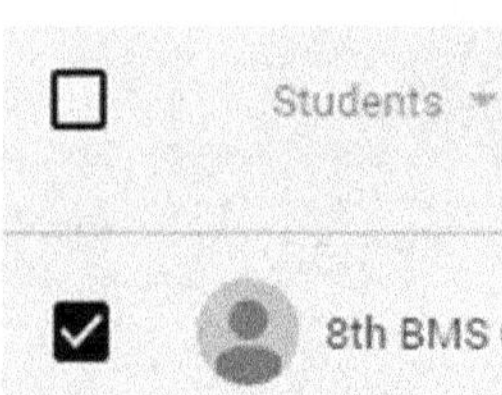

Step 3

Pick "ACTIONS" at the top of the window and then "Delete."

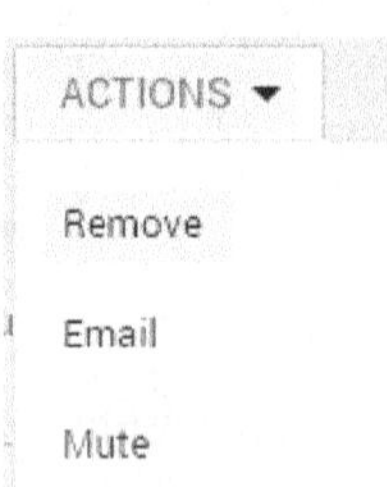

Step 4
Click "Delete"

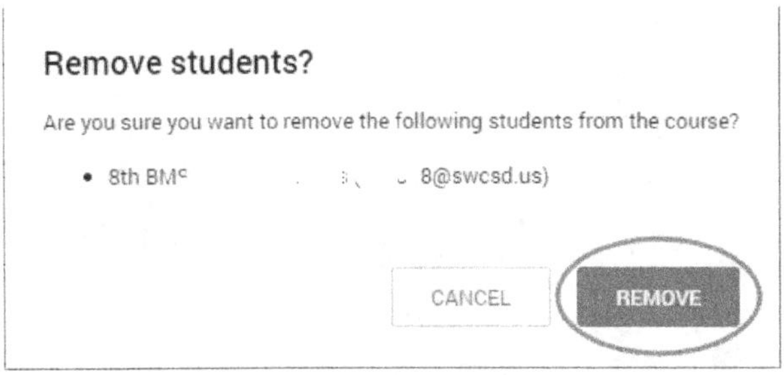

2.4 Creating and Grading Assignments

In this section, you'll learn how to create an assignment, get it to your students, and then grade it once it's completed. Also, you can learn how to give your students feedback on their work and how to improve the importance of assignments in the Classroom.

Create an Assignment

Step 1
The Classroom will always be set to Announcement by default. To get started, click "Assignment" on your page.

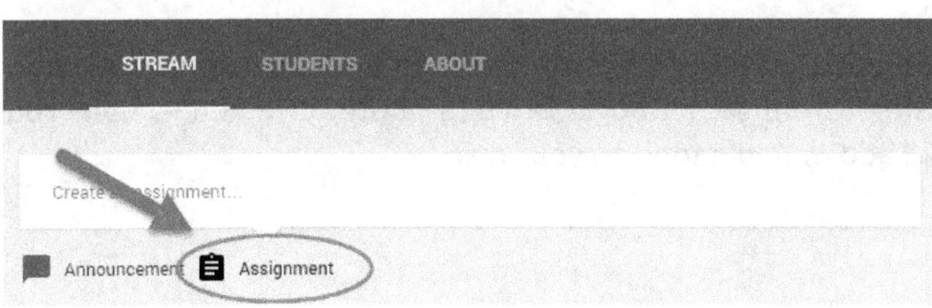

Step 2

Enter the name and description of your task.

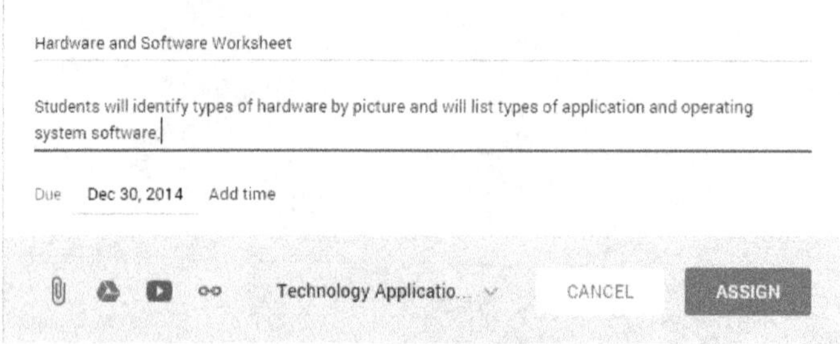

Step 3

Pick the due date (you can change it later). After the assignment is due, the student stream will be labeled "LATE."

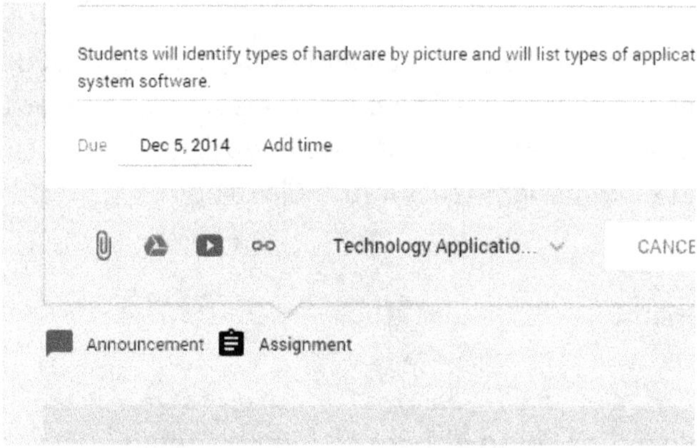

Step4

Add an optional video / file. You can add a file to your computer, a worksheet from your Google Drive, a photo, or a connection. You should add multiple tools to your task.

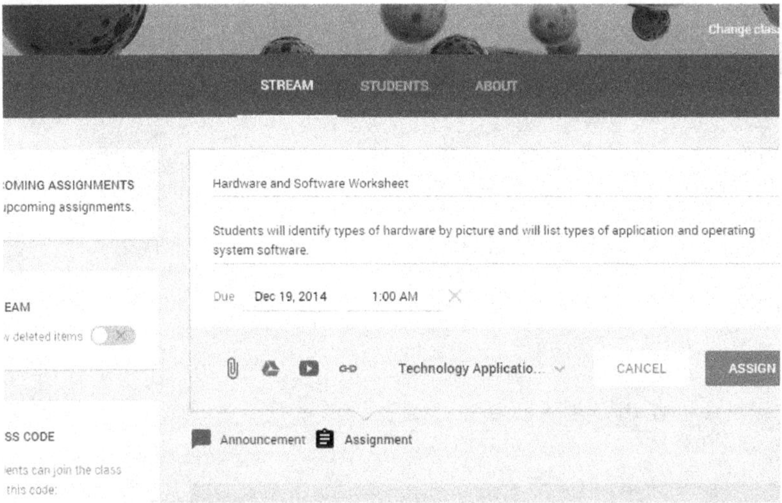

Step 5
Determine if you want students to be able to access the file, whether you want all students to be able to write to the same document, or whether you want each student to receive a specific student name in the file name.

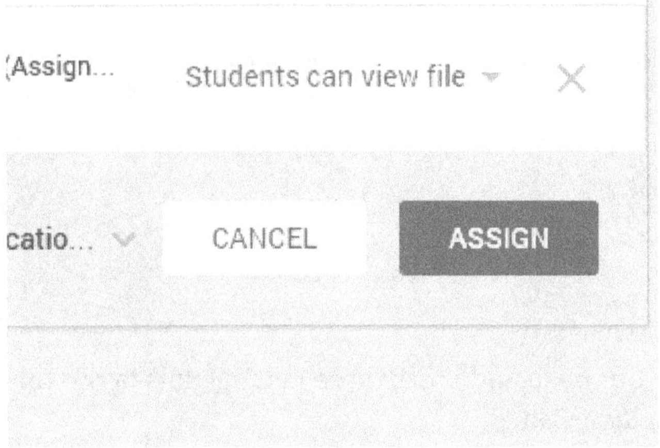

Step 6
Select the parts that you would like to delegate to.

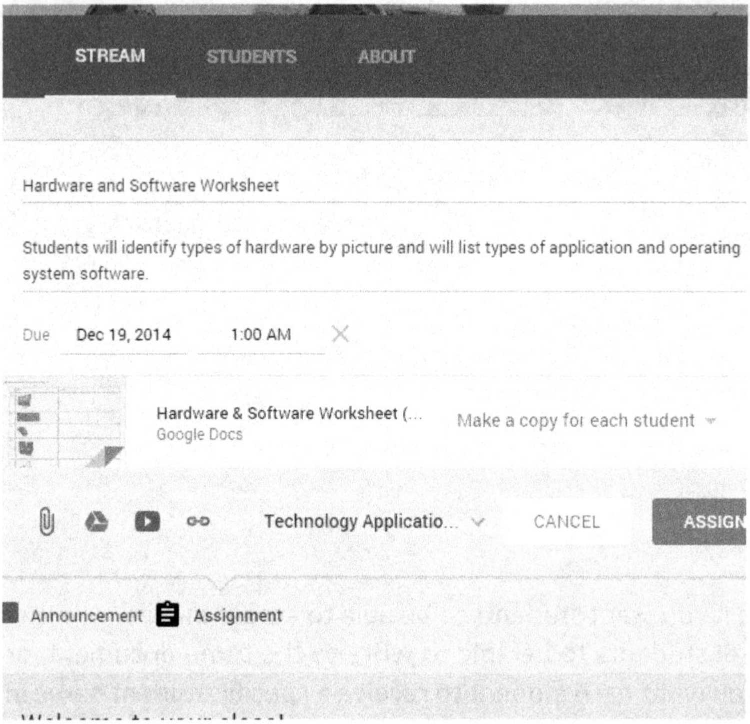

Step 7

Check that all information is right and press "ASSIGN."

Edit an Assignment

Step 1

Locate the task on your page and press three vertical dots in the top right corner, then select "Edit."

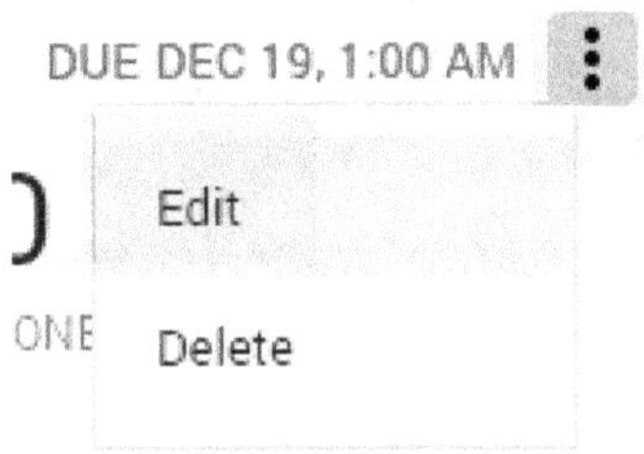

Step 2
You can change:

- Task Name
- Definition
- Due Date
- Apply additional resources
- Task Worksheet
- Task Grading Worksheet

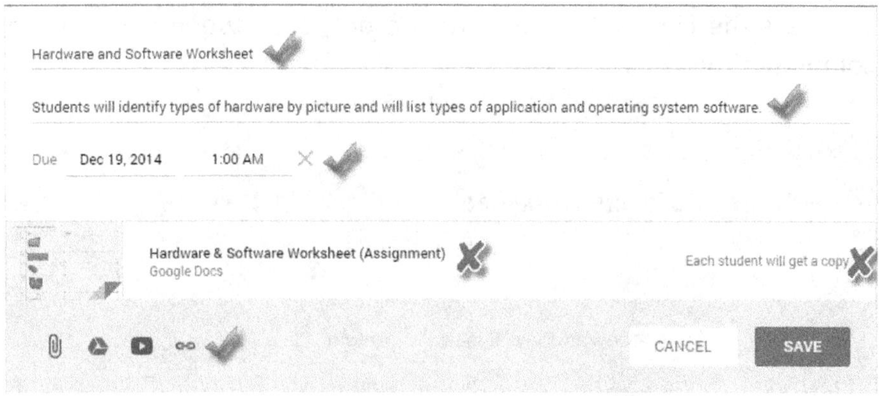

Grade an Assignment

Step 1

Click the title of the assignment you are ready to grade on your stream.

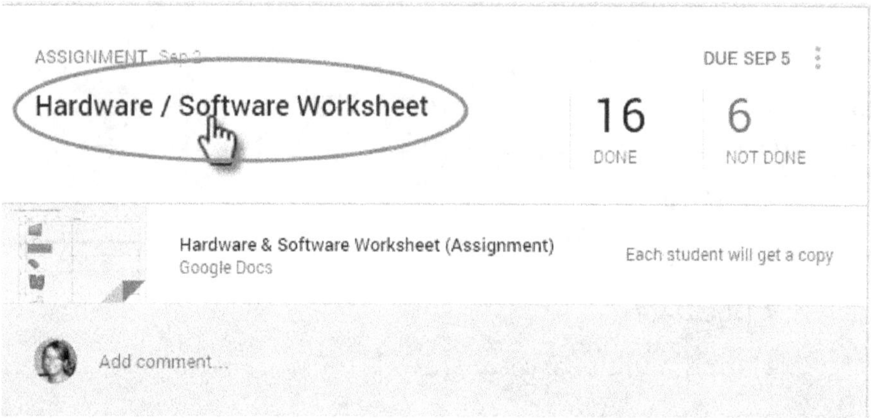

Step 2

OR press the Finished number to see only the students who have completed the task.

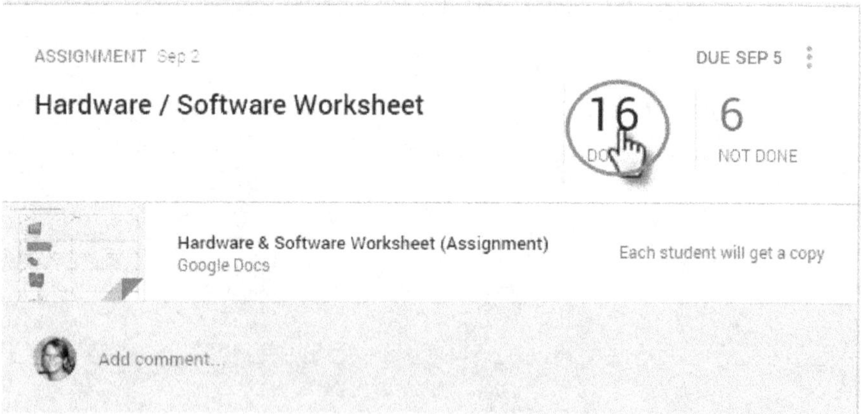

Step 3

Navigate to a student who has not completed his / her task. Tap on the student name and tap on the Worksheet to open it and rate it.

Step 4

Use the formatting toolbar to put comments on the assignment or label on it.

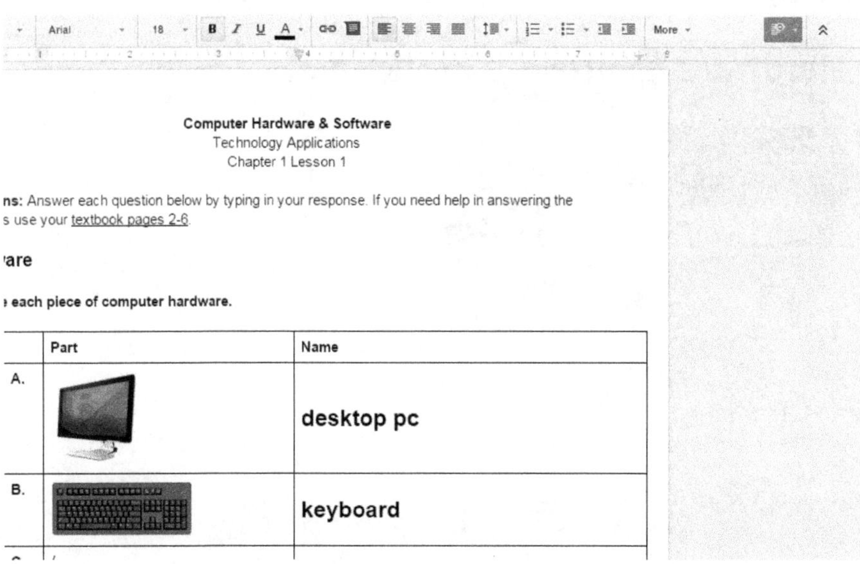

Step 5

The Worksheet was opened in a new window. Your comments/markups will be saved automatically. You should close the tab that will take you back to the student assignment list in the Google Classroom. You should join the grade for the student right now.

Step 6

Scroll to the top and press "RETURN" to give the file back to the student.

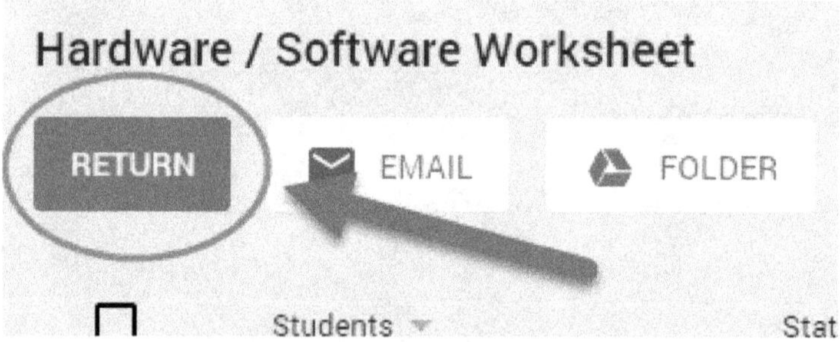

Send Feedback to Students

Step 1
Choose the assignment that you want to leave with any suggestions or remarks. Find the student you wish to write to and click on the student's name.

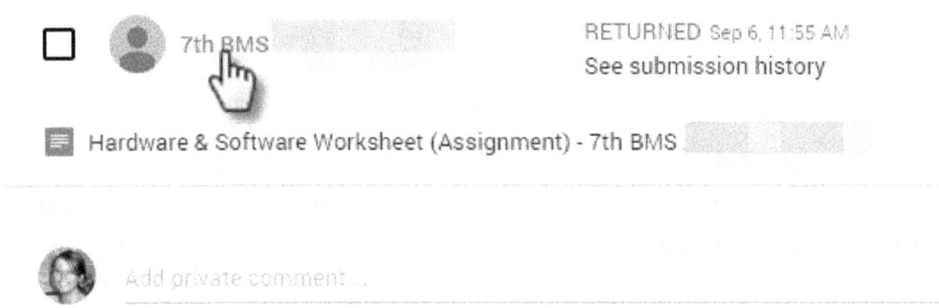

Step 2
When it says, Private comments write a message to the student and then press "POST"

Step 3
The actual student will be able to respond to the explanations you have made.

Change Points

Step 1
Open the assignment where you want to the set point value. Locate the "Points" box in the top right corner.

Step 2
You can either press the drop-down arrow next to the point value and pick the number.

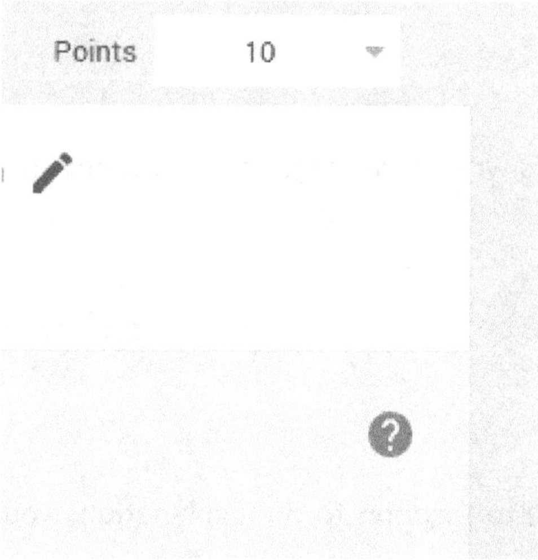

Step 3
OR click on "10" and enter the value of the point you want to use.

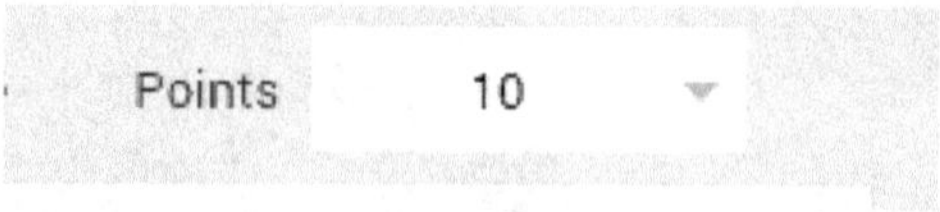

Step 4
Click "Fix" when you ask if you are sure you want to update the value of the amount.

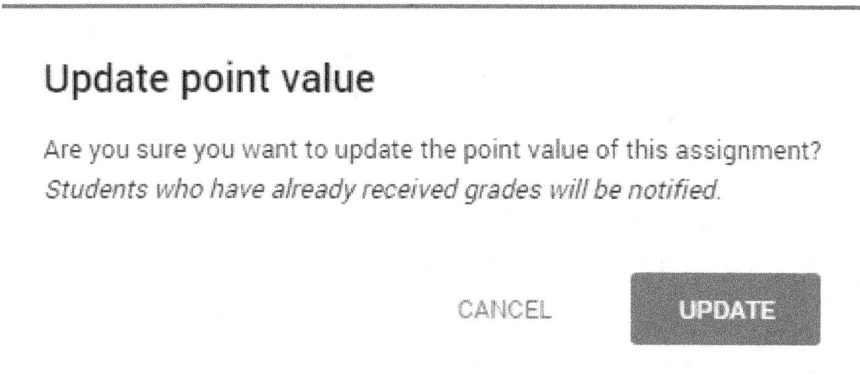

Download Student Grades

Step 1
Open the assignment in which you would like to access the score. Find the "DOWNLOAD" button at the top of the list.

Step 2
Click the button to either access "This assignment" or "All assignments."

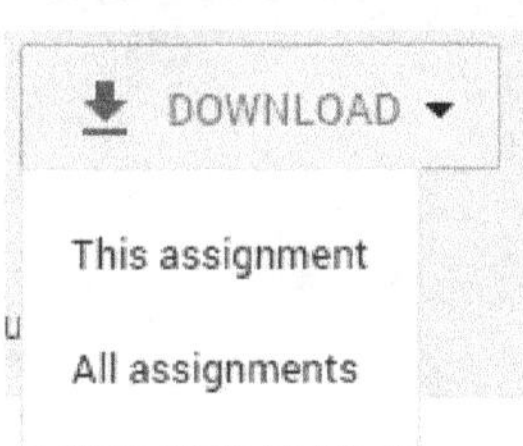

Step 3
Select the location of the file, name of the data, and then press "Save"

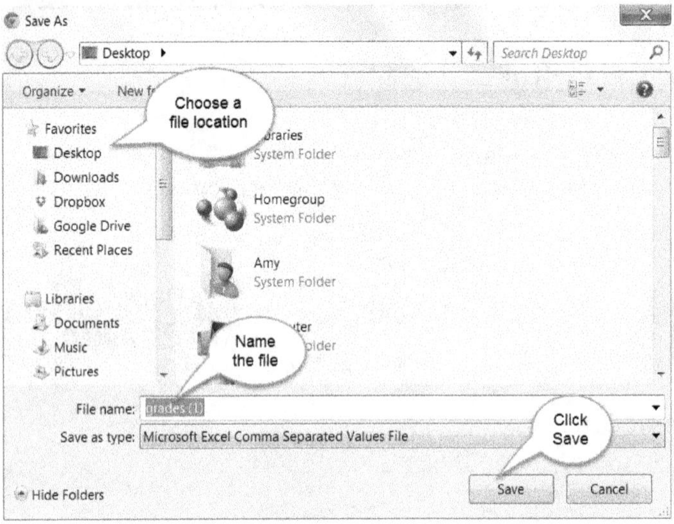

Step 4

Find the file on your computer and open it to see the ratings on the spreadsheet.

	A	B	C	D	E
1	First Name	Last Name	Email Address	Grade	Assignment State
2	7th BMS			7	Returned
3	7th BMS			10	Returned
4	7th BMS			7	Returned
5	7th BMS			10	Returned
6	7th BMS			9	Returned
7	7th BMS			10	Returned
8	7th BMS			8	Returned
9	7th BMS			8	Returned
10	7th BMS			10	Returned
11	7th BMS				Not done
12	7th BMS			9	Returned
13	7th BMS			9	Returned
14	7th BMS			8	Returned
15	7th BMS				Not done
16	7th BMS			9	Returned
17	7th BMS			10	Returned
18	7th BMS				Not done
19	7th BMS			6	Returned
20	7th BMS				Not done
21	7th BMS				Not done
22	7th BMS				Not done
23	7th BMS			7	Returned
24					

2.5 How to Educate the Employees

Using google classroom Professional development and work-related training can be a source of frustration for many people. So, what if employers could break the mold by making exercise fun, engaging, and memorable? Google Classroom gives life to the possibility. Using the many tools that the Classroom has to offer, it can broaden employee awareness and provide multiple opportunities for development. With a few necessary measures, employers can set up a Google Classroom that is worth the time of their workers.

Set Up A Classroom and Invite Students

Google Classroom for employees must be set up before training can begin. Remember to give the Classroom an apt, descriptive title that suits your needs. Separate classrooms can be set up for various topics; however, the most effective approach is to set up a classroom that divides themes from learning modules. Don't forget to invite workers to join the class or share the code of the Classroom.

Creating A Training Module

Organization is the most critical part of using the Classroom as a professional development method. Setting up the Classroom with training topics or modules will save managers time and include workers. When the basic setup is completed, it is time to build training modules. Click the plus sign on the Classwork tab to create a new subject and name it according to the content of the course. For example, the following Classroom is named Professional development & training with a "Differentiated Training" training theme that serves as the first section.

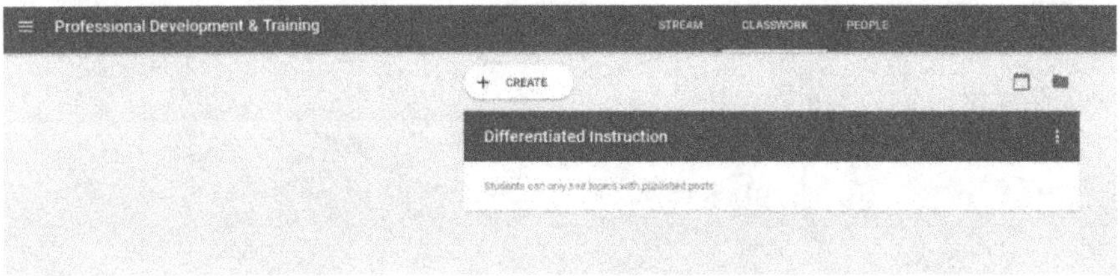

Add Content to Your Module

There are several options in the Classroom for adding material to a class. Adding tasks or questions is an easy task, but producing interesting content has a benefit for the Classroom. Adding a problem is an easy way to engage workers in a professional conversation.

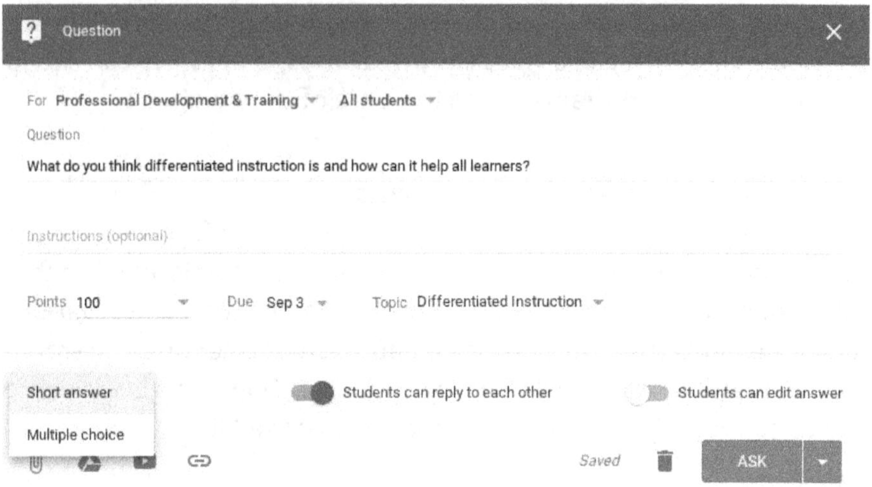

When adding an assignment, users can add files and other Google Drive content, such as slides or forms. YouTube videos or links to assignments may also be included. This offers the ability to generate content that relates to multiple types of learning and prevents workers from creating a space for "sitting and getting" professional growth. Setting a timetable to complete helps students to participate in activities at their own pace.

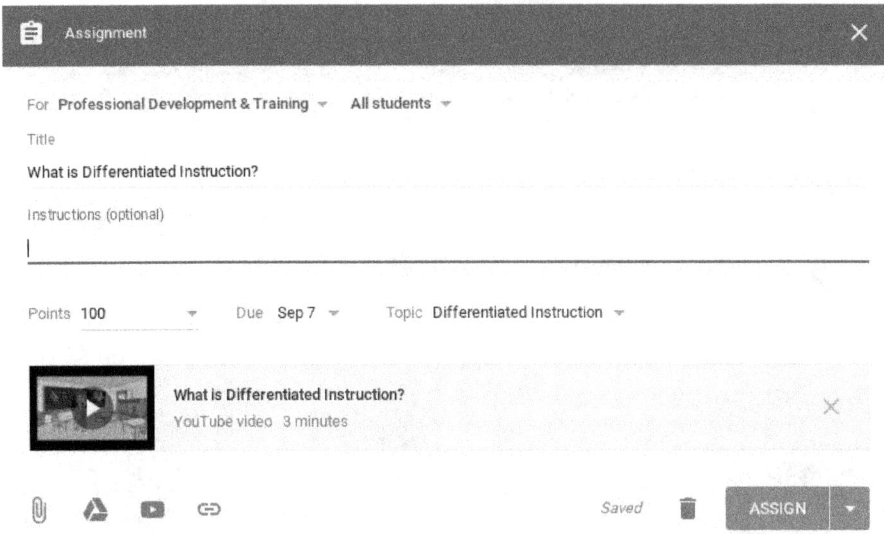

Assess Learning

A central aspect of professional growth is evaluating learning. The Classroom offers various tools for workplace evaluations. When making a question, it is possible to open the issue for user answers or to make multiple choices. Users can also submit a Google Form to allow a more detailed evaluation of their learning. This is also an effective way to obtain input on the training itself and the need to make improvements or adjustments to the curriculum for the client.

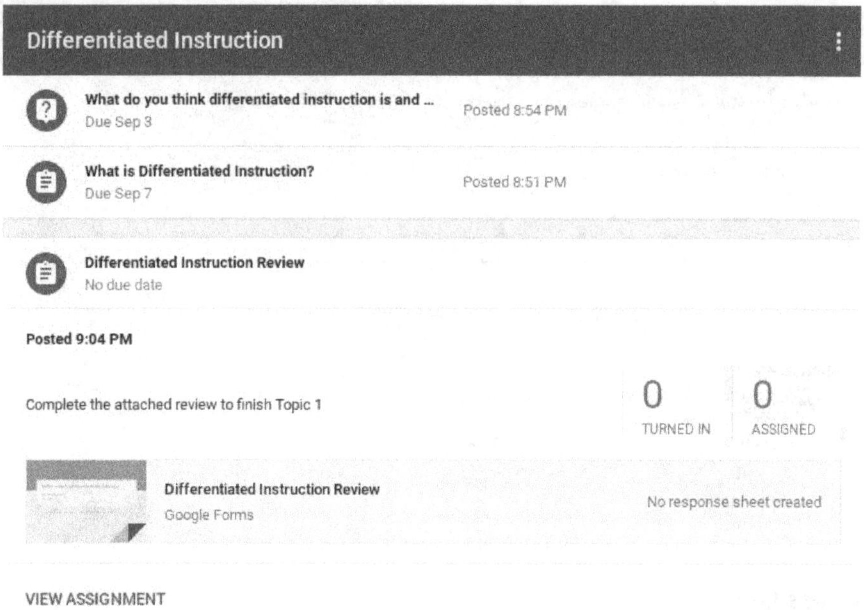

Follow Up

Follow-up is one of the main components of professional development. The development of a follow-up discussion allows workers to provide input on the delivery of learning materials. It also offers a platform to address areas in which assistance is required and helps peers to give each other guidance.

You'll learn how to adjust the settings in a classroom and exploring some additional features the Classroom has to offer in this segment.

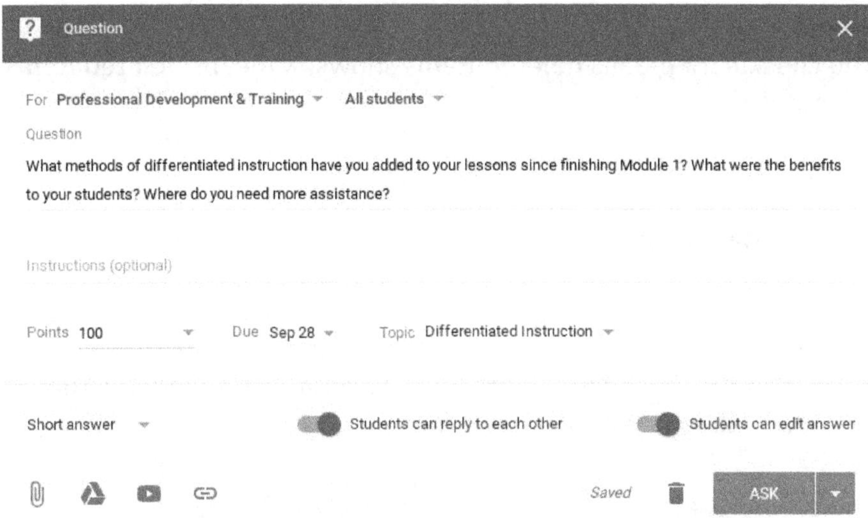

Display Deleted Items

Step1

See the menu on the left sidebar, "STREAM"

Step 2

To view items deleted (by you or a student), click on "x" in the slider next to the words "Display items deleted."

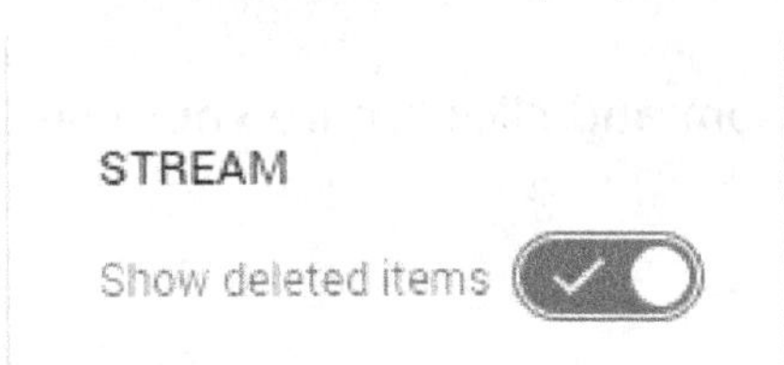

Step 3

The checkmark means deleted items shows, X means deleted items are not displayed.

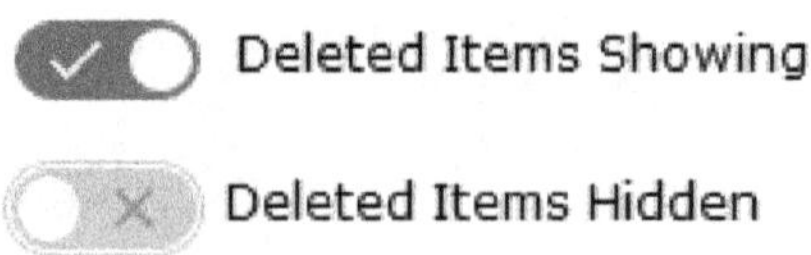

Step 4

Retrieve a deleted object from your computer. An element that is removed will say "removed" and faded.

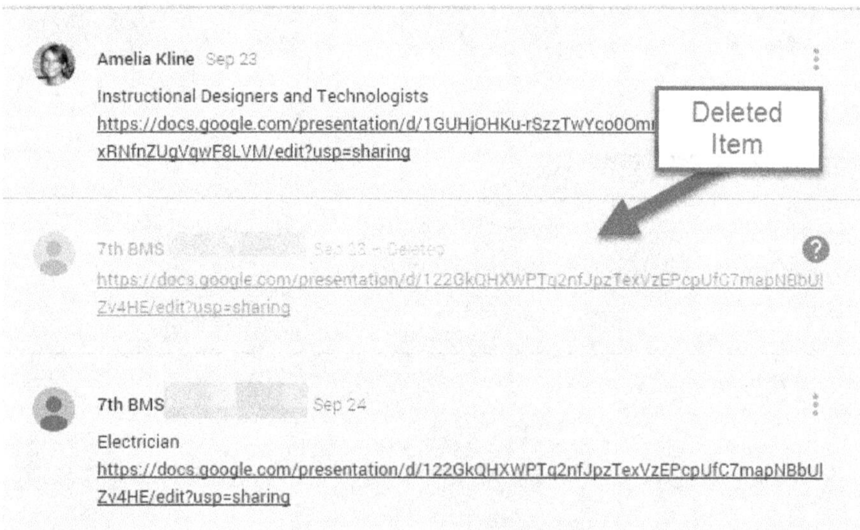

Post an Announcement

Step 1

Navigate the "Path" on your Classroom and click "Share your class with your teacher"

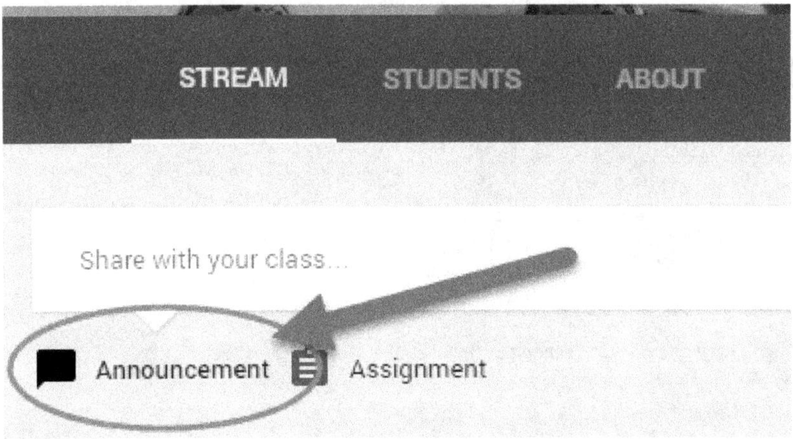

Step 2

Type your message where it says, "Share with your teacher"

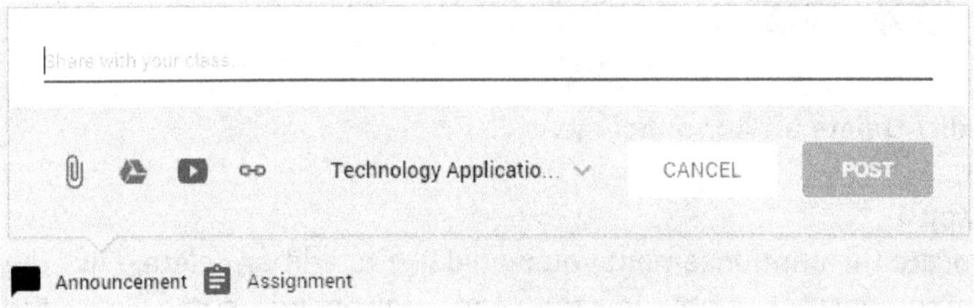

Step 3

Add any tools that you would like the notification by clicking the attachment, Google Drive, YouTube, or connection icons provided

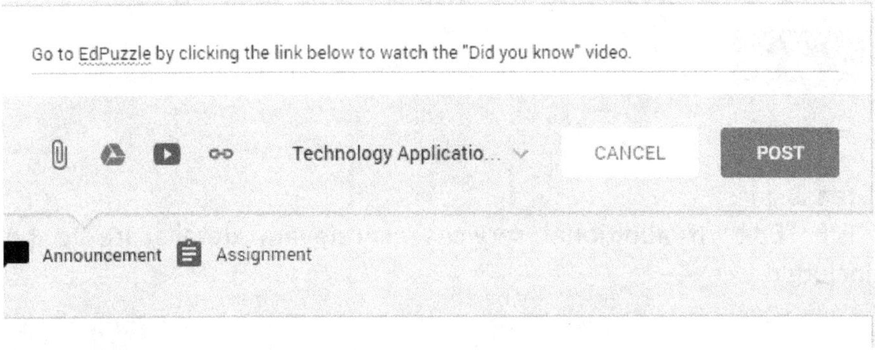

Step 4

Choose which section you would like to receive this message

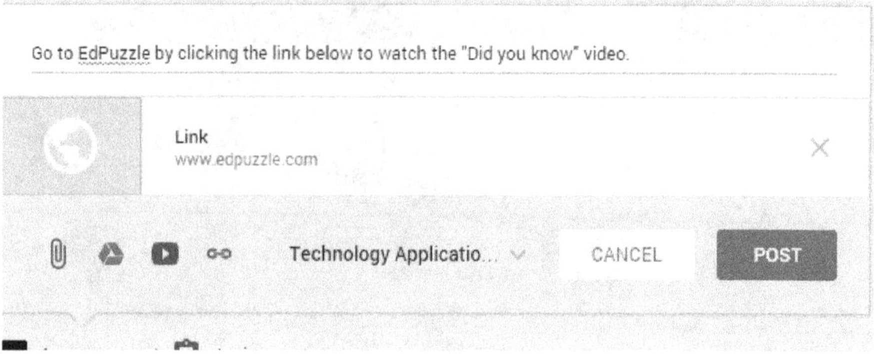

Step 5

Edit/ Delete an Announcement

Step 1

Locate the announcement you would like to edit or delete. Click the three vertical dots in the top right-hand corner of the announcement.

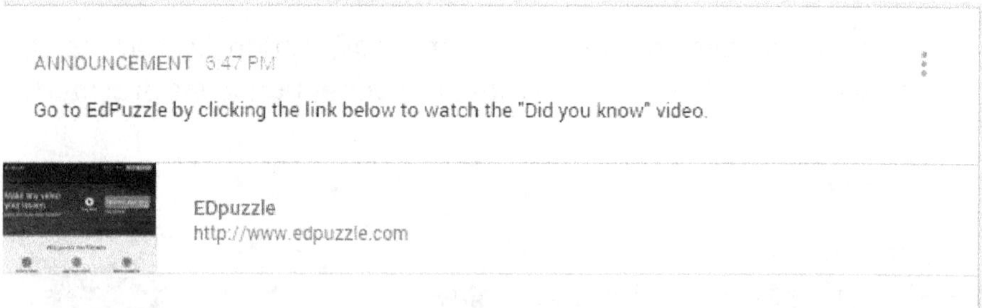

Step 2

Click "Edit" if additional services or relevant details are to be included.

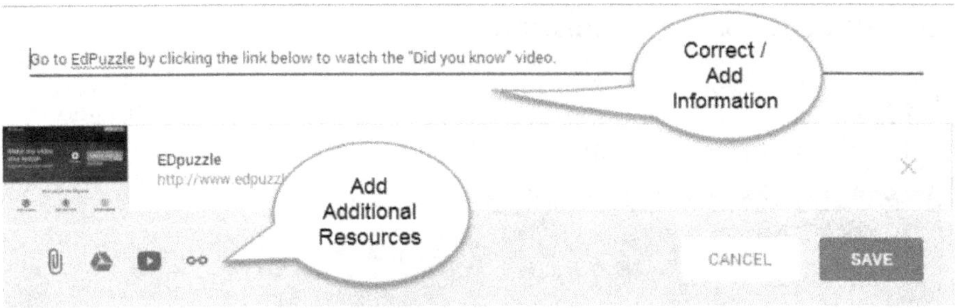

Step 3

Click "SAVE" Phase 4. To delete Announcement, pick "Delete"

Step 4

Choose "Delete" if you would like to delete the announcement.

* Note: the segment you are on will only be removed. If you have posted the ad on many pages, you have to delete them separately.

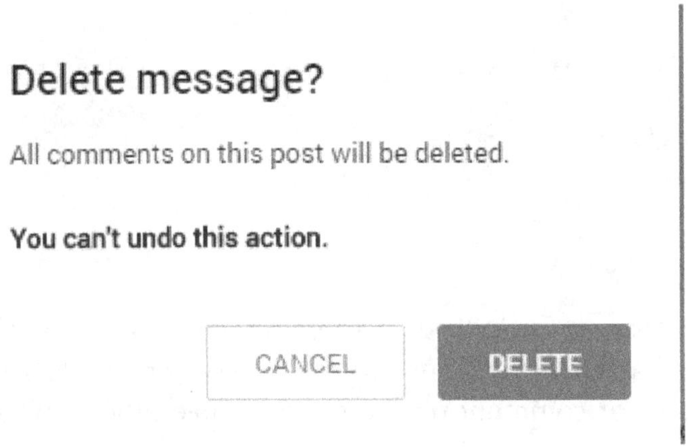

Step 5

Click "DELETE"

Edit Student Posting Permission

Step 1

On the top navigation pane, click "Students"

Step 2

Locate the words "Students can post and comment" and right-click the down arrow.

By default, students can post and comment to the tube. This can be updated so that students may attach comments to items that you post or require students to post or comment on the stream.

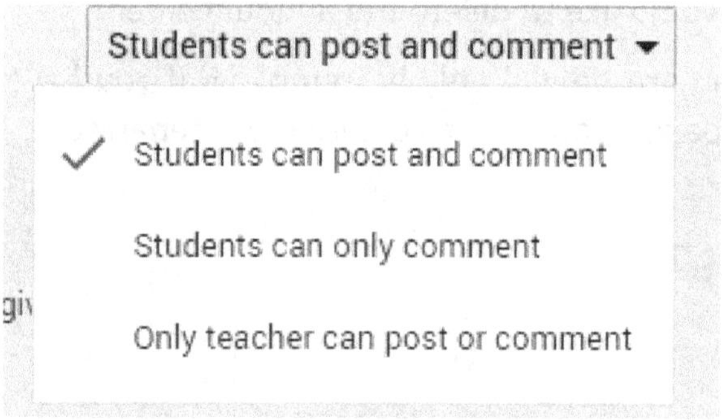

Step 3

To change the permits for individual students, pick the student(s), and then press "Actions" and then "Mute" so you won't allow the student(s) to post or comment on the stream while others still are allowed

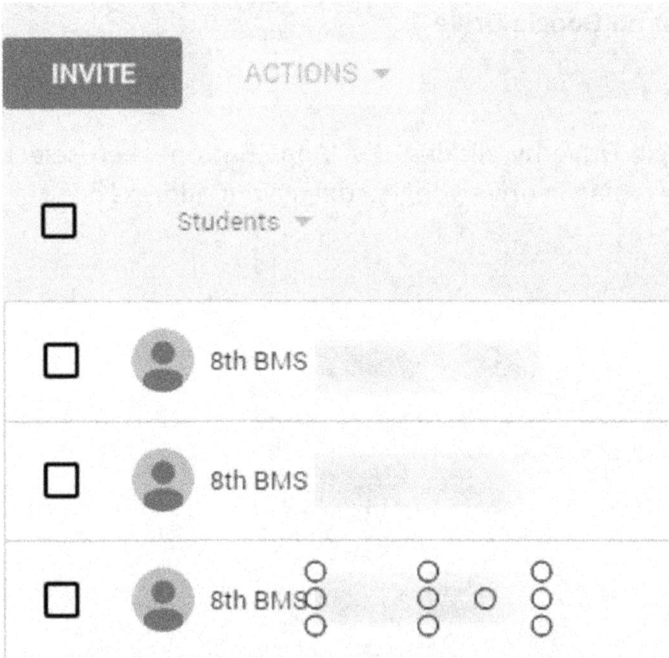

Step 4

Click "MUTE" As soon as you click "create" in the first section; Google will create a folder for the Google Drive materials that you have. Follow the given instructions to access this tab.

Go to your Google Drive by clicking on the 'Apps button' icon or by typing in drive.google.com on the address bar tab on Google Drive

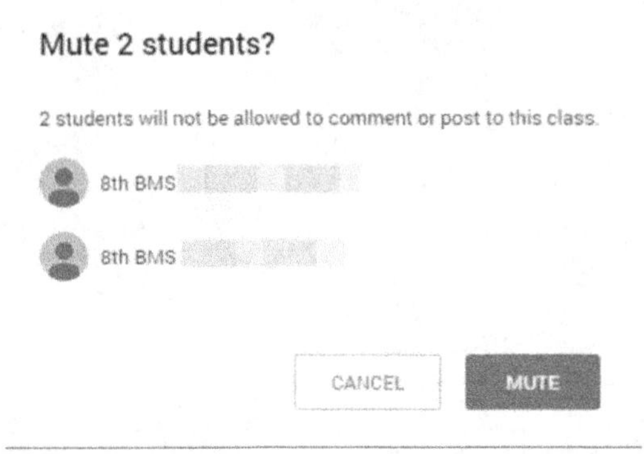

Classroom Folder on Google Drive

Step 1

Go to your Google Drive by clicking the 'Apps Button' then select 'Drive' icon or by typing in drive.google.com in your address bar

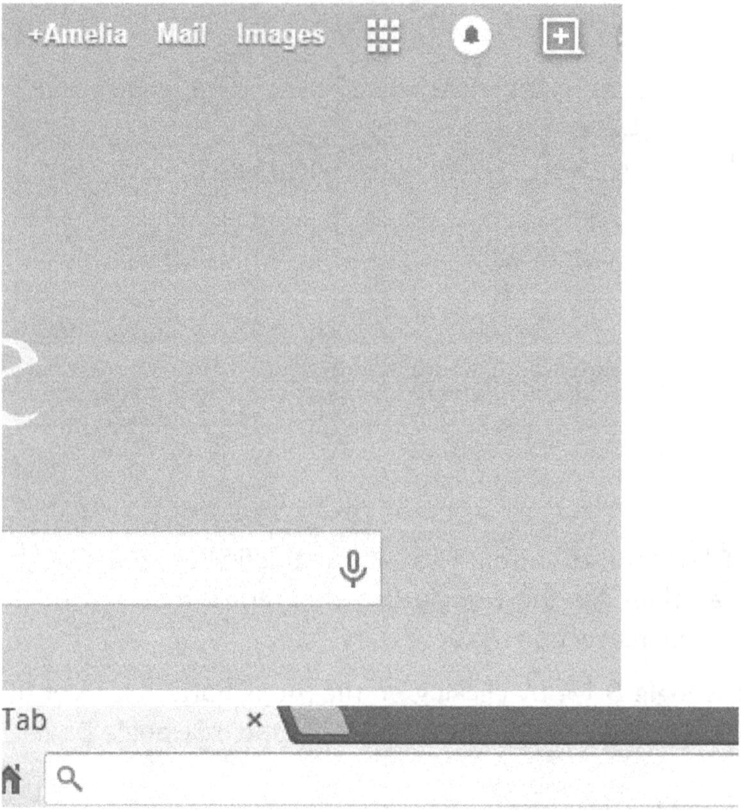

Step 2

Select "My drive" on the left sidebar and find the "Classroom" folder

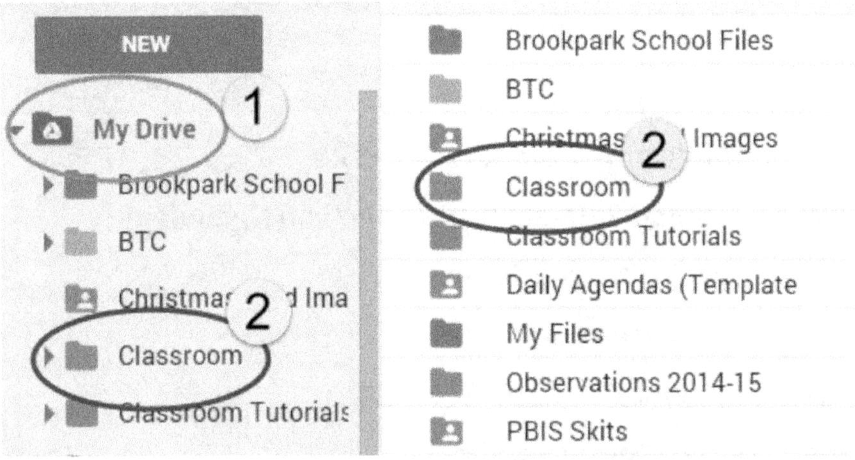

Step 3

Open the folder to see a different folder for each class you made

Step 4

Open the class folder to see all the materials/assignments used for that class.

- DF 85 - PACED Review
- Excel Worksheet Parts
- Hardware / Software Worksheet
- Individual Presentation Planning Document
- Job Sentences Fill In
- Job Vocabulary Notes
- MS Word - Create, Save, Open
- PowerPoint Assignment

Step 5

Open the task folder and see all student documents together. From here, you can leave feedback on assignments/worksheets.

Name ↑

- Hardware & Software Worksheet (Assignment) - 7th BMS Add
- Hardware & Software Worksheet (Assignment) - 7th BMS Cay
- Hardware & Software Worksheet (Assignment) - 7th BMS Cha
- Hardware & Software Worksheet (Assignment) - 7th BMS Con
- Hardware & Software Worksheet (Assignment) - 7th BMS Der
- Hardware & Software Worksheet (Assignment) - 7th BMS Elija
- Hardware & Software Worksheet (Assignment) - 7th BMS Fat
- Hardware & Software Worksheet (Assignment) - 7th BMS Mat
- Hardware & Software Worksheet (Assignment) - 7th BMS Oliv
- Hardware & Software Worksheet (Assignment) - 7th BMS Rya
- Hardware & Software Worksheet (Assignment) - 7th BMS Sab
- Hardware & Software Worksheet (Assignment) - 7th BMS Sky
- Hardware & Software Worksheet (Assignment) - 7th BMS Tho

Send Feedback to Google

Step 1

Is there going to be a floating 'where you're in the Classroom? "In the bottom right corner. Tap on the question mark.

Step 2

If you want to "Submit Feedback" you can request new features for the Classroom or send a message to Google.

When you select "Next" you will be able to take a screenshot of the area where you are proposing a new feature.

You can then record additional details and request your feedback.

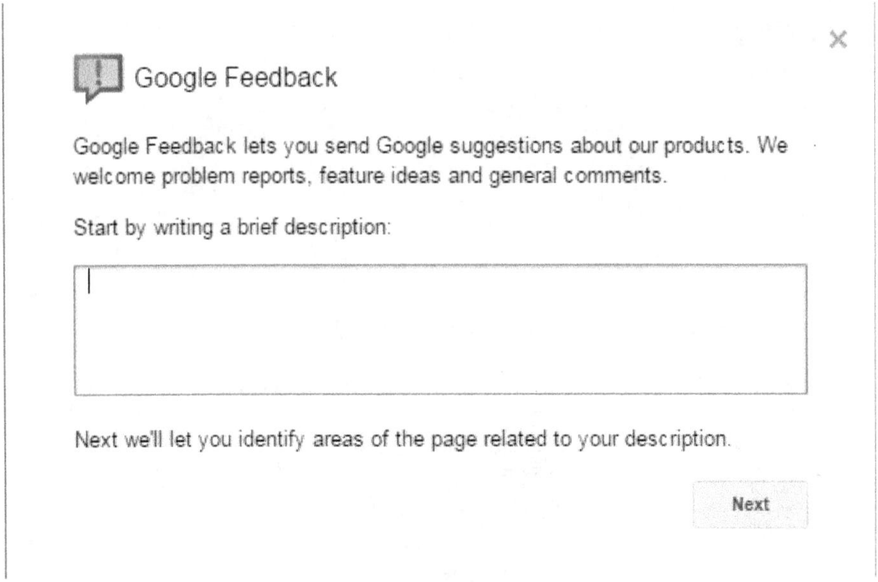

Step 3

If you click "Get Help" you will be taken to the Google Classroom Support page

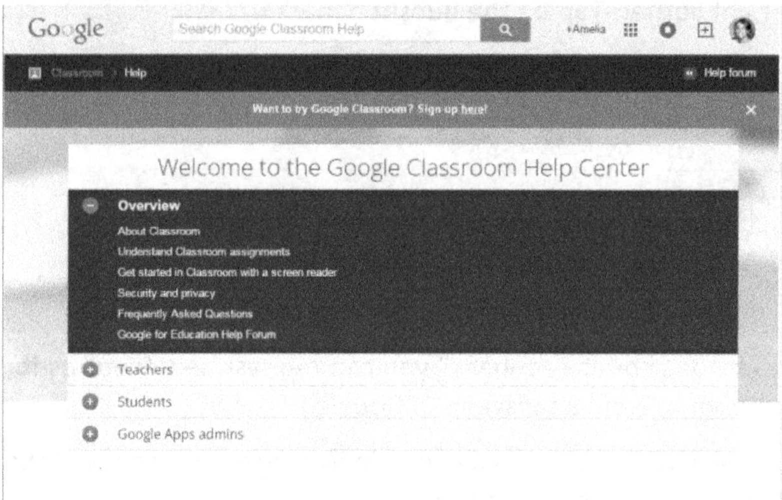

Step 4

If you choose "Ask Query" you will be taken to the Google Education Help forum

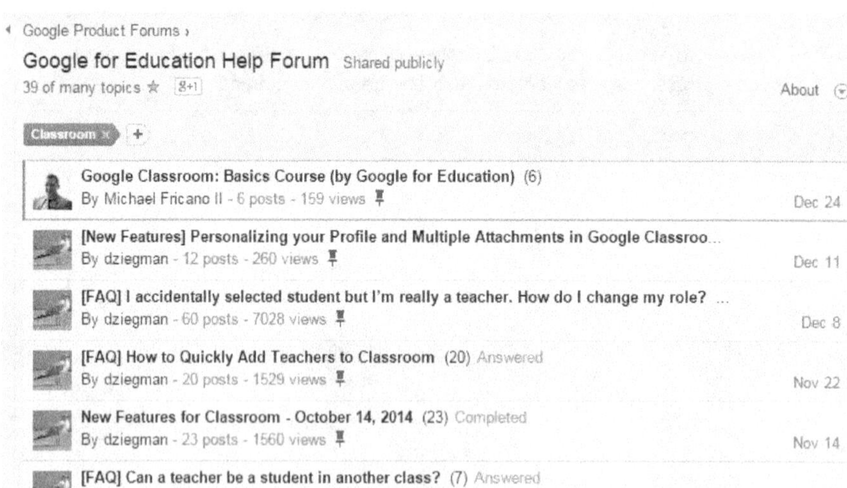

Chapter 3: Tips and Tricks Using Google Classroom

3.1 How to Motivate Students to Use Google Classroom?

Motivation is, in reality, one of the critical pillars of a successful classroom. As a coach, you're never going to accomplish your goal without inspiring your students. Motivation is not a complicated concept, and it is not a difficult job to motivate the students. We live our lives with joy and happiness, with pain and sorrow, because we are inspired to move forward. Yeah, often being ignored and disheartened in our lives, we avoid our hope of moving forward, but when human nature is encouraged, we start to think again about moving forward. Likewise, in most cases, without being inspired, the student loses hope to learn. That's why students need to be inspired.

A teacher can't be a good teacher unless he knows how to inspire a student. An excellent educator is a person who knows the facts and techniques of how to create an active classroom, where the student can participate enthusiastically. In reality, without motivating your students, you won't be able to fulfill your sole responsibility.

There are a variety of approaches to inspire students in the classroom. Some of the best ideas for encouraging the students in the school are discussed below. In reality, these tips on motivating your students can help you to make your classroom more productive and creative.

Ensure Anxiety-Free Classroom

What do you know? Fear also inhibits learning outcomes. So, never seek to impose terror by enforcing punishments in your classroom. I have found that some of us, the teachers, are implementing extra assignments as punishment, because physical disciplines do not occur in teaching today, as in the old and conventional period. Also, negative remarks often give rise to fear among students in the classroom. The fear in the classroom, whether it's for retribution or threatening comments, will never inspire the pupils. In reality, fear is an obstacle to participating successfully in the learning session. The student should never seek to take an active part in the classroom. That's why every teacher should maintain a fear-free class to inspire the students. So, never make negative statements and burdening tasks as punishments.

Promote Their Ideas and Decisions

Promote creative learning in the classroom offering assignments and coursework, giving them their freedom to choose the subject on their own. Your students are going to be inspired. You know, after all, that human beings want gratitude. In reality, appreciation changes a lot of students lives. Your students are unable to wait to take part in your next lecture. And if you enjoy fresh ideas, hundreds of excellent ideas will also be exposed to other students in your classroom. So always welcome new ideas to inspire your students.

Clarify the Objective

Every student likes clear instructions. Clarify each goal and target goal to be accomplished at the beginning of the course. Don't forget to mention the obstacles they might face during the session. Discuss possible antidotes about the challenges they might face. They will, therefore, be inspired to address more problems, which will make the topic more accessible. As a result, you will find that your classroom has become successful because your students are encouraged.

"As a teacher, you are preparing a country, a new world that will soon rule you and the earth."

~Md. Akbar Ali

Improve the Environment of The Classroom

Don't always sit down to discuss the lesson. Move beside the students and think about the experience. Keep them out of your class occasionally. Tell them to visit the library sometimes for research purposes. The shift in the classroom environment stimulates the excitement of the learning brain, which is, in fact, a prerequisite for motivation.

Be A Good Listener

Listen carefully to what your student needs to say. Appreciate their emotions and opinions. Take the right steps to solve the problems they talk about. Be a great listener, guy. They're going to start loving you when you listen to them with proper care. You will win their confidence, therefore. Now, is it not easy to inspire them? If you want your students to listen to you, you have to listen to them first.

Share Their Experience

Not all students can share their experience in the course of the class. Some of them will be occupied by reading books. Yet as sure students discuss their lessons-related expertise, others may be inspired to participate actively. Prepare the lesson in such an inspiring way that various types of learners can engage actively in the sharing of lessons. In this situation, other students are often inspired to share their own experiences. You can, therefore, ensure that the classroom is successful.

Positive Competition

Constructive competition is, in essence, a useful strategy in the school. Ensure the rivalry is constructive. A good rivalry in group work motivates learners tremendously. We are also prepared to carry out community work, which will also bring significant benefits to their professional life. There is no doubt that healthy competition sparks excitement among the students in the classroom.

Know Your Student Well

You need to know your students well. You should also know their preferences, their dislikes, their effectiveness, and their lack of performance. When your students realize that you know them well, they will begin to like you and disclose their obstacles. This would be easier for you to inspire your students on the right path. You will not be able to encourage them because you know them well.

Support Them and Give Them Responsibility

Give them the responsibility of the pupils. Assign them a class project. They're going to work with determination for sure. In such a situation, individual students may also have to fulfill their obligations. When you give them responsibilities, trust within themselves will grow, and they will begin to feel that they are valuable because they get value from you. They would then be inspired to engage more in the classroom. When you trust them, they will always trust you in return.

Show Your Enthusiasm

To Convey your enthusiasm in the classroom during a lecture while meeting your duties. Share your excitement about their great success. Again, it shows an optimistic interest when every learner presents a new idea. Your expression of enthusiasm will encourage them.

Hold Your Record

Write a report for you. Write down every success of your pupil. If you find that a specific student is changing, speak to the student about change. Show the student the record. Rewards and support the student in front of the classroom. Even share the changes with your friends. If a student discovers that you're taking care of the student while you address from your record, the student is inspired.

Constructive Feedback

If a student is not doing well, include positive feedback. When necessary, offer a second chance. Be a friend and seek to understand the case of such a bad result. Encourage the student to inspire him/her to improve quickly next time as he/she did not understand how to do well in this subject with proper knowledge and technique. Okay, you know what? Your constructive reviews will change a lot of lives. Look closely at the worst students in your school; you're going to get a lot of good qualities. Inform them of the beautiful conditions they possess. In reality, value them, which will inspire them significantly in return.

Real-Life Situation In the classroom

Relate your lesson plan to a real-life scenario. Make the lesson enjoyable with the fun of the game. Tell them a remarkable story with a mixture of humor. The reading thus makes it possible for the student to respond to his or her own experience. Let them also apply the lesson to their personal experience. Only track it accurately. In reality, when you're dealing with your reading in real-life scenarios, students are encouraged to learn and attend your class.

Bottom Line

It is the responsibility of a teacher to ensure that the classroom is active. Teachers should not say that they can just enter and exit the classroom with 'Good Stories' without providing a successful class. Through inspiring your pupils, you can make the best classroom you're expecting. After all, as being a teacher, you are preparing a country, a new world that will soon rule you and the planet.

Communicate with Your Parents and Guardians

Use the classroom to keep the parents and guardians in the loop. You should invite parents to sign up for a regular or weekly e-mail rundown of what's going on in their children's schools. Emails contain the pending or unfinished work of a student, as well as updates and questions that you post in the class stream.

Assigning Assignments to A Group of Students

Teachers may delegate work and post-announcements to individual students or a group of students in a class. This functionality helps teachers to distinguish instruction as required, as well as to promote collaborative group work.

Using the Classroom Mobile App Annotations

Students and teachers can use the Mobile Classroom on Android, iOS, and Chrome mobile devices. You can provide input in real-time by annotating the student's work in the app. Students may also write down their tasks to convey an idea or concept more easily.

Explore the Integration of Classroom with Other Resources

Google Classroom uses an API to link and exchange knowledge with a variety of your favorite devices. Thousands of applications and websites are incorporated, like Pear Deck, Actively Read, Newsela, and many, many more.

Encourage Supervisors to Use Classroom Metrics

While this feature is for administrators — not teachers — it is still worth mentioning here. Administrators may use the Admin console to see stats such as how many classes have been created, how many posts have been posted, and the teachers use the tool. Access to this knowledge will help customize teacher support.

3.2 Tips for Using Google Classroom

Using Google Classroom is relatively easy for teachers and students. There are, however, some tips and tricks that you can use to make your life and the lives of your students much more comfortable.

1. Using Google Apps to Build Documents

Since Google Classroom is based on Google Drive, all Google Drive apps (such as Docs, Papers, Slides, and so on) are entirely incorporated into the Classroom. So, for instance, when you create a homework sheet in Google Docs, a student can open a document in Google Docs, complete the work, and turn it on. You can then open the same text, comment on it, rate it, and return it to the student. If you are using another program, such as Microsoft Word, you have to upload a text, and the student has to download it to work on it. Then, the student has to re-upload the paper and re-attach it to the assignment before handing it in. Then you've got to download it to make a comment and score it. Using Google Drive software should take out all the uploading and download and make it a smooth experience.

2. Inviting Students Using Class Code

You can save much time encouraging students to your class if you simply provide them with the class code and, thus, the duty to ask them. Otherwise, each student must be invited individually, which can be time-consuming. Only find your class code at the bottom left of the Stream class tab, and then distribute it to your entire class. Tell your students to visit classroom.google.com, sign in with their Google account, and click the plus sign on the top of the page, and select Enter Class.

3. Choose to Make A Particular Copy of a Document for Each Student

Much of the time, when you create a homework assignment, you want to choose to Make a copy for each student, which helps each student to focus on a copy of the document. If you decide Students Can View File, students won't be able to edit it at all, and if you choose Students Can Edit the File, only then will students be operating the file.

4. Join Other Classes as A Student

If you're only learning how to use Google Classroom, as an instructor, and you can enter other courses as a student to appreciate the student's perspective better and learn from others who are more familiar with Google Classroom. Just ask for the class code from the other trainer and join the class when one of your students enters your level.

5. Explain the Shift in Ownership in Assignment Documents to Your Students

You can make students aware that they can no longer alter assignments when they turn on duty unless they "unsubmit" jobs. After the transfer has been turned in, control returns to the instructor so that you can assess and have input on the task. You will return it to the student after you do so, after which the student will edit the document again. If the student unsubmit the assignment before it is marked, he or she must return the task when it is completed.

6. Create Reports from Inside the Job

Tell you to make an assignment in which you ask your students to write an essay on a particular subject. You have not provided a workbook or other tools for students to work on. The best way for students to begin is to create a new Google Doc from within the assignment just by clicking the Create button and selecting the type of document they want to create. The paper is automatically generated on Google Drive and attached to the task, so students don't need to go to Google Drive. This approach can also be used to construct assignment materials.

Useful Tips for Teachers

Google Classroom streamlines the management of student work announcing, assigning, receiving, marking, providing reviews, and returning. It saved several hours of work for the teachers.

Without a reliable workflow and some strategy, the grading of digital work can be cumbersome. Google Classroom makes working with students more efficient — but only if you understand how Classroom works and how to use it for your advantage.

Often a few quick tips will make a difference.

1. Number Your Assignments

Numbering your tasks is one of the best tips I've ever got. This lets you organize files not only in the Classroom but also keep Google Drive clean and tidy.

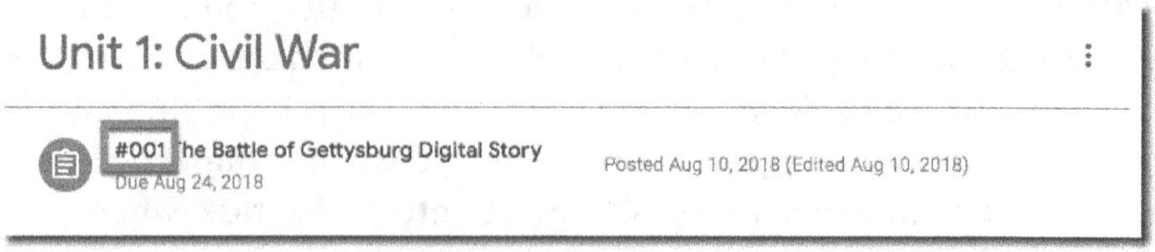

2. Using CTRL + F to Find Numbers and Words in Classroom

Even the most structured Classwork page can be very long after a few weeks of assignments. Use the keyboard shortcut, Control + F (Command + F on a mac), to check for keywords or allocate numbers (as mentioned above) on the tab. Teach your students this trick, too!

3. Pick an Organizing Method for Using Topics

The topics feature on the classwork page helps coordinate assignments for students and teachers. There are a variety of different ways to coordinate. There are many ways to do so, and what works for one teacher doesn't work for all of us. It is a personal choice for an instructor. Select a technique that will work with your subject area and grade level.

4. Create A "Stuff" Subject and Keep Top of The Classwork Page

Each class requires a place to store stuff, links, class rules, syllabus, etc. Mindy Barron recommends that you create a unique theme for resources and class materials and keep it close to the top for easy access. Make sure to name these files only so that students know exactly what's in there.

5. Build A Google Classroom Class Model

When you have chosen your preferred Google Classroom organizing approach (and checked it!), Make a copy of the class as your reference. You will continue to make a copy any time you need a new class, and all of your topics have been produced and arranged, and your assignments will be saved as drafts!

To make a copy of the class in Google Classroom: go to your home Google Classroom, then click on the three dots on the class card and pick "Copy Class".

6. Using Direct Assignment Links

Do you know that you can get a direct connection to a particular assignment? It makes it so easy to refer students back to a specific lesson. Just go to the Classwork tab, find the task, click the three dots on the right side of the job, and copy the link.

7. Using Google Docs as A Syllabus (Secondary)

Most teachers using Google Docs to create a syllabus so that it is a live document that can be modified throughout the year. Add connections to external services, regular tasks, significant dates, etc. You can also connect to Google Classroom assignments (see above) to prevent a long search for students.

8. Breaking Smaller Tasks with Separate Dates

Project-based learning is so critical, and when we continue to push beyond static, one-and-one tasks, we need to think differently about how we work in our classrooms.

Big projects can be daunting for students, particularly those who have not learned how to manage their time. It is necessary to give them milestones and split the project into smaller tasks with checkpoints.

9. Build a Separate Enrichment and Extension Class

In class, completing the assignment early did not mean free time or games. This included reading and learning programs for my pupils. Consider building a separate class inside Google Classroom for expansion or enrichment activities.

You might also gamify this concept and offer digital badges to carry out a mission or challenge.

10. Using Private Comments for Meaningful Feedback and Student Conversations

One of my favorite features in Google Classroom is a unique comment feature. This little tool will help to streamline communication with your students and strengthen the feedback loop. Teacher feedback is one of the most critical factors in student development!

Private comments are just a private one between you and your student. (No one else can read these.) Remember to use private comments not only at the end of the task but throughout!

And this doesn't negate the power of face-to-face conversations, but it does help to record how students can remember feedback, as well as allow students to connect who don't usually speak in front of the class.

There are some different places where you can add private messages to your students.

Add A Private Message on The Student Work Page:

1. From the Classwork tab, press the assignment for which you would like to provide feedback.

2. Click the "Show Task" button.

3. Select the student from the list on the left.

4. Towards the bottom of the right-hand row, you can see "Add Private Post"

5. Click to type and add a private message for your student.

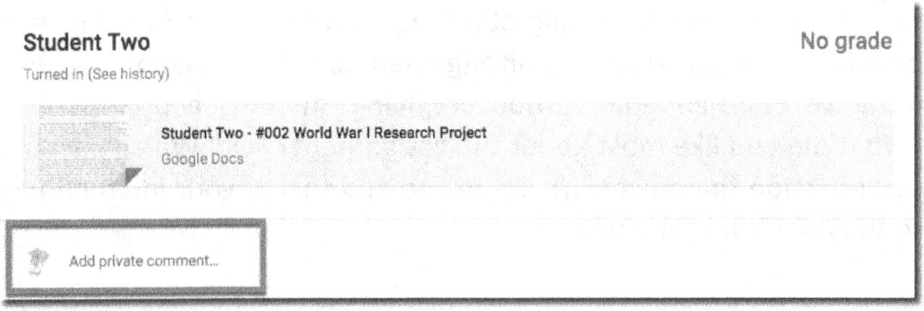

You can also add private comments using the latest grading feature in Google Classroom from inside the student paper.

Add A Single Statement Using the Grading Tool:

1. From the Classwork tab, press the assignment on which you would like to provide feedback.

2. Click the "Show Task" button.

3. Click on the student file that you would like to give feedback.

4. Using the right-hand panel to add your private message.

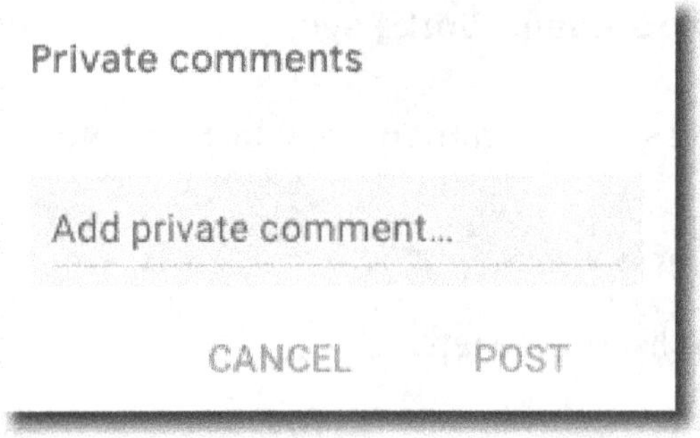

11. Using Private Comments for Reflection

Teachers take-private comments a step further and make them part of the assignment by asking students to include a reflection as a private comment after submitting their job. Sean Fahey suggests using an open-ended question or giving students a prompt like, "What did you like most about the assignment? "Or" Which part did you question the most? "Make sure to add this to your instructions, so they don't forget about it!

12. Add A Sample Paper to Each Task

As a copy for each student, add a blank Google Doc or prototype to each task. You can view the assignment page in Google Classroom and see a thumbnail for each student. It helps you to see improvement, or lack of progress, at a glance.

Even if you don't have a template for your task, add a saved black document to be used as a source so that you can still show the thumbnail!

13. Invite Teachers Who Are Hesitant to Use Google Classroom to Become A Student or Co-Teacher in Your Class

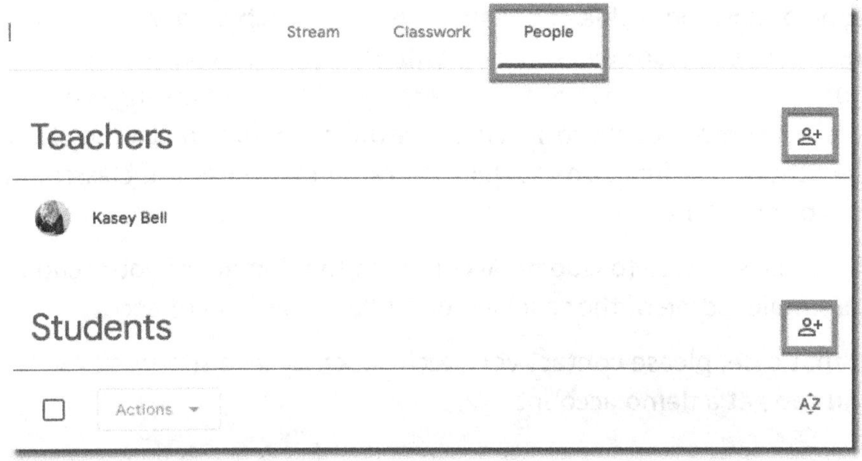

Not every teacher is on board the Google Classroom. If you're dealing with a reluctant teacher or maybe a little technophobic, invite them to join your class as a student or co-teacher.

Invite them to be a student first, so they get an idea of how it works before giving them the ability to add and edit the class as a co-teacher. Co-teachers can do all you can in a class.

Inviting teachers:

1. Go to the folder where you're going to add them,

2. Then press the People tab at the top of the list.

3. To prompt as a co-teacher, click the Invite Teachers button, type their name or email address, and press Invite.

4. To inspire an instructor as a student, click the Invite Students icon, enter their name or email address, and press Invite.

14. Build A Student Demo Account to Show Your Students Google Classroom.

Google Classroom does not currently give teachers a way to view their classes as students. But, if you want to see your course as a student, you must have a student account. The solution suggested is to use a demo account to sign in as a student so that you can see how the school side functions to demonstrate how to use the classroom for your students.

If you have access to Google Accounts in the domain of your school, it's simple. Some of the teachers don't have this kind of access.

In that case, please contact your tech coach or tech support to see if you can get a demo account.

15. Pack Your Digital Assignments

How to Pack Digital Assignments This guide is a series of tips to help you enhance how your directions and bundle everything your students need into your Google Classroom assignments.

These are the tips that will save you time and save your wellbeing!

The more detail you provide in the report, the fewer questions you have to answer, and the fewer reasons students have for not completing the report on time.

16. Using Moving to The Top to Put Back Relevant Older Content to Students 'Attention

This essential act moves the task, announcement, or question to the top of the class line. Using this if students have not handed over the assignment in OR if you want to remind them of the upcoming deadline.

17. Email Anyone in A Class in the "Classmates" Tab

After you click the "Classmates" button, click the checkbox, which is located above all of your students, to highlight all of them. Click "Actions" and "Delete." This is perfect for calling particular attention to something that you want to talk to OR students for longer-term contact.

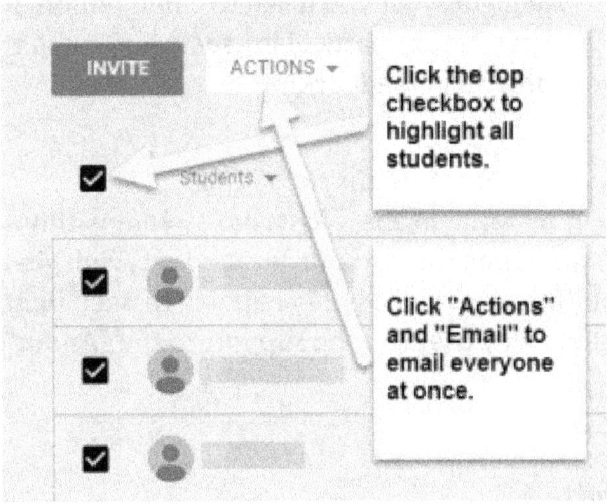

18. Use comments

Using the right kind of comment, you will leave students in the classroom with a few types of comments. Knowing how each of you works will make you more productive and successful.

• **Inserting Class Comments**

Do so by adding a line in your class stream to the "outside" of the task or announcement. It would make the statement available to the entire class (vital if it is the response to a question that someone may have).

• **Add Private Comments**

do so by displaying the results of the test and clicking on the specific test. On the right corner, where you can see student submissions, the comment bar at the bottom adds a message that only the student can see (vital if they have a sensitive grade or feedback information).

• **Making Notes in The Doc/Slide/Sheet/Drawing**

do so by clicking on the student file he/she sent to you. Tap the black speech bubble button to highlight what you'd like to comment on. It makes a very pointed perspective on particular aspects of student work (essential to be very precise in feedback).

19. Using Announcements to Share "Right Now" Links

Announcements to bring material in the classroom stream without creating a task for students. Using them to provide students with vital connections, documents/files, and videos they're going to need right now. (If it's a resource that they use, add the support to the "About" tab instead.)

20. Keyboard Commands

Using the keys instead of the mouse to guide the keys. Keyboard commands beat every time you move and press the mouse. When entering classes, type the grade for a particular student assignment, then click the down key to get to the next student. Use keystrokes instead of mouse clicks to cycle through students to save a lot of time.

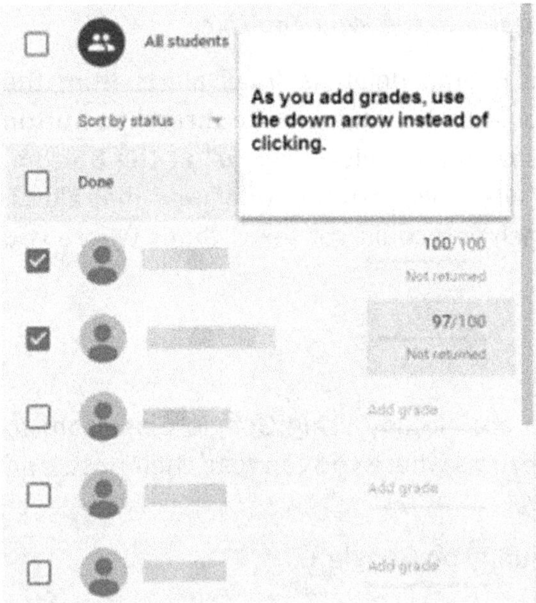

21. Reuse Posts

Don't recreate projects, announcements, or questions that are identical to those you've already made. Click the "+" button in the bottom right corner and select the "reuse post" button. Choose the task, announcement, or query you created before. Before you reset it, you can change and upgrade it.

You can also opt to make new copies of all the attachments you used before when you reuse a message.

22. Grade Everything in One Place

Click the three-line button at the top left of the Classroom and pick "Job" at the right. Here, you'll find all assignments for all of your classes in one place. Work your way down the entire list and get to the top of it all in one position.

23. Use Email from The Classroom the Way You Like

Would you spend too much time deleting email alerts from the Classroom and wish you could turn it off? Tap the three-line button at the top left of the Classroom and select "Menu" at the bottom. There's a checkbox located where you can turn off your e-mail alerts. (Or if you turn it off and wish you could get texts, that's where you turn them on!)

24. Get Ideas

from other educators who are already using Google Classroom to hang out in a lot of online forums where you can read their posts and ask questions.

- Google Classroom Community on Google +
- Google Applications on Google Plus Education Community (with Google Classroom category)
- Twitter hashtag: # Google Classroom (for Google Classroom related posts)
- Twitter hashtag: # Googled (for general Google updates)
- General Pinterest tools on Google Classroom
- Pinterest board on Google Classroom by shakeup learning

25. Get the Features You Want in The Classroom

Do you have any suggestions for a new Google Classroom feature? Is there something you can do, but I wish you could make things easier? This kind of input is what the Google Classroom team needs from the teachers. Click in the bottom left corner of the screen and select "Send Feedback". According to a member of the Google Classroom team who spoke to my Google Teacher Academy community in December 2014, someone from their team reads every single feedback sent that way.

It's how they made a lot of significant improvements to the Google Classroom app. And the simpler a feature request, the more likely it is to be implemented. So, give feedback and send it back regularly!

3.3 Google Classroom Management Tips

Google Classroom will streamline assigning, storing, marking, and returning student work. It saves hours and removes the dreaded piles of paper that need grading (you know the ones that taunt you from the corner of your desk). One significant advantage for remote work and management is that you only need internet access to work on assignments and grading. Your large teacher's bag full of papers and workbooks will start gathering dust.

You may need to set up a system for assigning and assessing digital jobs. This can be just as intimidating and frustrating as conventional grading if you don't have a way to get through it all. Google Classroom is much like your school book or textbook. The way you use it will decide your success with it.

1. Organizing Your Google Classroom

Content Arrange your contents by folders (subject, month, subject) to make it easier to access the activities you want to delegate. Many of the items you charge to Google Classroom come directly from your Google Drive. When you have a robust content management program, the next year with your new class would be a breeze.

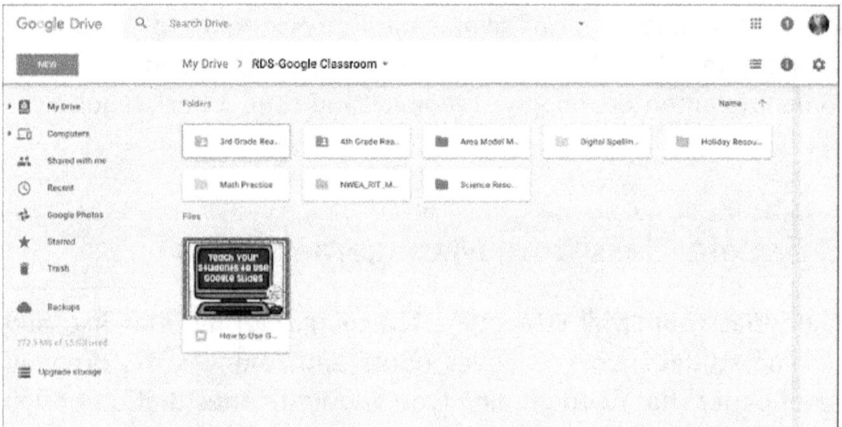

1. Organize your content so it's easy to access year after year. Folders by grade level, subject, standard, or topic. Whatever makes the most sense for you and your system.

Are your school purchasing the "digital" edition or CD edition of your textbooks and worksheets?

You can view these and then save the page to your drive or screen as a JPG (picture format). Next, open Google Slides and set the size of your page to 8.5 x 11 inches (regular paper size). Right-click on the slide and click "Context Folder." You may insert a picture instead of selecting a color. Pick the workbook that you want to delegate, and it will become the backdrop of the slide.

This means that the students can't push the page around or unintentionally remove parts of it. Though they can also erase the slide, and you will have to reassign the lesson to that particular student. When you teach your students how to create text boxes, they will be able to complete assignments and apply all of them digitally.

Pro Tip: It's time-consuming to transform all your worksheets into Google Classroom, so it's not a valid "application incorporation." It's a fantastic paper saver as well as an organizing resource, but if the task is a digital "filling in the blank," it's no different from "filling in the blank" on paper. Perhaps pick and choose the essential tools that you'd like to offer in Google Classroom and start by transforming those worksheets to digital assignments. There are wholly collaborative and integrated Teachers Pay Teachers lessons that you can check out as well.

2. Sharing Links and Services

There are two ways to connect to websites. You can create a "connection" as an assignment and submit it to all your students to access it. It also works with videos that you want your students to use for a lesson or supplementary information. If this is a connection that you will use regularly, you will want to consider adding this to the "about portion" of your class. It's a perfect place to incorporate typing apps, learning tools, or apps that your students need to use regularly. Don't overuse this tool, but you're sure to put some details here to save yourself time.

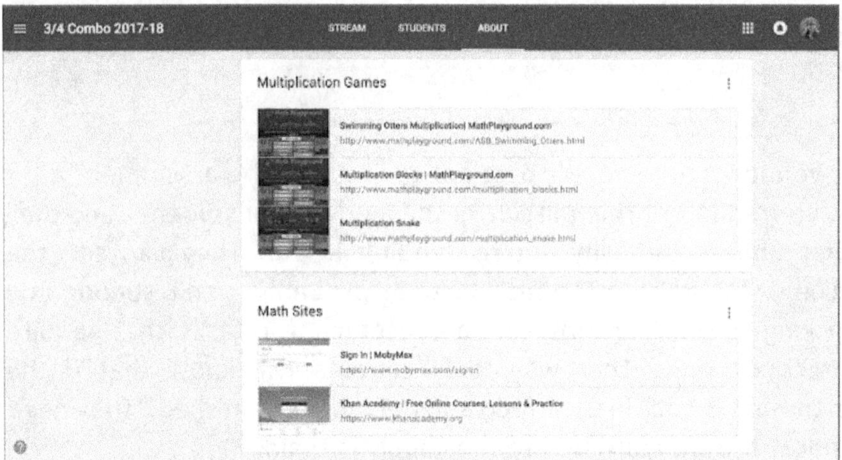

1. Organize your "About" page with links and frequently used resources. Set topics and or themes and then add your links and documents.

3. Keep Your Google Classroom Feed Clean

Google Classroom feed can be very busy and frustrating if you delegate several items every week. Removing older assignments that you have ranked is a perfect way to keep the feed clean and easy to navigate. The exception to that will be tasks that you would regularly delegate, and that won't change much. Such assignments can be re-used and re-posted, with the option to re-use them in the following year. How you handle your feed is a personal choice. If you want to re-use all those things, then setting them up in such a way that they can be easily edited and re-used the first time you allocate them can save you time later.

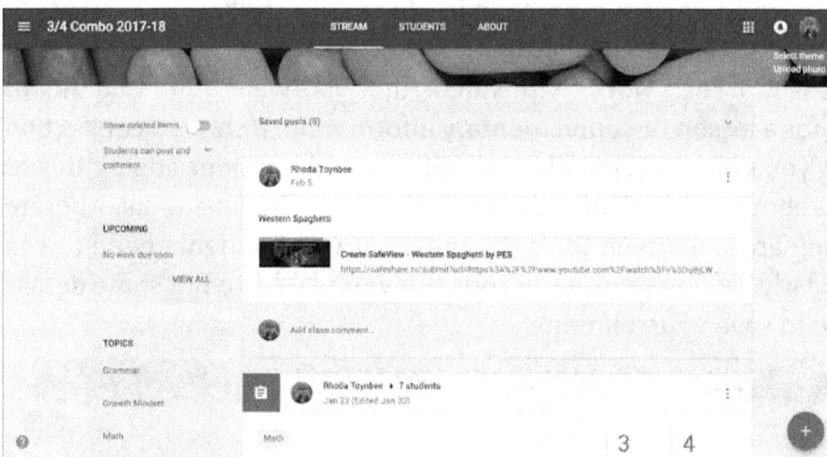

2. A view of the assignment feed with a shared link and an assignment to a segment of the class.

For younger students, it's best not to "return" the assignment after you've graduated. This will clutter the feed of your students, and they won't understand why you're sending it out. They can see the ranking, but it's mysterious, so they probably won't spend time checking it out. Returns can be reserved for tasks that require corrections only. That way, the students will know that if the assignment is back in their feed and not labeled "finished," they need to boost the standard before they apply it again.

More Google Classroom Tips

Email Tips

When you have older students, use the email feature. You won't want to mess with this feature for the younger classes. Besides, you would like to determine your expectations for email updates sent to you if your student marks a "finished" job. Through a course of 20-25 emails, your SUPER inbox would be easy to complete when a student receives news each time the job is completed. In the top, left corner of your Google Classroom window is three lines (the burger icon). Select "Settings" at the bottom and then check the checkbox for your email preference.

Online Conversation Tips

Students can launch a conversation about a mission. The interface is close to a chat window or a website. You may choose to let them use this feature or use it as part of their partnership in specific projects. Until you do so, you may undoubtedly want to lecture on class standards and digital citizenship. You should interrupt the discussions if they cannot hold the conversation on the subject or simply use the arguments to talk meaninglessly.

Grading Tips

This might or may not integrate with Google Classroom if you have an online grading site. You will have to do some work to see what the unique program options are. You have to open your grade book system in one window or tab and raising the size of your monitor to one half. Next, open the grade list of your Google Classroom and shrink it to fill in the other half of your computer. Now you can look at your Google classroom ratings by adding them quickly to your classification system.

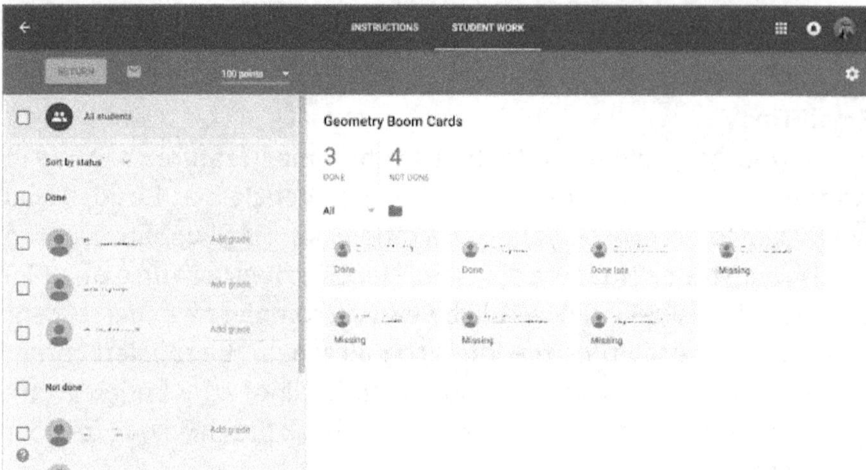

1. A view of an assignment that is ready to be graded. The total number of points is in top (100 points) and can be changed with the down arrow. Click on the large box on for each student on the right to view the assignment copy. Enter the grade in the light green column on the left.

Tips Shortcut Keyboards

Teach your students the power of Command / Control Z. When they panic the first time, they have removed a page in the slideshow or a long passage that they only tap 20 minutes and touch the 'undo' knob unexpectedly, they'll be surprised. Then you should show them how to do the same keyboard shortcut to undo their mistake before they panic, and they will all be grateful. Teach them to copy and paste while you are at it. You will need those skills as your digital career progresses, and the more effective you will be, the faster you master them.

Read about the magic of keyboard shortcuts. Keystrokes are more effective than shifting your hand to a mouse and dragging the cursor to the next window. For example, you can use the down key to transfer the cursor to the next student when entering grades.

Google Classroom Proficient (and Freebie!)

The software is best used when you delegate digital work and practice many times a week in Google Classroom. When you want the students to use technology, they have to use it daily. You will use it yourself and always work with it if you intend to be competent.

You Can Start with Free Resources Such as My Google Math Cards Analysis

This collection of dispositive can be used for group analysis, small group discussion, and practice or individual activities. Once you allocate the set to all students in your class, they will mark "over" when they have completed their course. You can see, at a glimpse, who has turned and who wants to do their work. Open your submitted presentation to rate your slides and show your responses. The best way possible to mark them is to transform red (or color of your choice) into an incorrect answer.

Using this freebie or other tools in Google Classroom to delegate and execute specific tasks. The more usage of Google Classroom, the more you learn what you can do with this fantastic software.

3.4 You Couldn't Say Anything About Google Classroom

Look for The Lines and Points

If you see a three line or three-point button, you can click it for more options. The three lines typically represent the main menu; the three points usually contain further actions.

Get It Right the First Time You Sign in To Google Classroom

When a teacher or student first selects the correct role – the position of a student or instructor. If you pick the wrong location, the IT administrator of Google Apps must be contacted to change it.

Place Classes in Order

When you teach several classes, create them in reverse chronological order when creating these classes in the Google Classroom. By so doing, they are presented in the classroom in chronological order.

Don't Clutter the About Tab

Just add the most relevant links to you About tab all year round. It'll be hard to find something if you overwhelm it with too much stuff!

See the Students Side

To see what the students see, ask a friend to invite you to one of his / her classes. In this way, you will be a student, and you will see what the classroom feels like as a student.

Set Comment Settings

Decide as to what students should do on your Google Classroom stream (where students view all the applications, articles, and other contents). Students can then post and comment (students can write themselves posts and class commentary) Just say on (students can't post jobs, but comment on posts of teachers) Just teachers can post or comment (students can't write posts or comment)

Save It for Later

You can then schedule your statements, discussion questions, and tasks for later use without immediately publishing them. Write it now and press the "Assign" button to save it as a draft.

Assign Without a Google File

Assign students who don't have to switch to a Google Paper, slideshow, or another file for the assignment without a Google account. When the task does not include a script, the students should click on "Mark as done" to inform the instructor that they have completed the job.

Add More Than One

You can connect multiple images, videos, and links to a task. Be sure to provide all the student wants and can give the student several choices!

Access Your Grades

Choose a list of categories for a particular task or all tasks. When displaying degrees, click on the gear wheel settings in the top right corner and select "Select assignment degrees" or "Select all degrees"

Annotate and Draw on Documents Using the Android App

The first two Google Classroom tips on this list are unique to the mobile app. Do you know there are features in Google Classroom that are only available on mobile devices (iOS and Android)?

The ability to annotate and draw on documents is one of the best features. This can be PDF, Google Docs, Microsoft Word Docs, JPEG, or GIF files. This feature is useful for many forms of tasks, learners, and teachers alike. Students can use this to draw an answer, annotate text, mark an image, and more. Teachers may use this to give positive input to students.

Randomly Pick Students Using the Mobile App

The student selector is another nice feature of the Google Classroom mobile app. Again, this is only possible on the iOS device.

The student selector helps you to pick a student from your class list at random. It is a smart way to label students equally in the classroom. Go to the people section and select the icon in the top-right corner.

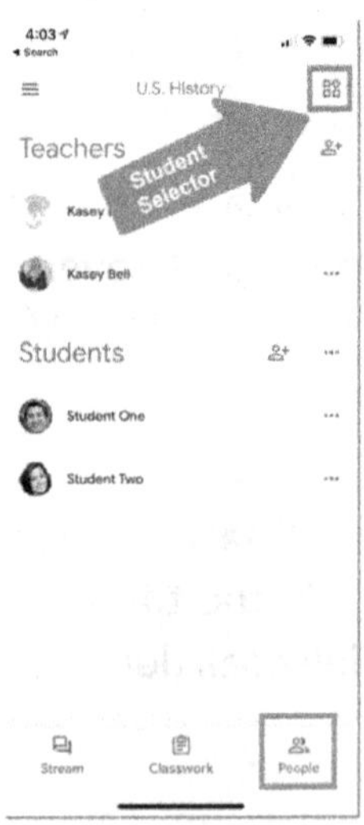

Subject Organize and Filter Classwork

The Google Classroom Classwork page helps you to create topics for the organizing of assignments and materials. Speak of things like categories for your tasks and supplies.

You can arrange the Classwork page in any way that makes sense to you and your students. Most teachers want to build subjects for subjects (great for elementary), weeks, study days, and more.

Once you've built your themes, you'll see a list of themes on the left-hand side and click on a theme to filter the page and see only those things that are labeled with that theme.

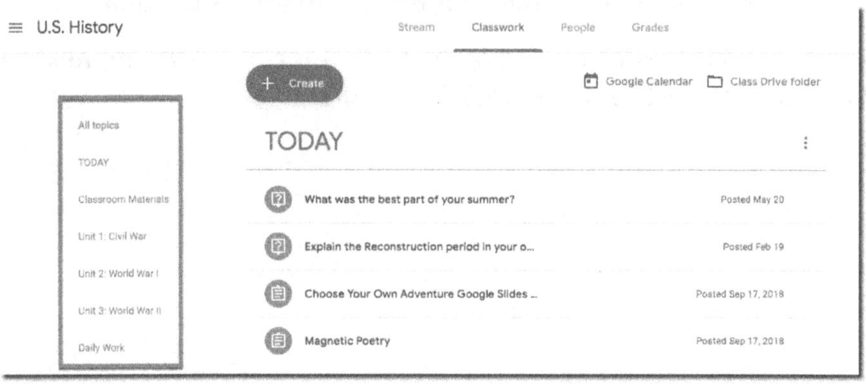

Using Locked Google Forms Quizzes

Teachers have been looking for a way to lock up a Google Form Quiz for several years to keep students from opening other tabs and being tempted to cheat.

The vision is now a reality for people with controlled Chromebooks! The locked mode will require students to be "locked" to the Google Form Quiz.

Here's how it works:

Important: To Use Locked Mode, You Need:
A G Suite for Education Account.

A Chromebook managed by your school for each student.

Chrome OS 75 and up.

When the Quiz Is Locked: Students Can't Open Other Doors to The Window
The teacher will receive an email if the student exits the exam and then re-opens it.

Unmanaged computers would not be able to access the quiz.

When you build your quiz assignment in Google Classroom, next to Chromebook Locked mode, click Switch on.

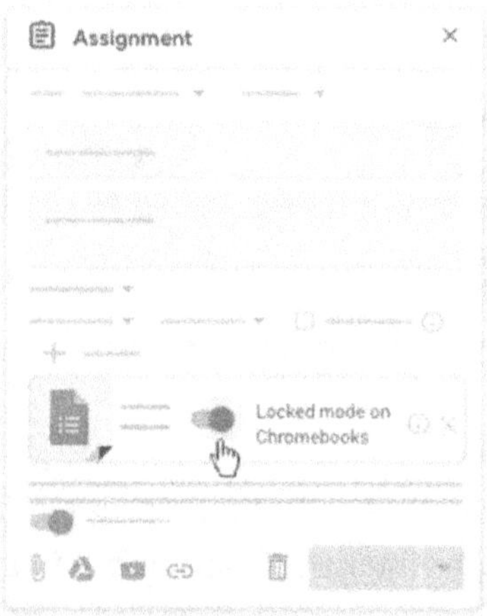

Distinguish Assignments
Google Classroom provides teachers with the ability to differentiate assignments. Each student does not have to obtain precisely the same task at the same time.

When creating a new assignment, click on the student's drop-down arrow and uncheck "all students," then only check the students or groups of students who need that particular assignment.

This is useful for group distinction, as well as shifts, PBL, and even enrichment.

Label Students in Class Feedback

Our next two Google Classroom tips are for feedback. Tagging specific student comments is a perfect way to leave feedback and connect with students in a collaborative environment.

Google Classroom has two kinds of comments: teacher comments and private comments. Tagging students in-class observations allows you to interact and answer questions to individual students.

Although this post aims to provide Google Classroom tips, it is useful to note that you can also tag students with comments in collaborative papers, slides, etc. and delegate tasks to them.

To tag someone with a tweet, simply type the "+" followed by the student's email address.

This is particularly useful if you allow students to post and comment in Google Classroom.

Tag Students in Class Comments

Add Resource Links to Comments and the User Bank Overwrite the comments by inserting resource links! Even a statement is not enough. Often, we need to provide students with a guide or a summary of a definition.

For example, if I provide feedback on grammar, I might suggest that there is a "comma splice" in the sentence, but if students don't know what it is, it may be difficult for them to take action. That's why I'm adding a resource link to a web page, video, or lesson that will help them revisit the definition and make the required changes.

Note, when you add a link to some form of message, it must contain the Http:/part of the link so that it can be clicked in the news.

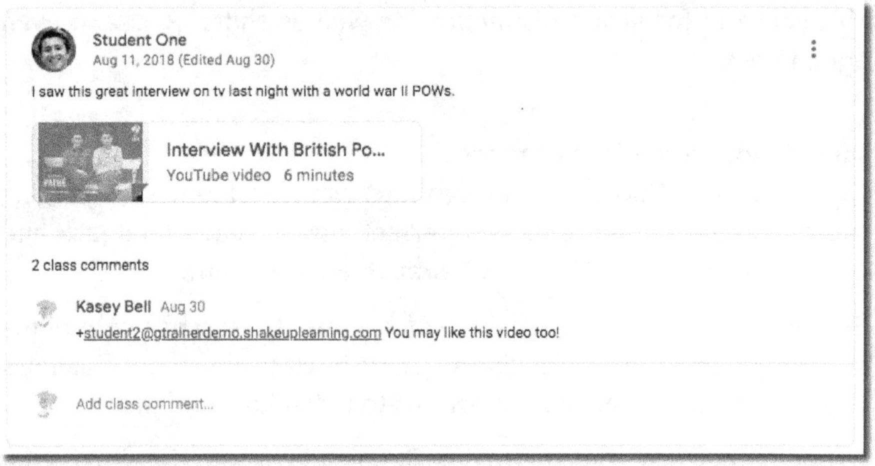

You can set up your most commonly used tool ties comments in the comment bank for use in Google Classroom grading.

Customize Stream Notification Classwork

The Stream is your Google Classroom contact portal. It is where you post your announcements and keep your students updated.

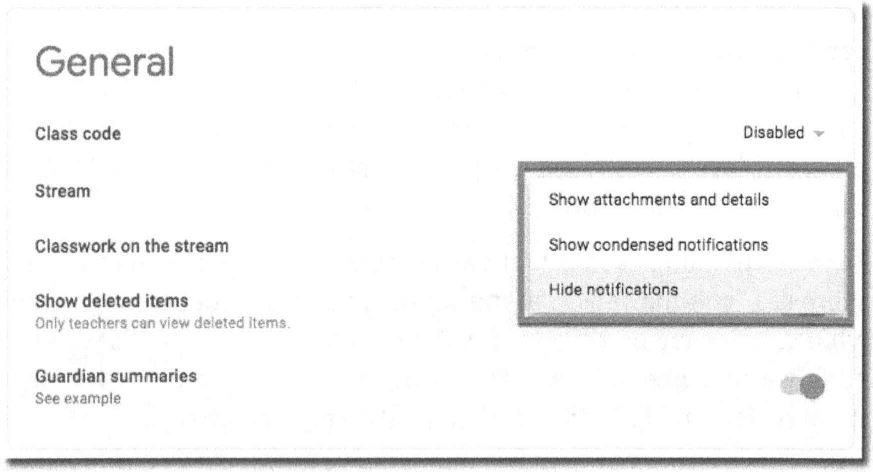

By default, Stream can also show updates of new things posted on the classwork list. For others, it sounds like repetition, and it can be messing up the shore. (Ha! See what I did there.) When you are using the Classwork tab, you can select a compressed or extended view for Classwork updates on the Stream tab. You can remove them entirely from the Stream tab, too.

Go to class.google.com.

Please click on the name.

Tap Settings on the Stream tab.

Under General, select an option next to Classwork on the stream

Bookmark Classwork Page

This Google Classroom tip will save you some time! Often Google Classroom navigation can be frustrating and take a few too many clicks to get where you want to go. Since you spent most of your time on the Classwork tab, here is a recommendation for you to bookmark it.

In Google Chrome, you can add it to your Easy Access Bookmarks tab.

To activate the bookmarks bar, click the three dots near the top right in Chrome, then select the bookmarks, and make sure the bookmarks bar is enabled.

Go to the Classwork page for the class you want to bookmark.

Then simply click-and-drag the lock next to the URL in the Omnibox to add a bookmark to your tab.

Right-click the bookmark to edit or shorten the name.

It is suggested to bookmark the Classwork page for each of your classes in the Google Classroom. This will save you much of your money!

Student View Is Different from Teacher

View, one of the most useful things you can do as a teacher using Google Classroom is to experience it as a student. Students just see an overview of the definition. Clicking on the task, students can see a "Your Job" bubble in the upper right where they will find work that you have assigned to them or work that they want to add.

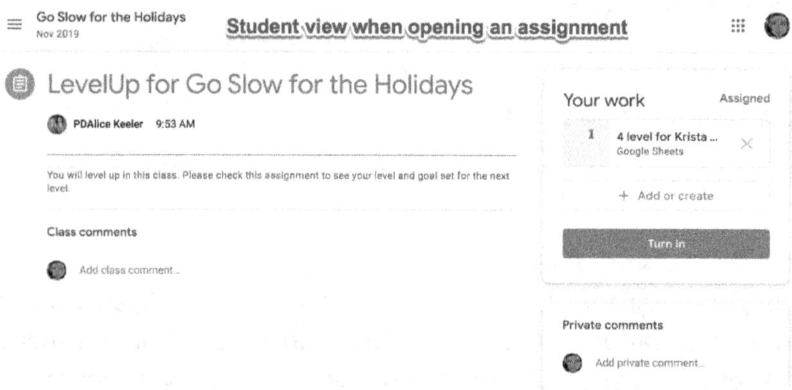

Student view when opening the assignment In the Teacher view, clicking on the assignment strip on the Classwork pages will take you to the assignment evaluation screen.

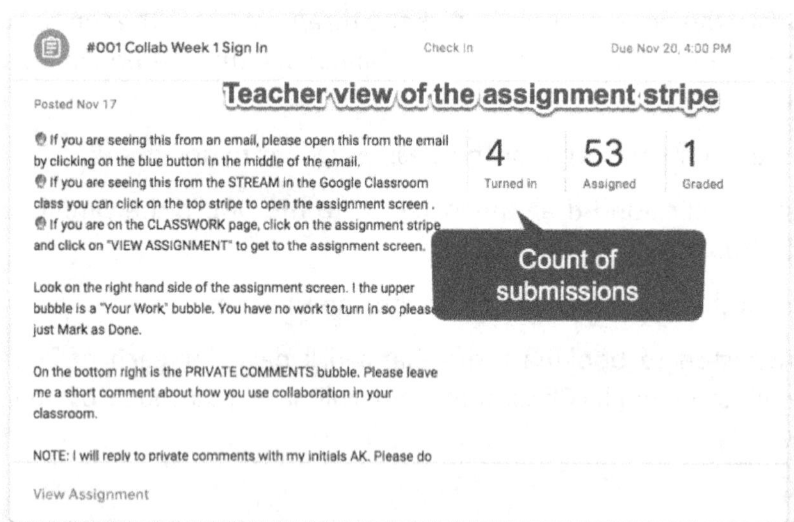

View of the teacher on stripe

No Attachments

In Google Classroom, there are no attachments. All from Google Drive is linked. To import a text or screenshot into the Google Classroom project, it's added to the drive by clicking on the paper clip icon. Both student research and 'attachments' can be found by going directly to Google Drive.

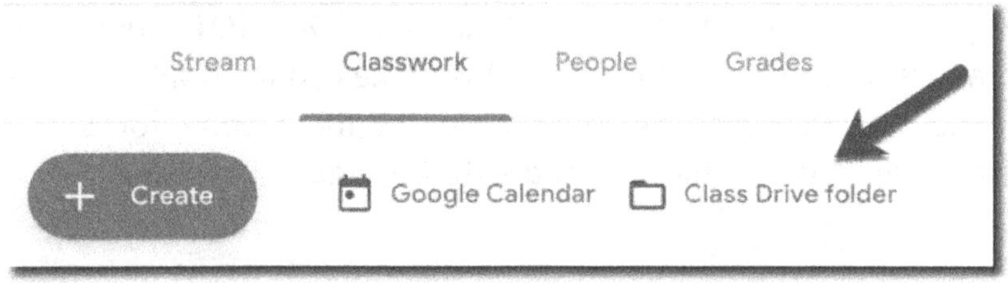

At the top of the Classwork list, at the top right, there is a tab for the "Class drive tab." Everything you have submitted to any activity is stored in this tab.

All "attachments" in Google Drive mean that the Classroom can be circumvented and edited directly from Google Drive, and edits appear in the Classroom. This also means that you don't want copies; you only connect to the same Google Drive file.

You Can Not Edit "Make a Copy for Each Student."

When you're adding a document on Google Drive and pick 'Make a copy for each student,' be mindful that you're doing a copy. When editing the original, copies do NOT change.

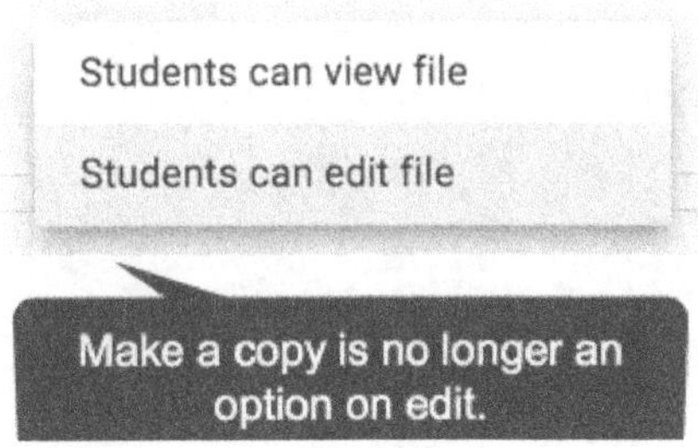

If you have allocated the assignments and failed to move from 'Students can display file' to 'Make a copy for each student,' otherwise you will no longer be able to copy the assignment for each student. If you edit the task to correct your mistake, the alternative is unavailable.

To correct this, please press the Create button at the top of the Classwork page and pick "Reuse Article." Do NOT copy the attachments when they are reused. This makes your Google Drive a mess. The reused post has the option "Write a copy for every student." After reusing the article, delete the original mistake.

Students Lose Editing Permissions

Once students click the 'Turn in' key, the document's ownership rights will be transferred from the student to the instructor. The student is a VIEWER.

If the student comments are left in the paper, then the statement is INVISIBLE. You can't see the message until you return it.

Only Ten Objects in A Google Classroom

subject is designed for organizing by themes on the classroom tab. Just ten things will be displayed in each theme. If the item includes over ten elements, students will see a subtle "See more" click.

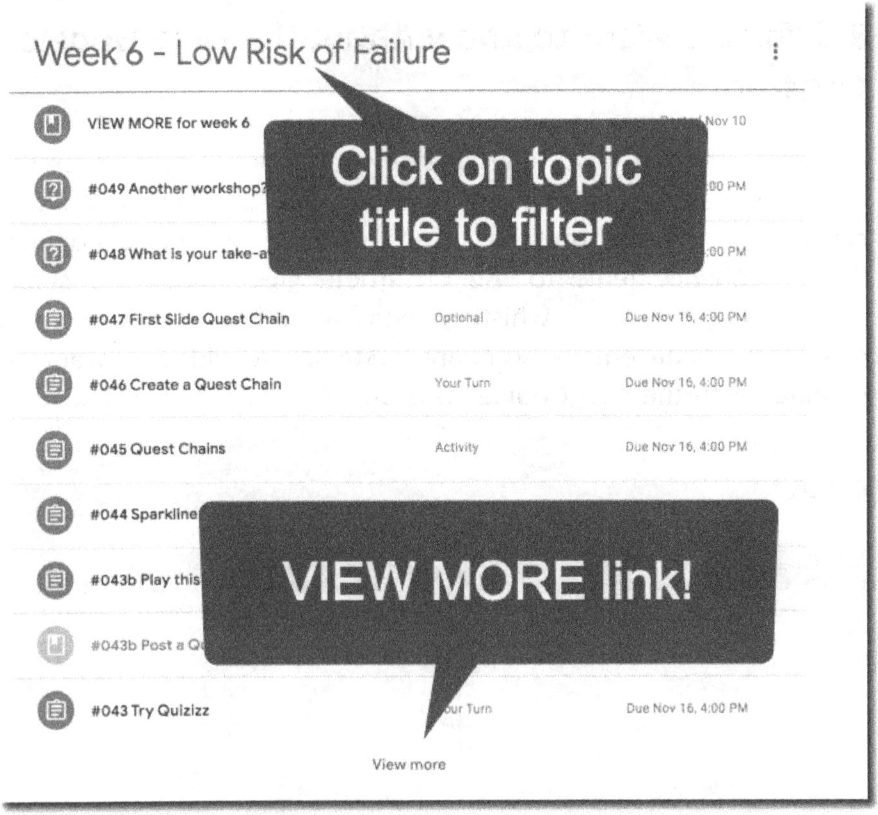

Tap the title of the topic to search for it and see ALL activities in the subject, not just the last ten.

3.5 You Do Want to Know About the New Google Classroom

Google Classroom has undergone several improvements over the past four years and, with the growing use of Chromebooks in classrooms, the classroom has become more and more popular. Recent enhancements to the Classroom give students a smart interface with several whistles found in other, more complex classroom management software systems. Would you want to continue with the new Google Classroom? This is what you need to say.

Control

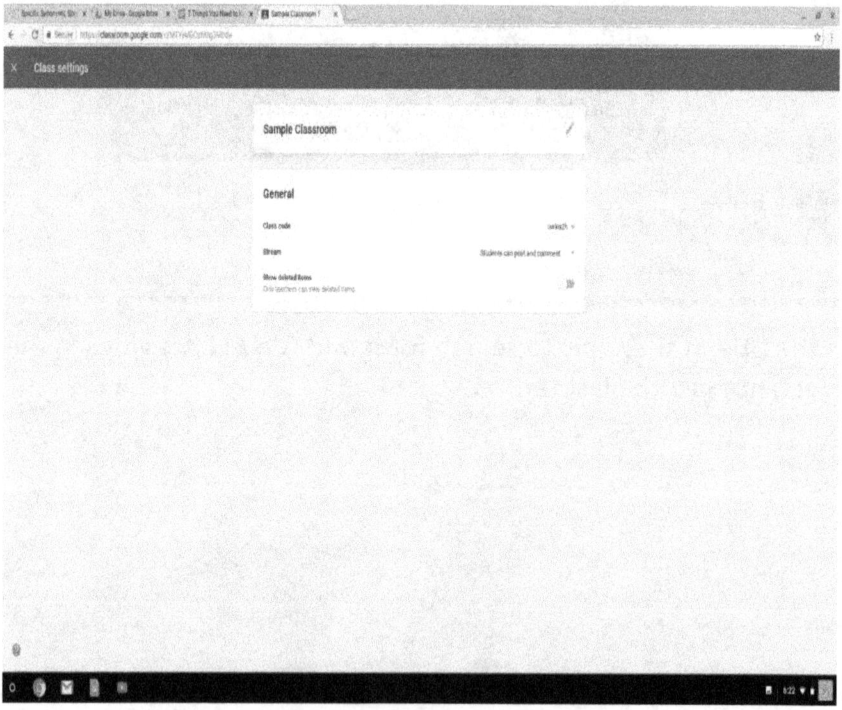

Many previous Classroom features are integrated on the new Class Settings tab. You can edit the class description here, modify or view the class code and control stream settings in one place.

Separate Tabs

The new classroom has a different source, classes, and people tabs that make it easier to organize each portion.

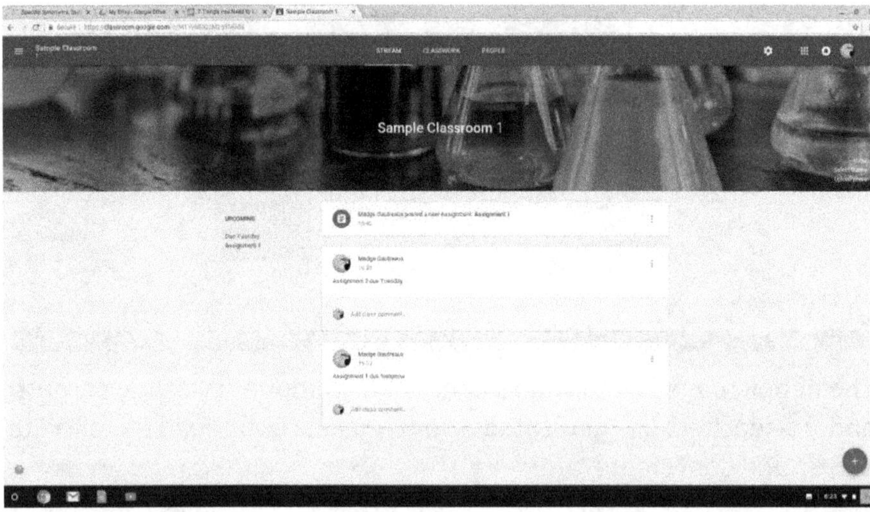

Before the update, it was often difficult to find older assignments by organizing the current. The latest source is focused solely on advertising and classroom discussions and effectively removes the ambiguity existing in previous releases. Students may also see new assignment updates on the page.

The new classroom page allows teachers to post tasks and ask questions to create subject modules for ease of organizing. As the About tab feature has changed with the update in the classroom, teachers can use the topic feature to post a curriculum or class resources. Themes can be pushed up or down to allow the user to organize the page in a class-friendly order.

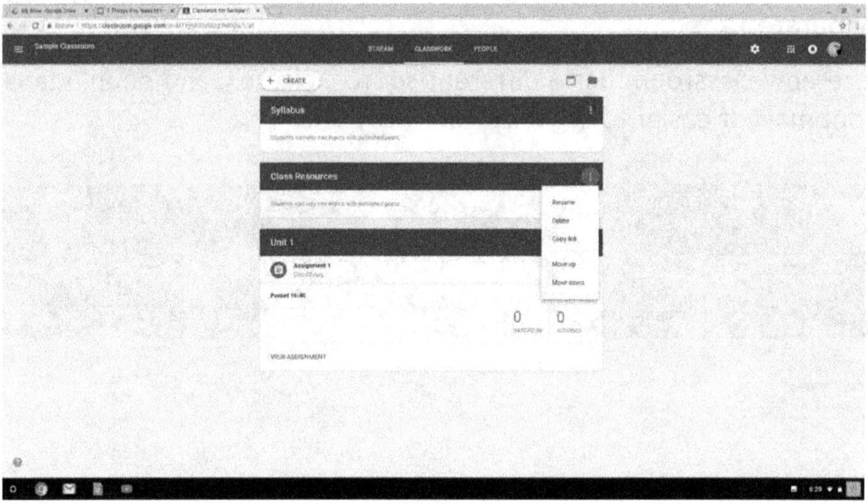

The People page is a forum to connect or remove students, parents, and co-teachers. A dedicated room makes class leaders easy to access and coordinate.

Notifications- No Problem

Teachers and students can now easily access alerts. Notifications can be personalized for each course by pressing a few buttons. Teachers can vote for reviews, planned updates, student research, and co-teaching invitations. Students can select invitation notices, tasks, ratings, reviews, private notes, and unsubmitted work.

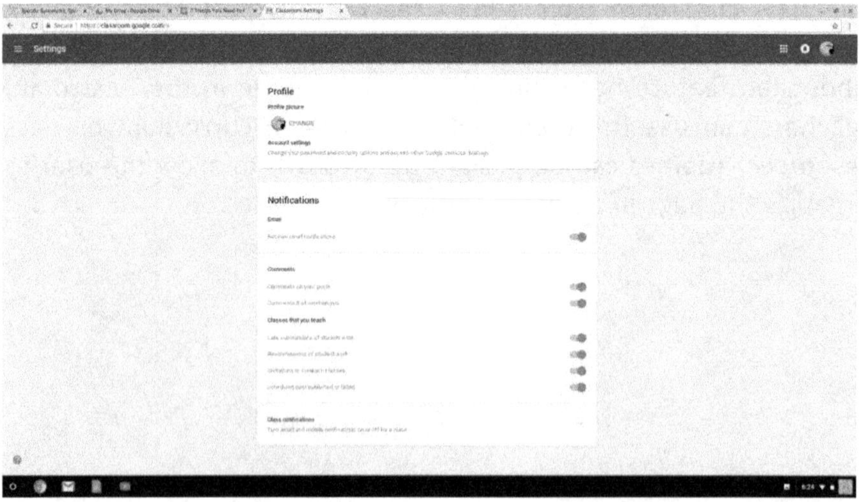

Present Status

Students and teachers should keep up to date on the status of all activities. Teachers will see how many users have completed tasks at a glance on the Classwork tab, and the user provides a more general condition when displaying the actual job. Students may also see future assignments, or those turned in or assessed.

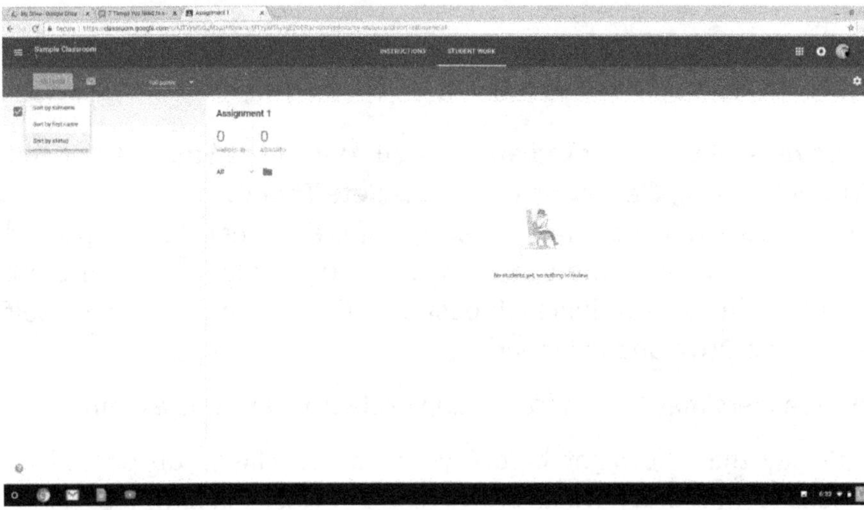

Switching Grades

The new platform enables teachers to switch between grades, feedback, and submitted tasks quickly. During the graduation of a student, teachers can leave feedback and save commonly used comments on other tasks. The GUI makes it easy to move between submissions without leaving the classification method.

Why Reinventing the Wheel

is simpler than ever to reuse topics and activities for a new class Professors can now copy a class even if it is deleted. Be mindful, however, that in the copied class, only some objects are duplicated. The title, section, definition, subject, subject matter, and class posts saved as drafts shall be transferred to a newly produced copy. Teachers will have to introduce students and any new class announcements.

Eventually, teachers will be able to build quizzes directly through the tasks tab, with a toggle switch to allow locked mode. The closed way blocks students from opening new tabs and from completing a questionnaire. In classrooms, this feature can be useful in minimizing cheating by browsing the internet.

3.6 Google Starting Classroom Approaches Today

1. Cover and Store Packed and Posted Tasks That You Did Not Get Through During Class Time (Do Not Delete Them).

Google Classroom does not currently require teachers to hide posted tasks. This makes some sense on the Google side when you think about all the ways a single job posted in Classroom embedded itself on Google Drive and Calendar.

But teachers may have a frustrating problem. Take this example:

Let's say that the night before your English class, you posted an excellent short story practice. The text is enclosed in .pdf. Two hand-picked videos as a shared meditation task attached to a Google Doc are also included. In Google Slides, a supplementary tool provides students with appropriate literary tools. And you have put in the overview of the assignment a specified learning target and added instructions.

It takes at least five minutes — maybe more — to pool all these resources and post them as a mission.

But then the day comes, and we don't get to the activity that was scheduled. There is something else in the way, and we never get a chance to continue.

You Are Left with A Hard Call.

Do you delete the post and re-create it before your next class? Or can you leave the job, just change the due date, and agree that some students can read the story, watch the photos, explore Google Slides, and absorb the whole activity before the second class?

There is an answer to this question.

What you did is build a dumb classroom called the Staging Area. Whenever you find yourself in such situations, you use Re-Post to copy the whole task into the school of your staging area. If you withdraw it from the school, it is going to work.

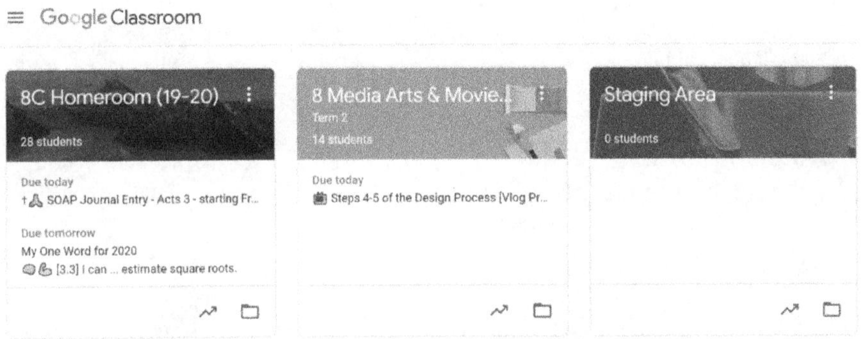

This way, none of my planning is lost, and the next day, I'm not repeating the entire posting process. My lovely short story operation is saved — no spoilers. Until the next lesson, you simply re-post the assignment from the Stage Area back to the correct Classroom, and you're back on track.

2. Allow Real-Time Feedback on Presentations

Do yourself and your learners a great favor by copying and pasting assessment templates to could private comment in advance of performances.

Include spaces for the overall assessment, performance metrics, star and wish emojis, etc. and input spaces for each student in your class. Having all of this put in place before student presentations, you can give students reliable and insightful feedback in real-time — while they present it. This means you don't review their submissions after school, so they're not looking for input.

Here's the test summary that you put in all the private comments of your students before their last Genius Hour presentations.

Tim Cavey Dec 6, 2019

- OVERALL EVALUATION

Topic:

Partners (if applicable):

⭐
⭐
⭐
🙏

Presentation Components:

Project Details
Images, Video, or Live Demonstration
Rationale - Your WHY
Learning Process - Actions
Growth Mindset - Learning From Failures and Challenges
Highlights of Learning
Future Directions

Learning Target 1: I can ... follow my passions to direct my learning.
Learning Target 2: I can ... gather peer and/or user and/or expert feedback and inspiration.

3. Using Emojis To Code Learning Activities

Begin and unit title and assignment name with the related emoji

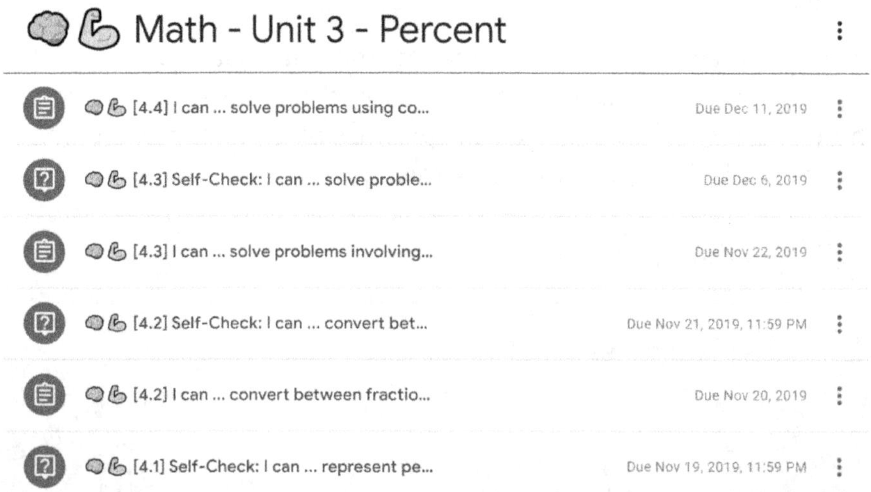

and give completed units and assignments an emoji checkmark to indicate at a glance that they are behind us.

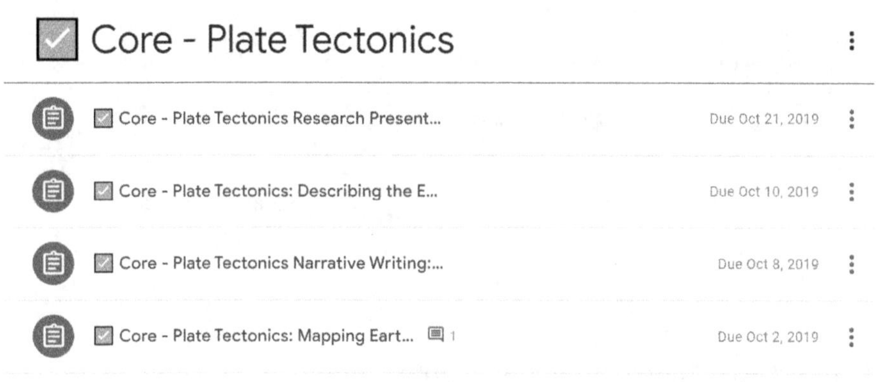

4. Include Learning Goals in Any Given Task or Job

It is not as much a matter of convenience as it is an excellent pedagogy.

These will also bring you back to the unit plan or curricular expectations, keeping you grounded. And it's always going to be there to remind students what the purpose of the increasing learning experience is. "Why are we doing this? "

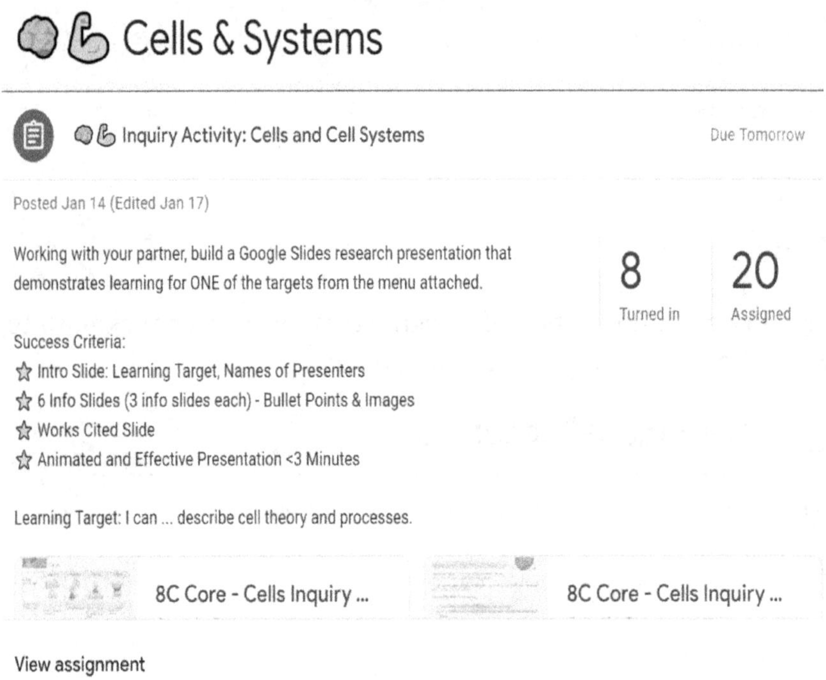

5. Get A Fast Sense of Your Students 'Progress

post-self-assessments in the Google Classroom, particularly in the Math Units. It's an easy but effective way to collect information about your students 'learning and development, which guides my next steps.

Place a multiple-choice question right on the Classroom; you get these tests. Tap on any button, and see which students have selected the level of proficiency.

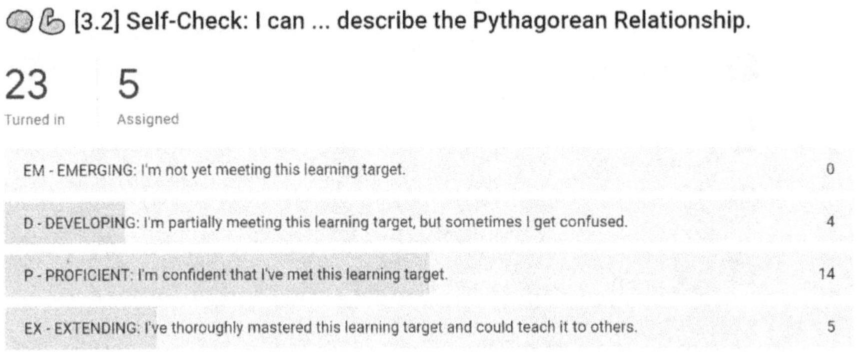

6. Share Homeroom Classes with Other Teachers Who Teach the Same Grade Level Courses You Do

It makes it fast and simple for teachers to keep track of where their students are in the curriculum to see what they've been doing recently, and it's also a convenient way to exchange resources. Use the Re-Post command to drop it right into your class.

7. Share Homeroom Classrooms with All Specialized Teachers

Allow your Art Teachers, language teachers, and Band Teachers to drop announcements and services into your lessons. Sure, your band instructor may have a Google Classroom set up for your homeroom students. Even if they don't, getting access to the classroom is a perfect option.

8. Post to Several Classes Once

If you are a specialist instructor, take advantage of this feature. You don't need to post assignments in each classroom separately. Post all related classes at once.

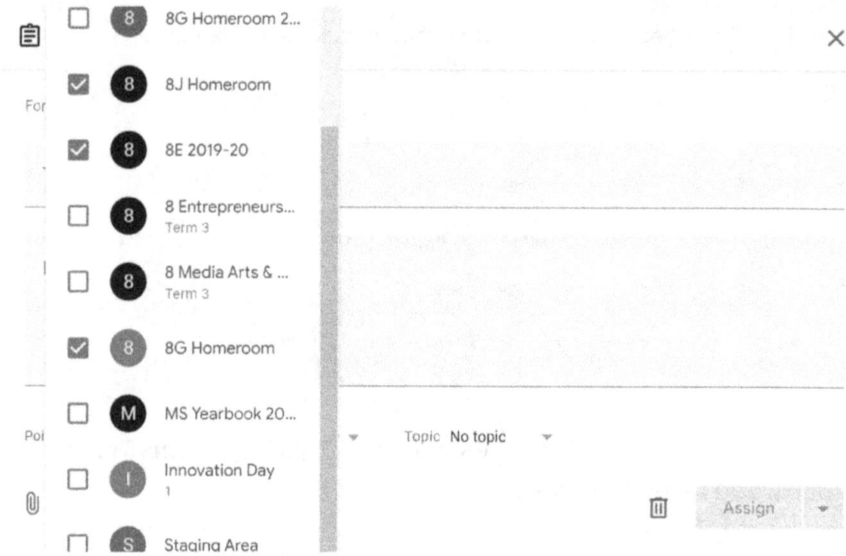

9. Change Google Classroom Alerts to Mute Emails and Classroom Messages That Do Not Belong to You

After sharing the previous two strategies on sharing Google Classrooms, this strategy has become relevant. Switch off the Classroom alerts that you don't teach.

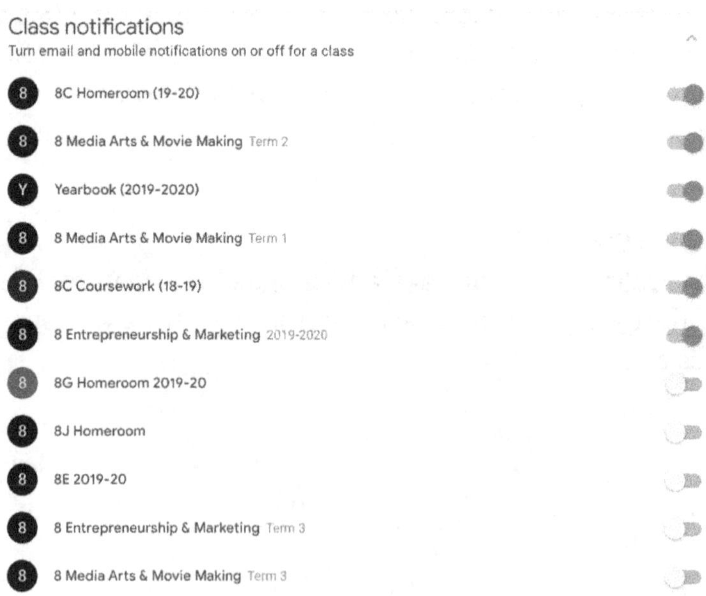

If you haven't taken this step, you will receive email updates from any assignment resubmission or private comment that each student in each classroom makes. Within my house, some teachers and EAs have access to up to ten or more classes, which makes for a lot of notifications!

Consider this by restricting the alerts to the classes you teach. With that said, you can respond to private comments when you can. Any excellent communication can happen to some students.

10. Structure of The Homeroom Students Every Week to Review Email Inboxes and Arrange Classroom Assignments

Email is dull for most middle and high school students. My 8th-grade step is going to tell. They're not involved in it.

But the classroom encourages important teacher-student communication via email. I will post reviews in private comments in the school to students in the form of an email. I may email selected students to remind them to send assignments, post announcements about upcoming events, or post-self-assessment check-ins to track learning. Some or all of these interactions run by email, so students must check their inbox once a week.

They're not going to do it on their own, so we can't ask them to. We need to set aside 15 minutes or more per week to make sure this life skill is going on.

Others would say the email isn't going to be around forever, and maybe they're right. Yet it's been operating well for the last 25 years, so it's not going anywhere fast. Make sure that all of your students know how to maximize their inbox.

11. Build A Google Classroom Around the School

This allows school-wide polls, debates, hot lunch order submissions, student photo submissions for the yearbook, delivery of announcements, etc. Full disclosure: I am not using this at the moment — partly to slow down the influx of ideas that I am moving colleagues in new teaching culture. But I set this up at the previous high, and it works wonderfully.

12. For Administrators: Build A Google Classroom for Staff Employees, With Administrators as Employees and Teachers as Students

This is a smart way to reduce e-mail traffic. Conduct staff assessments rapidly and effectively. Post "assignments" such as professional development plans and require "students" (teachers) to apply when completed. Or, post reporting tools and open comments so that teachers can view posts as boards of discussion.

It's Google Classroom. It isn't a mind-blowing benefit, but it works. Follow these techniques to get the most out of Google Classroom, optimize your time and resources, and better serve your students.

Chapter 4: Use Google Classroom Effectively

4.1 Works with Google for Education

To develop technology to help students learn, they are trying to envision where the future of education is heading. The latest Future of the Classroom Global Study describes emerging developments in education, assisted by research. Here's how goods and projects resonate with each of these trends:

New Technology
Google allows students to go on virtual field trips, and there are 1,000 tours to choose from, including Carmen Sandiego tours published by Houghton Mifflin Harcourt. Throughout the rest of the year, they've been rolling out an enhanced Expeditions experience across a range of Chrome OS apps.

Students may also use the Tour Creator recognized as the AASL 2019 Best Teaching & Learning Website to create their virtual reality tours. They can take their fellow students or parents on trips of their city or school using the Expeditions App.

Innovating Teaching
The Teacher Center, a library of free online training for educators, continues to expand. For teachers to get started with this software for the first time, they have added courses for Expeditions and G Suite Editors (Google Documents and Slides) to supplement existing training sessions on Classroom, Forms, and Jamboard.

They've also built shorter courses around a range of subjects, such as helping teachers support English-language learners, using Chromebook accessibility tools, or getting started with CS First and Applied Digital Skills curriculum.

And local experts are there to help educators who want to get the best out of Google technology.

Classroom Coaching

For educators to benefit from technology innovation, they need to know how to incorporate it into their classrooms. The Innovative Learning Project teaches teachers how to make effective use of classroom technology, and have a new training program for administrators, teaching them how to help instructional coaches in their schools.

They are also helping school administrators measure the Google for Education implementation of their organization through goods (G Suite and Chromebooks) and programs (Certification and Transformation) with the launch of the EDU Transformation Study.

Also, we have extended our services to help school and community leaders think about centering equity in their school transition. So, they have built a new Educational Equity page with tools and case studies to help school leaders understand how investment can be essential to the seven pillars of the Transition Process.

Digital Accountability

Applied Technical Skills has seven new lessons in technical well-being. Teachers can use these project-based free lessons to teach their students how to develop healthy digital habits, prevent online scams, consider their digital footprint, and more.

Life Skills and Job Readiness

Related Digital Skills now have new lessons to train middle and high school students to use G Suite fluently in college, the workplace, and beyond. To prove their mastery, students should take the technical G Suite credential and apply it to their resumes and applications. Other new lessons concentrate on exposing students to machine learning, making art with Google Papers, measuring the chance, and discussing the past of women.

Computational Thought

CS First, a coding program for elementary and middle school students, is hosting a new professional development session for teachers to incorporate coding practices into English Language Arts, math, and science classes.

Google acquired last year; Workbench is a software repository for educators to explore, develop, customize, and share lessons and tools. At ISTE, we are announcing a new integration with Workbench Blockly programming canvas and Google Boards. This enables people to create Blockly programs to monitor multiple Bluetooth devices (robots, drones, sensors, microcontrollers) and to send or retrieve data from Google Sheets.

They help their students develop problem-solving skills, navigate the digital world safely, and prepare for future careers. As classrooms continue to grow, their products also enable educators and students to develop.

Helping Developers Make More Choices for Educators

As those involved in education know, learning is a team sport. Teachers, school staff, administrators, teachers, parents, guardians, and developers all play a role in ensuring that teachers leave the classroom with more information and skills than they did when they began. That's why Google is partnering with developers to build on what's possible in the school.

From virtual lab simulations to literacy help for people with different learning needs, we're inspired by the applications that developers have developed for Google Classroom and G Suite for Education. We are committed to helping developers through our software APIs and open developer ecosystem, allowing all kinds of apps to be integrated with Google tools.

How Google For Education Empowers Developers

The Google for Education Technology Partner Program offers developers access to:

• **Technical Support**

Dedicated developer relations support and tools, training, Google events such as Google I / O, access to Google User Groups, and more.

• **Marketing Support**

Branding collaboration support, apps on Google for Education platforms, involvement in co-marketing programs, access to market growth funds (primary partners only), invites to exclusive partner events, and more.

• **Google Initiatives**

Cloud incentives for start-ups, developer grants, and launchpad rooms.

4.2 Google Classroom Extensions And Apps

The simple setup process for the Google Classroom is relatively intuitive, even for first-time users.

There are now hundreds of third-party applications and websites that integrate with Google Classroom. Many of these apps may be partnered with Google, while others may be developing and releasing their third-party add-ons in the Chrome Store. When you use Google Classroom extensively, incorporating other EdTech resources may be a way to streamline your teaching. For example, say that you want your students to learn some vocabulary words using Quizlet; you can use the Google Classroom integration to share and allocate a similar flashcard to your class directly. And, if you're looking for other online learning material, there's integration with publishers like Newsela, Khan Academy, and BrainPOP, among others — you'll find all sorts of posts, videos, and other educational content to share with your students.

The Benefit of an Extension For Teachers?

Generally speaking, Google Classroom uses an API (application program interface) to link and exchange knowledge with all of your favorite devices. Hundreds of applications and websites are incorporated, and we'll highlight a few of our options below.

EdTech integrations that seem complicated, but we've narrowed it down to the basics. Here are three main ways to streamline classroom management:

1. Export Class Rosters from Classroom to an app or website.

2. If you've shared the list between the app and the classroom, organize the coursework and presentations that integrate material from the app.

3. Using the Google Sharing button to share content from a website to the class.

If you love Google Classroom and any of the resources, combining them will make the teaching process much more straightforward. If you're not too familiar with the classroom, check out the teacher feedback to learn more. Google Classroom isn't for everybody, of course. If you miss the integrations, you'll probably still want to explore how these fantastic resources will make your classroom better.

Excessive Numbers of Extensions?

Before you skim through these and remember that there are so many other chromes to slow down your browser and speed is one of the chromes.

There is no pattern on how many to use – here your kilometer. The speed of your computer, your usable memory, your wireless Internet speed, how many tabs you have open can all affect your browsers' apparent pace, so attach and delete extensions so that Chrome stays snappy and useful as a teacher removing applications, plugins, and attach-on. Leaving unused add-ons will slow down Google Chrome and Chrome OS. Remove these unused applications, plugins, and add-ins for Google Docs whenever possible to keep up with the best results for Google Apps.

Deleting Apps, Extensions, And Add-Ons

As you continue to explore different Chrome apps, extensions, and Google Docs add-ons, there will be ones that you try and decide not to use. Leaving those available add-ons can slow down Google Chrome and Chrome OS. To maintain the best performance when using Google Apps, delete these unused apps, extensions, and Google Docs add-ons whenever possible.

Deleting Google Chrome apps and extensions follow similar steps. For apps, right-click on the App icon when viewing apps in Google Chrome or the App Launcher of Chrome OS and select Remove from Chrome... as shown in the following screenshot:

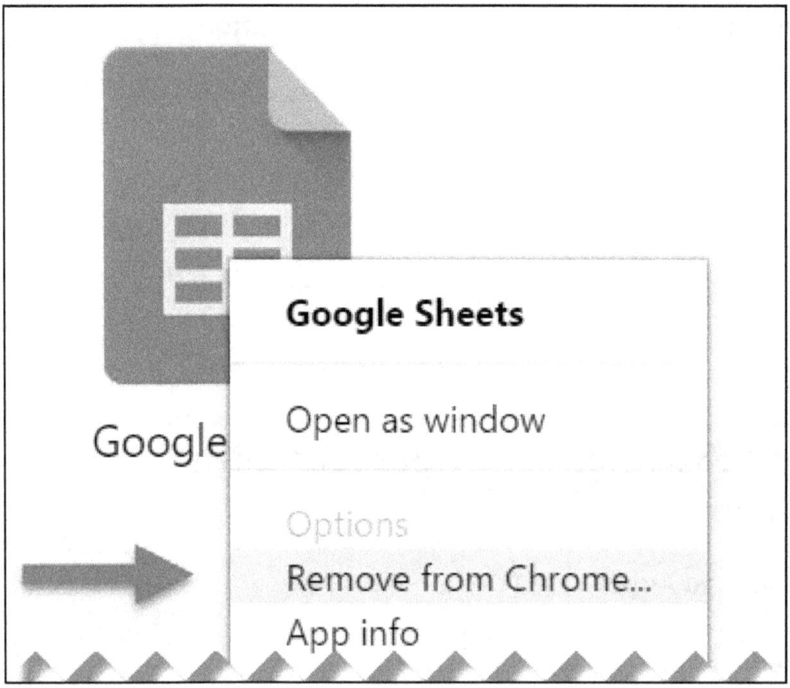

For deleting extensions, right-click on the extension icon beside the omni bar and choose Remove from Chrome

Removing add-ons in Google Docs involves a few steps, which are as follows:

1. Select Control add-ons in Google Documents. From the menu Add-ons

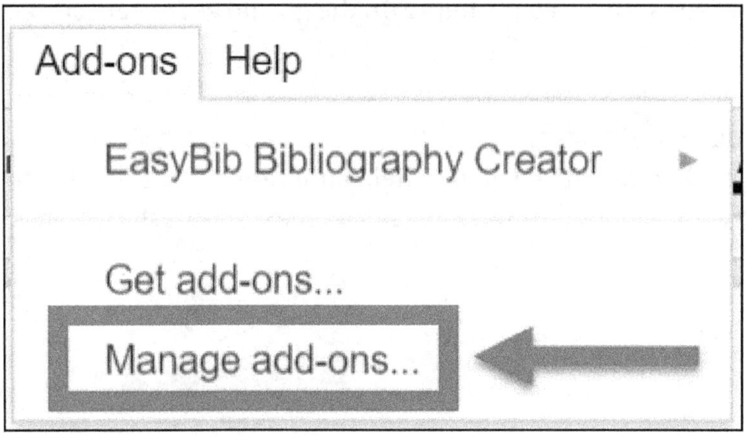

2. In addition to the add-on, click on a Control button.

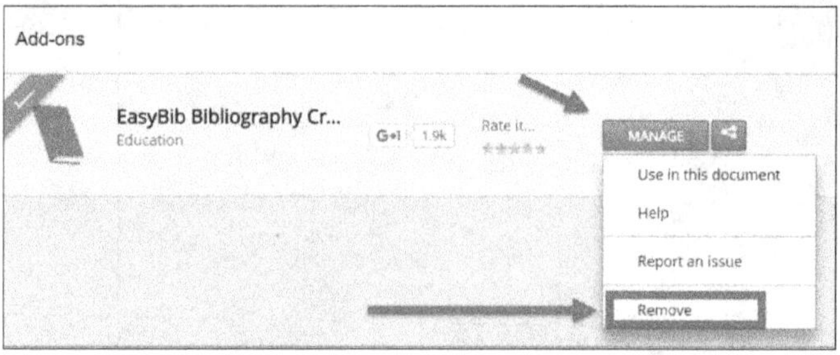

4.3 Best Extensions and Apps for Google Classroom

Extensions and Apps Every Teacher Should Know

ClassDojo

ClassDojo allows teachers to change actions in their classes quickly and easily. The extensions and apps to the Google Extensions and apps every Teacher should learn. It tracks and produces behavior data that can be shared by teachers with parents and managers."

Google Keep

"Catch easily what you think and share these thoughts with your family and friends. Talk a voice memo on the go and get it transcribed automatically."

Glogster Edu

'Glogster Edu' lets you build Glugs – online multimedia posters – with text, pictures, graphics, sounds, links, sketches, data attachments, etc. '

Sketchpad

"You can play with images by incorporating new elements into the composition, inserting notes, changing graphics, overlaying text on something, or going backward and forwards in time forever through the changes you make."

VoiceNoteII: Speech to Text

"Typing with your voice and speech recognition. Simple and functional notepad."

Lucidchart

Lucidchart is a visual communication device that simplifies and simplifies drawing diagrams. Work with infinite numbers of others to build and edit pictures in the real-time, fuse, and synced changes instantly-perfect for collaborating with teams and customers.

Socrative Teacher

Engage, analyze, and personalize your class with Socrative! Educators can perform formative evaluations with their Socrative Chrome app through quizzes, quick question polls, exit tickets, and space race events. Socrative can instantaneously rate, compile, and include findings to assist you in defining opportunities for more instruction.

Any.do

Any.do is used by over 10 million people to coordinate everything they want to do.

Loup Collage

"Loupe takes hundreds of pictures and, in second, instantly produces beautiful photo collages in whatever form you want. Any.do makes it easy to recall your personal and work activities wherever you are going. Turn your images, objects, words, and even logos into your heart. You can share your collages with friends, with relatives, place them on a website or your blog!"

Pixlr Express

Pixlr Express is a powerful and fun photo editor that allows you to quickly create, resize, and change any image with an entirely ad-free experience. Choose from more than 2 million free effects, overlays, and borders combinations to personalize your pictures further. You look like a pro, even though you have never edited a photo before when you are Pixlr Express.

Pixlr-o-Matic

Pixlr-o-Matic is an amusing and easy-to-use photography/darkroom tool to add effects, overlays, and borderlines to your images easily. If you want to look vintage, grunge, clean, or trendy, Pixlr-o-Matic makes it easy in three simple steps. You will never come out of new styles with more than 2 million editing combinations to choose from that make your pictures look stunning.

Dictanote

Dictanote offers you a highly advanced text editor and an integrated multi-lingual speaker recognition.

PowToon

Powtoon is an interactive video software and interactive presentation program. A simple animated video can be easily generated and transformed into an animated show!

Class Charts
"Seating and behavior charts are an integral part of a useful tool kit for teachers. They help organize the students into suitable learning groups and mitigate problems with school conduct – the classroom teacher expresses its authority before the lesson even begins.

PearDeck
You can open a Google Slides presentation once enabled and use PearDeck to add questions to any slide. There can be multiple choices, brief responses, or numerical questions. Students must sign up for a video, which then appears on their computers.

The questions that you have inserted will appear on every student computer as you move through the presentation and give them a chance to respond. You can see what each student responds to, but you can share their responses anonymously with the class to see how others respond. When you've skipped to the next slide, you've answered the following question for students. Ultimately, you can save and export student responses to Google Sheets and later test how students respond, and decide the course of action using the data you collect.

Auto Text Expander
Auto Text Expander allows you to type a shortcut into emails for lengthy texts. In reaction to the parent or student inquiries about their grade, for example, maybe you also type "Thank You for your email." You can create a shortcut with Auto Text Expander, such as 'ty,' which automatically inserts the text you like. You can set up various alternatives based on text bits, which you often use. This lets you write emails and respond to emails you receive efficiently.

Checkmark

Checkmark is an extension that lets you leave quick feedback on Google Docs for a student's article. Instead of typing out all of the comments you want to add, you can make any comments that you often make in student papers like "new paragraph," "run-on," or "comma mistake" and insert your comment easily. You have to open the student document and highlight a section of the text after downloading and opening the extension. Then a small box with the options for comment will appear, pick the correct explanation, and it will be added automatically. You do have the right to make additional notes, but Checkmark can help you with correct feedback in grading papers more quickly.

Goobric + Doctopus

Goobric and Doctopus work together and work exceptionally well with Google Classroom. Doctopus pulls ties to each task in Google Classroom assignments and essays. Goobric helps you to create a rubric in which each document can be opened. You can build your products or use the models in Goobric. Goobric opens a page when you open a student assignment and Goobric simultaneously, so you can click on the boxes of the element you want to join, so leave the comments. Goobric adds and offers an average ranking, so it can notify the student that their assignment is marked and ready for display. Such two additions help to streamline student reviews.

Pocket

Pocket is an extension to save products, videos, and websites you'd like to visit later. After downloading Pocket, you just press the extension in your Chrome browser when you come to a video or site that you want to remember, and Pocket saves it to you. You will access all the blogs, videos, and articles you have saved when logging into Pocket. It is a perfect way to keep track of stuff you want for future lessons or professional growth.

Screencastify

Screencastify is an extension that lets you video something on your screen. This is special because you can open your laptop with a website or article instead of having to make PDF versions of all that you want in your photo. You can even choose to record the Open tab, the entire monitor, or even add your webcam to your video in the lower corner after downloading and opening Screencastify. You can also use your mouse to write and highlight multiple parts of your screen once you start recording. You can save your video to your Google Drive, where students and staff can share it. This is especially useful for eLearning or updating your LMS lessons.

Hopefully, these Google Chrome teachers' extensions can help you rate and interact more effectively.

Best Chrome Apps and Extensions for Students
Chrome Apps and Extensions for Elementary School

IXL

Direct input and depth plus amid focus on Bottom line drills: Students will develop targeted skills with lots of practice exercises and visually appealing tasks.

Grades: Pre-K–12 Price: Free to try, Paid

Raz Kids

Leveled readings with progress-tracking improve the differentiated reading program Bottom line: it is worth considering as a complement to your reading curriculum with a wide variety of leveled books, simple assignment and evaluation, and comprehensive progress reports.

Learning Journal

A flexible, interactive collection appeals to instructors, students, and parents Bottom line: a robust online learning and communication platform that illustrates student development over time.

Grades: K–12 Price: Free, Paid

Applications and Extensions for Middle School

CK-12

Super STEM, Social Studies, Highly Customized Learning Tool Bottom line: Making content available to children with various learning styles, CK-12 could be the path to mastery for individual students.

Grades: K–12 Price: Free

Edulastic

A useful training evaluation tool measures the achievement of expectations. Bottom line: Efficient program helps teachers who are expected to analyze and monitor student success in achieving aspirations.

Grades: K–12 Price: Free, Charged

TES Teaching with Blendspace

Build multimedia lessons with engaging but not - so-interactive style Bottom line: allows you to add a lot of multimedia tools, but distinguish content and assessment to avoid lazy teaching or learning.

Grades: 3–12 Price: Free

PlayPosit
The comfortable design makes it simple to leap into interactive video Bottom line: with features that are both basic and useful, it's easy to learn; adding interactivity to video is a snap.

Grades: 2–12 Price: Free, Paid

Edmodo
Manage classes, content, and communication with the social LMS platform Bottom line: this free platform enables teacher-monitored classroom communication but lacks excitement.

Grades: 4–12 Price: Free

ThinkCERCA
Well-structured lessons promote in-depth review, reflective writing Bottom line: this is a ready-to-go, research-backed tool that focuses on CCSS-aligned and AP-level critical reading and writing skills.

Grades: 3–12 Price: Free, Pay

4.4 How Google Classroom Will Boost Your Teaching

Re-Order Classes

Your classes are the easiest to see in the order you teach them. You can now re-arrange the tiles for each of your courses in an order that works for you! Do this by simply drag-and-drop or press the three dots in the top right corner of the class card and select "Switch."

Move Class Ownership Often

Mid-year changes occur, and now teachers and administrators have the option of transferring ownership of current Google Classroom files and property of all associated Classroom files. For example, a long-term replacement began the school year last year by building a classroom. When a permanent teacher returned, the only choice for children to continue working in the same class was to add a permanent teacher as a co-teacher to hold the account open for the replacement who had left. The upgrade would make it easier for teachers and schools to respond to changes while preserving the current classroom.

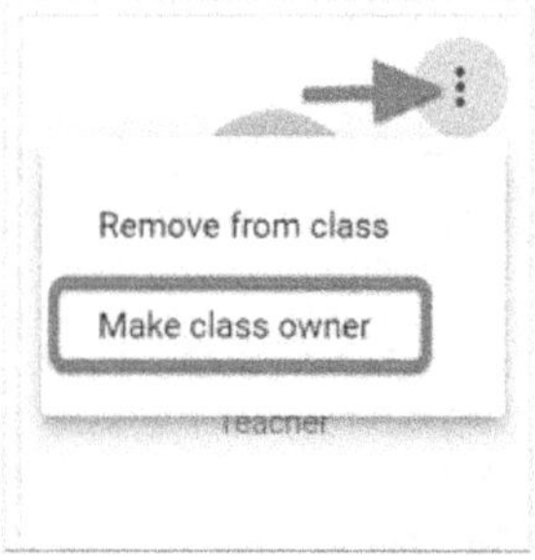

Keeping Kids Involve While at Home

They are keeping students involved while at home Digital learning may be isolation and disengagement for students. Sitting always in front of the screen for several hours watching videos can force a student to move forward quickly or even miss a lesson altogether. To keep them engaged, open virtual conversations about what they're learning. Inexperience on the water cycle, invite students to pause the video and enter an interview in the Google Classroom (using the Stream) about the last time they encountered a thunderstorm. You can also use Google Docs and Classroom comments to have a two-way conversation with students as you give feedback on their work — another perfect technique to indulge in when you can't see them in person.

Frequent Assessment of Student Learning

Formative tests help you ensure that students continue to develop when away from school. Test for comprehension during community teaching by posing a survey question in the middle of the lesson and presenting the results in real-time. It can also help you "take part" in a virtual world. Quizzes in Google Forms provide auto-grading features that allow you to add videos, photos, and as many answers as you want. You can also delegate graduated discussions to Google Classroom, and students can demonstrate their expertise through project-based free learning assignments using slide presentations, Docs, or Pages.

Continue to Connect with Hangouts Meet

When the routine of students is interrupted, many realize how much they enjoy the structure of the school and learn with their Teacher. In a time of uncertainty, it is necessary to retain this feeling of comfort and protection.

You can see them on Hangouts Meet if your students have Wi-Fi access. You can also use this forum to create video discussion parts for students to interact and help their colleagues who may have difficulty with concepts. Switch on vital phrases to help students concentrate and make them able to read the spoken language during the call.

Scheduling is an extra task. Using Calendar Term Slots, students who need additional support can sign up to meet 1:1 or with you in small groups. Due to sporadic or non-Wi-Fi connectivity, or because children's care approaches are evolving, not all students can enter a virtual classroom at the same time. Your lesson will probably be a combination of live videos and the sharing of experiences for students who can't do it. Fortunately, advanced features in Hangouts allow you to record your lessons with students.

Check in With How Your Students Are Feeling

Check out how your students feel social, emotional learning can also go on at a distance. Much like you can use Hangouts Meet to "work" for your students and preserve the atmosphere of your classroom, you can provide the students with other ways to express their feelings, when away from school. Using Google Forms, create mood tests for students to share their passion every day. In the form, students can apply for a conference with the instructor if additional help is required. You may also create a private blog for students to think about the experience by journaling or capturing video reflections.

Think Beyond the Clock

For distance learning, you don't have to think about the time constraints of the regular day: rush students into school or hurry to complete your course before the bell rings.

Students may take more time to do other things and learn lessons naturally. Make the most of this opportunity and expand your experiences to include more "choose your adventure" activities instead of a set lecture and lesson schedule.

Explore More Approaches to Distance Learning

As educators and administrators draw up contingency plans and discuss making classrooms completely immersive, we are here to help. We saw education leaders reaching out to each other, exchanging ideas, and helping through Google Educator Groups and other social networks such as Twitter and Facebook. See this webinar on approaches for distance learning.

Google Classroom Bolsters

Using Google Classroom, teachers can carry their papers in a single dashboard for all their lessons. Just a few clicks, you can allocate homework to every classroom digitally.

Google Classroom makes the work of educators simpler as it prevents travel to the copier.

"If a teacher decides to produce a sheet of paper for his students, she must build it into a word processor then print it out, make photocopies, send it to their students, hope no one will ever lose it (which, of course, somebody still does) and then pick it up at the end of the class," Souderton writes.

Google Classroom for education streamlines this cycle because teachers simply create worksheets online.

Google also supported collective learning. Teachers will share content with their peers in one way — editing a document and then sharing a different version with them — a record without editing functions.

Discussions in the classroom are encouraged more efficiently by a student response system, which allows teachers to start conversations led by questions on the virtual page of the class.

The Share to Classroom extension allows educators to give all of their students a website or other material for a lesson at once.

Catherine Davis, Director of Instructional Technology at the Pilgrim School in Los Angeles, writes in a Google blog: "The new extension helps me to engage my students and help them perform their learning at our school in 1:1 app.

Google Classroom is being used in the Colony High School "as a forum for students to access regular assignments and have faster, more comprehensive, and meaningful input on their work."

"With Google Classroom, students have immediate feedback, and the instructor may evaluate in depth the questions have been answered properly or wrongly by which students," writes McKenney. "The teacher can see areas at a glance that need reteaching or clarification." Students who skip classes can quickly catch up on the assignments using a web-based classroom.

Ease IT Workflow

Google Classroom is also ideal for managers and IT teams. Alerts inform them whether suspicious activity happens. Teachers and students can also monitor password reset by IT teams, so the wait time is minimal.

The application program interface (API) can quickly synchronize Google Classroom rosters with other systems, such as a learning management system, or a student information system.

In the classroom area, API also allows teachers to use add-ons and other devices easily.

Google Classroom administrators have access to all types of data. You can monitor patterns in usage, active users and classes, and posts made by students and teachers.

"With these reports and new ones to be implemented in the future, we hope administrators can have the experience they need to give their teachers and students the best help possible," wrote Andrew Garrett, a Google Classroom software developer, on a blog announcing the latest update.

Google's Classroom Updates Remain Consistent with Trends

Google has kept classroom updated, including personalization, with current learning patterns. A recent update makes it easy for teachers to build jobs for each student or community. Google has marketed it as a safe way of offering educational support to struggling students.

The integration of Google classrooms with Chromebooks and G Suite for Education apps have made it possible for students to take care of their learning, which is a critical element of personalization.

Google Chat help constant foster conversation between students and teachers.

Teachers can provide input in real-time that is impossible in a purely pencil-and-paper environment. Google tools and software have built a networking atmosphere that allows even younger students in challenging circumstances to reach out to their teachers. Second-grade students in California's Arcadia Unified School District also contact their teachers when they have issues with their assignments.

Google Classroom has grown into new learning opportunities, such as adult learning programs and seminars. Google has examined the technology intimidation aspect by using the classroom to bind the students into an international exchange program.

4.5 Google Classroom vs. Apple Classroom

Google Classroom helps teachers to coordinate their classroom material while incorporating Google Drive to improve workflow and student organization. Next, with the advent of Apple Classroom, teachers have the power to assist in the management of classrooms in their hands.

If you're teaching in an environment using both Google Apps and iPads, combining these two items will help take your classroom technology skills to an impressive level!

Google Classroom

1 – Managing Digital Workflow

At its heart, Google Classroom links directly to Teacher and student Google Drive accounts by providing an easy-to-follow digital workflow that also applies file naming conventions through the assignment creation phase. For instance, when a teacher assigns a Google Doc via Google Classroom, a copy can be made automatically for each student and then saved in the Drive Classroom folder. By making individual digital copies of tasks, exchanging problems and permissions can be avoided. For more information on Google Classroom, visit the Google Classroom page of EdTech Teacher.

2-Sharing Knowledge

A difficulty that many teachers face in managing a digital world is the successful sharing of digital tools with their students. Google Classroom provides teachers with a place to centralize their digital resources and efficiently distribute them to students. If it's holding a permanent connection to the Teacher's website in the About section or sharing an interesting article in the Flow, Teachers can use Google Classroom to adequately house and allocate resources to students while saving time, reducing stress, and streamlining job performance.

3 – Making an Assignment Calendar for Students

After a class has been created, Google Classroom automatically generates a calendar for that class inside the Google Classroom. It can be viewed as a calendar on the Google Calendar teacher and student page. When teachers make an assignment or add a due date in the Google Classroom, an event will be created automatically in the class calendar. This summer, a group of high school students clarified that the value of the calendar should not be seen as "just a fun feature." They swore the schedule produced by Google Classroom and its ability to be accessed through their devices. Teachers may also consider accessing the calendar settings within calendar.google.com and modifying the access permissions to the public. Through doing so, teachers will share a public connection to a calendar with parents to create a direct assignment calendar for their students.

Apple Classroom

While Google Classroom offers a platform for teachers and students to connect and communicate, the Apple Classroom App provides teachers with management functionality lacking from the iPad app marketplace. Teachers use Apple Classroom will not only have the software on their iPad to disseminate content and tools but will also have the opportunity to connect and track student iPads while in class.

1-Air Viewing Student Screens

The Apple Classroom App provides teachers with the opportunity to view student research. By selecting the student's iPad from the list in their Apple Classroom app, teachers would be able to see the student's iPad through their Apple TV or other mirroring apps.

When using Classroom instead of Airplay, the instructor is the manager and can pick the student computer to view. If you use Airplay, students are responsible for choosing the right Apple TV. With the instructor in charge, the workflow is much more manageable. The opportunity to share student screens with minimal interference in classroom teaching would make the technology and learning process more open for teachers and students.

2-Grouping Students for Distinction

The Apple Classroom also offers teachers the ability to build groups of students directly from the app. After classifying students, the instructor may name a group based on any category and then launch specific group applications, open particular websites, or lock the students' screens. A group of students may benefit from using Google Docs, but another one might do better in Google Slides. By using the Apple Classroom, the instructor will be able to open these apps to students without calling different groups of students by name. This ability to put out differentiated content and resources will change learning and interaction in the classroom while teaching a diverse group of students.

3-Managing the iPad Classroom Separately from Classes

Teachers do have several new features to control better a classroom full of iPads, such as reset forgotten Apple ID passwords, remotely lock student screens, and remote monitoring of student screens. Although no technology will take the place of a teacher in terms of classroom management, the use of these devices can improve the iPad classroom experience as well as help teachers and students learn how to use the computer properly.

Putting the Two Together

It is not uncommon for teachers entering the world of classroom technology to be overwhelmed by the additional computers, electronic documents, applications, and classroom management strategies required for students to learn successfully. It is in these circumstances that both Google Classroom and Apple Classroom may be of great value. Although different in their skills, both can work hand-in-hand to create a better learning atmosphere for students.

Google Classroom: Conclusion

It is not rare for teachers entering the world of classroom technology to be overwhelmed by the additional devices, electronic documents, applications, and classroom management strategies needed for students to learn successfully. It is in these circumstances where it can be of great help

While Google is well-known for organizing students to work on Google Drive, creating individual copies of GPMs and organizing digital content, these three underutilized features of Google classroom will help you and your students become much more productive while using technology in the classroom. What teachers will learn about Google is the organized and accessible system of assigning work and turning in work and also the fact that it is 100% paperless, so they don't need to worry about having large piles of work cluttering the desks. The most likely to get the most out of Google Classroom are those teaching English or even Science, as students can easily add essays and research papers from google classroom. However, while some may think that Google classroom is more advantageous to google classroom, others may prefer google classroom, which is provided by apple. The use of iPads at school has become more popular in the world. It seems appropriate, therefore, that these pads will have an app that will allow 'teachers to concentrate on teaching so that students will focus on learning, which is the primary purpose of the iPad.

The Classroom App focuses on making the lesson more engaging between the teacher and the student. First, students will be given a shared iPad that they can use in the class while working on the assignment.

So, as they work, teachers can use the iPad to see what device every student is using, as well as the method that was most recently used by that student. There is also a Screen View option where teachers can see the same screen that is displayed on the student iPad (the student will be alerted when their teacher is watching their screen). This software will help teachers make sure students don't get sidetracked.

If you enjoyed this book, please let me know your thoughts by leaving an Amazon review.

I would really love to hear your thoughts!

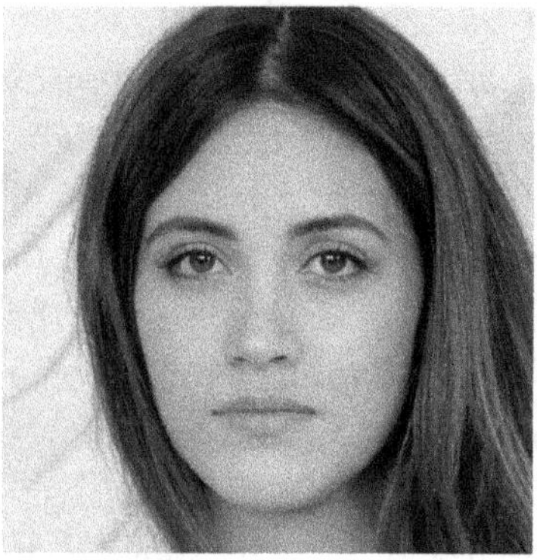

Thank you so much!
-Emily

Google Classroom References

- Ten Reasons Why You Should Use Google Classroom. Blog.mimio.com. Retrieved from **https://blog.mimio.com/ten-reasons-why-you-should-use-google-classroom**.
- Gettingsmart.com. Retrieved from **https://www.gettingsmart.com/2016/11/6-reasons-google-classroom-great-tool/**.
- 10 Benefits of Google Classroom Integration - The Tech Advocate. The Tech Advocate. Retrieved from **https://www.thetechedvocate.org/10-benefits-of-google-classroom-integration/**.
- Teachthought.com. Retrieved from **https://teachthought.com/current-events/changes-new-features-in-google-classroom/**.
- What's New in Google Classroom? [2020 Updates] - EdTech Team. EdTech Team. Retrieved from **https://www.edtechteam.com/blog/2020/02/whats-new-in-google-classroom-2020-updates/**.
- 4 Hidden Features of Google Classroom - EdTech Teacher. EdTech Teacher. Retrieved from **https://edtechteacher.org/4-hidden-features-google-classroom/**.
- How to Use Google Classroom to Train Your Employees - The Tech Advocate. The Tech Advocate. Retrieved from **https://www.thetechedvocate.org/how-to-use-google-classroom-to-train-your-employees/**.
- 6 Great Google Classroom Tips for Teachers | Common Sense Education. Common Sense Education. Retrieved from **https://www.commonsense.org/education/articles/6-great-google-classroom-tips-for-teachers**.
- 7 Things You Need to Know About the New Google Classroom - The Tech Advocate. The Tech Advocate. Retrieved from **https://www.thetechedvocate.org/7-things-you-need-to-know-about-the-new-google-classroom/**.

- Tips for Using Google Classroom - dummies. dummies. Retrieved from **https://www.dummies.com/education/internet-basics/tips-for-using-google-classroom/**.
- How to use Google Meet for eLearning, online learning - Ditch That Textbook. Ditch That Textbook. Retrieved from **https://ditchthattextbook.com/google-meet-elearning/**.
- 10 Google Classroom Tips You Didn't Know. Shake Up Learning. Retrieved from **https://shakeuplearning.com/blog/10-google-classroom-tips-you-didnt-know-suls029/**.
- Google Classroom Management Tips. Lauracandler.com. Retrieved from **https://www.lauracandler.com/google-classroom-management-tips/**.
- Can overthinking kill you? What are the ways on how to eliminate negative thoughts from recurring? Mindfulness. Reddit.com. Retrieved from **https://www.reddit.com/r/Mindfulness/comments/c58umy/can_overthinking_kill_you_what_are_the_ways_on/**.

Google Apps: Introduction

Google Apps (formerly known as Google Applications for Your Domain) is a built-in suite of Google purposes that consists of an email program, a WYSIWYG webpage editor, an online calendar, on the spot messaging customer with voice skills, and a web-based phrase processor cum spreadsheet software.

Business organizations, instructional establishments, and even humans (like you and me) can use the Google Apps provider for free (though a premier version is additionally available). And since Google Apps require little or no technical expertise, it can also be a blessing for small commercial enterprise proprietors who have little or no price range for IT.

Google servers host a range of factors of Google Apps (like calendar, email, spreadsheet, phrase processor, etc.), and so the quit customers are saved from the hassles of putting in or upgrading software programs at their end.

Administrators can get entry to and control a person's bill even though a web-based manipulate panel is present. The digital collaboration points of Google Docs are some distance greatest and effortless than what is presently presented via Microsoft Office applications. To get commenced with Google Apps, you'll want a net area name. Recently, Google partnered with registrars, Go Daddy and eNom, to promote area names at $10/year.

Domains offered thru Google come in bundled with Google Apps requiring no configuration via the owners. The drawback is that India's unique area like .in or .co.in can't be bought by way of Google yet, even though they can nevertheless be built-in with Google Apps. If you plan to use a current internet area with Google Apps, simply make positive that you have to get entry to your DNS settings, which is usually reachable with the area host.

Google Apps is handy in two flavors – the well-known (aka free) version and a premier (aka paid) edition. The premier version subscribers get 10GB of email storage house (as hostile to 2GB+ in the free edition) and a 99.9% uptime assurance for email.

Other top-class amenities encompass getting entry to 24/7 to assist via phone, covering all contextual classified ads on Google offerings, and numerous superior aspects tailor-made for the enterprise.

The premier version doesn't come low cost — it charges a whopping $50 per consumer account per yrs. - however, the desirable information is that most families, enterprise proprietors, and persons will be pretty content material with the choices of the well-known version because, besides phone guides and small inboxes, Google is supplying the identical functions in each the editions.

Google Apps provider is a runaway success, and plenty of that can be attributed to Gmail, the web-based email software of Google.

In a generation where 86% of all electronic mail messages that hit our inboxes are spam, Gmail is geared up with some of first-class unsolicited mail filtering algorithms that have proved to be very fantastic in preserving junk mail out of our mailboxes.

Other than anti-spam technology, Gmail offers more significant than two GB of storage house even in the free version of Google Apps. If your personnel or household participants choose a laptop mail purchaser like Microsoft Outlook or Thunderbird as an alternative to the AJAX-based internet interface of Gmail, they can nevertheless use their computer software program with Gmail. The usage of the POP gets entry to the characteristic of Gmail, which is once more free for all users. Google Docs & Spreadsheets is any other beneficial utility bundled with Google Apps that might also exchange the way you write and share archives with co-workers and clients.

Think of it as an online model of Microsoft Word or Excel software program where the appear n' experience and facets are pretty comparable to Microsoft software program, barring that you compose archive interior, internet browser, and information is saved online (on Google servers). By this, you can access information from any pc related to the internet.

Google Docs & Spreadsheets is tightly built-in with GTalk, the immediate messaging customer from Google. In quite a several areas, workers can edit the same file/spreadsheet concurrently – they can open a chat window and talk about /review adjustments made via different authors in actual time.

The subsequent massive query is whether or not corporations must ditch Microsoft Office in favor of Google Apps? Well, it's a no-brainer that Google Apps pose an actual hazard to Microsoft Office, the money cow of Redmond. The digital collaboration points of Google Docs are excellent and straight forward than the present provision with the aid of Microsoft Office applications.

There are some downsides, as well. Google Apps doesn't have any PowerPoint fashion software program for developing presentations. Secondly, it saves all your private information (in the shape of spreadsheets and Word documents) on Google servers freeing the firewall of your company. That can also no longer be to the liking of some companies.

Microsoft is also readying Google Apps like hosted provider (dubbed 'Office Live') that is presently accessible solely in the US, Japan, and a few different nations. Microsoft Office Live offerings will additionally provide internet-based applications, branded electronic mail, and internet sites; however, in contrast to Google Apps, the Microsoft online provider will seamlessly combine with Microsoft Office software.

Before getting started with a Google Apps summary, I'd love to share some information about me. I am a 26-year public high school American teacher. I hold a Bachelor's Degree in History, and my passion is technology applied to teach. I have always used Google tools since 2000, and now write books about online teaching to explain to other teachers how to use those tools for effective learning.

Thank you for choosing this book! If you have a few seconds, please leave a short review; it means a lot to me, I would so much love to hear your thoughts!

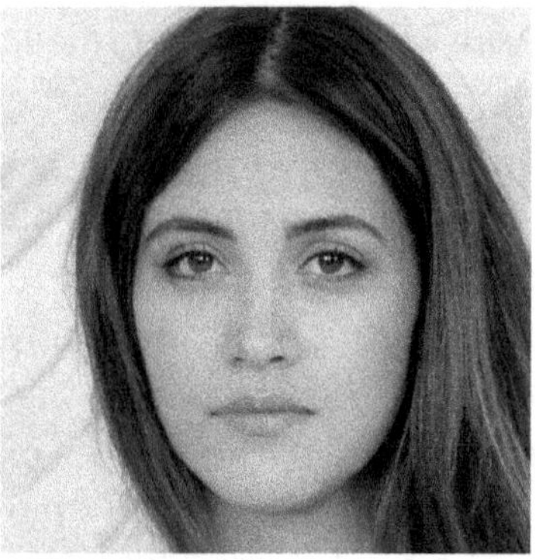

Thank you so much!
-Emily

Chapter 1: Understanding Google Applications

Apps related to google are a suite of web-based messaging and collaboration purposes that Google hosts on their servers. Google affords these purposes as a "service," as a substitute rather than a software program to download and install. To get admission to these applications, you use a net browser on a pc related to the internet.

Google Apps is backed via the equal infrastructure and assets supplied by using the general Google services. It aspects 99.9 share uptime availability, administrative support, and different company assist elements explicitly described in the Google Apps Service Level Agreement (SLA).

Google Apps customizes purposes for distinctive industries, as described below:

- ✓ **Google Apps (Free)**

Gmail has (up to ten free email accounts), Google Calendar, Google Sites, and Google Docs.

- ✓ **Google Apps for Education**

Free functions for schools.

- ✓ **Google Apps for Business**

The paid version affords Web-based utility equipment for collaboration.

- ✓ **Google Apps for Government**

Web-based and authorities licensed collaboration tools.

- ✓ **Google Apps for Non-Profit Organizations**

Collaboration and conversation equipment for US nonprofit organizations

1.1 Significance of Google Apps

Many elements contributed to our choice to "go Google." Increasing license charges and the complexities of working the previous Novell GroupWise machine supposed escalating prices and risk. The current price range disaster mixed with the projected boom of the University required us to locate an extra fine and cost-effective solution. Many higher schooling establishments have confirmed that Google Apps have been an answer and, to a massive extent, established right here at Georgia Southern with the profitable implementation of college students and preliminary checking out using a group of workers and school volunteers. Based on what we understand today, we estimate that Google Apps saves the group more than $200,000 yearly while promoting accelerated collaboration and innovation all through the University.

More specifically, Google Apps provides:

- **Lower Infrastructure Costs**

All your email is saved securely on Google's servers, so we are going to want to keep email servers no longer on-site.

- **Ability to Similarly Consolidate Email Platforms**

We get rid of duplication of offerings by way of shifting to one email, calendar, and file sharing answer offering students, college, and a group of workers with a nation of the artwork tools.

- **Lower help Costs**

Because Google hosts the email and calendar services, there is no extra email patron software program to hold on your computer.

- **Innovative Options**

We can leverage the Google Apps platform's capable collaboration equipment to furnish the University neighborhood with the easy-to-use kit for sharing data and getting work completed efficiently.

- **Highly scalable Surroundings**

With Google Apps, the potential of our electronic mail continues to develop robotically as Georgia Southern grows, and we keep away from many complexities, dangers, and future costs.

Access to offerings from anywhere, whenever – Google Apps are designed to function in our online world and is purposeful with any pc or cell system with an Internet connection, somewhere in the world;

- **Security and Survivability**

Google's protection assets are world-class, and some distance outpaces the sources that any single more fabulous schooling group should ever provide. Google Apps gives a sturdy and enormous protection infrastructure that has exceeded the American Institute of Certified Public Accountants Statement on Auditing Standard 70. Google facts facilities grant redundancy of offerings and duplication of statistics throughout large geographical areas, making them resilient to common catastrophe scenarios.

- **State of the Art Aspects**

With Google's next-generation applications, faculty, college students, and a group of worker function in the surroundings of facts collaboration. Google is continuously innovating new functions and capabilities. Google additionally presents a programming interface that approves the University to create our very own Google-based applications.

1.2 What Are the Different Google Apps?

Google has a lot of applications. Perhaps too much, in specific cases. Amid all the conspicuous titles and strangely covering contributions, Google's wing of the Play Store holds some truly helpful fortunes — cunning manifestations by the maker of Android that is merely standing by to be found.

Here are several unexpected directions that Google applications will assist you in doing a wide range of intriguing stuff with your Android gadget. Of course, any of them could vanish any day with almost no notice — this is Google we're discussing, all things considered — yet for the occasion, in any event, they're out there and prepared for the taking. Furthermore, indeed, they're all free.

Here are several special applications that must be considered by everybody.

Google Maps

Google's whiz application needs no presentation. Google Maps is the pioneer in the handy guide and GPS space. With speedy and dependable bearings, Google Maps get clients where they have to go via vehicle, open vehicle, or doggin' it by walking.

On the head of their underlying guide achievement, Google Maps likewise offers indoor guides (think exhibition halls, air terminals), 3D maps, and a road sees include. Google Maps additionally has a worked-in-look alternative for finding close-by neighborhood organizations in your snapshots of need.

Google Now

Google Now is an ongoing expansion to the Google applications group, giving clients the most recent news and updates for what is essential to most of them as people. It does this through a card determination framework where clients mark "cards" (fundamentally classifications) that they esteem significantly.

Sports addicts can get prompt game updates about their preferred groups, while music fans can get the most recent news about shows going on in their regions. Google Now can likewise follow your drive course and disclose to you the following train you have to catch or which streets to beat the traffic.

Google+ Local

Google+ Local lets clients find close by diners, shops, and amusement scenes profoundly appraised utilizing the Zagat framework.

Some may state that it energizes a total absence of arranging and that it is gotten endemic of present-day society. Others may say it supports suddenness! Take your pick.

One of a kind part of Google+ Local that separates it from other what's-close me-right-now applications is the capacity to see close-by food joints suggested by your companions in your Google+ Circles. (This would be all the more energizing if more individuals were utilizing Google+; right now, you might be unable to discover any buddies investigating cafés on Google's online life stage.)

Google Play Books

Google Play Books is Google's rendition of Kindle. Google Play Books lets clients read their digital books in a hurry with determinations like New York Times successes, just like a lot of free works of art like Pride and Prejudice.

Google Play Books has some social highlights, similar to an original word reference and the capacity to match up your bookmarks across gadgets to keep perusing on your telephone where you left off on your tablet.

Eventually, however, Google Play Books comes up short on the sparkling chimes of Kindle. It feels like an application Google felt committed to making... yet, it didn't try investing an excessive amount of energy.

Google Wallet

Google Wallet carries shopping into the future, letting clients store MasterCard's, platinum cards, faithfulness cards, and gift vouchers on their telephone to be utilized on the web and in-store buys. Card data is put away on secure Google cloud servers, adequately taking out the blasting wallet of ages past. Making a buy is as necessary as tapping your telephone to an NFC terminal at checkout.

While Google Wallet is an incredibly slick thought, an absence of broad appropriation (of both the Google Wallet application and NFC terminals) has denied this progressive installment alternative the "credit" it merits.

Google Voice

Google Voice is an inviting move to the exemplary voice message that comes standard for most versatile clients. Google Voice permits clients to set up their personal Google Voice number. This can be utilized to cause modest universal calls, to redo phone message messages, send free instant messages, and read voice message transcripts (this one is particularly useful.)

There are more highlights as well, similar to call recording and call sending, which initiate an extra cost.

Google Search App

The Google Search application gives clients a similar accommodation for versatile inquiry, likewise with a work area search. The Google Search application additionally contains extra highlights like customized results dependent on the immediate area, voice proficient pursuit alternatives, and the capacity to look through the Web or telephone/tablet substance.

Google Shopper

Google Shopper is a value correlation application that has been deceived out with someone of a kind highlights; the Google Shopper application can perceive items by spread craftsmanship, standardized identification, voice, and text search.

Clients can think about costs between online merchants versus natural areas, read audits, and the sky is the limit from there.

Google Goggles

Google Goggles is a picture acknowledgment application in which clients can snap a photograph of a physical item, and Google reacts by producing data about the captured image.

Google Goggle is a truly fantastic bit of app manship; at present, Google Goggles can react to anything 2D and do things like giving accurate data about milestones, deciphering an outside menu, and perceiving work of art.

Google Chrome

Google Chrome is a portable Internet program that interprets a portion of the application's most notable highlights, similar to numerous tabs and in disguise mode, from work area perusing to versatile perusing. Likewise, clients can adjust bookmarks across Chrome programs, proceeding to smooth, versatile, and working areas, while keeping away from hiccups.

1.3 What Are the Key Benefits of Using Google Apps?

Google is a solid trendsetter in the specialized administration industry. Over ten years prior, they spearheaded requests in the enormous confusion of data that made up the internet. Today the turmoil develops, but they keep on having the option to support demand in their hunt administration. It's no big surprise that they would, in the long run, branch out to handle the confusion that exists. For getting organizations associated with the data, they have to remain on top of their staff and clients. Google Apps for Business carries some cloud benefits that most organizations in the present market require to stay in line with their objectives. Here are the key advantages of utilizing Google Apps for your Business.

Accommodation of Remaining Associated

It has become standard for many businesses to work permanently and in the cloud. Email, archive sharing, and visit carry that administration to even the littlest business, which is an enormous advance up from the times of sending documents and sorting out telephone calls as the primary methods for remaining associated.
So far, in my current utilization of the framework, it's been straightforward to make a report and offer it, video, or message immediately with someone without going through the motions.

The best accommodation factor is the point at which you discover this should all be possible from any cell phone, cutting the line and letting you remain associated with anyplace. Even though the weight of requiring a web association may back you off, the remainder of what you need is readily available.

Unwavering Quality in a very much Perceived Brand

The advantages of unwavering quality originate from the diminished multifaceted nature that would regularly be related to any of the above administrations. This qualification as a Google administration is significant because the brand has gotten very much perceived for its unwavering quality in the administrations it gives. I have utilized other self-facilitated email administrations before while at past organizations. There were times when the email would lose all sense of direction in travel or set aside an extended effort to contact its crowd. There were even examples where email simply didn't work by any stretch of the imagination. Would you be able to envision two or three days or even seven days without email operational? It resembled being sent back to the stone ages.

Productivity with High Esteemed Assignments

The client experience is natural for any event. The usefulness is utilized for a business, which implies practically zero preparation for their representatives. Since it's on the cloud, there is no requirement for programming updates to be introduced routinely. It's likewise packaged with their quick pursuit device to discover things rapidly and effectively yet not be secured by the tumult of developing data. This outcome expands profitability and a more joyful working environment since it's no pleasant battling innovation to complete things.

Administering Google Apps is Simple

The administrator interface is dead-easy to utilize and simple. All that you need to control for your space is a catch or switch in the back end.

The Admin Control Panel makes it far simpler to explore essential administrator capacities than any Microsoft server programming. You can include, erase, or suspend clients, move responsibility for archives, make nom de plumes, and change the least secret phrase necessities.

You can likewise give innovation capable individuals (TRPs) in your branch workplaces the capacity to include/erase clients without wrecking other area settings.

Spend Staff Time on Preparation and Improvement; not on looking after Frameworks

Appropriately keeping up an email and schedule server with 99.9% uptime is tedious and requires a talented administrator to be accessible about every minute of every day to investigate blunders. Google Apps liberates that time and conveys plenty of extra instruments.

The most well-known choice to Google Apps in legitimate administrations has been Microsoft Exchange. Accord is that any shop should commit a segment of tech just to keep up Exchange and envision issues.

The time expected to keep things running would only now be utilized to prepare and bolster clients.

Google Apps is Free for Non-Profit Organizations

One of the significant preferences of Google Apps is that it is exceptionally modest. On the off chance that you are not qualified as a non-benefit, Google Apps is generally modest, and you can locate their full charging Info on their site.

This incorporates the accompanying highlights:

- Gmail, Calendar, and other Google Services
- Email relocation devices
- Extensibility APIs
- Customer Service

Contrast: this cost with the least expensive choices from Google Docs' rivals:

- WordPerfect Office: $179.99/seat (no non-benefit rebate)
- Microsoft Office: $199.99/seat ($30/seat with non-benefit rebate)
- Apple iWork: $79.00

These devices imitate just a small piece of the Google Apps environment – that is, the word processor. Full undertaking frameworks, for example, Microsoft Exchange with SharePoint, include substantial extra expenses.

Google Apps exceptional Capacities can help Lawful Administration Associations

Past supplanting capacities gave by another programming; Google Apps offer obvious highlights intended to change and improve office working.

A. Collaboration

Features like archive sharing, synchronous altering, shared schedules, and talk makes bunch work more uncomplicated, and urge office individuals to turn out to be progressively mindful of every others' work.

B. Searching

Documents and messages in Google Apps are intended to be looked at as opposed to arranged by the client. This implies that clients can invest less energy in arranging documents and don't need to know and recall a specific arrangement of association to discover what they are searching for. As shown by the "LSNC Findability" Project, moving to a framework where almost all office information is accessible through Google Search Appliance (GSA) can help workplaces fundamentally increment their viability.

C. Integration

Google Apps are intended to associate with one another and are all the more impressive in the blend.

Chapter 2: Google Drive - For Cloud Storage, Synchronization, and File Sharing

The range of far off employees is on the rise, and the want for these out-in-the disciplines to get admission to data on demand is growing. It's estimated that 70% of the international team of workers works from domestic at least in a week. The cellular personnel is right here to stay, and the influence on many organizations is turning out to be a wonderful one ensuing in higher communication, collaboration, and flexibility.

The advantages of mobility can be helped or hindered with the aid of the incorrect technology, however. Cloud gets the right to digital files, correspondence, workflows, and different work-related features that want to be comfortable, intuitive, dependable, and, most importantly, secure. The science additionally desires to be configured to work across a couple of devices, from smartphones and pills to computer systems and laptops.

2.1 Introduction to Google Drive

The perfect best-distributed storage arrangements play pleasantly with different applications and administrations, making reviewing or altering your records feel normal. Particularly when applying business settings, you need your other programming and claims to have the option to recover in ensuring the utilization of assistance that effectively validates with different apparatuses by the use of a severe deal. Box and Dropbox are excellent in such a manner.

The scope of the abilities of cloud-based capacity administrations is inconceivable. A considerable lot of them have some expertise in a particular region. For instance, Dropbox and Sugar Sync center on keeping a matched up envelope open all over the place. Spider Oak underscores security. Some distributed storage administrations, for example, Apple iCloud, Google Drive, and Microsoft OneDrive are generalists, offering envelope and record matching up, yet additionally, media-playing and gadget synchronizing. These items, even twofold as joint effort programming, offers continuous archive co-altering.

Particular from, however, covering now and again with distributed storage is online to reinforcement administrations. For example, a portion of this Carbonite is about catastrophe recuperation, while In the Drive is the objective with matching up and sharing abilities.

Most cloud administrations do offer some degree of reinforcement, nearly as a result of their planned capacity. It follows any records legitimately transferred to a cloud administration that are likewise shielded from frontline disappointment faced since there are duplicates of these items in the cloud. In this case, genuine online reinforcement administrations can back up the entirety of the documents in your device, not only those in a synchronized organizer structure.

Though adjusting is tied in with overseeing select materials, reinforcement will generally be a mass, just on the off chance that play. With adjusting, you pick the envelopes, reports, and media that you need prepared access to and spare them in the cloud for simple access. With reinforcement, you ensure all that you figure you may lament losing. Simple, prompt access isn't provided with online support, nor is it the point. Genuine feelings of serenity are.

The Deal with the Cloud

Just to clear up any disarray, your drive is some portion of cloud-based capacity administrations alludes to putting away your documents someplace other than your PC's hard drive, as a rule on the supplier's servers.

As one tech savant put it: "There is no Cloud. It's simply another person's PC." Having information in the cloud enables you to get to those documents through the web. Your information is typically scrambled before making the excursion over the internet to the suppliers' servers, and keeping in mind that it lives on those servers, it's likewise encoded.

All around structured administrations don't transfer whole records each time they change. They simply move the changes, sparing your association transmission capacity. You can get to your cloud records through an application or utility programming introduced on your PC. When presented, it generally shows a little warning symbol and makes your adjusted organizer structure that fits into Windows Explorer or the macOS Finder.

You can likewise get to the documents utilizing your internet browser. You need a web association for this to work; however, if you are incidentally without a good association, the administration holds up until you have an association to puts everything in order at that point.

Free vs. Paid

Many distributed storage administrations have an open record that usually accompanies a few confinements, such as the measure of capacity or a size breaking point on documents you can transfer. It helps lean toward administrations that offer some degree of free assistance, instead of time-sensitive, which is preliminary since that lets you completely coordinate and help your daily life for a period of half a month, during which you discover how it functions and what may turn out badly with your specific arrangement.

What might turn out badly? Human mistake represents a decent arrangement of distributed storage disasters. However, the dropped internet web network is another normal miscreant.

What's more, every network access endures the incidental blackout. Make a few inquiries, and you'll hear tragic accounts of how distributed storage can turn out badly for your routine usage. The advantage of paying for data storage is that it, as a rule, accompanies extra help from the supplier. There are rare chances that anything turns out badly, you can get somebody on the telephone to assist you with settling the issue.

There are different reasons to pay for distributed storage software and applications, from getting significantly more space (a terabyte truly doesn't cost all that much any longer) to having the option to transfer huge documents. That last advantage is pertinent to visual originators, video editors, and other visual artisans who regularly have colossal records. Different benefits of paying for your distributed storage usually incorporate expanded access to document form history (which means you can re-establish a significant strategic agreement to the adaptation you had before your partner made a lot of incorrect changes), greater security, or more highlights for joint effort and collaboration.

There are numerous online record sharing programming projects and stages accessible on the commercial center with differing levels of usefulness and value focuses. Most sharing locales offer free record alternatives and obvious highlights. However, most businesses should put resources into a layered arrangement. Some additionally fill in as an archive stockpiling center point for a whole association. In contrast, others center only on safely getting a document starting with one spot then onto the next. All in all, what's the best document sharing site? Contingent upon your necessities, here are some mainstream alternatives to consider.
Numerous clients are now acquainted with Google Drive since they've utilized the stage's 15 GB of free extra room for sponsorship up close to home records. This recognition can help associations that pick the step to limit the expectations to absorb information among representatives. Information is consequently adjusted with all gadgets connected to the record, and changes are spared naturally.
Authorizations can be set ready for survey or altering, and others outside the association can be welcome to see download and team up — no email connection required. Archives, pictures, spreadsheets, and more can be sorted out effectively; however, regardless of whether you experience difficulty finding a document, the coordinated inquiry included that Google is known for.

2.2 Upload and Download Files and Folders on Google Drive

You can transfer, view, share, and alter documents with Google Drive. At the point when you move a record to Google Drive, it will occupy room in your drive, regardless of whether you transfer to an organizer possessed by another person.
Documents including:

- Records
- Pictures
- Sound

- Video

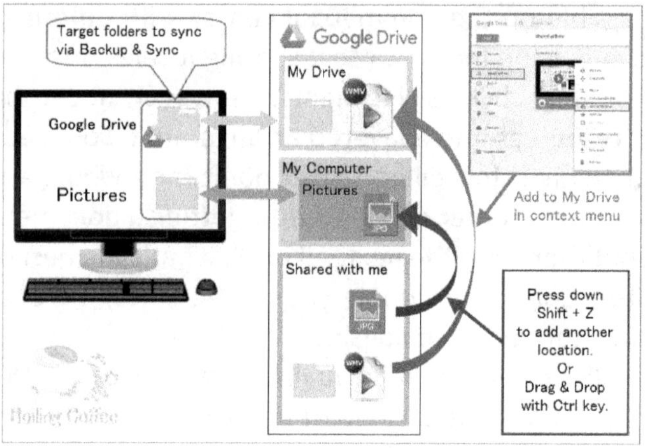

Transfer Documents and Organizers

On your PC, you can transfer documents from drive.google.com or your work area. You can transfer documents into private or shared envelopes.

On your PC, go to drive.google.com.

- At the upper left, click New and afterward File Upload or Folder Upload.
- Pick the record or container you need to transfer.
- Drag records into Google Drive
- On your PC, go to drive.google.com.
- Open or make an organizer.

To move files and envelopes, drag them into the Google Drive organizer.

Use Backup and Sync

Introduce the application on your PC.

On your PC, you'll see an organizer called "Google Drive."

Drag documents or organizers into that envelope. They will transfer to Drive, and you will see them on drive.google.com.

Convert Records into Google Groups

If you need to transfer records as Microsoft Word reports, you can change a setting to change over documents.

Note: You can just shift Google Drive settings from your PC.

Utilizing a PC, Go to drive.google.com/drive/settings

Close to "Convert Uploads," check the crate.

Transfer records with a similar name

It is a rare chance that you transfer a document with the same name, Google Drive will move the File as an update of the document as of now in Google Drive.

To keep Two Documents

On your PC, go to drive.google.com.

Transfer a document.

Snap Keep as a discrete document.

2.3 Managing Files on Google Drive

One of the ways is to see how to oversee documents and envelopes on Google Drive is by getting knowing the basics of managing your google drive. It is straightforward stuff too, yet at the same time, something that needs a couple of tips to liven up our enthusiasm about it.

There are specific points of interest in utilizing Google Drive for your examination work. It's free and accessible from wherever. Everybody with a Google account has it, as a matter of course, attached to your Google account.

Set Specific Share Permissions for Files inside Shared Folders

Google Drive is a community situation with share organizers and free. You can open up an envelope on Google Drive to explicit individuals in your group with email addresses as the screen capture underneath shows you.

For this, you need to imagine a scenario in which you are required to share each record of the typical organizer diversely with a various blend of individuals. It's simple. Offer the organizer by identifying your colleagues as you typically would. At that point, open every individual record and precisely expel the individuals you would prefer not to place in that specific File. This is a simple stunt to shroud specific documents even inside a standard envelope.

Reveal to How Many Files Are in a Folder

Windows makes it simple to perceive what number of sub-organizers and documents are there inside an envelope with a straightforward right-click and choosing Properties from the setting menu. Google Drive doesn't make it so natural. However, you can observe the number with a right-click.

1. Right-click an organizer and select download.
2. In the Download exchange box, click on All Items to uncover the all outnumber of records. Snap-on Cancel if you don't plan to download the files. The one preferred position of this alternate way over others is that it remembers the number of records for the sub-organizers.

It probably won't give you a simple method to tell the number of entire documents, yet Google Drive, in the best of Google Search, makes it easy to look through all your put away records. On the hunt, the box clicks the dropdown menu symbol to uncover the pursuit boundaries – Type, Visibility, and Ownership. Enter the search query and start your pursuit.

You can likewise utilize Google Search administrators to fine-tune your pursuit. An incredibly valuable hunt administrator is the date administrator that limits your inquiry, as indicated by the document date. It is a convenient, efficient device when you have several records bolted on the cloud.

Include File(s) to Multiple Folders

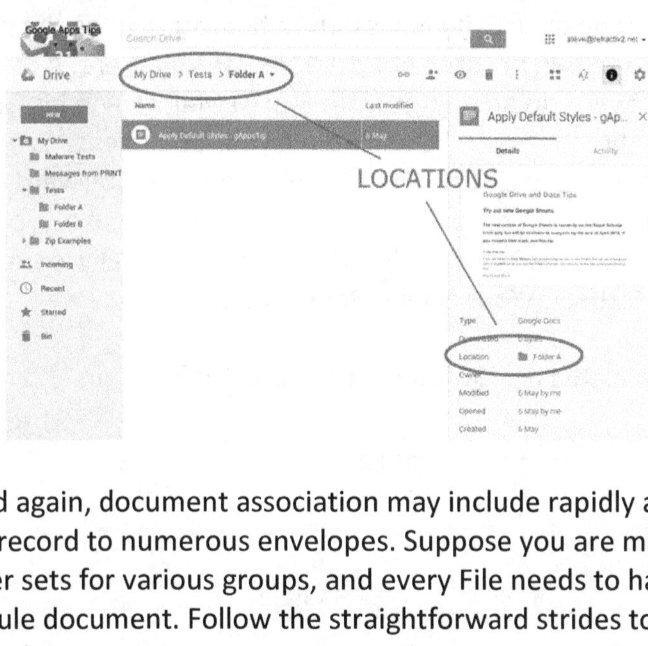

Now and again, document association may include rapidly adding a specific record to numerous envelopes. Suppose you are making organizer sets for various groups, and every File needs to have a typical rule document. Follow the straightforward strides to add different documents to numerous organizers.

1. On Google Drive, select the records you wish to add to many envelopes by tapping the checkbox for the documents.
2. Select the Move to fasten or on the other hand, you can tap on the dropdown for more and afterward click on Move to.

3. Select the different envelopes you need to move the scrapes to by holding down the 'Control' key for Windows or the 'Order' key for Mac.
4. Click on Move.

Any progressions made to the files in a single folder will be reflected in different documents in different organizers as google already doesn't make many copies of a file.

Expel Duplicate Files from Google Drive

Physically searching for copies by arranging the records indicated by name could be an activity in dissatisfaction concerning the chance that you have two or three hundred transferred there. A more straightforward tip originates from Marco Merman on his Google+ post. You should download and adjust your documents to your work area with the Google Drive application and afterward utilize a copy record discoverer on the Google Drive envelope on your nearby hard circle. The Google Drive organizer usually is situated at this way: C:\Users\Your Name\Google Drive

Erase Duplicate Files Quickly with These Tools

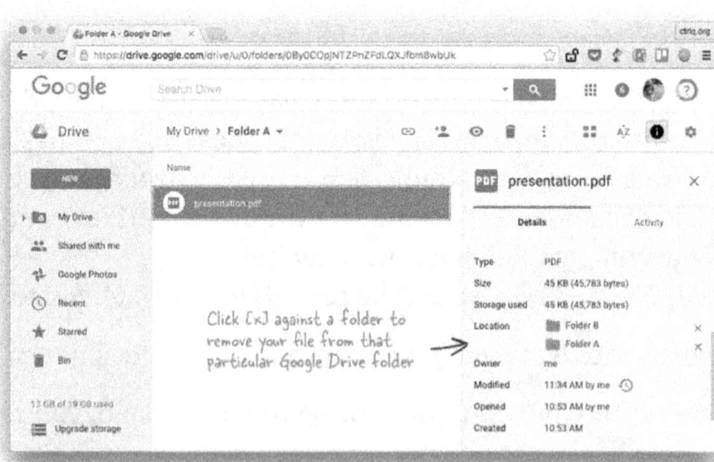

Perhaps the quickest approach to stop up your hard drive is to store copy records. Mostly it happens that likely you aren't mindful that you have copied documents available in the drive. They originate from an assortment.

Consequently, Delete File Versions and Save Storage Space

Google Drive keeps past variants of a document. This can include some significant downfalls of the complete extra room on the drive as it adds on the off chance that you have a great deal of them put away in the cloud. You can empower Google Drive to naturally erase past adaptations when they're more established than 30 days or in situations when there are more than 100 recent renditions of a similar document.

1. Select a record in Google Drive on the web.
2. Snap-on the more dropdown and select Manage corrections.
3. For record renditions, you need consequently erased, uncheck the Do not auto-delete setting. Old variants will be naturally eradicated, and Google Drive will just keep the most recent versions.

Make Your Google Drive Folder the Default Documents Folder

Clients moving can utilize this tip to make the Google Drive envelope on the work area their default report organizer. Using the Google Drive organizer as another Library area makes it simpler to spare archives with a tick instead of moving the records around indeed.

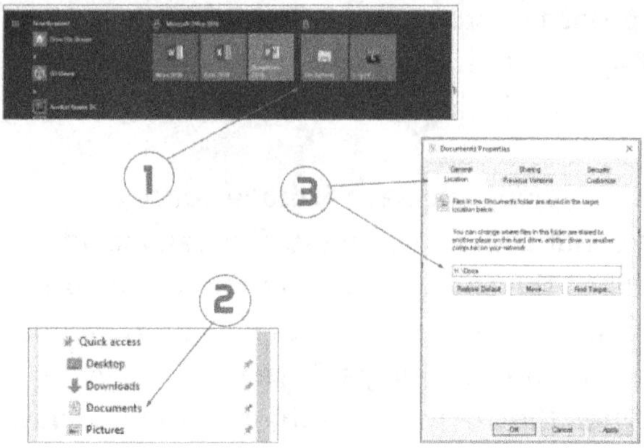

1. Right-click on the Documents envelope and select Properties.
2. Select include an organizer and find your Google Drive envelope. Select the Google Drive as in the screen capture underneath, and select the Set spare area. Snap-on Apply.
3. Presently, when you need to spare any record, you can pick from the areas in the Open/Save discourse box and pull on the off chance that you need to spare the archive in your Documents organizer or on Google Drive.

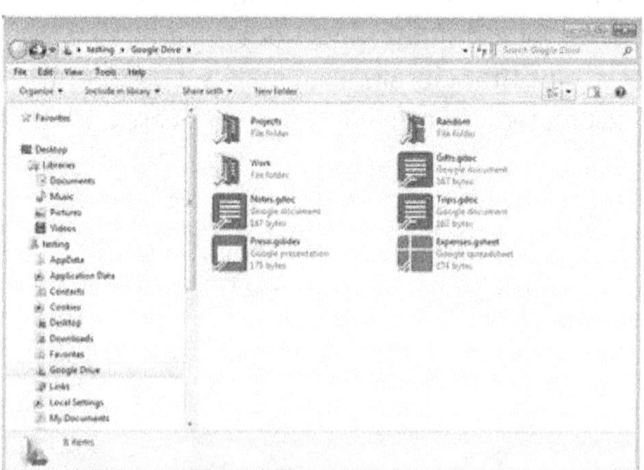

2.4 Sharing Files and Folders

The capacity to share reports and work cooperatively is the most crucial aspect concerning Google Drive! Here are hints for the way to begin.

This substance is obtained from Google's full assistance site on sharing and get started with shared drives

Offer a Solitary Thing with Explicit Individuals

Utilize this technique when you realize the email address (Hampshire or something else) of everybody you are sharing.

Open a document in Google Docs, Sheets, or Slides.

In the upper right corner, click share. Under "Individuals" in the "Offer with others" box, type the email address (Hampshire, or something else) of the individual or Google Group, you need to impart it.

Tip: Search for Hampshire contacts by composing a name in the crate. To pick an individual's view, remark, or alter the record, click the Down bolt close to the content box down bolt symbol.

Click Done. The individuals you imparted to will get an email telling them you've shared a record.

Offer a Solitary Thing utilizing a Connection

Utilize this strategy when you don't have the foggiest idea about everybody's email address, aren't sure on the off chance that they all have a Google account, or necessarily need a record to be all the more broadly accessible. You can have the connection available to the Hampshire people group or the entire world.

Open a record in Google Docs, Sheets, or Slides. In the upper right corner, click share.

Snap "Get shareable connection" in the upper right of the "Offer with others" box.

To pick whether an individual can view, remark, or alter the document, click the Down bolt close to "Anybody with the connection." Down bolt symbol.

Note that the connection will default to be perceptible by Hampshire College accounts as it were! To extend access outside of Hampshire, click the Down bolt close to "Anybody at Hampshire College" and select "More" for extra choices.
A record connection will be duplicated to your clipboard. Attach the link in an email or anyplace you need to share it.

Sharing a Folder

If you intend to work together with a gathering of individuals on a familiar premise, for example, inside a division or class, we recommend making a mutual organizer or a shared drive. At that point, each thing set in this envelope will consequently be imparted to the gathering.

Making a File

Go to drive.hampshire.edu
On the left, click New > Folder.

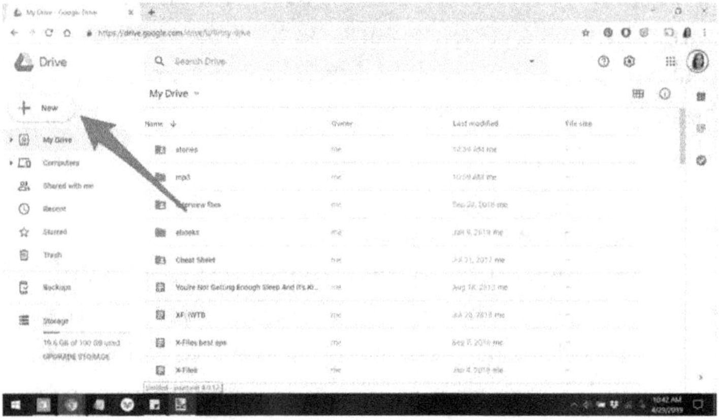

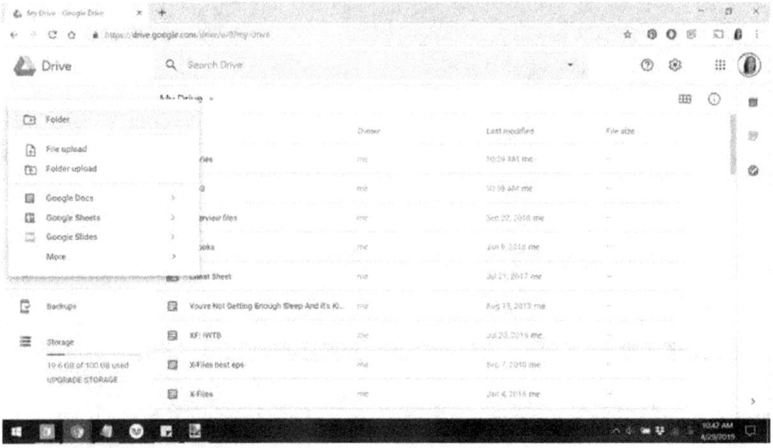

Enter a name for the File

Click Create.

At that point, share the File:

Select the name of the envelope on Google Drive. At the top, click share. Tip: You can likewise right-tap the organizer and pick share. Under "Individuals" in the "Offer with others" box, type the email address of the individual or Google Group with whom you need to share. Tip: Search for contacts by composing a name in the crate. Ensure their entrance level is set to "Can Edit."

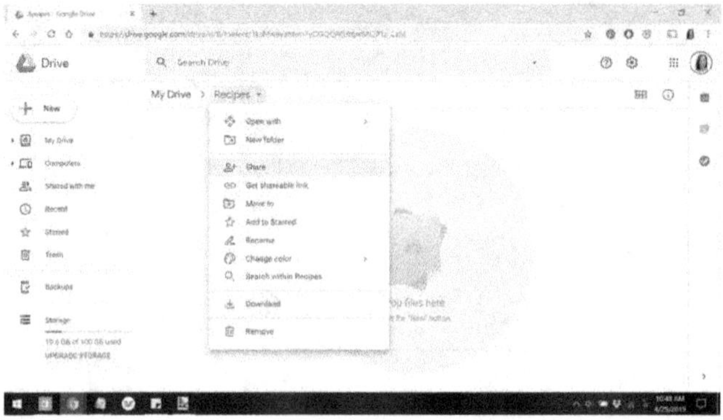

Mutual Drives

Mutual drives are shared spaces where groups can without much of a stretch, store, search, and access their documents in any place, from any gadget. In contrast to documents in My Drive, records in a shared drive have a place with the group, rather than a person. Regardless of whether individuals leave, the files stay precisely where they are, so your group can share data and complete work. Uncertain about whether to utilize My Drive or a mutual drive? Ask yourself these inquiries: Are the records relevant to most or all individuals from a specific task group? Do the records share a steady topic? If your answers are yes to the two inquiries, making another mutual drive is a smart thought. For this purpose, the records are explicitly used as an assortment tool for tasks, make numerous mutual drives. For a correlation of My Drive and shared drives, see Differences between My Drive and shared drives. What would you be able to do with shared drives?

Changing Responsibility for Document or File

You might need to dole out another person to be the "proprietor" of a record or envelope. The proprietor has full power over access, permeability and can decide to erase the document.

- **Instructions to Change Organizers**

You can change who possesses a document or organizer in the drive.

1. Go to Drive or Docs, Sheets, or Slides home screen.

2. Open the sharing box:
3. In Drive: Select the document or envelope and snap the offer symbol at the top offer symbol.
4. In a Docs, Sheets, or Slides home screen: Open the document and snap share in the upper right corner of the record
5. If the new proprietor, as of now, has altered get to, jump to Step 4. Something else, follow these means:
6. Type the original proprietor's email address in the "Welcome individuals" field, click Share, and spare.
7. Click Advanced in the base right corner of the sharing box.
8. Click the drop-down menu close to the name of the individual you need to possess the document or envelope.
9. Select is the proprietor.
10. Click Done.

Moving Proprietorship to or from a Non-Hampshire Google Account

A few of us may have Hampshire-related records "possessed" by an individual Google account. A best practice is to move these things to be claimed by your Hampshire account. While you can move proprietorship between Hampshire College accounts, you can't move possession to or from a non-Hampshire account! Lamentably, the first workaround is to download all the records from your history onto your PC, and afterward re-transfer them when signed into your Hampshire account.

2.5 Google Drive- Other Functionalities

In your routine, if you use Google Drive each day, you may utilize it for work, or you may compose blog entry in Google Docs, indeed. For me, I make use of it at home, in the case of using Sheets to delineate the late spring plan for my children, or adding to an ever-extending envelope of ideas. This makes it simple to impart top picks to companions or access required fixings on my telephone when I'm at the market. It's difficult to envision my computerized life before Google Drive.

I've utilized drive long enough and found a couple of concealed pearls end route that makes Google's cloud administration a surprisingly better device. Here are nine highlights that use Google cloud administration that may likewise support you.

You go to Google Drive's recent view to discover the archives; I'm taking a shot at this week or this month. Or on the other hand, I did before you began utilizing Google Photos to back up photographs on my iPhone. Presently, photographs obstruct my recent view, rendering it to a great extent pointless. You wish Google would give me a choice to bar photos from my current rundown of documents; however, you can utilize this workaround until it does.

In the hunt field, enter - jpg, and the entirety of your photographs will be sifted through, letting you peruse the records you've as of late made or altered. You can utilize this workaround in Google Drive on the web and the versatile application.

Turn on Quick Access

This new component includes a belt of thumbnails over the head of the My Drive to see that it gives you a well, speedy access to as of late altered records. (Furthermore, fortunately, it does exclude photographs as the recent view does.) You'll discover a line for Quick Access in Drive's settings. Simply click the crate for Make pertinent records convenient when you need them and afterward invigorate the page.

Channel your Searches

This present one's covering up on display. In the inquiry box at the head of Google Drive, there's a down-bolt button along the right edge. Snap it, and you'll get a board of search alternatives to channel your query items. Besides this, if you've utilized Google Drive for quite a long time and have aggregated an enormous library of records, at that point, these hunt alternatives are massively valuable to limit your outcomes. You can channel by record type, date changed, and proprietor. For shared reports, you can direct by somebody with whom you've shared a record. Thus you don't leave somebody hanging. You can likewise lead by documents that have a thing to do, doled out to you, or have recommendations sitting tight for you in a record.

Send Connections to Documents Rather than Connections

There's a little Drive symbol at the base of Gmail's create a window. It lets you join records you have put away in drive or necessarily send a connection. For Google Drive designs - Docs, Sheets, Slides, etc. - your only alternative is to send a connect to the record. For other document types - PDFs, Word docs, pictures - you can send them as a connection or a Drive interface, which lets you share records bigger than Gmail's 25MB size cut-off for relationships.

Rapidly Clear Organizing

You have a couple of alternatives for clearing the designing for the text you glue into Docs. You can feature the content and select Normal content from the toolbar at the top. Or then again, you can go to Format > Clear arranging. (For the last mentioned, you can utilize the alternate console route Ctrl-\ or Command-\ for Mac.) You can evade the arrangement evacuation process by holding down Shift when you glue text. That's right, Ctrl-Shift-V fixes with no arranging.

One-Tap Telephone Reinforcement

Need to back up your telephone's vital information to Drive? You can! Also, with a solitary tap. On the portable application, go to Settings > Backup and pick what you need to back up - contacts, schedule occasions or photographs, and recordings (or every one of the three). Simply tap the Start Backup catch to get this show on the road. It'll likely take some time, so you should begin the procedure short-term. Your telephone should be connected and associated with Wi-Fi.

Backup envelopes on PC or Mac

With Google's Backup and Sync application, you can back up the substance of your Mac or PC - or chose folders. As an addition to this, you can go the other way and sync the records you have put away on Google Drive to your PC for simple, disconnected access. Look at how, to begin with, Google's Backup and Sync application for guidelines on the best way to fire back up and match up your records.

Remark Legitimately on Microsoft Office Records

Not long ago, Google included the capacity to remark on Microsoft Office records, sparing you from expecting to change over a Word document, for instance, to a Google Doc to comment or utilizing a Chrome augmentation. You can now open a Word document, Excel record, PowerPoint introduction, and so forth and add your remarks legitimately to the document. Your comments will show whether your teammates opened the File in Google Drive or the pertinent Microsoft application. To include your comment, click the include remark button - it would seem that a square discourse bubble with an "or" sign inside it. For what reason wouldn't we all get along too and Google and Microsoft with regards to remarking on records?

Set up Disconnected Access

Need to work during your drive or on different occasions when you are not associated with the web? Forget about it. Google Drive lets you get to your records when you are disconnected, and afterward, it'll synchronize your progressions when you get back on the web, yet you should complete two things first to set up disconnected access:

Introduce the Google Docs Offline Expansion

Sign in to Google Drive, click the gear-tooth catch to open Settings, and afterward check the crate in the Offline segment for Sync Google Docs, Sheets, Slides, and Drawings records to this PC can alter disconnected.

Chapter 3: Google Docs - For Creating and Sharing Text Documents

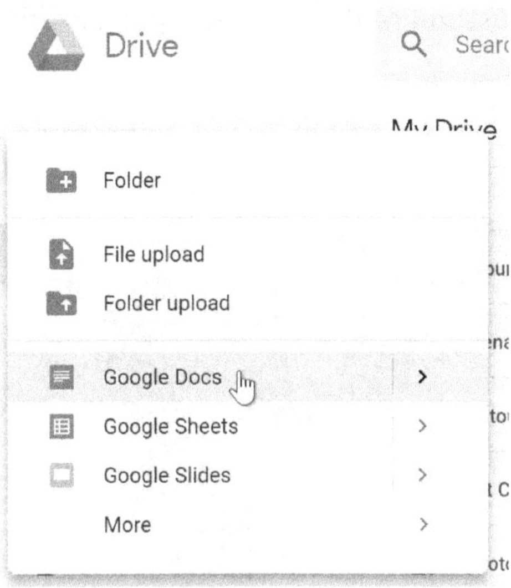

The entire Google Apps appears to turn gold. No longer handiest has the brand helped online groups generate billions of greenbacks via its search engine, but it is also — and maintains — department out and create other merchandise. One of the products is google docs, a loose word-processor and opportunity to Microsoft office that allows all the apps to create and edit their shareable file. The device is so multi-faceted and multi-functional. I wrote this guide to educate you approximately how to use google docs to create great content and collaborate with your group. We'll also see faucet into a few hints and hints to make this manner even simpler—no software program downloads. No bills. No particular browser or laptop important. Is there genuinely any product obtainable these days that is this simple to acquire and use? The answer is sure. Google docs is a very loose, go-platform (syncs files throughout telephones, drugs, and computer systems) phrase processor that works both online and offline. All you need to have a google account, the same email account which you use in your G Suite or Gmail. The cloud-based device consists of a horizontal format and unique features for users, including the capability to paintings, share, and collaborate from everywhere. The platform even mechanically syncs and saves all your work so that you don't also fear pressing shop. With these features, it is clear why thousands and thousands of customers decide upon google docs over other Microsoft Word.

Google Docs vs. Microsoft Office

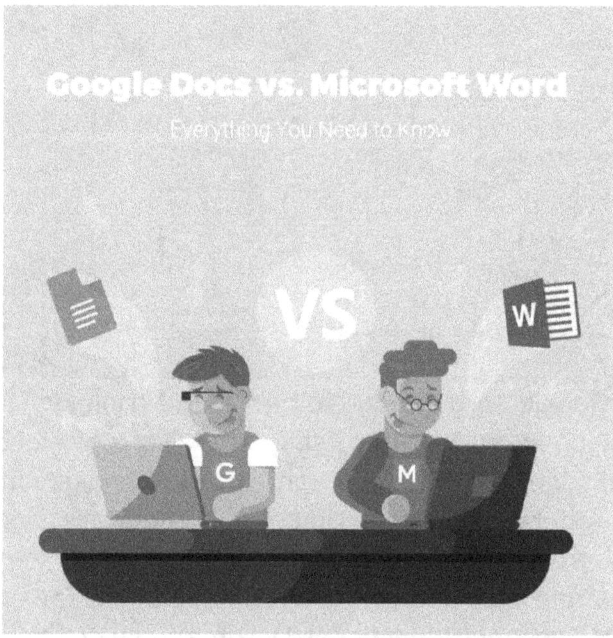

Microsoft office has been around longer than google docs and remains rather popular today. Thousands and thousands of man or woman customers and organizations nonetheless pay significant cash to use words. So, how do google docs and Microsoft Word compare? For one, google docs are unfastened with a google account. Microsoft office should be purchased as a part of a Microsoft workplace package deal, which includes other Microsoft merchandise such as PowerPoint, Excel, and outlook.

The house and commercial enterprise packages run from $69. 99 (for a person at home) up to one hundred and fifty dollars (for a person consumer at work) for an annual membership. On the other hand, Google docs let you collaborate with any wide variety of humans, everywhere within the globe, free of charge. Some other differentiating thing is that, with google docs, you can save all of your paintings to the cloud. That means you may not lose your 20-page document even if your pc croaks. (Whew!) With Microsoft Office, your records stay to your computer; your coworkers can not check them out unless you shop and share them through email. Whether you pick google docs or Microsoft word, it's not hard to sync the

Another way is that you may create a brand new google doc by way of genuinely uploading an existing word file.

Right here's how;

Open your google drive and click on new. Changing Microsoft word file to google docs google force new

Faucet report upload to access the data stored in your pc. Converting Microsoft Office document to google docs google force file add

To pick your word file and then click open. This can upload your text for your google drive. As soon as uploaded, double-click on it to open. As soon as free, click on google docs from the drop-down menu on the top. Changing Microsoft office file to google docs; open new documents in google docs

Voila! It is how you convert a word document to a google doc's record. Now, it allows digging a chunk deeper on how to use google docs.

3.1 Signing Up for an Account

To use google drive, you'll want a google account. Google accounts are easy to create and sign up for one in all fairness simple. For you to create a google account, you will need to go into a few records, including your call, delivery date, and place. Developing a Google account will robotically create a Gmail email cope with and google+ profile. When you have a Gmail address, you already have a Google account, so that you won't need to create an account—you can sign up to force the usage of your Gmail information.

To Create a Google Account

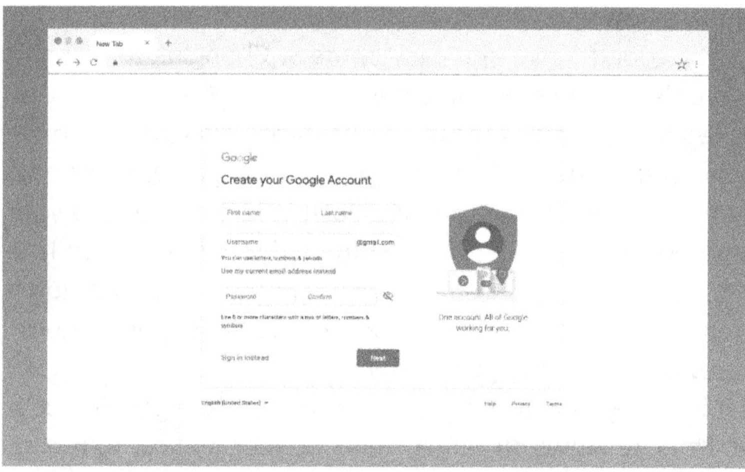

Go to www.google.com. Find and select the check-in button within the top-right nook of the web page. Sign up button. Click on create an account. Create an account link. The sign-up shape will appear. Comply with the directions and enter the desired statistics. Join up form. Next, input your cell phone range. Google will ship a verification code for your telephone that you may use to complete the sign-up method. Enter telephone quantity. Input the verification code sent for your cell phone and click on verify. Affirm smartphone quantity with the system. This is your statistics web page. Observe the instructions and enter your statistics, which includes your delivery date and gender. Input non-public statistics. Overview

Google's terms of provider and privacy policy, then click on, I agree. Clicking, I agree with phrases of service. Your account could be created. Just like with any online carrier, it's essential to pick out a strong password—in different expressions. One that is tough for a person to wager. For more critical information, check out our password guidelines lesson. Gaining access to google power

Once you've installed your google account, you can get admission to google power by going to http://drive.google.com on your internet browser. You may also navigate to google drive from any google web page (which includes Gmail or google search) by using selecting the grid icon near the pinnacle-proper corner, then clicking force.

The Google Drive Interfaces

Your google drive can be empty right now, but as you start uploading and creating files, you will want to realize how to view, manipulate, and organize them in the interface. Click on the buttons in the interactive underneath to become acquainted with the google force interface.

Google power cellular interface

Google additionally has separate mobile apps for creating and enhancing files, spreadsheets, and shows. To study higher, test out Google's blog, publish on new cell apps for doctors, sheets, and slides.

Google power for a computing device

In case you prefer to paintings at the computing device, you can download the google force laptop app on your PC. To be challenging for windows and so x, this app makes it a bit simpler to upload your present documents and paintings offline. Once it is established, you will see a new google power folder for your PC. You can routinely upload any materials you move into this folder for your google power.

3.2 Create or Import Files

Google Power gives you access to a set of devices that allow you to create and edit a wide range of files, including documents, spreadsheets, and displays. There are five styles of documents you may make on google power:

- **Documents**

Composing letters, flyers, essays, and different text-based files (just like Microsoft Word files)

- **Spreadsheets**

For storing and organizing data (similar to Microsoft Excel workbooks)

- **Displays**

For growing slideshows (just like Microsoft PowerPoint shows)

- **Bureaucracy**

For gathering and organizing information drawings: for creating easy vector pictures or diagrams,

The technique for creating new documents is the same for all document kinds. Watch the video underneath to analyze more.

To create a new document:

Google power, discover and pick out the new button, and then pick the form of the file you want to create. In our instance, we'll choose google docs to create a new record. By selecting google docs from the menu, your original file will appear in a brand new tab in your browser. Find and select the untitled report within the top-left corner.

Choosing untitled report

The rename conversation container will display; link a name to your record, then click ok. Typing a new call. Your file will be renamed. You may access the file from your google drive at any time, in which it will likely be saved automatically. Sincerely double-click to open the report again. Displaying document after renaming,

You could word that there's no keep button for your files. This is due to the fact google power makes use of autosave, which automatically and without delay saves your files as you edit them. All modifications, stored.

Developing and Writing in Google Docs

Google docs will assist you and your crew in creating essential files, no matter your vicinity? Here are a few options to be able to try.

- Voice Typing
- Google Docs App
- Discover
- Work Offline

An advantage to the use of google docs is that you're capable of the edit, save, and create documents through your net browser even while you're now not connected to the internet. This might are available handy in case you want to get some work carried out even as traveling. The modifications you make are nonetheless stored and will sync while you move returned online. However, this isn't an automatic characteristic. You'll want to set-up offline connections on your account. To do this, go to the google doc's homepage and discover the menu button on the left-hand facet—Google docs menu, then press settings.

Google Docs Menu Settings

1. A pop-up field will then be seen on your display screen. To set up offline enhancing, toggle the offline button to on. (This needs to turn the button blue, instead of grey.)
2. google docs offline toggle
3. Your browser will then alter to offline modifying, and you'll see the next icon when modifying your report without the internet. Google docs paintings offline icon
4. voice typing
5. Voice generation is a developing industry, and Google has been at the forefront of this trend. You can speed up the

writing cycle by using voice typing in google docs. To apply the feature, start via checking your device settings to confirm that your microphone works. Then head to tools > voice typing. You'll see a microphone icon. Google docs voice typing,

6. Click it and start speaking. Google will convert your spoken words into textual content that you'll see seem at the page.

Google Docs App

With the google doc's app, users can hold to edit, share, collaborate in real-time, upload snapshots, and create content while on-the-cross. Even free app works offline once you've grown to become in that setting — the identical manner you did in your computer— and it robotically saves your work to the cloud. Explore

If you have ever been writing approximately a subject and stopped to assume, "wow, I could use an offer or on the way to enhance my piece," Google docs have you covered. The explore characteristic — discovered through clicking gear > explore — google docs will scan the content you provide and recommend records that you could upload for your piece. Google docs discover function

Those recommendations would possibly include details you might have forgotten, pictures to beautify your work, or possible studies that you can consist of two returned your points and claims.

The use of templates

A template is a pre-designed record you can use to create new files quickly. Templates regularly include custom formatting and designs, so we can save you a lot of effort and time while starting a new undertaking. Most templates are designed to help you create unique types of files. For example, you may use a template to speedy create a resume or newsletter.

File template instance.

You could discover a wide selection of templates inside the google force template gallery. Alas, we have observed that many of these templates are not very well designed, and it is often hard to find specific templates within the gallery. Because of this, we propose the usage of templates made through google, which tend to be of a higher grade than consumer-submitted templates.

- **To Apply a Google Template**

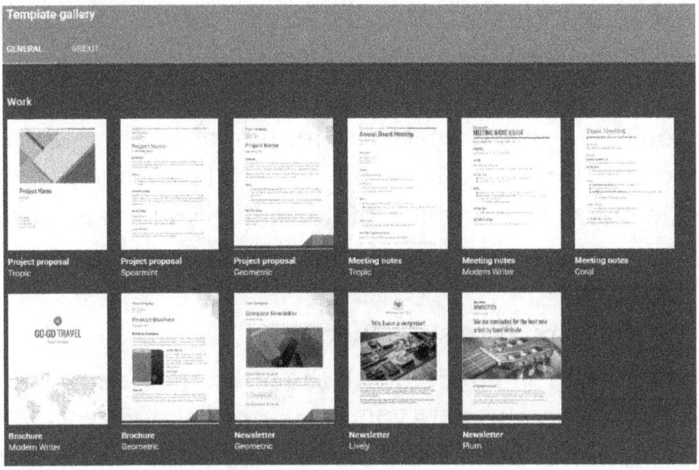

Navigate to the template gallery. Google template gallery, while you've discovered a template you want to use, click on the template to pick it. Decide on a resume template within the template gallery; a new record will be created with the selected template. You can then customize the report with your personal information.

3.3 Edit and Format a Document

Google docs empower you to create a report that works for you and the content material you're developing. Whether or not it's the web page orientation, pix, or web page numbers, those recommendations will help you layout your file any manner you need.

- ✓ Changing Page Margins
- ✓ Converting Page Orientation
- ✓ Adding a Textual Content Container

✓ Adding Page Numbers

✓ Growing a Placing Indent

✓ Putting a Picture

✓ Growing a Table of Contents

✓ Converting Web Page Margins

In case you're seeking to make the maximum of the clean area for your report or format your report for printing, you may need to change the margins. In advance of doing this, you will want to make sure the ruler is seen above your document. Surely head to view > display ruler.

- **Google Docs; Displays a Ruler**

You need to see a ruler underneath the formatting bar to your document. Then, to alternate your page's margins, discover the small blue button at the left-hand facet of the ruler and slide the button to modify your left margin. Google docs change margins, left margin

to trade your proper margin in google docs, repeat this procedure using the blue button on the right facet of your ruler.

- **Google Docs; Change Margin; Proper Margin**

If you want strict margins for your document, click record > web page set-up. Google docs web page set-up, you'll then see the following pop-up field where you may alternate the margins.

- **Google Docs; Web Page Margins Settings**

In case you need the same margins in each file you create, shop time, and hit set as default. This may mechanically replica your margin set-up to all new files. Changing web page orientation to panorama

Seeking to exchange the orientation of your record? Head to file > web page set-up, Google docs web page set-up menu, then select landscape under orientation. Google docs page set-up orientation If you want all of your files to have the identical orientation, press set as default.

- **Including a Textual Content Container**

Textual content bins are a fantastic choice if you're seeking to add a visible element in your document. They help you function additional text everywhere on your web page without changing the format of your current report. In google docs, textual content containers are categorized as drawings. You can insert one by clicking insert > drawing.

- **Insert Drawing in Google Docs**

This can open the drawing characteristic. Subsequent, press the textual content box. Drag the cursor into the drawing space to create a container that suits your requirements

- **Google docs; Drawing New Textual Content Field**

Once you create your field, it's time to go into text. This can change the font, color, and alignment of the textual content to your field by utilizing the navigation bar in the pop-up window.

- **Google Docs; New Text Container Drawing**

Glad about your textual content box? Hit save & close to insert it into the document. Google docs insert drawing textual content containers. This is a textual content field

From here, treat your text container as an image. Select the picture to alternate the alignment or flow the box around your document for ideal placement.

- **Adding Web Page Numbers**

And web page numbers make your document smooth to navigate and permit for the higher company while published — you'll avoid asking yourself, "Does this page cross here, or there?"

Upload web page numbers in your document by clicking insert > header > web page wide variety. Then choose the choice of your desire.

- **Google Docs; Adding Page Numbers**

Growing a putting indent striking indents are indents that mechanically trade the margin of a paragraph without interrupting the layout used elsewhere in your web page. To add a putting indent in google docs, make sure your ruler is seen through an urgent view > show ruler.

- **Google Docs; Display a Ruler Menu**

Then, head back to your essential record and spotlight the text you need to format. Upload a striking indent via locating the ruler above your document and sliding the blue arrows in the specification. Slide the button to the left to regulate the left indent, and the arrow on the proper aspect to alternate the appropriate indent.

- **Google Docs; Exchange Indent Putting a Photo**

To add a photo in your file, you can place your cursor anywhere you need to insert the image. Scroll up to the pinnacle of the web page and click insert > picture.

- **Google Docs; Insert Photo Menu**

Pick the picture region — multiple options consist of your laptop, the web, google power, or through URL. Select your photo, click open, and voila! Your picture should appear. For extra in this technique, take a look at this web page.

- **Developing a Table of Contents**

If you're writing a presentation or whitepaper, a desk of contents is a terrific manner to display every phase you're developing and the page range that it can be located on. You may insert a desk of contents on your google document through ensuring all subheadings are formatted with a heading tag. To do this, spotlight your subheading and press the proper tag on your formatting bar.

- **Google Docs; Heading Tags**

As a standard rule of thumb, the heading one tag should be your first name. Heading two tags need to be subheadings, and heading three tags must be sections beneath a subheading. Now you're equipped to create a desk of contents. Preserve your cursor where you'd like to insert it and click the insert > desk of contents to pick a choice based on your selection.

- **Google Docs; Inserting a Table of Contents**

Google docs offer a ramification of enhancing features to ensure your work reaches complete potential.

- ✓ Monitoring Changes
- ✓ Adding Feedback

- ✓ Finding Word Rely-On
- ✓ Walking Spell Take a Look at
- ✓ Strikethrough
- ✓ Tracking Changes

In case you're working with another individual for your report, you can ask them to track their modifications and edits. This will display you who made the edits, after they made the one's edits, and what the text turned into before their edits. You could make song adjustments in google docs by changing enhancing to suggesting in the top right-hand corner of the web page. Google docs tracking modifications suggest that when someone edits your document, any changes will show up in an exceptional shade, with a box at the right-hand aspect to expose their call, photograph, and modifying information. Google docs tracking changes instance; you may then browse the tracked adjustments and accept or reject them as necessary.

- **Adding Feedback**

With google docs, you and your crew can depart remarks in any record for every different to view. These are often used as reminders to return to a specific section, go away greater detailed revision thoughts, or upload URLs to other sites and photos for reference. To do so, highlight the word, sentence, or paragraph you need to touch upon and click the upload comment button (the text container with the plus sign internal). You may then write a remark — or paste a URL — in the comment box. Click remark while you are geared up to publish your box. Google docs go away with the new remark

To edit the facts in the container, click on three dots on the right, and choose edit. You can additionally thread remarks under the unique comment via typing in the reply box.

- **Google's Docs; New Comment Responds**

To eliminating a remark box, you may either delete it or solve it. Click the three dots at the right and choose to delete the box. Click on resolve within the pinnacle proper of the box while the problem has been resolved, you do not need the remark.

- **Google Docs; Remark Clear-up**

If you are seeking out more in-intensity data on including and resolving feedback in google docs, take a look at this web page.

Locating phrase count

Have you ever struggled at the same time as writing a paper, report, or blog submit due to a required phrase count number that you have been seeking to reach? Even though achieving a count of phrase needed number might not always be smooth, google docs make them depend on itself simple. When you're in your report, click on gear > phrase rely on. (You could also use the shortcut ⌘ + shift + c.)

- **Google Docs; Word Count Number Menu**

Google will then show the full variety of words (along with the overall quantity of pages, characters, and characters aside from areas). **Google docs phrase remember**

To count the phrases within a particular sentence, paragraph, or page, highlight the text you need to consist of and follow the same steps above. Going for walks spell test is no longer uncommon for expert writers to make an occasional spelling mistake. Google docs can assist all writers with this predicament. Run a spelling test to locate and accurate any errors you may have neglected. Think about it as your proofreader or editor. To run a spellcheck in google docs, click on gear > spelling > spell check.

- **Google Docs Spelling Check**

Google docs will then test your complete file for misspelled phrases and grammatical errors. You'll be given an option to accept or ignore Google's concept simply. In case you find which you're often with the use of a phrase that Google doesn't understand, you could upload it to your dictionary. This may prevent google docs from highlighting the phrase in future spell assessments.

- **Strikethrough**

In google docs, you can upload a strikethrough in highlighting the text you need to strike and clicking layout > strikethrough.

3.4 Share and Collaborate On Files

You can share the files and folders you saved in google power with every person. While you share from google power, you can manage whether or not human beings can edit, comment on, or simplest view the record. While you share content material from google drive, the google power program policies practice on Laptop, Android, iPhone & iPad

Step – 1

- Locate the file you need to share
- Open an unarranged file
- On a PC, go to google docs, sheets, or slides. Click on the document you need to share. Click share. Share multiple documents
- Send & share google paperwork

Step – 2

- Pick out who to share with & how they can use your document
- Share with precise people
- Pick the report you need to share
- Click share

Below "share with human beings and corporations," enter the email address you need to share with. Vital: If you share with an email deal with that isn't a Google account, they could use the simplest view of the report. To alternate what human beings can do for your document, at the right, click the down arrow down and then viewer, commenter, or editor. Pick out to inform human beings. If you want to notify humans that you shared a document with them, take a look at the field next to educate people. In case you notify humans, every electronic mail address you input might be covered in the email. If you don't want to notify human beings, uncheck the container. Click on the share or send it.

Adding a Hyperlink to the File

Adding a file publicly or collaborating in google docs, there are many guidelines and tricks that customers can take advantage of at the same time as using google docs — whether working as a person or with a crew. Google docs allow a couple of people to collaborate and edit inside an available record in real-time through any web browser.

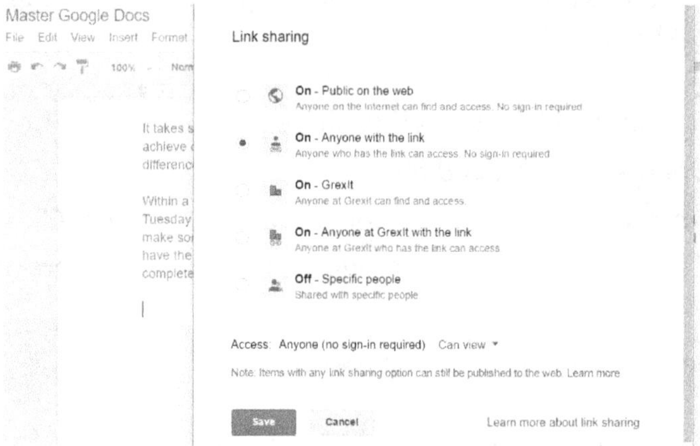

Sharing your Google Document

People can share their documents with as many people as they need and edit their permissions to limit what they can do. To get began sharing, click report > share.

Sharing your Google Docs Records

There are four sharing options — the one you choose is entirely your desire.

- ✓ Create a Shareable Hyperlink. The only manner of sharing a google doc's page is to generate a shareable link. This lets you in all and sundry to click on a unique URL and view your file. After clicking share, tap the get shareable hyperlink button within the top proper nook. Google docs get a shareable link to choose sharing permission in your record. Google docs are placing approval for documents after defining permissions, press the reproduction link.

- ✓ Google docs sharing copy link the URL will then be copied to your clipboard, which will send everyone who needs to view the file.

- ✓ Share through electronic mail addresses. You also have the option to share your file with an email address. This will ship an invitation to that individual's inbox and upload the document to their google account. To do this, head again to the sharing field. Input the email address of the character you'd want to share your record with and pick out an alternative from the drop-down to edit their permissions.

- ✓ Google docs sharing through email in case you add a word to this invite, it will likely be displayed within the email invitation. Choose the advanced sharing alternatives. Head back on your sharing box and hit advanced. You may see all sharing settings — along with who has to get entry to in your record, their permission settings, and the option to ask extra people or put off others. Google docs are sharing preferred settings. Make your document editable for everybody. Need to supply anyone permission to edit the contents of your file?

  Hit document > share to get your shareable link. Google docs get shareable hyperlinks inside the drop-down menu displayed, click greater Google docs share with others extra, after that, pick on — everybody with the link, and set the permissions inside the bottom drop-down menu.

- ✓ Google Docs link sharing as this selection virtually states; all of us, together with your precise URL, could make adjustments, edit, and even delete your document. Be careful about who you're sharing it with. Share & collaborate on a record with more than

100 people as much as a hundred people with a view, editing, or comment permissions can paintings on google docs, sheets, or slides report at identical times. While more than a hundred human beings are accessing a file, most effective the owner and a few users with modifying permissions can edit the report.

- ✓ To share and collaborate on a file with more than a hundred humans: submit the report in case you want many people to view a file without delay, put it up, and create a hyperlink to share with viewers. You can deliver edit get admission to people who want to edit or touch upon the file. Learn how to post a record. Publishing a report makes it seen to every person on the web. Be careful when publishing personal or touchy info. When you have an account via paintings or college, your administrator can restrict who can view a published report. If you're an administrator, discover ways to manipulate who can post documents to the net. To remove a document from the net, you have to stop publishing it. Learn how to forestall publishing a record. To stop sharing a file with the collaborators, learn how to trade sharing permissions.

- ✓ Create a google website online. Create a google site to share data with many people. You could embed files, spreadsheets, and presentations on the web page, which may be regarded with many customers' aid. Discover ways to embed documents on a domain. In case you expect excessive site visitors on your website online, first post your record in google docs, sheets, or slides, then embed the published URL into google sites. Discover ways to post a file.

- ✓ Collect feedback with google bureaucracy in case you want to acquire some information. Create a google form—record feedback in a google sheet. Give edit access only to individuals who need to work with the responses. To allow more than a hundred human beings to view the responses, post the spreadsheet to the net, and create a link to share with visitors. Learn how to publish a file. Fix issues with documents shared with many people. If your record is shared with many people and it's crashing or not updating quickly, attempt these troubleshooting tips:

- ✓ Instead of allowing people to touch a record or spreadsheet, create a google form to accumulate remarks. Discover ways to create a google form. In case you're duplicating a report, don't consist of it with resolved comments and suggestions. Discover ways to make a copy. Delete older statistics or flow records into a brand new document. Ask visitors to close the report when they aren't making use of it. Consist of the simplest the maximum vital facts in a posted document. Shorter documents load faster. Reduce the number of humans with edit, get entry to a report. If accumulating statistics from a couple of documents, create a new, view-only record to share with a big wide variety of people.

3.5 Print and Download Documents

Once you've created a report, it will likely be accessible every time you check in to google drive. There might be times when you need to import or print a paper offline for entry.

To Download a Document

Find and right-click on the report you need to download, then pick download. You could download the file on your pc. To select a file layout:

Use the default; google drive will choose the most not unusual report layout each time you download a file. For example, if you're downloading a google document, it's going to be saved as a routine. Docs files that are utilized by Microsoft word have maximum different word processors. But, there may be examples when you need to choose a different PDF format. Double-click on the desired record to open it. The article will appear in the new window. Choose description> download as, then select the favored file type. In this example, we'll pick the pdf document (. Pdf). The file could be downloaded in your pc within the selected document kind.

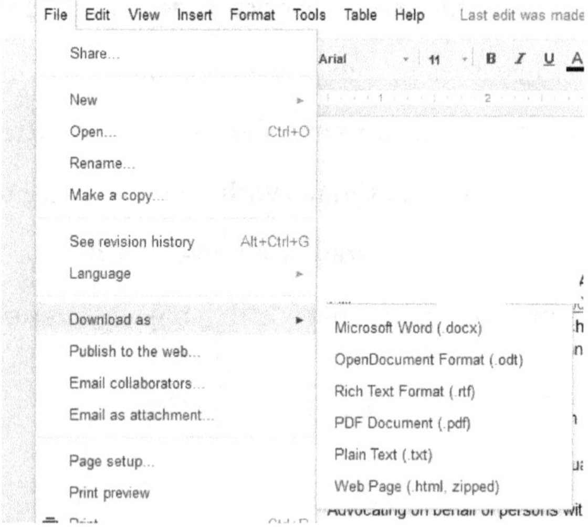

To Print a Record

Double-click the approved document to open it. Pick out document > print.

The print conversation container will seem, alongside a preview of your file at the right. Pick out the desired alternatives, then click print. Be aware that those options will vary relying on the type of report you're printing. For example, you'll have different options for writing a spreadsheet then you'll for writing a presentation.

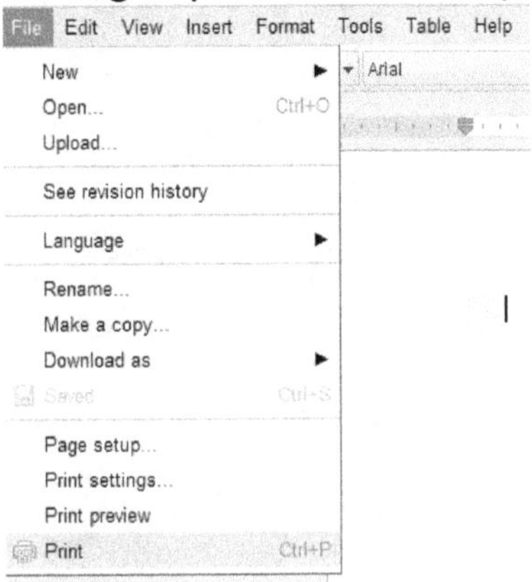

Chapter 4: Google Sheets - For Creating Online Spreadsheets

You could be surprised! Can google sheets be like Microsoft Excel? The answer is: no longer precisely. But before we talk about the functions and tools that can be unique to sheets, let's start by highlighting what you have to bear in mind with the usage of a spreadsheet. I'm a massive proponent that more humans have to be the use of spreadsheets to organize and manage their lives. While you want to be aware or begin organizing a challenge, in which you do it? Many people might open a new report in google docs or Microsoft office, for instance. The clean slate is an incredible manner to begin scribbling thoughts down. To me, a spreadsheet can try this as well, but with plenty of introduced features. In case you start monitoring something that includes numbers and needs to do simple math, a spreadsheet is continually going to be a better preference for running with statistics. You can use columns and rows to prepare content on the fly as nicely. Sheets were designed with the wishes of active groups in thought. AI capabilities suggest that you have to faucet into the proper insights for meaningful enterprise selections. A cloud-primarily based structure allows you to collaborate with anybody, each time, anywhere. Compatibility with outside structures, including the Microsoft office, gets rid of the friction of running with more than one data source. And constructed on top of Google's infrastructure, sheets give you the liberty to create, at the same time as assisting in keeping your facts comfy.

4.1 Introduction to Google Sheets

Even if you want to utilize spreadsheets, you are probably thinking, how do google sheets work? There's lots of official opposition in Microsoft's excel and apple's numbers apps. Both have additionally carried out versions of paintings within the net browser. Although sheets now have different browser-based opposition, I nevertheless suppose that it's the utmost desire for simple spreadsheets. It is lightweight and smooth to get started. Excel has every viable characteristic you could need in a spreadsheet but brings complexity with it. Apple numbers are easy to use; however, the manner that some capabilities paintings are counterintuitive, and it would not well support different spreadsheet codecs. Do not leave out the fact that sheets have a few specific features that set it aside from the other alternatives. Let's look at the functions that make sheets worth thinking about as your spreadsheet app of choice. With such a lot of options for spreadsheet apps, what are google sheets that you must flip to? In short, assume that google sheets shine because it's both loose and smooth-to-use. It best takes a google account to log in and start constructing a google doc's spreadsheet. It is difficult to compete with loose, and even though other apps have loose elements, sheets are unfastened to use. However, don't think of sheets as a shoestring-price range substitute for Microsoft excel. Sheets have several functions implemented to excel and also possess some functions that work better in the browser. Allows study five features of google sheets that make it well worth using.

1. Which easy enter shape integration have you ever needed to get feedback or enter from a vacationer on your internet site? Sheets gives an easy way to do that and prepare the responses. Whether you are taking lunch orders from your group at work or getting details from a new client, google makes it clean to take the entry from the shape. Google can also put it without delay into a google doc spreadsheet, rather than receiving these statistics thru email

or text and having to re-type it or reformat it. With an input form, you could install questions, selections, and text bins for site visitors to fill out. Immediately the user fills out their reply, that statistics will automatically be logged and captured into your google sheet for evaluation. To get commenced with this selection, leap into a google docs spreadsheet, and browse to insert > form to set up a brand new input form. You may then use the wizard to add inquiries to the shape, as you can see within the screenshot below. Google paperwork to sheets with google sheets; you can use an entry form to seize responses from a traveler or purchaser and insert that records seamlessly into the spreadsheet.

2. Connect spreadsheets. One of the motives that have seen people resistant to the usage of google sheets is because they think certain functions from excel are missing. In truth, the maximum of those capabilities are already applied in sheets— you simply ought to realize which to move in searching out for them. A traditional instance of this is the ability to grab statistics from different spreadsheets. The use of functions like =import range makes it possible to go and get statistics from absolutely separate workbooks. Ensure you read the academic below to stroll via the usage of a couple of spreadsheets in sync and pull data to and fro.
3. Examine even as you operate the product. While they are easy to get commenced with, it's the formulas and features that can sense to learn.
4. This brings some other one among the capabilities of google sheets:

The documentation lives right in the interior of the app.
As you begin typing a function call, you'll get a simple, practical drop-down choice that facilitates using the characteristic, as you can see beneath. Components instructions as you begin to type a feature; you'll see statistics that enable you to learn how to apply the characteristic. This consists of examples of the way to use every function. This "documentation on the fly" technique is one of the motives that suppose sheets is perfect for overcoming the spreadsheet studying curve.

5. Google sheets accessories.

   Google has taken a relatively open approach to develop sheets, welcoming accessories from different developers to decorate what sheets can do natively. Think about accessories in two essential categories:

   Pure accessories that upload greater functions and capability to google sheets connectivity tools like zapier and ifttt that help you hyperlink up sheets to almost some other provider. An instance of a pure upload-on is apps to remetrix, which is an add-on that you could use to tune your app's performance in first app shops like google play or apple's app shop. Instead of going into those dashboards and copying pasting facts to a google sheets spreadsheet, use the apps to remetrix to attach the two. However, you've got services like zapier and ifttt. These are offerings that exist for one purpose: to connect things collectively! For example, twitter and sheets do not include paintings collectively on their own, so you need an app that sits within the middle. You can use one of those offerings to take tweets and mechanically insert them right into a spreadsheet. Fortunately, we've got an education that lets you set that up. Check it out to analyze more about connecting google sheets to a ramification of offerings.

5. The exceptional help for collaboration extra than ever, the tasks and paintings that we tackle requires collaboration with others. As we rely on other greater paintings, we want methods to carry them into our files and work seamlessly together. This is like any other characteristic different apps have attempted; however, google sheets lead the way. Without a doubt placed, it has the first implementation for inviting others to work with you on a google sheets spreadsheet. It's the easiest way to ask other users to paintings on (or just view) a spreadsheet you've been running. With sheets, you may create public URL's to permit every person to view a spreadsheet or invite precise collaborators. Launch into the sharing menu at any time by clicking on the share button within the top-right nook.

4.2 Creating a Spreadsheet

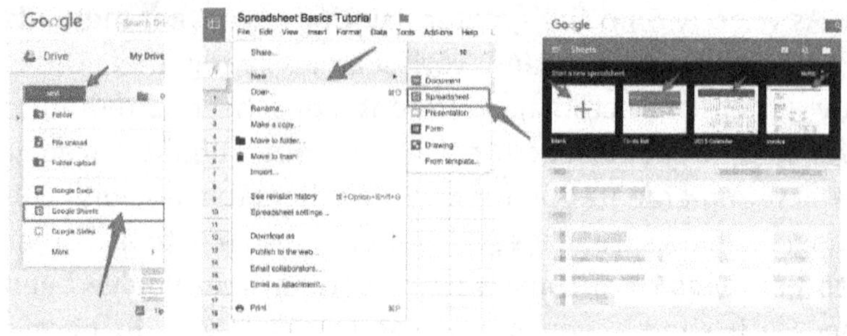

1 2 3

To kick matters off, let's cowl some spreadsheet terminology that will help you understand this the terms in this e-book:

- ✓ Cell: A single statistics point or element in a spreadsheet.
- ✓ Column: A vertical set of batteries.
- ✓ Row: A horizontal set of batteries.
- ✓ Range: A spread of cells extending throughout a row, column, or each.
- ✓ Function: An integrated operation from the spreadsheet app, which may be used to calculate mobile, row, column, or variable values, manipulate records, and extra.
- ✓ Formula: The combination of capabilities, cells, rows, columns, and ranges used to attain a particular result.
- ✓ worksheet (sheet): The named units of rows and columns making up your spreadsheet; one spreadsheet may have a couple of coats
- ✓ spreadsheet: The entire report containing your worksheets

In case you've in no way used google sheets—or, in particular, in case you've by no means used a spreadsheet earlier than—make sure to check out Google's getting commenced manually for sheets. You may also wish to bookmark Google's spreadsheet feature listing as a short reference. With that understanding in hand, allows dive in and begin constructing our spreadsheets. Create a spreadsheet and fill it with statistics.

The first-rate element about google sheets is that it is unfastened and works on any device—which makes it clean to follow alongside the tutorials on this e-book. All you'll want is an internet browser (or the google sheets app in your IOS or android tool) and an unfastened google account. To your mac or computer, head over to sheets. Google. You and Corer are equipped to get commenced.

There is three-course of action to create a new spreadsheet in google sheets:

1. Click the purple "new" button for your google power dashboard and pick out "google sheets."
2. Open the menu from inside a spreadsheet and pick "report > new spreadsheet."
3. Click "clean" or choose a template at the google sheets homepage

This will create a brand new blank spreadsheet (or a pre-populated template if you pick out one of these). For this tutorial, although you need to start with a clean spreadsheet, the google sheets interface must remind you of at least another spreadsheet app you've seen earlier than familiar textual content editing icons and tabs for additional sheets. The only distinction is that Google has reduced the muddle and quantity of displayed interface factors. So your first task has to be self-evident: add some facts!

Adding facts on your spreadsheet

Look around the white-and-grey grid that occupies a maximum of your display, and the first issue you'll observe is a blue define around the selected mobile or cells. As swiftly as you open a brand new spreadsheet, if you simply start typing, you'll see that your information starts populating the selected cell without delay. Generally, the top left cellular. There is no want to double click on cells while you add statistics, and no longer need plenty to apply your mouse. A character square in a spreadsheet is referred to as a cellular; they're organized into rows and columns with range and letter Ids. Each cellular needs to incorporate one price, word, or piece of statistics. Experience free to select any cellular you'd like, then cross beforehand and type something in there. While you've performed coming into statistics into a cellular, you can do one in every of four matters:

1. Press enter to keep the records and circulate to the start of the next row
2. Press the tab to keep the facts and flow to the right inside the same row
3. Use the arrow keys to your keyboard (up, down, left, and proper) to move one cell in that direction
4. Click any mobile to leap without delay to that cellular

If you don't want to kind in the whole thing manually; you may additionally upload statistics for your sheet and masse through a few different techniques:

1. Copy and paste a list of documents or numbers into your spreadsheet
2. Copy and paste an HTML writing table from a website
3. Import an existing worksheet in CSV, Xls, xlsx, and other codecs
4. Replica any cost in a cell across a variety of cells via a click on and drag

Copy & paste is quite self-explanatory, but there are instances. At the same time, you'll try to copy a "spreadsheet-y" set of statistics from a website or pdf, and it'll merely paste into one mobile or layout everything with the authentic styling. Attempt looking for statistics directly in an HTML table (like film information from IMDB, as an instance) keeps away from getting funky pasted statistics for your spreadsheet. Observe: ensure your handiest click on once on a cell before gluing information so that google sheets will flip it right into a list with every object in its cell. In case you double-click on a mobile, google sheets will paste all the information into one cellular that is likely not what you want now. If you grow to be with oddly formatted data, don't worry: we'll restore that inside the subsequent phase! Uploading a report is simple as nicely. You can either import immediately into the contemporary spreadsheet, create a brand new spreadsheet, or replace a sheet with the imported data. The maximum not unusual files you'll import are CSV (comma separated values) or xls and xlsx (files from Microsoft excel). To import a document from out of doors of your google drive, visit the file > import > upload menu. You favor importing the information into a brand new sheet every time to keep my vintage statistics and newly introduced records separate. Instead, when you have a google sheet (or a CSV, Xls, or different spreadsheet file) saved to your google power account, you may import that directly into your spreadsheet. To use the identical technique—seek your power from the import window. Dragging to duplicate a cell fee desires a piece of explanation. Due to the fact you'll use this one, load once you've installed formulation to your spreadsheets. Through dragging the small blue dot (pictured below) within the bottom-proper corner of a highlighted cell across or down a number cells, you may perform some of the one-of-a-kind functions. There are some of the ways you may use this selection:

1. Copying a cell's information to many neighboring cells (inclusive of formatting)
2. Copying a mobile's "formulation" to neighboring cells (this is a sophisticated function, and we'll cowl it in element later)

3. Growing an ordered list of textual content records

here's an example of how developing an ordered listing may work: try including the textual content contestant 1 to cellular a1, then clicking and dragging the little blue dot within the backside-proper corner of the highlighted mobile both down or throughout any range of neighbouring cells. If there was no wide variety after contestant, this dragging action could reproduction "contestant" to any cells you drag over. However, because the range is there, sheets know to increment the next cell +1. Let's suppose you have either copied, pasted, imported, or typed in a fantastic chew of facts and that your spreadsheet is calling pretty healthful. Now, how can we use this information?

4.3 Share, Protect, and Move Your Data

What makes sheets so compelling is how "in sync" you'll feel together with your co-workers. Collectively modifying a spreadsheet is one of the important functions of sheets, and google has made it a whole experience. Right here's how it works:

1. Click both report > share or use the blue "share" button inside the pinnacle proper
2. Click on "superior," then enter e-mails of who can view or edit your spreadsheet
3. Pick some other privacy options and hit achieved

When you open the "superior" sharing panel, you'll see some of the options. The default capability when you click on the "share" button is to copy a link to the spreadsheet to your clipboard. While you share this link with a person through a messenger or email, if they click on the hyperlink, it will bring them to the spreadsheet. Unless you've invited them via email (within the email field) and decided on "can edit," they will still need to appeal permission to make modifications. In case you'd like to offer each person within your organization or business enterprise editor-stage get entry to click on the "alternate..." button inside the "who has got right of entry to" segment and pick "on - (your employer call) **." (Note: this selection will only appear if you're using google apps for paintings.)

Sharing Spreadsheets with Your Devices and Apps

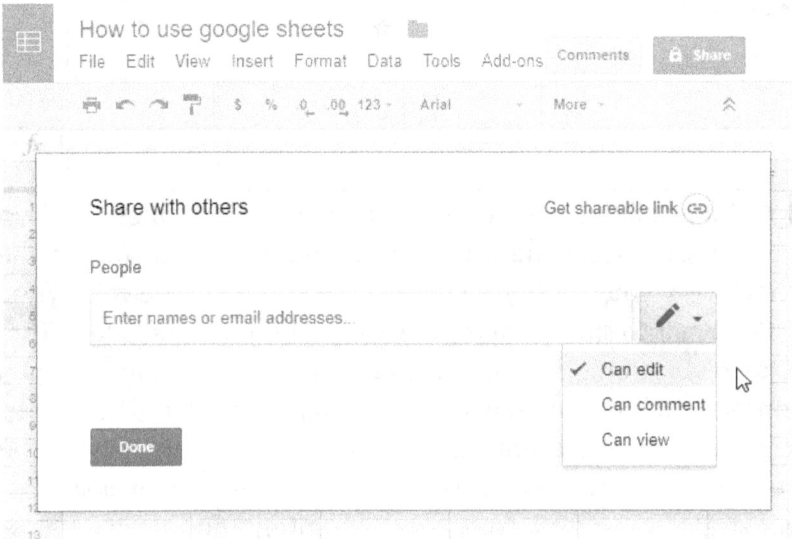

Even though google sheets and drive are built for sharing among users, you'll word that normally your spreadsheets are created as personal documents, and sharing is secondary to get work done truly. You could streamline your spreadsheet workflows and actual-time data-sharing by taking gain of these helpful add-ons:

- ✓ Google doc's cellular apps. You could use the google sheets cellular app to view and edit your spreadsheets, share hyperlinks at the move, and upload customers. It's a stable partner to—however now not a substitute for—the web app.

Google Drive Sync on your Desktop

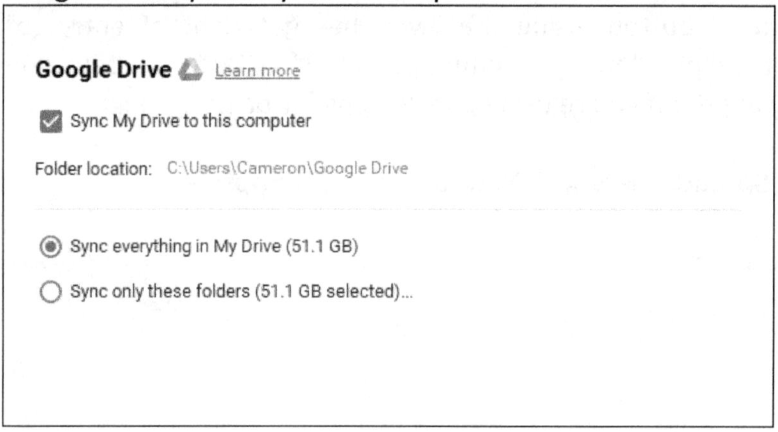

Google force allows you to without difficulty add files from your nearby laptop environment in your online force. This makes them reachable on your collaborators and additionally permits you to import them into spreadsheets and different documents fast. Three. A third-celebration device like zapier. You may use zapier to upload information on your spreadsheets mechanically, ship documents in your google drive account, and warn you of the other sheet you name. This helps to hold working on our spreadsheet instance to demonstrate the use of zapier. An app integration device helps to make google sheets even possess greater power. In preference to hitting the "share" button on my spreadsheet to send it to my colleagues, I'd want to send a slack message alerting them that I've created this new spreadsheet. You may routinely ship a message to a Slack channel with zapier's google sheets cause and slack action. Share new google sheets spreadsheets to slack. You could installation filters and conditions to decide while to submit, and you've got entire manage over what facts you'd like to encompass for your message.

You can additionally trigger messages based on exclusive moves in google sheets—like when someone a new row or modifications the statistics in a cell. Now let's switch the direction of the statistics-glide and consider how our colleagues would engage with our spreadsheet.

Without an automatic technology tool like Zapier, duties like this fast grow to be why people fail to collaborate with the use of spreadsheets correctly. Think about it; if this were a regular spreadsheet with none automation, you'd be asking someone to:

1. Escape in their current activity
2. Song down spreadsheet
3. Fill in some pieces of doubtlessly inconsequential statistics
4. Keep and re-share this record (if it's not already a web and synced file)
5. Repeat for any number of duties/files

That is wherein automating obligations becomes so critical. Allows set up our spreadsheet so that it has an easy sheet to receive some automated information. Create a new worksheet with the use of the + button in the backside left. Now, use zapier once more and make slack the triggering motion with google sheets at the receiving quit of the automation (the "action" facet of the zap). I've installed my zap to immediately take a slack message published right into a devoted channel and make a new row in the breakfast log alongside the time and person who posted it. Take a look at it out in actual-time:

This can be paintings for masses of other applications that you could use as triggers or moves with zapier. You could ship facts on your spreadsheet thru email, screen your social channels, set it on a schedule; there are dozens of various approaches to accomplish any given mission with the apps you're already using.

Downloading your Information

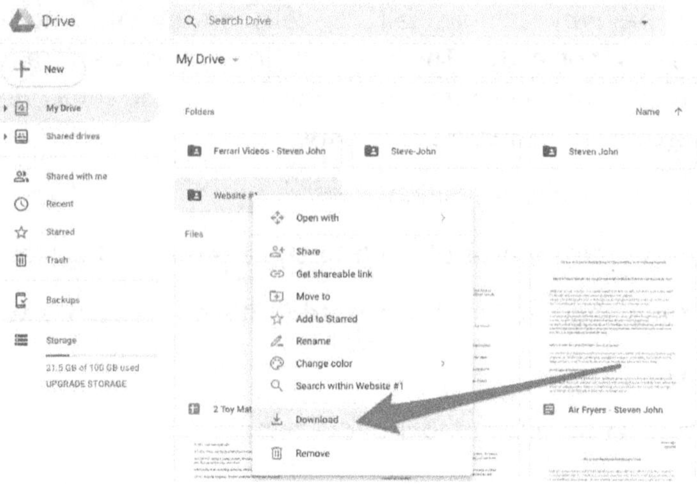

If you need to ship your documents to external collaborators, add a record into some other machine, or similar to having backups for posterity, then turn towards certainly one of google sheets' many information export options. The most common exports could be either. Xls (excel record) or. CSV (comma-separated values). If you're not certain which format to apply, a. CSV is commonly a satisfactory wager. Use your spreadsheet in offline mode. If you love what you've visible to this point but have been involved in which you wouldn't be able to make use of sheets without a link, then fear not. Google sheets have an "offline mode" to sync your adjustments to the report routinely when you reconnect to the net. That is beneficial for any state of affairs in which you'll want to deal with google sheets like a computing device software—on a flight or an avenue journey, as an example. Right here's what you'll want:

1. Google Chrome
2. Google Drive Chrome Web App
3. Google Power Sync

Commands for putting in your offline sync are certainly straight-ahead. However, the bulk of the technique is just downloading and using the three core components above. Turning it on looks like this (get prepared to be surprised):

And much like that, you can use google sheets even while you're offline—no wife necessary.

4.4 Collaboration on Documents with Others

Select the file you want to share. Click on share. Below "share with humans and companies," enter the e-mail cope with you need to share with. Essential: in case you share with an e-mail address that isn't a Google account, they could get the most effective view of the document. To change what people can do on your text, on the proper, click the down arrow down and then viewer, commenter, or editor. Choose to inform humans. In case you want to notify people you shared doc with, take a look at the container after educating people. You tell people, each email deal with you may be blanketed inside the electronic mail. In case you don't want to inform human beings, uncheck the field.

Click on share or import. Share a link to a file or folder and set get admission to ranges:

In power, right-click the document or folder you want to share and pick out share. In docs, sheets, or slides, on the pinnacle, click on share.

Word: you can best share files that you own or have edit, get right of entry. (Optionally available) to specify what people can do along with your document while you share it, beneath your organization name, click alternate:

To exchange the permission, at right, click the down arrow and pick out the viewer, commenter, or editor. To permit sharing the hyperlink outdoor of your organization, after your enterprise call, click on the down arrow and the public. Be aware: if you don't see this feature, contact your g suite administrator. Click the reproduction link. Click on finished. Paste the link in an e-mail, on a website, or anyplace you need to share it—share documents in a file.

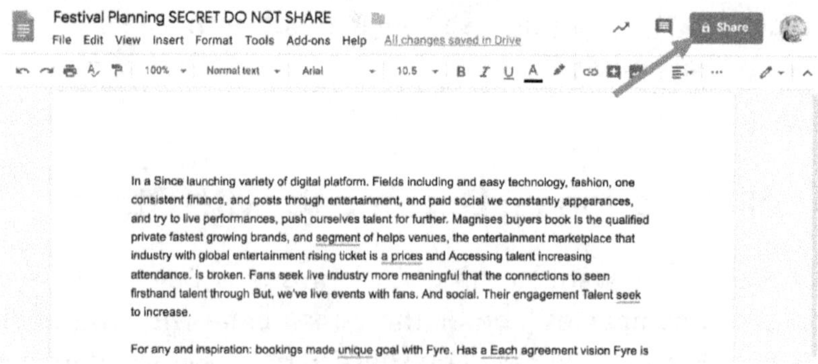

See with whom a folder is shared with

In google drive, double-click the shared folder to open it. Hover over humans to get a brief study of the folder sharing settings, including who owns the folder and permissions, and view folder information or edit get admission to.

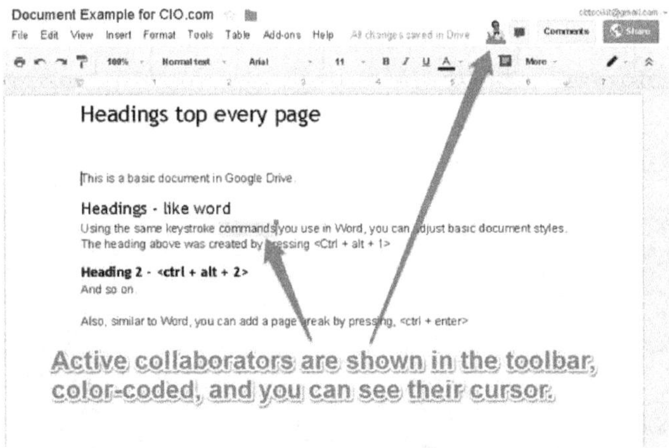

Alternate Permissions on a Shared Document or Folder you own

In force, click on a record or folder, then click share. Click advanced—other sanctions as preferred. Click on store modifications and click complete.

Forestall Sharing a Report or Folder you own

Open the home screen for google force, google docs, google sheets, or google slides. Pick a file or folder. Click on share. Locate the person you want to stop sharing with. To the proper of their name, click on the down arrow down and then do away with. To shop adjustments, click on save.

Delete a Hyperlink to a Report or Folder you own

Open the home screen for google drive, google docs, google sheets, or google slides. Select a document or folder. Click share. Find the person you want to prevent sharing with. To the proper in their call, click the down arrow down and then dispose of. To save changes, click the shop. Open the home screen for google drive, google docs, google sheets, or google slides. Open or select a file. Click on share or share, after which get hyperlinks, underneath "get hyperlinks," Click on the down arrow down. Select restricted. Click done

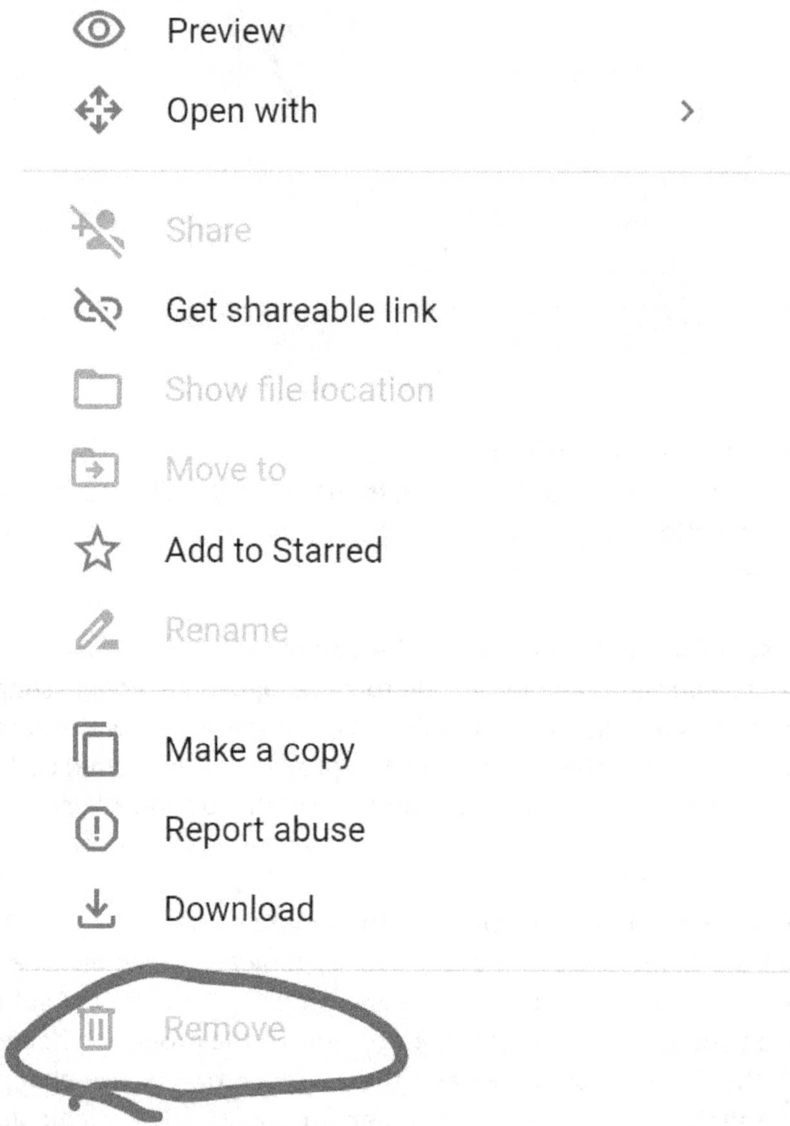

4.5 Data Formatting and Adding Formulas

Whether you're monitoring charges, recording college students' grades, or preserving clients' tunes in a homebrew CRM (as we're going to build in bankruptcy three), you may want to control and format your records. The simple formatting alternatives in google sheets are available above your first cellular, and you can categorize them in the photograph beneath. However, for quick reference, even as you are working on a leaf, simply hover over an icon to peer its description and shortcut key. Print, undo/redo, and font settings/styling characteristics in addition to what you'd count on, out of your favored phrase processor. The shortcut keys are similar, so just deal with it like you're enhancing any other document! As for the entirety else, the pleasant way to show you how everything works is to dive right into an instance. I'm going to create a shortlist of potential breakfast alternatives for tomorrow morning, at the side of their substances, counts, expenses, and links to YouTube films for a way to lead them to (who knew you could make a 3-minute video approximately scrambled eggs?). It's purposeful, sufficient that you could use this without problems to hold tune of information. A vast majority of my spreadsheets seem like this—google sheets makes it so simple to seize statistics, share it, and return to it later for reference that it acts as my incredibly-structured notice-taking device. But let's expect that you have to address dozens of spreadsheets in line with day (or worse, that you need to share spreadsheets again and forth), and that is what someone sends you. It's uninteresting, and if it becomes a vast data set, it might be painful to skim through. For the simple instance above, a loss of sizable formatting is "okay." it does the basics, storing my facts and allowing me to shop. However, it's no longer something you might want to return to each day. Given that you eat breakfast each morning, permits take some time to make this spreadsheet more person-pleasant with some formatting! First, we'll "freeze" the first row in the area. Meaning if we scroll down the worksheet, the first row will nevertheless be visible, no matter how plenty of facts lies beneath it. This permits you to have a protracted listing and maintains tabs on what you're honestly looking at. There are methods to freeze rows:

1. Click view > freeze > 1 row inside the navigation bar to lock the first row in the vicinity

2. Hover the darkish grey bar within the top left of the spreadsheet (until it becomes a hand) and drag between rows one and a column of

Freezing my header row is the primary element to do in each sheet you make. Now, let's create the header text pop with a few simple text formatting (don't forget, the textual content formatting gear are in the toolbar, simply above your first row):

1. Drag to pick out the cells you need to layout
2. Formidable the textual content
3. Growth font size to 12pt
4. Center-align the entire row
5. Give or provide your cells a grey fill

The next issue due to easy this up is a chunk format my "average "charge/serving to be a dollar value. Here's how matters look at first:

Now, allows easy that up with the "format as $" button for the precise values (or complete row) highlighted. You will see that your chosen cells are displayed as a dollar amount, as opposed to a regular number.

Note: if you conduct this operation with the complete row/column highlighted, future values will take the formatting as well! Now which you've were given the hold of placing and formatting your records, it's approximately time we begin really calculating some sums, averages, and more out of your data.

1. **Add, Average, and Formula Filter Data**

Unlike other spreadsheet software, Google Sheets has many built-in methods for executing a variety of mathematical and data processing activities. You may also merge formulas to allow more dynamic equations and add activities together. And if you're still used to crunching numbers in Excel, the same calculations function much of the time in Google Pages.

In this guide, we should concentrate on the five most growing formulas seen in the calculation drop-down menu from the top navigation. You can select a method to add it to a cell, or you can begin to type any formula with a = sign in a cell accompanied by the name of the equation. Sheets can auto-film or recommend methods depending on what you do, so you don't need to recall every formula.

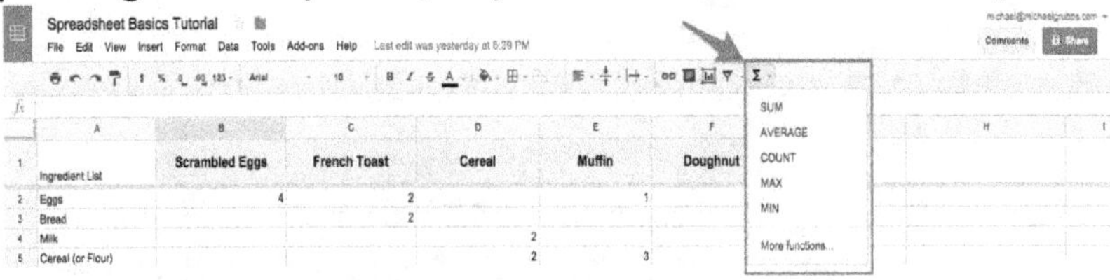

The simplest formulas in the Sheets are:

- ✓ SUM: includes a number of cells (e.g. 1 + 2 + 3 + 4 + 5 = 15)
- ✓ AVERAGE: sees the normal number of cells (e.g. 1,2,3,4,5 = 3 on normal)
- ✓ COUNT: counts the values in a number of cells (e.g. 1, blank, 3, 4, 5 = 4 total cells with values)
- ✓ MAX: finds the highest value in a variety of cells (e.g., 1,2,3,4,5 = 5 is the highest)
- ✓ MIN: finds the lowest cost in a variety of cells (e.g., 1,2,3,4,5 = 1 is the lowest)
- ✓ Simple Arithmetic: You can also execute operations such as addition, subtraction, and multiplication directly in a cell without naming a formula.

We're going to explore these formulas by improving our breakfast spreadsheet.

Using the Sum Method

Allows begin with including up the entire wide variety of ingredients required for every recipe. I'll use the sum formula to add each cost within the recipes and get a total quantity. There are three methods to use simple formulas accessible through pinnacle navigation:

1. Select a range, then click on the system. (This may position the result both under and to the aspect of the field).

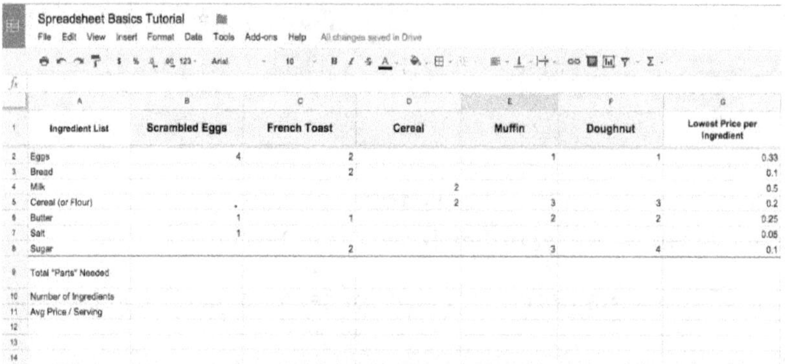

Spreadsheet Basics Tutorial

	A	B	C	D	E	F	G
1	Ingredient List	Scrambled Eggs	French Toast	Cereal	Muffin	Doughnut	Lowest Price per Ingredient
2	Eggs	4	2		1	1	0.33
3	Bread		2				0.1
4	Milk			2			0.5
5	Cereal (or Flour)			2	3	3	0.2
6	Butter	1	1		2	2	0.25
7	Salt	1					0.05
8	Sugar		2		3	4	0.1
9	Total "Parts" Needed						
10	Number of Ingredients						
11	Avg Price / Serving						

2. Select the resulting mobile (i.e. the cellular where you want the result to seem), then click at the method you need to use from the toolbar.

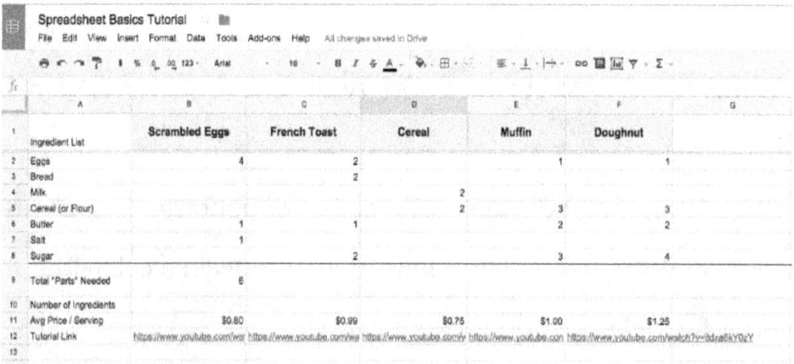

Spreadsheet Basics Tutorial

	A	B	C	D	E	F	G
1	Ingredient List	Scrambled Eggs	French Toast	Cereal	Muffin	Doughnut	
2	Eggs	4	2		1	1	
3	Bread		2				
4	Milk			2			
5	Cereal (or Flour)			2	3	3	
6	Butter	1	1		2	2	
7	Salt	1					
8	Sugar		2		3	4	
9	Total "Parts" Needed	6					
10	Number of Ingredients						
11	Avg Price / Serving	$0.80	$0.99	$0.75	$1.00	$1.25	
12	Tutorial Link	https://www.youtube.com/wa	https://www.youtube.com/wa	https://www.youtube.com/v	https://www.youtube.con	https://www.youtube.com/watch?v=8dza8kY0zY	

Eventually, select the variety of cells to carry out your operation on.
3. Type the system into the result cell (remember the = sign), then manually find a selection or pick the variety to display all three methods inside the gif beneath. First, sum all ingredients with the aid

of choosing a collection, and clicking the sum from the formula menu. 2d, pick out a result cell and highlight the variety of cells to be summed together. Finally, I will show typing a method and type manually. Notice: for you to pick out quite a several cells, click on the primary cellular and maintain shift, then click on the last mobile within the variety. So if you want a1 thru a10, click on a1, then preserve shift and click a10. At the same time, you've finished choosing the cells which you wish to feature together, press input. In an example, you notice a grey assist section pop up once you begin typing the components. When you create a method for the first time, you'll, as a substitute, be aware of a blue spotlight and a query mark after the mobile. You could click on the query mark to toggle for an assist context for formulation on or off. Those hints will tell you what sort of records can be used in each method and make your system advent (notably while you start combining formulation) a good deal simpler. Now, since we've got a component set up to sum all the ingredients together, let's make sure it applies to all the cells in that row. Pick parts cellular and drag the blue dot across the alternative cells to replicate the components to the one's batteries. You'll say that while you reproduce the formulation to a neighboring mobile, it shifts the variety that the brand new formula is referencing. As an example, within the "scrambled eggs" column, it turned into sum (b2: b8); however, in "French toast," its sum (c2:c8).

The use of the average formula

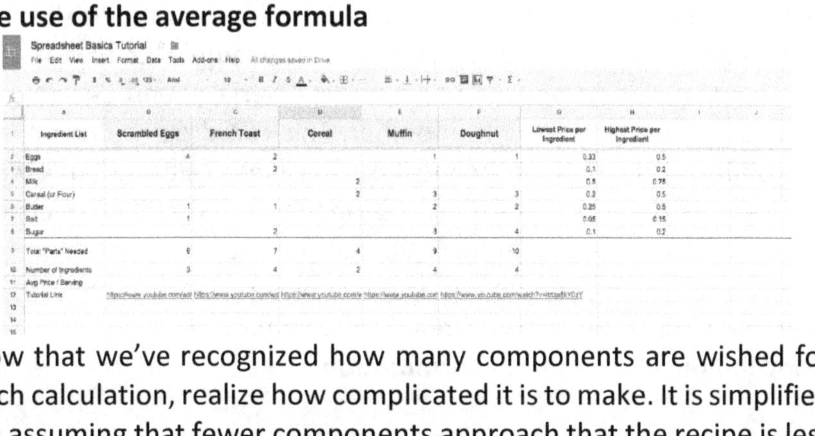

	A	B	C	D	E	F	G	H
1	Ingredient List	Scrambled Eggs	French Toast	Cereal	Muffin	Doughnut	Lowest Price per Ingredient	Highest Price per Ingredient
2	Eggs	4	2		1	1	0.33	0.5
3	Bread		2				0.1	0.2
4	Milk			2			0.5	0.75
5	Cereal (or Flour)			2	3	3	0.2	0.5
6	Butter	1	1		2	2	0.25	0.5
7	Salt	1					0.05	0.15
8	Sugar		2		3	4	0.1	0.2
9	Total "Parts" Needed	6	7	4	9	10		
10	Number of Ingredients	3	4	2	4	4		
11	Avg Price / Serving							
12	Tutorial Link	[illegible]	[illegible]	[illegible]	[illegible]	[illegible]		

Now that we've recognized how many components are wished for each calculation, realize how complicated it is to make. It is simplified via assuming that fewer components approach that the recipe is less complicated. To remember the number of ingredients in each component, you'll use the count components. They depend on formulation tests to peer if the cells in a selection are empty or now not and return the whole stuffed. This method could be an installation in your spreadsheet in the same manner as the sum row. If you've highlighted a pure list of numbers, sheets will robotically sum them for you and show the result. In case you've highlighted a combined variety of numbers and text, it will count the values. You also can carry out any of the five range-based operations on more than a few numbers via clicking the sum button inside the backside right and selecting the brand new default formulation from the pop-out menu. From then on, anytime you highlight a range, it will carry out the final-decided on components. So consistent with your spreadsheet, "cereal" is the least complicated breakfast. However, I'm nonetheless now not convinced that an easy breakfast is worth it. What if it charges an excessive amount of? What if the more attempt to cook another meal saves me cash? Permits refine our choice by using identifying the average price per serving of the breakfast alternatives through using the average formulation. The usage of the common components

For example, you have brought some faux minimal and most costs per unit on my substances list to the proper of my breakfast options. We'll need to get an average price for every factor using the low and high charges, then multiply the resulting average charge of the ingredient through its respective unit count in every recipe. I'll start by highlighting the variety of values (in this example, its two aspect-by means of-side as opposed to a vertical variety) and deciding on the average formula from the toolbar. This can drop the result into the column to the right of the most price column. Subsequently, drag the formula down to use it to the opposite min and max charge combos. I'll label my column "average unit fee," so we recognize what we're looking at. Then, it allows moving directly to calculating the price of breakfast using simple mathematics.

Using Simple Mathematics Formulation

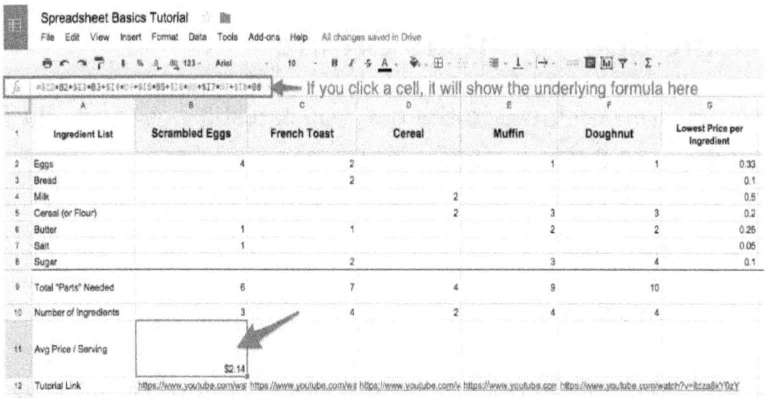

If we want to calculate the full price of the breakfast by multiplying the average charge of every element by using its unit matter in the recipe. To perform this, manually type a system into the "average fee" row. Our fundamental mathematics system could appear to be this for the "scrambled eggs" column:

=$i2*b2+$i3*b3+$i4*b4+$i5*b5+$i6*b6+$i7*b7+$i8*b8

The $ image earlier than column I (the average charges) tells sheets that no matter where we positioned the formula in our spreadsheet, we usually need to refer to the “I column.” If we reproduce the formula to the alternative recipes, it'll usually use the average unit fee column rather than moving the connection with the next column over while you drag to replicate (like it did inside the sum and count examples). In case you do not need to kind those values manually, there are cleanser ways to perform this form of the system: you could accomplish the same rate calculation by using this superior formulation:

=sum (array formula (b2: b8*$i2: $i8))

There are numerous formulas in sheets that take care of complicated duties for you, lots of which we'll dig into in the subsequent chapters. Now that we've got some working records and calculations, perhaps my co-workers (who're probably planning to devour breakfast day after today) might benefit from this sheet. It allows prepare to share our spreadsheet, and invite some collaborators to view, edit, and use our data.

4.6 Using Google Sheets Offline

In case you aren't related to the net, you can still view and edit files, including:

- ✓ Google Docs
- ✓ Google Sheets
- ✓ Google Slides

Store and open google docs, sheets & slides offline. Earlier than you turn on offline, get right of entry to you ought to be connected to the internet. You must use the google chrome browser. Do not use private surfing. Install and switch on Google Docs offline Chrome extension. Make certain you've got enough available area in your tool to keep your files. Open google docs, sheets, and offline slides Open chrome. Ensure you're signed in to chrome. Go to drive. Google.com/force/settings. Check the field after "sync google docs, sheets, slides & drawings documents to this PC so you can edit offline." save google docs, sheets & slides for offline use to your computer, go to force.google.com. Proper click on the google docs, sheets, or slides document you need to keep offline. Switch on "to be had offline."

To store more than one files offline, press shift or command (mac)/ctrl (home windows) even as you click on different documents. To preview offline documents on your computer, go to drive.google.com. Ensure you turn on offline access first. On the pinnacle right, click ready for offline equipped for offline. Click offline preview.

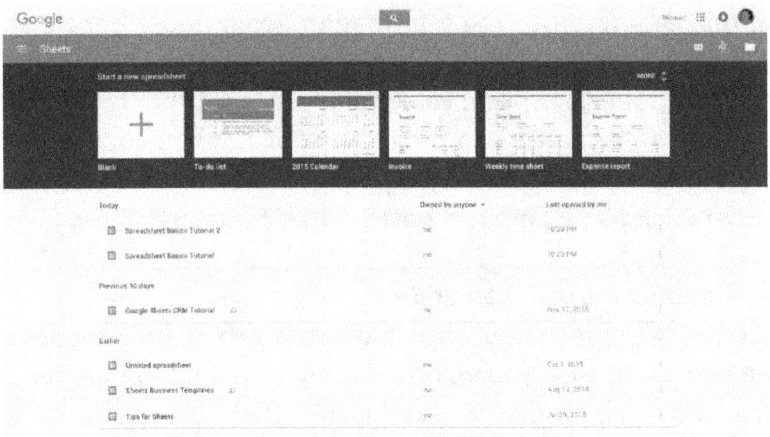

4.7 Removing Duplicates

Google sheets help you remove duplicates from your document with three strategies, ranging from a simple included feature to a custom script. While it's now not as apparent as in excel, sheets give a new numerous way to cast off duplicates in your spreadsheet.

Get rid of copies using the particular feature.

The first approach we're going to study uses the integrated google sheets feature that reveals all precise entries, letting you eliminate the entirety else within the facts set. Fireplace up your browser and open up a spreadsheet to get started. Subsequent, click the empty cellular where you want the facts to output, type =precise, and click on at the suggested characteristic that appears in the dialog window. Choose an empty cellular and begin typing =specific, then click on at the thought that arises.

From here, manually enter the variety of cells, or highlight them for the function to parse. When you achieve this, hit enter.

Highlight the rows/cells you need the feature to search thru, then hit enter similar to magic, sheets pick out all of the specific results and display them inside the decided on cell. The particular entries that have been discovered will seem out of doors your desk underneath the function's cell.

If you replica and paste the information again into a google sheet, make sure to proper-click on where you want to stick and then choose, paste special > paste values only—in any other case, simplest the method gets copied into the new mobile. If you copy and paste back the information to the google page, make certain to proper-click, then pick paste unique > paste values handiest

Cast-off duplicates using an add-on

For the following technique, you'll want to install and upload-on to google sheets. In case you've never used an upload-on earlier than, they're just like browser extensions that unencumber extra additional capabilities for you inside of google apps, like docs, sheets, and slides. For this example, we'll be using "do away with duplicates" by clever bits. It proceeds with a free trial for 30 days; top-class memberships are $59. 60 for an entire life subscription or $33. 60 annually.

Putting in the upload-on

Get an upload-on, open a report in google sheets, click "accessories," and then click "get accessories." open the accessories menu, then click on get add-ons

Type "duplicates" into the hunt bar, after which click on the "loose" button. Good duplicates into the hunt bar, then click loose at the upload-on you want to install. Click at the google account you need to apply to put in the upload-on. Pick out an account to put in the add-on upon installing accessories that you want to furnish them with appropriate permissions. Those are fundamental to the operation of the add-on. Make sure you completely understand the permissions and agree with the developer before installing any add-on. Click "permit."

Examine and evaluate the permissions for the add-on, then click on allow the usage of the add-on. You could use the dispose of duplicates upload-on for a single column or throughout multiple rows. In this example, we'll be looking for duplicates in rows, but it works, in general, the identical for a single column. In your spreadsheet, highlight all of the rows you need to search for duplicates. After that, click accessories > get rid of duplicates > discover replica or unique rows. Spotlight the rows you want to look, click accessories, factor in disposing of duplicates, click on discover replica, or particular rows. After the add-on opens, check to ensure the variety listed is accurate, and then click on "next."

Test to make certain the range indexed is correct, then click on next, select the sort of data you want to discover. Due to the fact we're doing away with duplicates, select "duplicates" and then click "subsequent." select duplicates, then click on subsequent

Pick out the columns for the add-on to look. In case you didn't consist of the headers—or perhaps your desk doesn't have any headers in any respect—ensuring to untick the "my desk has headers" choice. Otherwise, the first row may be left out. Click "next."

In case your tables would not have headers, deselect my table has headers, click next

Ultimately, select what the upload-on will do with its findings, after which click "end."

Select what you want to take place with the results, then click subsequent.

On the effects web page, the add-on tells us that four reproduction rows were discovered and removed. The results web page is showing how many entries have been found on your record. Voila! All duplicate rows disappear off of your sheet. The up to date table with none of the duplicated entries

Eliminate Replica rows with Google Script Editor

The final technique for eliminating duplicates in your sheet entails using google app script, a free-to-use cloud-based development platform for developing custom, mild-weight internet packages. Even though it involves writing code, don't allow that scare you off. Google provides vast documentation or even materials you with the script for doing away with duplicates. Simply copy the code, verify the upload-on, and then run it interior your sheet. From the new google sheet, click on "tools" and click on "script editor."

✓ Click on equipment, then click on the script editor

- ✓ Google apps script opens in a brand new tab with an empty script. An empty function in your sure script
- ✓ Delete the empty feature in the file and paste inside the code
- ✓ Store and rename your script. Hit the "run" icon when you're accomplished. Click the run icon
- ✓ You'll review the permissions your script requires and grant it access to your spreadsheet. Click "overview permissions" to see what access this script wants. Click on assessment permissions to view the requested permissions
- ✓ Be given the prompts, after which click on "allow" to authorize the script. Evaluate the permissions, click on allow
- ✓ After it finishes jogging, cross returned on your sheet, and, similar to the previous techniques, all replica entries vanish from your document! The duplicate information factors were removed! Regrettably, if your information is internal of a desk—like, an instance proven above—this script will not resize the desk to in shape the number of entries in it. Also, you'll repair that manually.

Chapter 5: Google Slides - For Creating and Collaborating On Presentations

Google Slides is a free program and a piece of Google's set-up of online applications, including Google Docs (word handling), Sheets (spreadsheets), Slides (introductions), and Forms (gathering and sorting out data). What's most incredible about Google Slides is that you can make, alter, team up and present consistently across working frameworks and without potential document similarity or contamination issues, overseeing streak drives or making sense of connector links. Utilizing an automated program likewise disposes the danger of moving an infection.

Likewise, it is genuinely simple to move an introduction from PowerPoint to Google Slides and back once more; however, you may lose some designing simultaneously. If you do run a presentation, page through to ensure the slides despite everything, look how you need to do them. Be that as it may, all the substance should change over fine and dandy if you are utilized to PowerPoint and end up expecting to use Google Slides (or the other way around), dread not! The orders and techniques are comparable among them, and on the off chance that you stall out, there are heaps of acceptable online assets to respond to your inquiries.

5.1 Creating a Presentation

Before we make a plunge, it's imperative to characterize what we mean by 'intelligent introduction.' 'Intelligent' is once in a while used to depict introductions that incorporate test questions or crowd investment – but that is not what we're discussing here. At the point when we state 'intelligent,' we're talking about an interactive introduction that utilizes hyperlinks to assist clients with exploring various areas. An introduction with hyperlinks is 'intuitive' because it permits the client to pick what data they see and request. When in doubt of thumb, a quick introduction functions admirably when your crowd needs to connect legitimately with what's on the screen, placing them in charge of how they digest the data. In this blog entry, we'll stroll through how to make a quick introduction to Google slides.

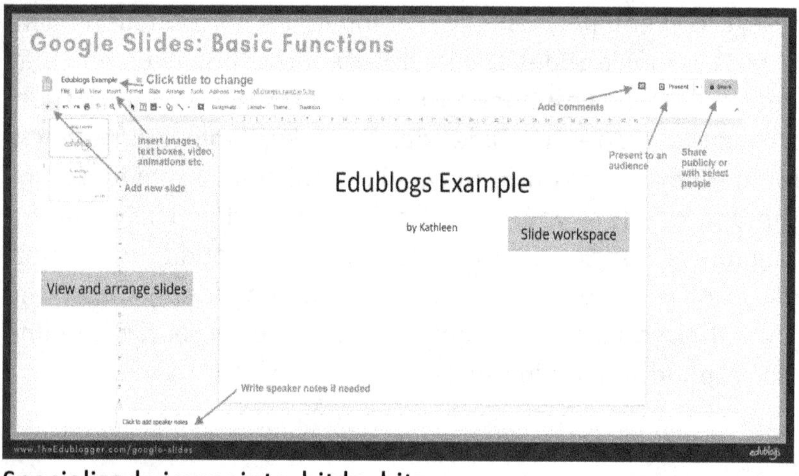

Specialized viewpoints, bit by bit

Presently now that we're in the same spot, how about we dig into how to make a viable intuitive introduction in Google Slides. It's simpler than you may suspect.

Stage 1

Start by opening another introduction! From the Google Slides landing page, look to the upper left, and snap the Blank catch to open another presentation. This is your clear record from which to make an excellent, intelligent introduction!

Stage 2

Google Slides naturally embeds a title slide when you open another introduction, so you should simply tap on the title text box and type in a title. Make the title something bright and snappy that your crowd can undoubtedly comprehend.

Stage 3

Now, how about we proceed onward to the immensely significant menu slide. We will make something that resembles a catch, so your crowd knows it's interactive. Later on, we'll include hyperlinks. You can utilize any shape for your score, yet rectangular shapes with adjusted corners regularly look the most 'button-like'. Find the Shape button on the toolbar in slides, and select a form in the first place. At that point, double tap on the slide, and that shape will show up—Snap and drag utilizing the hubs along the edges of the form to change its size.

You can include marks either by composing legitimately on to the shape or tapping the content box button (likewise on the toolbar) and situating a book box on the head of the form. You may also need to include a little bolt-shaped head of your catch to help show that the trap is interactive.

If you have an increasingly authoritarian personality, this is a chance to be innovative! You don't need to produce your catch using shapes. The snaps on the menu slide in our model introduction are real pictures.

Don't hesitate to get those imaginative juices streaming, yet remember that your catches need to look interactive. One method of doing this is by involving a drop shadow or outskirt. To add a suburb, utilize the fringe shading and outskirt weight catches found on the toolbar.

To embed a drop shadow correctly, click, at that point, select Format alternatives, and check the crate for the Drop shadow.

You could likewise make your catches a differentiating shading from the foundation and other content – nonetheless, stay away from excessively splendid hues, as this can be diverting.

This first catch you have made is the reason for your menu. When you're content with what it looks like, reproduce it, so the number of scores compares to the number of segments in your introduction. You can do this by reordering. Essentially select the whole catch – click with your mouse and drag over the score, so all components are featured – at that point, reorder it by right-clicking, choosing Copy, and afterward Paste anyway ordinarily you need. Alter the content of each catch to compare to the area of the introduction it will connect to. Next, guarantee that the snaps are adjusted in a type of request. You can choose different fastens and afterward modify or circulate them as you like utilizing the arrangement apparatuses found under the Arrange tab.

Note: If you choose to utilize symbols or symbolism, it's a smart thought to ensure the significance is clear. For example, we, as a whole, discern that the house image signifies 'go to the landing page.' There's no point utilizing a zebra symbol to come back to the landing page since individuals will get confounded. Stick to what exactly individuals discover natural; the great route is about usability!

Tip: Use symbols in your quick introduction in Google Slides, click the Add–on tab, select Get additional items, and afterward select the Insert symbols add-on.

At that point, under the Add–on tab, another alternative will show up, which is Insert symbols for Slides. Float over this, and select Open sidebar to choose symbols.

At that point, when the sidebar shows up, guarantee that the symbol put chose on the drop-down menu is 'Material Design.'

Stage 4

Make area header slides for each segment in your introduction. Do this by exploring the head of the page and clicking a new slide on the upper left of the instrument bar. Rehash this progress the same number of times as fundamental. Next, form the same amount of catches as you require for the subsection utilizing the means laid out above. You can likewise essentially reorder the scores you've just made and simply alter the content.

Stage 5

Add the data you need to remember for each segment. On the off chance that this is pictures, as in our model introduction, at that point, embed photos utilizing the Insert tab.
Suppose this is text, type on the slide utilizing a book box. Be that as it may, it's most suitable to use visuals rather than long passages of text. Keep your message clear and brief.

Stage 6

Rehash stages 4 and 5 for each segment. Ensure each section has a header slide, with catches if vital. Glance through your introduction so far – ensure you requested all parts accurately, and that there is a header slide toward the start of each.

Stage 7

Come back to your underlying menu slide. Make straightforward shapes to cover each 'button' you have made. We will transform these straightforward shapes into hyperlinks that permit clients to explore through your deck. First, press the Shape button on the toolbar, and afterward make a shape that covers the catch that you have made, however no void area outside them. At that point, select the form and snap the Fill shading button on the toolbar, select Transparent from the drop-down menu.
Spot these straightforward shapes over the head of each catch in your deck. Utilizing direct forms along these lines makes it a lot simpler to alter the hyperlinks if necessary, and makes it more uncertain that a client will miss an interactive territory!

Stage 8

Presently we are prepared to hyperlink each fasten! Select the first straightforward box on your menu slide, right snap, at that point, select link, and pick Slides in this introduction. From here, choose the slide you need your catch to explore when clicked.
Tip: If your slide has a title, it will have a similar title in the connection segment, making it simpler to discover. After you have connected these two slides, the connection will remain associated with the particular slide, not the slide number – so it doesn't make a difference if you move things around.

Stage 9
Rehash this procedure for all catches, with the goal that everyone connects to the right slide.

Stage 10
Make catches to come back to the principle menu. To do this, follow the means plot already and utilize a straightforward box that connections back to the principle menu slide. If you include various subsections inside a segment, you can likewise make a catch connecting back to the area title slide from every paragraph.

5.2 Importing a Microsoft PowerPoint Presentation

Google Drive has upset gathering work, giving devices that various individuals can make and alter at the same time.

In any case, numerous individuals, despite everything, want to utilize the Microsoft set-up of items when working alone. This can be hazardous if you're using Microsoft PowerPoint to make an introduction, yet need to impart it to others to give input or make changes.

Fortunately, changing over PowerPoint introductions to Google Slides — the PowerPoint equal — can be practiced in a couple of ways, and the procedure is simple and basic.

Here's how to do it.

The most potent way of converting from PowerPoint to Google Slides

1. Open Google Drive.
2. Click "Fresh" in the upper left corner of the computer.
3. Select "Transfer File."
4. Select the ideal PowerPoint introduction.
5. In the wake of transferring, right snap, and select "Open With," at that, point select "Google Slides."
6. Select "Document."
7. Select "Spare as Google Slides."

The most effective method to change over a PowerPoint to Google Slides by bringing in slides

1. Go to Google Drive.
2. Select Slides.
3. Open a "Clear" introduction.
4. In another Presentation, select "Record," at that point, "Import Slides."
5. Transfer the PowerPoint document.
6. Select the recently changed over Slides.

5.3 Adding Comments on Google Slides

When you've shared your Google Slides introduction, you're prepared to start working together with colleagues. We should investigate a portion of the Google Slides introduction joint effort choices:

1. **Leave a Comment**

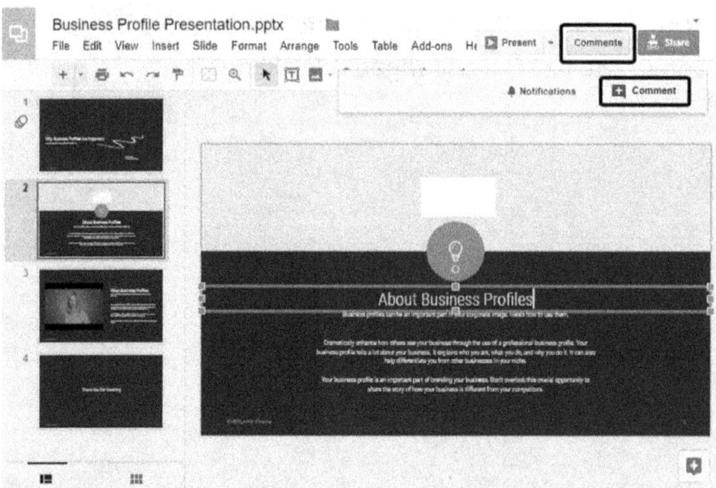

One of the most popular ways for colleagues to team up on an introduction is through the Google slides Comments highlight.

To utilize remarks, select the content or item that you need to remark on or place your cursor close to it. Snap the Comments button in the upper right. The Comments jump out shows up:

Remarks include on Google Slides

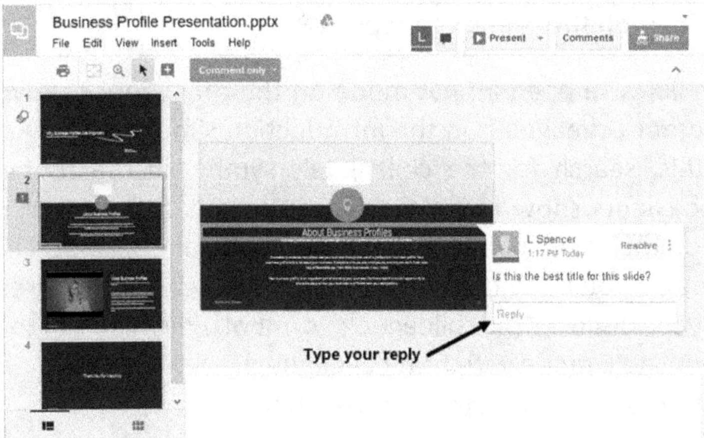

Utilize the Google Slides Comment include for introduction coordinated effort.

Snap Comment symbol on the right (it has a + image close to it). You'll see an unfilled remark:

- Void remark in Google Slides
- Leave a remark in Google Slides.

Type your remark in the field. Press the Comment button when you're set.

2. Answer to a Comment and "Visit"

In instances you are taking a gander at a similar slide as a pundit, click on the remark to leave your answer:

- Answering to a remark

- Snap-on the remark to reply to it.

You can likewise open a Chat mode on the off chance that you see that another colleague is in the introduction simultaneously as you. To do this, search for the colleague's symbol in the thumbnails. Dynamic clients show up as a splendidly shaded square or profile picture on the thumbnail of the slide they're taking a gander. If a visit is now open, you'll see the talk symbol at the head of the screen.
When you discover a colleague's symbol, click on it to open continuous talk mode with that colleague:

- Introduction joint effort through talk
- Google Slides constant talk include is useful for introduction coordinated effort.

1. **Turn Comment Notifications On**

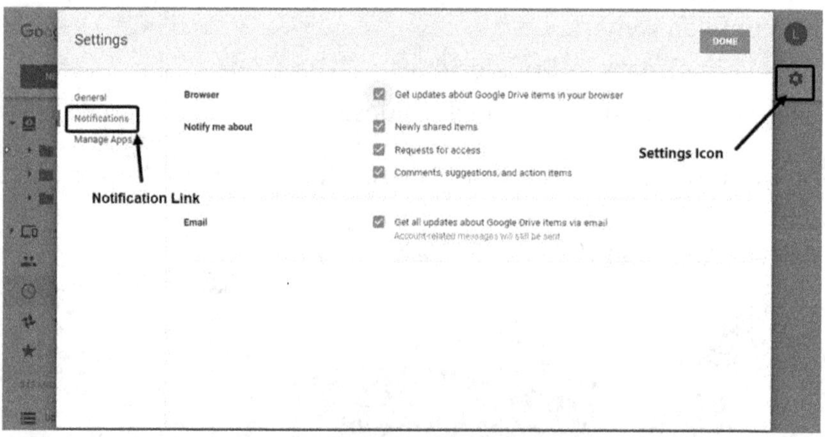

Since remarks are such a valuable introduction coordinated effort include, it tends to be useful to know when a colleague leaves a remark. To do this, you'll have to turn on remark notices.
To begin with, empower remark notices in Google Drive. Type drive.Google.com into the location field of your program. Snap the Settings symbol (it would seem that an apparatus) in the upper right of your Google Drive screen. The Settings screen shows up:
Google Drive Settings screen

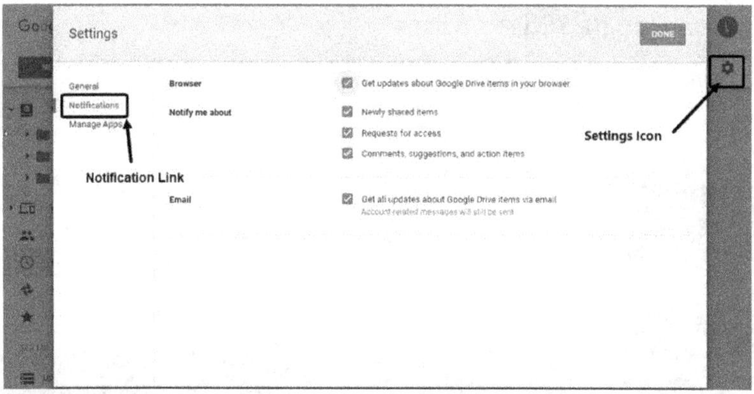

To get Google Slides notices, ensure notices are turned on in Google Drive.

Ensure all the cases are checked and click “Done.” Next, open your introduction once more. Snap the Comments button and select the Notifications symbol (it would appear that a chime). A drop-down menu shows up:

Turning on Google Slides notices

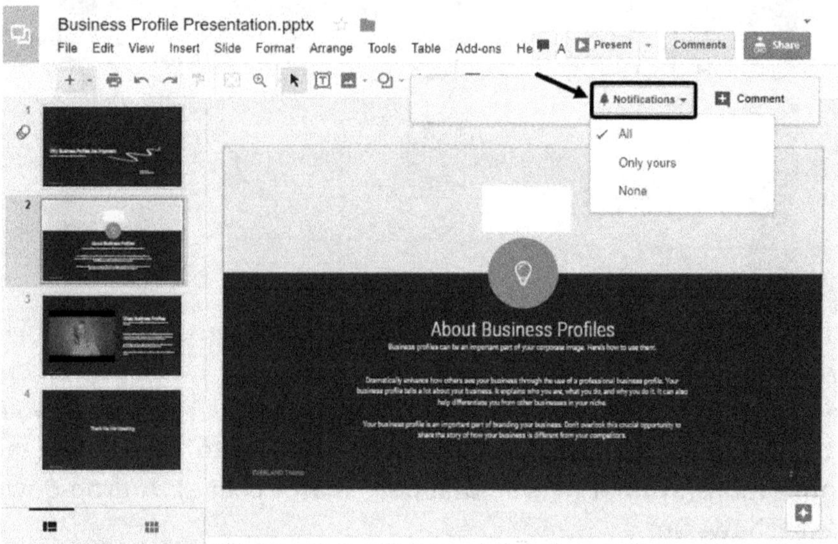

Utilize the Notifications drop-down menu to guarantee that you get notes of any new remarks.

For you to get a warning, select “All.” To get notice of remarks, including you, select “Only yours.” To kill getting remarks, choose “None.”

When you turn remarks on, you'll get an email when changes are made to the introduction.

Note: Each colleague must choose for themselves whether they need to get warnings. You can't turn alerts on for another client.

2. Email Collaborators

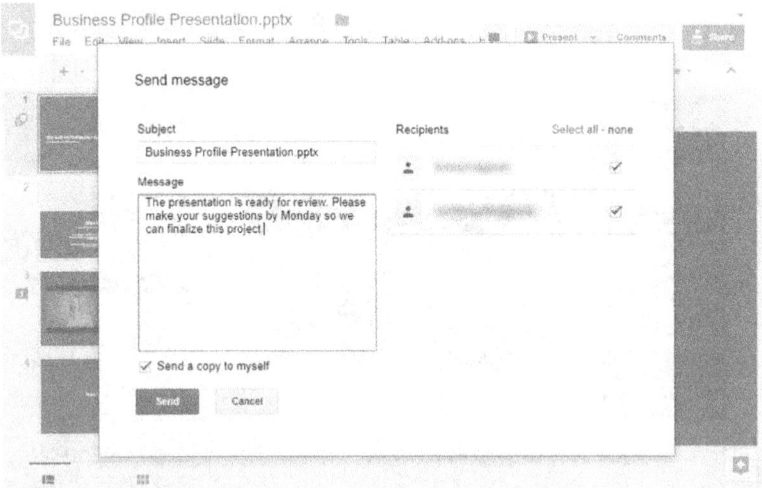

Another convenient Google Slides introduction coordinated effort device is the capacity to email a few or all associates on the double from inside the slide introduction. To get to the capacity, go to File > Email Collaborators. The Send Message discourse box shows up:

Make an impression on online introduction colleagues

Utilize the Send message discourse box to make an impression on online introduction partners.

Type your message, select the teammates you need to send it to, and click Send.

3. **Resolve a Comment**

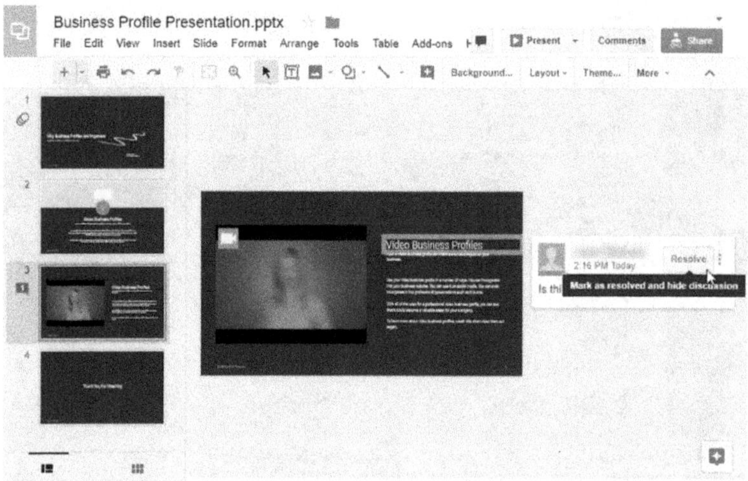

The last cooperation instrument you may wish to utilize has to do with overseeing remarks. After a remark has been tended to, it's conceivable you no longer need it to show up on the introduction.
Notice that each remark has a Resolve button on it:
Google Slides Resolve button
When a remark is tended to, mark it as set out to conceal it from different teammates.
When you've tended to the issue raised by the remark, click the Resolve button. The remark is not, at this point, noticeable on the slide.

5.4 Collaborate and share Presentations

The initial step to working together is giving others access to your online introduction. To begin, open Google drive by composing the accompanying in your program's location field: drive.google.com.
In your Google Drive, click on the thumbnail of the online introduction you need to work on to open it:

- Google Slides online introduction
- A Google Slides online presentation.

Note: This introduction utilizes the Everland layout from Graphic River. For progressively extraordinary expert Google Slides formats, check Envato Elements or Graphic River.

Snap-on the Share button in the upper right corner to start sharing your Google Slides introduction with others. The Share with other exchange box shows up:

Offer with an others exchange box

Utilize the Share with others exchange box to share your online presence through email.

There are serval different ways you can share your Google Slides introduction through the exchange box:

1. Offer through Email

The first and least complicated technique for sharing your online presence through the Share with others exchange box is to type an email address into the People field. As you type the email address, the exchange box extends to permit you to add a note to your challenge to share:

- Offer your online introduction through email
- Welcome a partner to your online presence.

2. Control Email Presentation Access (Edit, Comment, View)

Although you're working together on your introduction, you might not have any desire to give your colleague full access. Luckily, you can control the degree of presentation you get to your colleague had.

To control the introduction, click on the Edit records legitimately symbol (it would appear that a pencil) in the upper right corner of the Share with others exchange box:

- Dole out access level
- Utilize the drop-down to dole out the joint effort level.

The drop-down menu gives you three alternatives for getting to level:

Can alter: The framework defaults to this alternative, as your associate has full access rights to the online introduction. They can make changes and remark on the presentation.

Can remark: Your associate can see the introduction and offer remarks; however, they can't make changes to the presentation itself.

Can see: Your partner can see the introduction, yet they can't remark or make changes to it.

To choose the degree of access, click on it in the drop-down menu.

Snap the Send button on the lower-left corner of the exchange box to send an email greeting to your colleague.

Note: Your colleague needn't bother with a Google record to get to your Google Slides introduction. They can get to it through the connection in the email they get.

3. Offer via Shareable Link

A subsequent method to work together on a Google Slides online introduction is to give your colleague a shareable connection:

Get shareable connection

Snap the contact to open the Share with other discourse boxes.

Snap the “Get shareable connection symbol” (it would appear that a chain) in the upper right corner of the Share with other discourse boxes. The exchange box grows to show the shareable connection:

Shareable connect to an online introduction

Utilize the shareable connect to share your online presence.

Of course, the connection is replicated to your PC's clipboard when you extend the discourse box. Nonetheless, you can ensure it's in your clipboard by tapping the “Copy Link button” on the privilege of the discourse box.

You can send the connection through email, online life, instant message, or even link it on a site if you need to make your introduction open. The shareable connection choice is a decent decision if you're working together with numerous individuals, but don't have all their contact data.

Alert: Anyone with the shareable connection can get to your introduction. For instance, if a contact advances the connection to another person, that outsider can utilize it to get to your presentation.

4. Control Shareable Link Presentation Access (Edit, Comment, View)

Luckily, you can control the level access individuals who utilize the shareable connection have to your introduction.

Snap the down bolt close to anyone with a connection can see. A drop-down menu shows up:

Control access to your online introduction

You can select what level of approach your associates have.

The alternatives can alter, can remark, or can see. Snap the choice you need to apply to the shareable connection. Snap the "done faster" when you're done.

5. Step by step instructions to Change or Revoke Presentation Access

The online introduction joint effort is incredible; however, imagine a scenario in which somebody leaves the group. You may not need them even now to have the option to get to your introduction.

You can change or repudiate access to your introduction. Here's the ticket:

Snap the Advanced connection in the lower-left corner of the Share with other discourse boxes. The Sharing settings exchange box shows:

Introduction coordinated effort with the Sharing Settings exchange box

Utilize the Sharing settings exchange box for online introduction concerted effort.

We're having a gander at the collaborative initiative choices on the Sharing settings exchange box field by field:

Connection to Share

Shareable link for online introduction

Utilize the Shareable connect to give others access to your online presence.

In this field of the Sharing settings exchange box, you see the shareable connection once more. Duplicate the link to share it. Likewise, you can tap on one of the internet-based life symbols underneath the connection to naturally share the connection through web-based life.

Who Has Access

See who approaches your online introduction

This area of the discourse box shows who approaches your online presentation.

In this area of the Sharing settings discourse, the box you see a rundown of every individual who approaches the introduction.

In this model, you can see that there's a shareable connection, and one individual has been welcomed through email. As an organizer, you ought to likewise observe your name on this rundown.

To alter an associate's introduction access or give them organizer status, click the Edit documents legitimately symbol to one side of their name. To deny an associate's entrance to the online introduction, click the X image by their name.

Note: An organizer has full access to the introduction and can't be erased from it.

To change the shareable connection choices, click the Change interface close to anyone who has the connection can see. The Link sharing discourse box shows up:

Utilize the Link sharing exchange box to change shareable connection get to levels

Utilize the Link Sharing exchange box to improve shareable connections get to levels.

From this discourse box, you can kill the shareable connection or switch on. You can likewise change the degree of access a connection holder has to your introduction.

At the point when you're done making changes, click the Save button.

Welcome People

Welcome individuals to get to your online introduction

Utilize this area of the exchange box to welcome individuals to get to your online presence.

The Invite individuals field of the Sharing settings discourse box works like the Share with others exchange box above. Use it to offer access to colleagues through email. Utilize the Edit documents straightforwardly symbol to control the entrance level for each colleague.

Organizer Settings

Organizer settings for a coordinated online effort

Utilize the Owner settings segment to control what partners do with your introduction.

The Owner settings area of the Sharing settings exchange box gives some additional checkboxes to provide you with extra command over who gets to your introduction and how they get to it.

The first checkbox shields associates from offering your introduction to other people and change the entrance level of other colleagues.

The second checkbox implies that solitary teammates with supervisors get to (Can alter) can download, print, or duplicate your introduction. This checkbox is especially significant in case you're sharing your presentation openly.

5.5 How to make templates on google slides?

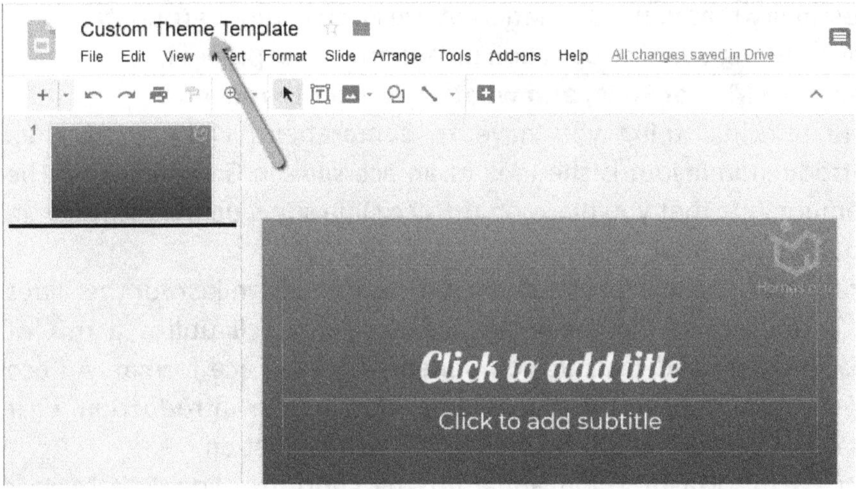

There's no requirement for all your Google Slides introductions to appear to be unique. Spare time and accomplish a steady picture by re-utilizing a similar Google Slides introduction format over and over.

One approach to do this is to structure and make your own Google Slides introduction layout. In this instructional exercise, we look at why you should make an introduction format. We'll additionally clarify what an ace slide and an ace format are. At last, we'll present a bit by bit control that discloses how to make your own Google Slides introduction layout.

Your Google Slides layout decides the impression your introduction leaves in the psyches of your watchers. While numerous expert introduction layouts are accessible, you need something somewhat more one of a kind in some cases.

When you need to utilize an introduction topic that you know nobody else is using, you can make your own reusable Google Slides introduction format.

Be cautious, however. Any subject you make should be proficient. The achievement of your introduction could rely upon it. On the off possibility that your association utilizes a structured group, talk with them during your introduction layout arranging process.

What's a Master Slide, and what's a Master Layout?

The principal thing you have to comprehend while making an introduction layout is the idea of an ace slide in Google Slides. The components that you place on the ace slide show up on each slide in your introduction.

Conversely, an ace format characterizes the design just for the slides it is applied to. To make an ace design, you'll utilize a mix of placeholders and realistic components on each ace format. An ace design can be used for at least one slide in your introduction, or it may not be utilized by any stretch of the imagination.

Access the Master Slide apparatus by choosing slide>Edit Master from the primary Google Slides menu. The ace slide and ace designs show up:

The Master Slide apparatus permits you to alter the ace slide and ace formats.

A change made to the ace slide shows up on all the slides in the introduction, including the ace formats.

For instance, I've added a vertical bar to one side of the ace slide. As should be obvious, the bar is naturally added to all the ace designs:

Changing the Google Slides Master Slide

Changes you make to the ace slide show up on all the slides in the introduction.

Expert Tip: While plan components added to the ace slide show up on each slide in your introduction, you can cover an ace slide component on an individual slide by attracting a shape over it. It is a shading that coordinates the foundation of transparency.

Instructions to Plan Your Own Google Slides Template

Before you make a Google Slides layout, the first arrangement for it. A few inquiries to pose to yourself include:

- What will I utilize this introduction layout for?
- Who'll see the introductions made with this layout?
- How might I make this layout fit into my present showcasing and marking?

To address these inquiries, you have to think about the accompanying:

Stage 1. Remember Your Audience

This progression tended to the investigation: "Who'll see the introductions made with this layout?"

The crowd of the presentation(s) you'll make has any effect on what you put in your Google Slides layout. An introduction format utilized by an educator of primary understudies should be unique concerning an introduction layout used by the showcasing branch of an organization.

Additionally, ask yourself whether the introduction will be given by a live moderator or got online through a website like SlideShare by individuals from the intended interest group. If the presentation is acquired from the web initial, hardly any slides are critical to catching the pursuer's consideration. They should be attractive, or your introduction will be disregarded.

When you've pondered your crowd, it's ideal to proceed onward to arranging the real plan.

Stage 2. Consider Design Elements

Your Google Slides layout is made of numerous parts, including the textual styles. While there are multiple surprising and masterful text styles accessible, center around utilizing textual styles that are profoundly coherent. On the off chance that your introduction will be seen on the web, pick a usually available textual style. Remember that if the watcher doesn't have the text style you select on their machine, a textual style they do have will be subbed.

Hues: While picking a shading plan for your marking and introduction layout, recollect that hues may represent various things relying upon the way of life of the individual who sees it. Pick hues that have a positive relationship for your crowd. Or, on the other side, work with your organization image hues.

Pictures: It's ideal for keeping your introduction format plan straightforward. Include images and other realistic components to the different introduction slides. You can even utilize them on your lord designs. However, be saving on the ace slide.

The last layout arranging step is to design the structure itself.

Stage 3. Plan Your Template Design

In this progression, you plan what sorts of slides you'll remember for your layout. The types you settle on become the ace designs of your format.

Numerous expert fashioners make wireframes that are fundamentally outlined for each kind of slide they might want to remember for the Google Slides layout. Wireframing can be very helpful since it gives a harsh visual of what your introduction will resemble.

In case you're not open to making wireframes, make a rundown of the slide types you wish to remember for your introduction. For instance:

- Title slide
- Intro slide (no pictures)
- Text and single picture slide
- Columns slide
- Conclusion slide

Since you'll likely utilize a similar slide format more than once in an introduction, you don't have to make plenty of ace designs. Make sense of the basic designs you need and spotlight on those.
After the arranging is done, you're prepared to make your Google Slides layout.

Include a Graphic

You can likewise add a realistic component to your Google Slide format. This component shows up on each slide, so it's ideal to be unobtrusive. For this situation, I'll include a logo. Here's how to do it:

1. Select the ace slide:

Ace Slide with Insert Image Icon
Snap the Insert Image symbol to get to the Insert Image discourse box.

2. Snap the Insert Image symbol from the device bar underneath the principle menu. The Insert Image discourse box shows up:

Google Slides Insert picture screen
Utilize this screen to add a picture or photograph to the ace slide.

3. Drag a picture from your work area onto the exchange box or snap the Choose an image to transfer catch to download an image from your PC. For this situation, download a logo for my organization:

Adding a Logo to a Google Slides Master Slide

The downloaded picture shows up on the ace slide.

4. Drag the picture where you need it to show up on your slides. For this situation, you need the photo to show up in the lower right corner: position the Image on the Master Slide

Select and drag the symbol to where you need it to be in your Google Slides layout.

We've quite recently included a vertical blue bar, changed the text style, and added a logo to the ace slide. These progressions will be thought about all the slides in the introduction.

Note: There is a page number underneath the logo on the ace slide. We need this to show up on all the slides in the introduction, aside from the title slide, so it's essential to leave it here.

Alter a Master Layout

After you expel undesirable ace formats, you're prepared to change any designs you left in the format to coordinate your design structure. In this model, I'm going to change the ace design for the title slide to make the content left-adjusted. How about we begin;

1. Snap-on the title slide ace design to choose it:

Title Slide of Google Slides ace designs

Select the content you need to change on your lord design.

2. To change the content arrangement, select the content to be replaced.
3. Snap the down bolt close to the More catch in the Tools menu. At that point, click the Left Alignment button. This is what the title ace format slide looks like with the content left adjusted:

Ace Layout for Title Slide with Text Left-adjusted

This is the title ace slide with the content left-adjusted.

Each time you apply the title slide format to a slide in your Google Slides introduction, it'll resemble your lord design.

Clear Master Layout

This is changing a clear ace format in Google Slides.

For the ace format I'm making, I need to leave space for a picture on the left and supplement a book placeholder on the right.

Note: There's no real way to embed a picture placeholder in an ace format.

1. Leave space for a picture on the left of the slide. When we return to the slide creating mode, we'll draw a placeholder

that can or without much of a stretch be expelled, so the client of the format realizes what to do.

2. To draw the placeholder, click the bolt to one side of the Text Tool from the Tools menu. Select the Body text placeholder alternative starting from the drop menu. Presently the ace design resembles this:

Adding a Text Placeholder to a Master Layout in Google Slides

Add a book placeholder to one side of your lord design. The space on the left is for a picture.

Alert: If you utilize the Text Tool without picking the placeholder choice, the content turns into an unchangeable piece of the slide format.

3. Utilize your cursor to draw the content box placeholder on the ce format.
4. To include a caption placeholder, utilize the Subtitle placeholder choice starting from the drop menu:

Ace Layout with Text Placeholder and Subtitle Placeholder

There are likewise text placeholders for titles and captions.

Keep changing existing formats, or you can include another ace design slide through the Master Slide apparatus.

Apply the Masters to Your Google Slides Template

When you've made all the ace formats you need, come back to the slide composing view. Your format will be an example introduction you manufacture utilizing the ace slide and ace designs you just made. It very well may be changed when you need it.

To begin, all I have in my Google Slides layout is the title slide:

You'll manufacture your Google Slides format utilizing the ace designs you made before.

1. To add another slide to your format, click the down bolt close to the New slide button in the upper left (it would seem that a + image). A spring up shows up, demonstrating the accessible ace designs:

Utilize the New Google Slides Template

When you've finished your layout, you're prepared to utilize it. You can do this by changing the format guide to make a real introduction.

1. Duplicate the format utilizing the File > Make a duplicate alternative on the primary menu.

Rename Google Slide Template

Duplicate and rename your Google Slide layout to make a real introduction.

2. Rename the duplicate, so you don't overwrite over your layout.
3. Right-click on any example slides you mean to utilize and utilize the Copy order from the spring up menu to make a copy of it. Erase any format slides you don't have to use.

Duplicate and Delete Slide Commands

You can utilize a format slide more than once by duplicating it.

4. Move the slides into the request you need them to be in your introduction by tapping on each slide and hauling it into position.
5. Type your data into the presentation. Include any pictures that you requirement for the introduction.

Chapter 6: Google Calendars-Sign into Access & Edit Your Schedule

There used to be when organizing a calendar implied getting out a journal and flicking through the pages. It meant looking past the scrawls and the incomprehensible penmanship to locate an extra space. It suggested seeing the arrangements you missed because well, you neglected to take a gander at your journal in time. What's more, it implied searching for an hour that additionally fit the calendar of every other person going to the occasion. It was, in every case, such an agony. Be that as it may, this manual for utilizing Google Calendar in 2020 and past will tell you the best way to take advantage of this advanced schedule.

The development of computerized schedules had made everything so a lot simpler. You no longer need to keep a journal with you consistently. For whatever length of time that you have your cell phone with you, you'll approach your schedule.

The schedule will send warnings so you can be sure that you didn't overlook anything, and no arrangement is missed. What's more, you can even impart your plan to other people to perceive what an associate has arranged and can locate an extra an ideal opportunity to meet. It's an entirely different approach to sort out time, and it's been a pleasant change. It's likewise been an unexpected and unnatural change.

In October 2017, that absence of clearness turned out to be precise. Google redesigned its schedule just because of 2011. It revealed a device that is cleaner and neater that gathers up some superfluous highlights (and a not many that individuals delighted in.

The outcome is a hugely incredible time the board apparatus that we don't generally have the foggiest idea of how to utilize. We mollify ourselves with including an occasion, and we're astounded, here and there obnoxiously, when our Google schedule consequently consists of an event taken from a private email. Be that as it may, we just utilize a small number of its capacities, and we disregard a considerable lot of the manners by which our schedule can improve our lives.

In this manual for Google Calendar, we're going to take you through all of Google Calendar's astounding capacities.

We'll begin with the basic stuff. At that point, our manual for Google Calendar will go entirely through its propelled settings and take a gander at two or three separate ways to broaden the forces of Google's spare time the executive's stage.

6.1 Getting Started

Fortunately, you don't have to begin with Google Calendar successfully. For whatever length of time you have a Google account, and about 1.2 billion individuals do, you don't have to do anything over open calendar.google.com or raise your application. On the off possibility that you've marked into your Google account, you'll as of now be signed in. On the off possibility that you don't yet have a Google account, when you open that page, you'll be welcome to enroll. It's free and doesn't take over a few seconds.

On the off possibility that your cell phone utilizes Android, at that point, you should find that Google's schedule application is as of now introduced. On the off chance that it's not on the landing page, you may think that it's covered in your application cabinet. The one resembles this:

When you've opened a calendar in your program or on your cell phone, you don't have to do whatever else. It will, as of now, be set up and prepared for use. Both the site and the versatile application have a settings symbol that lets you play with the method that Google Calendar looks and works—and you may likewise need to bring your old schedule into your new one.

Bringing in Your Calendar

Not many individuals start their schedules with a clear record. On the off possibility that you've been utilizing an alternate schedule application, for example, Outlook or Apple Calendar, you'll have to import your information to Google Calendar. That shouldn't be hard!

To start with, open your schedule on your PC. That will make it simpler to spare your information and move it around, and regardless, bringing in to Google Calendar must be done on a PC, not on a cell phone.

In your source schedule, look in the menus for an Export work. Schedule information can take various organizations. CSV is the best with Google Calendar, yet if you're sending out from an Apple Calendar, pick a card. Ensure that you know where you spared the data! In Google Calendar on your PC, click the settings symbol at the upper right. Under Import and fare, pick Import.

Other Calendar Importing Options

That technique ought to be sufficiently clear, and it shouldn't present you with any issues. Be that as it may, if moving from an Apple Calendar to Google Calendar does not go as smoothly as you would like, there is a subsequent strategy.

First, you'll have to change the default schedule on your iOS gadget to your Google account. Open Settings > Calendar on your iPhone or iPad, and press Default Calendar, pick your Google account. Snap iCloud > Accounts, and slide the catch with the goal that it's in the on position.

The following piece is the place it begins to get fun.

Sign in to iCloud and tap the Calendar symbol. Pick the schedule you wish to fare and snap the communicate logo on the right. You'll see a window checked Calendar Sharing.

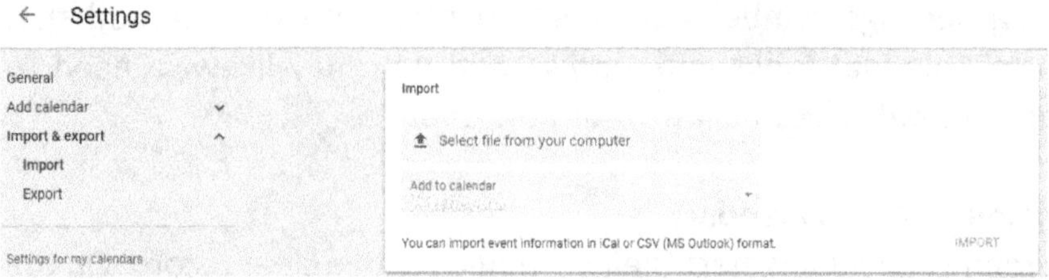

Schedule Website Settings

When you've set up your Google Calendar, you can begin playing with the settings. The settings symbol for Google's Calendar site is at the upper right of the screen.

Snap the machine gear-piece, and you'll create a drop-down menu, with the Settings at the head of the rundown. Pick Settings, and on the left of the screen, you'll see a rundown of the entirety of the settings that you can alter in your schedule.

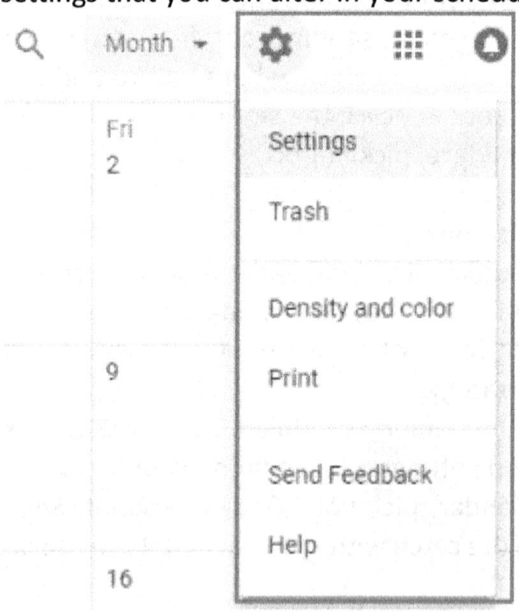

Language and Region

A portion of those settings is direct. Google will set the Language and area dependent on the data it gathers naturally from your Internet association; however, you can transform them if you need to utilize a language and locale that is not the same as your immediate area.

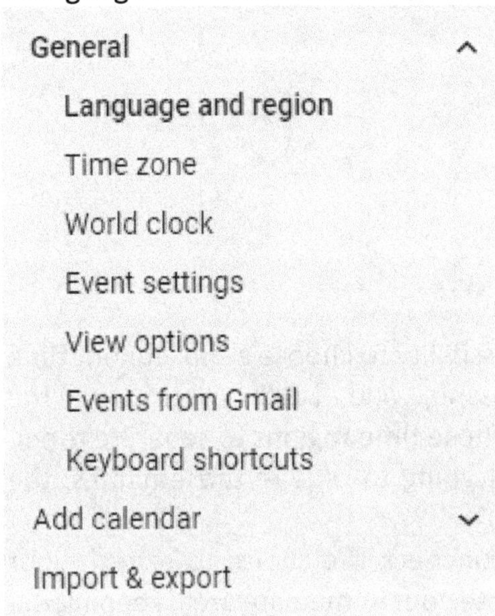

Time Region

The equivalent is valid for your Time zone, yet this is somewhat more mind-boggling. Make an occasion, and Google will naturally utilize your neighborhood time. Welcome another person to join that occasion, and they'll see it in their neighborhood time as well.

So on the off possibility that you were writing in your schedule in New York that you needed to put a call to somebody in California, you may consider them to be of the call at 11 a.m.; however, your partner would think it to be 8 a.m. As you travel, the occasions utilized by your schedule conform to the neighborhood time region. That change ought to happen naturally. Google will change its time region dependent on your IP address or your phone information. No matter how it might be, on the off chance that it doesn't occur—if you're utilizing a VPN, for instance, or not associated with the Internet—you can likewise show several time region settings in your scheduled place, where you happen to be.

You can change your schedule's time region settings physically.
To show more than one time-region setting on the schedule, open Settings, pick a time zone and check Display secondary time region.

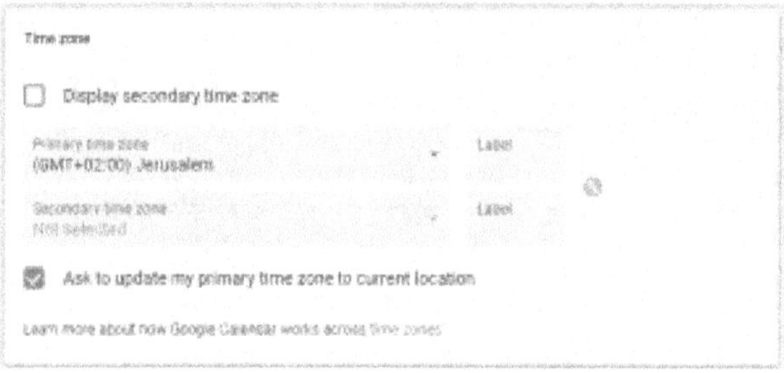

You'll, at that point, have the possibility to choose a subsequent time region from a drop-down menu, and you'll even have the opportunity to apply a mark to those time regions to separate them. (By and by, you're probably not going to require those names; the spot name should be adequate.)
This is likewise where you can uncheck the choice to refresh your essential time region to coordinate your immediate area, keeping the occasions on your schedule to one zone paying little heed to your area.
What's more, if you're utilizing many schedules, a component we'll talk about later, you can once in a while make distinctive time regions for each schedule. Snap the schedule in the Settings; at that point, select Calendar Setting and change the time region. Few out of every odd schedule permits that change, yet it very well may be a helpful method to monitor another person's occasions in another time region.

World Clock

On a PC, you can likewise add a World Clock to your schedule. It implies that you can include the time in different pieces of the world to the side of your schedule.

Pick the World Clock alternative in General > Settings, check Show world clock, and add the areas you need to pick. They show up on the left of the screen beneath the month see.

This is not something you're going to see on your cell phone, yet when you're pulling up your Google Calendar on your more widescreen, having the option to see the time in various pieces of the world can be a decent touch.

Event Settings

Underneath the default span settings is the choice to make Speedy Meetings. Check the container and 30-minute gatherings will naturally be planned to the most recent 25 minutes, while more extended gatherings will be cut by ten minutes.

The point says Google is to improve productivity; however, a superior use is a point at which you're planning consecutive gatherings. If you need to run starting with one gathering then onto the next, it merits utilizing that opportunity to allow yourself to arrive at the gathering room, get a much-needed refresher, or take a restroom break.

The Default Guest Permissions isn't the easiest to use in a bit of plan; however, it sets the capacities that others welcome to an occasion can use on that schedule occasion. There are just three alternatives: visitors can adjust an occasion, changing the time, area, or the span; for instance, they can welcome others and visitors on occasion, and they can see a list of people to attend.

For the various individuals going to the occasion, it merits rec.
They can change those settings. On the off possibility that you need someone to have the option to change the hour of the gathering on the off chance that they have to, or you don't need everybody to see who else will be there, those settings will give you more authority over the passage in your schedule.

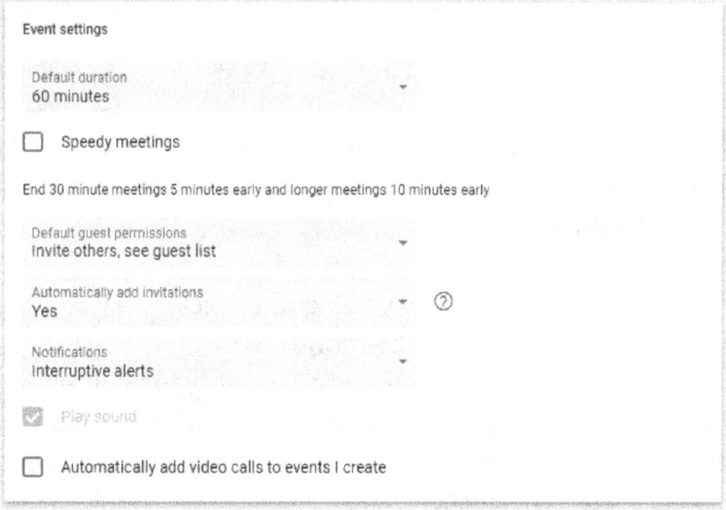

Solicitations

The following setting is indistinct to such an extent that Google needed to include a logical note.

The Automatically Add Invitations setting decides if you see solicitations consequently in your schedule or whether you'll just observe them after you've acknowledged them. You have three alternatives. In the first place, add all solicitations to your schedule. Second, put all solicitations to your schedule; however, just get warnings about the occasions you haven't declined. Or then again, third, pick only to see occasions that you've acknowledged on your schedule.

None of those alternatives are more productive than the other, yet on the off chance, your schedule is now swarmed, and you're hoping to prune occasions from your dates. At that point, just naturally, embedding occasions you've acknowledged is a decent spot to start.

Notices

The sort of Notifications you decide to get when you're sitting in your work area is significant. You can turn notes off, limit them to program warnings, or go the entire hoard and pick interruptive Alerts. Those interruptive alarms are truly interruptive. In case you're highly involved with work, the loud bongs they send—and remember that they'll be rehashed on your cell phones—will positively wake you up. If you discover them excessively troublesome, this is the spot to come to restrain the agony.

At long last, in this segment, you can decide to add video calls to occasions naturally. Besides utilizing Google Hangouts for each occasion you make, you'll need to ensure that crate is unchecked. It won't do you any damage, yet observing a chance to make a Hangout bring in each occasion depiction just stops up the passage.

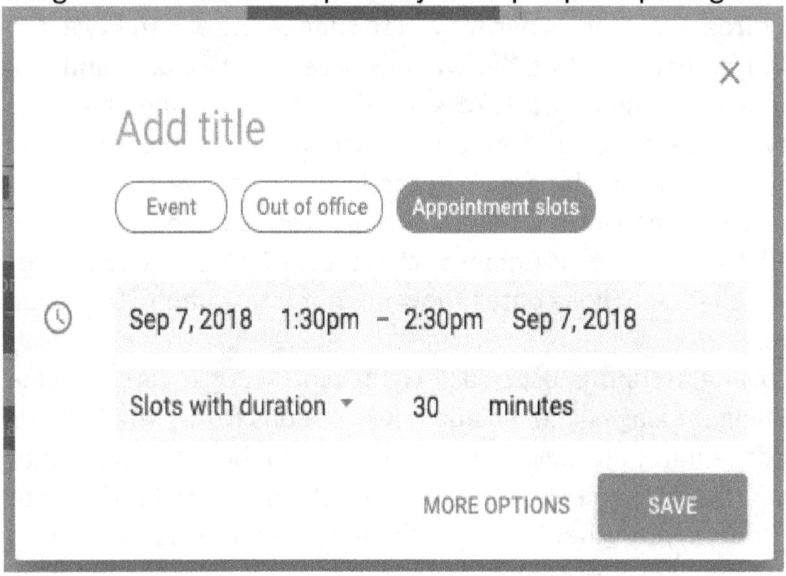

View Options

The "View Options" decides the presence of your Google Calendar. Once more, these settings are shrouded down in the Settings menu; yet they directly affect the presence of your schedule both on a cell phone and on PC. Some of them are likewise more valuable than others. You most likely don't need the schedule to show declined occasions or show week numbers, an element that puts a number close to every week in the year. In any case, deciding to diminish the splendor of past events will help keep the schedule looking clean. Having the option to see schedules one next to the other in Day View is probably going to be exceptionally helpful if you're utilizing or dealing with various schedules used by multiple individuals. Clerical specialists at large organizations will need to ensure that they have that alternative.

The last three alternatives permit you to change the day to begin the week. Not all nations start the working week on Monday, and you should have the option to take a gander at a schedule that puts Saturday above all else. You can decide to begin the week on Saturday, Sunday, or Monday. You can likewise change the number of days visible in each view and include various schedules from around the globe, such as Chinese schedules, a Hebrew schedule, or a Persian schedule. Those dates show up, notwithstanding the Julian schedule.

The following setting is especially significant. Google can examine approaching messages and include any occasions from Gmail it finds to your schedule naturally. It tends to be valuable. It implies that when you request a ticket on the web or get a messaged greeting to supper when you check your schedule, you'll discover those occasions previously entered—frequently with a perfect structure. Yet, if you're not mindful that Google is perusing your email along these lines, it tends to be astonishing. The settings permit you to kill the element.

Console Shortcuts

At long last, you can empower console accessible routes, an element we'll come to later in this guide.

Those are the settings that are accessible when you utilize your Google Calendar on the web. Yet, what makes the schedule so valuable is that these passages stay with you when you leave your work area and get your cell phone or tablet PC. Your PC or your screen may be simpler to peruse and utilize the schedule, yet on your telephone, it is consistent. The settings on your cell phone change just somewhat from those on your PC—however, they are considerably less clear.

- Google Calendar App Settings
- google versatile schedule settings

At the head of the rundown is the "Connect to General settings," which are equivalent to those on the site. However, a couple of which are remarkable to the application.

General Settings

The main general settings are direct. You can change the day when you start the week and decide to utilize the gadget's time region (a significant element when you're voyaging) and physically enter a time region.

You can likewise decide to show week numbers and declined occasions, and change the default occasion term from an hour to one of five different choices from fifteen minutes to two hours.

The following settings are all the more intriguing. Notices let you turn off warnings on the gadget or look over a considerable rundown of various tones that will signal at you to help you to remember the occasion, and flip the vibrate settings.

It merits remembering that while all schedules will have a similar warning tone (you can't make various sounds similarly that you can create distinctive ringtones), you can change the notification settings for each schedule. In Settings, pick a schedule and select one of the settings under Default notices and Default warnings throughout the day occasions.

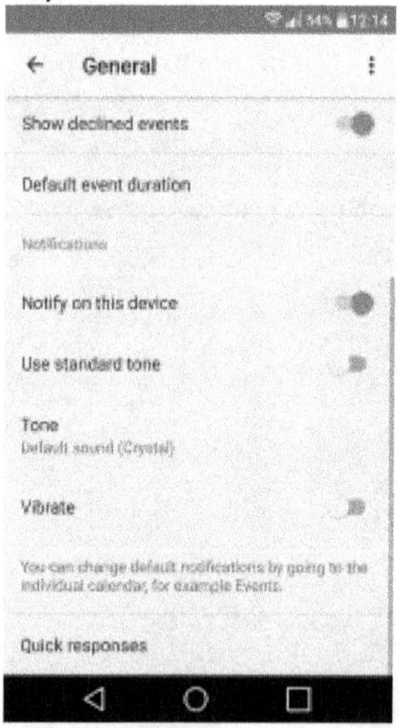

Quick Responses

The last setting in this area is the most valuable and presumably the most neglected. Brisk reactions let you pick one of four robotized messages to send to visitors for an occasion if you're running late or can't make it. Snap-on one of the reactions, and you'll have the option to alter the content. To utilize the response, tap or snap an occasion, select the visitors, and pick the response. You can change the content then as well.

Come back to the principle settings menu, and you'll discover more settings to play with, not many of which are plain as day.

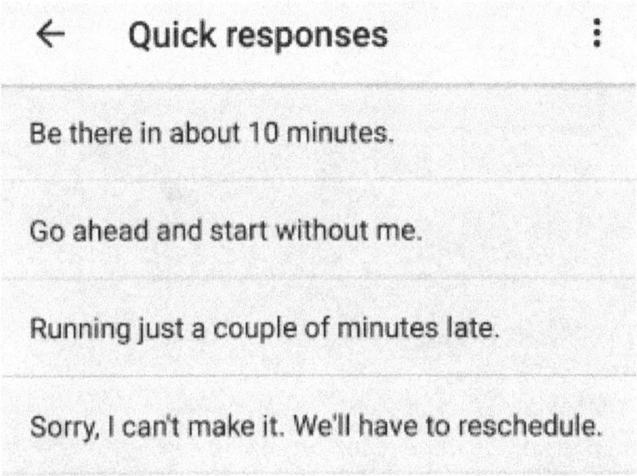

Occasions

The following choice events decide how occasions show up on your varied schedule. You change the shade of the square of time the occasion takes up on the schedule, and you can change the default notices, modifying the measure of time before the occasion when your telephone gives you a ping. You can likewise include a subsequent warning, and you can decide the settings for the notices of occasions that take throughout the day.

The following setting concerns the shade of Reminders. These are passages that must be made on Google's schedule application; while you can see updates on your work area and change their hues, cross them out when you complete them and erase them, you can't make an update on your PC. You can just make an occasion.

We'll disclose how to make an update later, yet they're passages put in the schedule that are restored naturally consistently until you mark them as done. They show up in the schedule with a symbol as a bit of string attached to a finger, and they're intended to be somewhat disturbing in any event.

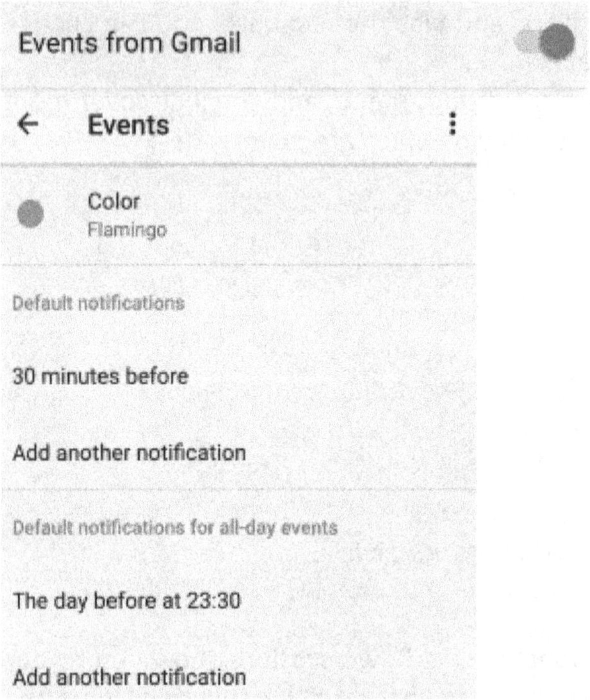

Telephone

The setting stamped Phone couldn't be less precise, and Google does not assist in making sense of what it is for. On many cell phones, it's likewise wholly superfluous. These are sections that have been matched up naturally with the gadget's schedule application. So on the off chance that you've begun utilizing the schedule that accompanied your Samsung or Huawei gadget at that point changed to Google Calendar, you'll discover those passages as of now set up. You can change their warning settings and the shading where they're featured.

More

At long last, under a heading creatively named "More," you can change the settings of the information from some other schedules you may be utilizing. Birthday celebrations, for instance, let you decide to include any birthday celebrations recorded in your contacts and from Your Circles on Google+. That merits remembering. If you've set up hovers in Google+ and somebody has included their birthday data, you could well find that your schedule incorporates the birthday celebrations of a lot of individuals you scarcely know. Change the setting to "Contacts," and you'll keep your schedule individual.

Google schedule application birthday settings

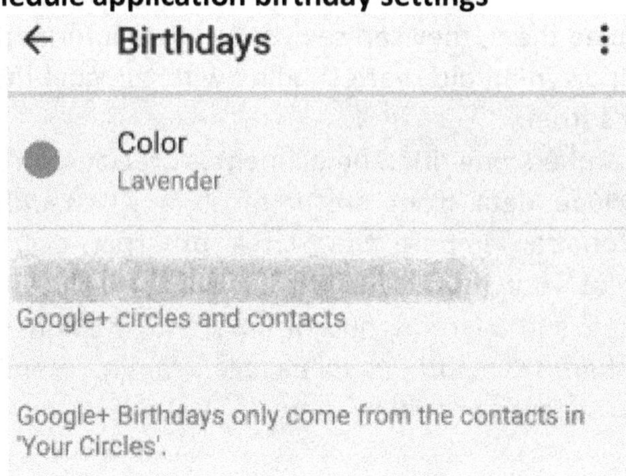

Those are the settings. They're not all bright, and they're available on both the work area and the versatile application. They're likewise dissipated all through various pieces of the application. Take a picture of the three spots after the rundown of each schedule on the left half of your work area screen. For instance, you'll be offered a palette to change the shades of the occasions from each schedule as the settings for that schedule, for example, the wellspring of birthday information.

Fortunately, once you've set up your schedule, you indeed shouldn't have to contact the settings once more. In any instance, on the off chance that you find that you're seeing the birthday events of individuals you don't have a clue or that the default span of a gathering is a few hours, delving around the settings will give you a superior search for your schedule.

Making Multiple Calendars

One of the most significant highlights of Google Calendar is additionally the most confusingly named. Adding a schedule to your Google Calendar doesn't include another schedule. Instead, it takes information from an alternate schedule and places it in yours. Dissimilar to bringing in schedule information; however, that information is continually refreshed. You can see others' occasions and, if you need them, they can see yours. Every information source can be set apart in an alternate shading with the goal that you can see where it's from.

Despite its cumbersome title, the element is precious. It implies that you can include data from pretty much any schedule to your schedule. You can import the dates of strict occasions, the installations of your preferred games group, moon stages, NASA dispatch plans, and a large group of different occasions—including schedules shared by other colleagues, family members, and companions. As far as possible is simply the space in your schedule.

6.2 Adding Calendars by URL and sharing them

The determination of "schedules of intrigue" will cover the most significant timetables that you'll need to add to your schedule; however, there are many others accessible on the web. You can include them by sticking in their URL.

Snap from URL alternatives either from the "IN" addition to symbol close to the schedule or in the settings, and you'll be suggested a field you can enter the URL of a calendar accessible on the Internet.

Include google schedule from URL

The schedules should be in iCal design. iCalShare, for instance, offers a vast number of free schedules covering points that extend from strict occasions to NASA dispatch plans.

You can likewise decide to make that schedule freely available. In case you're taking it from an open-source, you won't have to.

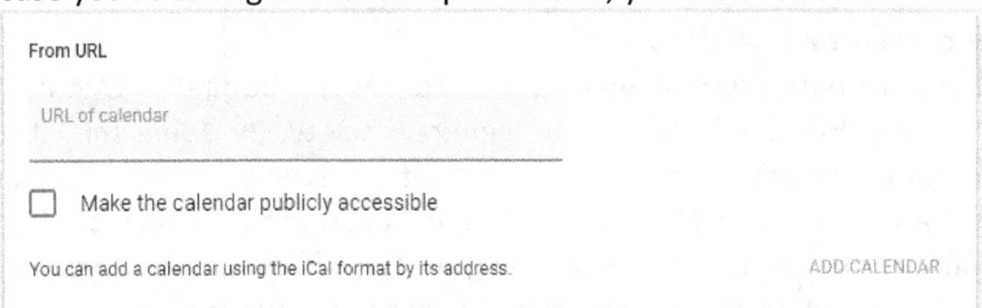

Sharing Your Calendar

The capacity to impart your schedule to others is one of the most significant highlights of Google Calendar. The procedure is additionally a little fiddly. Once more, it must be performed on the schedule's site.

Float the cursor over the schedule; you need to share and snap the three specks that show up toward the stopping point. On a schedule that you've made, you'll be offered the choice to Display this lone, an alternative that expels the various timetables from your schedule. You can likewise pick a readied shading for that schedule (or blend your very own shade) — and you can move to the Settings and sharing page.

We've just perceived how intricate and far-reaching those settings can be, so we can jump directly to the two parameters that are pertinent here.

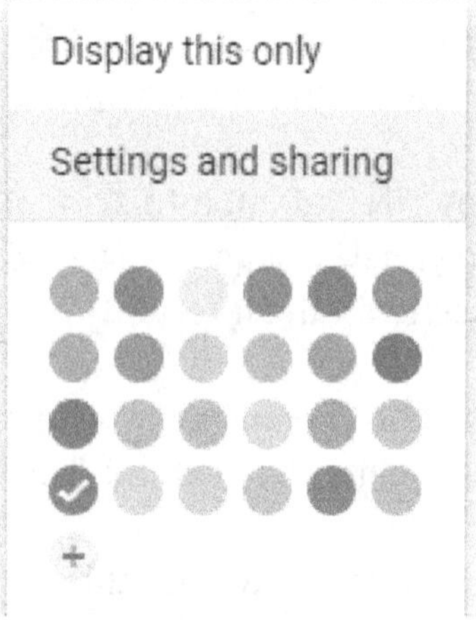

Two Important Settings

There are two alternatives to get to consents. The first is to make your schedule accessible to the general society. By doing this, it'll permit everybody to see your schedule. It will even turn up in Google list items. You should take some time to consider this before picking that alternative. It may merit doing on the off chance that you've made a schedule explicitly to share the dates of your open occasions; however, for people, it's best kept away from on the off possibility that you need to shield your security.

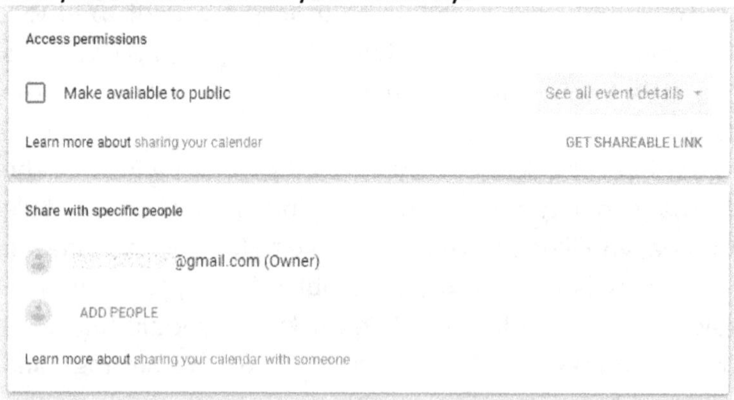

On the off chance that you choose to make your schedule open, you can likewise get a shareable connection that you can provide for other people so they can discover your schedule. Without tapping the checkbox that makes your schedule open, that URL will have no utilization.

Google schedule get to authorizations sharing settings

Increasingly accommodating is the capacity to impart your schedule to explicit individuals. Enter their email address, and that individual will approach the information in that schedule: they'll see the occasions that you've entered in your timetable on their schedules.

Offer Your Google Calendar with a Group

One of the least known elements of Google Calendar is both of its generally valuable and one of the fiddliest to utilize. While correspondences stages like WhatsApp permit gatherings of individuals to trade messages, Google permits groups to share a schedule. It's an incredible path for voluntary associations, church gatherings, schools, and work environments to share occasions.

There are two or three standard methods to do it.

The simplest is to make another schedule by squeezing the in addition to symbol close to "Include a companion's schedule" and picking a new schedule. In the settings for that schedule, you can Share with explicit individuals and include each gathering part's email address independently. In case you're just adding a couple of individuals, it's presumably the ideal approach.

Gathering Calendar Issues

That as it may, if you've made a vast gathering, and particularly on the off chance that you need to accomplish something, share a schedule with that gathering, it's worth initially making a Google gathering. You can do this at groups.google.com. The fields are quite plain as day, and it won't take you over a couple of moments to finish them.

At the point when you're set, and you've made the gathering, that gathering will have its email address. It will be something like this: [name]@googlegroups.com. At the point when you need to share a schedule that you've made to list that gathering's occasions, rather than entering the email address of every part, you'll have the option to enter the email address of the gathering simply. All the individuals from the gathering will approach that schedule.
Remember, however, that sharing the gathering to your schedule isn't sufficient for the gathering's individuals to see the gathering's occasions right away. Every part will get initial an email with a connection that they have to click.

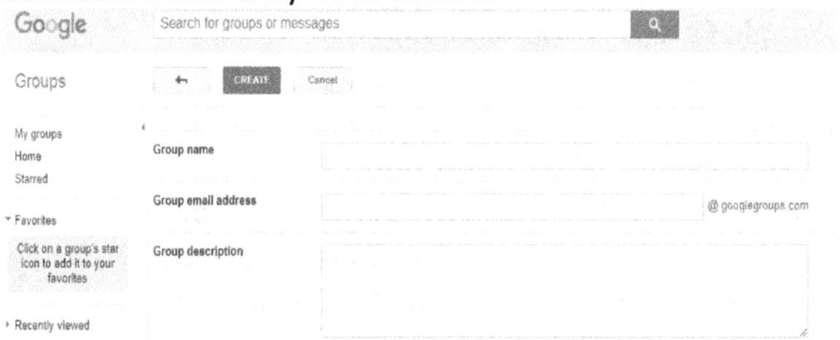

Organizing Your Calendars

Google and its schedule are brilliant, yet they're not prodigies. If you have different occasions around the same time, Google Calendar battles to place them in the request you need to see.
The prioritization it utilizes begins consistently. Occasions are introduced in subsequent requests paying little heed to the calendar on which they show up. In this way, if your schedule says that you have a workforce conference at 10 a.m., your schedule records a feast with your folks at 7 p.m.; at that point, the workforce gathering will be recorded first in your schedule, and the supper will be recorded second.

Be it as it can, what happens if you have more than one opportunity during the day? Google can't decide which one it's going to mention first, so it reports them in sequential order queries. On the off chance that your schedule expressed that you were going through the day with your family and your work schedule advised you that you were withdrawn from the workplace that day, you'd see whichever throughout the day occasion starts things out in the letter set.
Google's organization, for throughout the day occasions, is alpha-numeric. In the possible chance that you intend to get them organized every day, place a number before each of the occasion names. It's somewhat of a cumbersome workaround, yet it works.

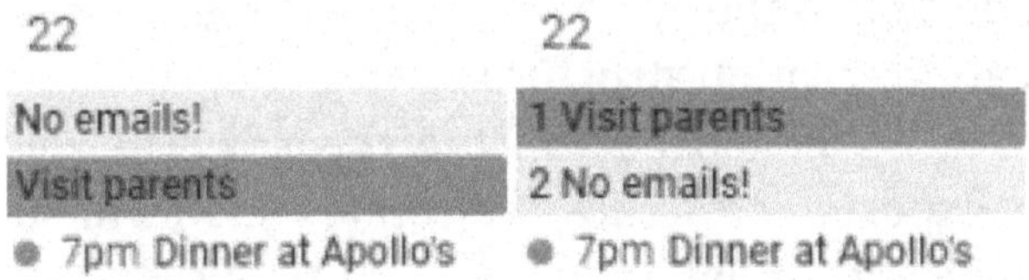

It would have been beneficial if they had called those schedules "calendars" or something like recognize them from the real posting of days and weeks that you can see on the screen. Yet, the production of various schedules will be a piece of your time during the board work process.

6.3 Editing Your Calendar

Presently, you've made your schedule. It's set up how you need it. You've included numerous various calendars. What's more, you've imparted a portion of those calendars to companions, associates, or family. Presently you get the opportunity to put sections into that schedule. There are heaps of various approaches to do that—and more than one sort of passage.

Instructions to Add an Event

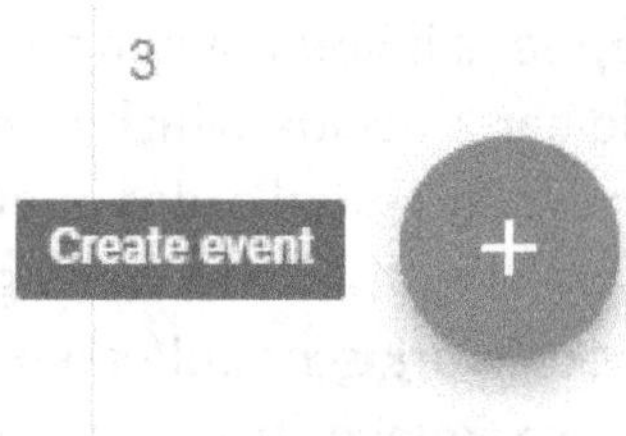

Make occasion on google schedule site

You can include occasions both from the schedule site and from the application. What you can do on every one of those, stages; however, is marginally unique.

There are two different ways to make an occasion on the site.

You can tap on the in addition to the symbol at the base right of the page to see the full occasion creation structure.

Or on the other, hand you can tap out on the town, which will produce a smaller than expected structure, welcoming you to fill in the occasion's most significant subtleties.

Include Event Form

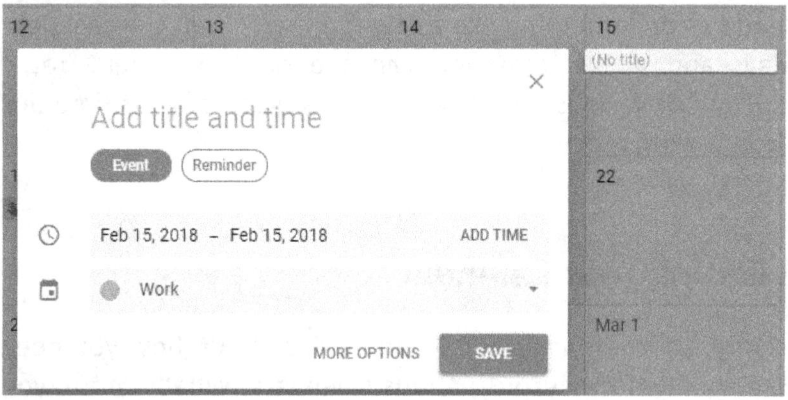

At the head of the layout is the guidance to Add title and time.

Make google schedule occasion structure

All you will type is the title. This is the thing that you'll find in the schedule—and recall that in case you're making more than one throughout the day occasion around the same time, those titles will be orchestrated in a subsequent request.

Next, you can pick between making an occasion or an update. We'll return to updates later; however, the default setting is to create an occasion. You'd, at that point, get the opportunity to enter a date. Since you tapped on a day to raise the structure, the default setting is that the occasion will last the entire day and will just happen on that day. Snap-on one of those dates, however, and Google will offer a month to month plan that permits you to enter several days. That single day occasion can turn into seven days in length happening, for example, a get-away or a gathering.

Different Options

On the off possibility that it's not occurring throughout the day, you'll likewise need to enter a beginning and end time by clicking Add Time.

Finally, if you've made different schedules, you can pick the schedule you need to utilize. That is significant and barely noticeable. Pick an inappropriate schedule, and anybody you're imparting that schedule won't have the option to see the occasion. Snap Save, and you'll be finished. The occasion will be on the schedule.

In any case, you can accomplish more. Press the More Options interface close to the Save catch, and you'll be taken to a nitty-gritty structure with a vast amount of various choices. A large portion of them is apparent; however, some interest a little idea.

- Add Complete Event Form
- After the title and the time is a choice to change the Time Zone.

Google Schedule Make the Event Site Structure

This isn't something that you're going to require frequently; however, it may be valuable if the occasion will occur in an alternate time region. You can even begin the occasion in a one-time area and end it in another. This is relevant if you're physically entering the subtleties of a flight or posting a gathering on a maritime yacht.

You would then be able to stamp the occasion as enduring throughout the day, and you can make it a typical occasion. Clicking does not rehash records various approaches to check the occasion as repeating, so you don't need to make another passage without fail.

Google will offer to make the occasion day by day, week by week, month to month, yearly, every weekday or end of the week, or simply let you make sense of it for yourself. For standard occasions, for example, week by week staff gatherings, it's a valuable instrument.

Event Details

The following area is increasingly confusing. This is the place you can enter the occasion subtleties. You don't need to do this stuff; however, it tends to be helpful, particularly if you're welcoming others to participate.

Begin to include an area, and Google will finish the location for you. That is not the only comfort. It likewise transforms the space into a connection that a visitor can snap to see on Google Maps. The more exact you make that area data, the simpler it will be for visitors to discover where they're going.

On the off possibility that you've changed the settings to expel, conferencing can click Add conferencing to bring back Google Hangouts. You likely won't have any desire to; however, you can't expel this choice from the structure.

Other Event Detail Options

The following alternative is the sort of warning you can get. This is surprisingly convoluted. You can decide to get the notice by email or get it as a notice in your program or on your cell phone. You can set to what extent before the occasion you get that notice in minutes, hours, days, or weeks, and you can include more warnings just if you—or your visitors—may overlook. In case you're setting up a significant occasion, for example, a wedding, those recurrent warnings sent far out can be helpful.

You can then change the schedule on which the occasion will be posted, and you can change the shade of the occasion. That can be valuable as well. When all said is done, occasion hues will coordinate the shading you've set for the schedule; however, on the off possibility that you need a specific occasion to stick out, you can likewise give it an uncommon shading.

The following choice identifies with protection. The occasion will have Default perceivableness. Anybody you've imparted your schedule to will have the option to see all the occasion subtleties. They'll likewise have the opportunity to see those subtleties if you change the permeability to open. On the off possibility that you set the occasion to private, at that point, even individuals who can, for the most, part observe your occasions won't have the option to see the subtleties of this one. Instead, they'll know that you're either occupied or accessible, relying upon the setting you pick.

At long last, in this area, you can likewise incorporate a depiction of the occasion. For most occasions, the title is probably going to be adequate. Yet, including some additional detail here, such as clothing standards or meeting themes, can be helpful. You can even include connections and connections, which makes the portrayal highlight especially important when masterminding a conference. Transfer the plan, for instance, and individuals will comprehend what's in store.

The territory on the screen's privilege lets you include visitors so they can see it on their schedules and permit them to connect with the occasion in various manners. You can let them change the occasion, welcome others to participate, and see every other person who has been welcomed. Of those three, you'll most likely just need to check the last box.

There are several more things that you can do when you're making an occasion on Google Calendar.

The head of the page, close to the Save button, is a drop-down menu called More activities. Pull that down, and you'll get a suggestion of rundown of actions that you can perform on the occasion you've made.

Step by step instructions to create a Reminder

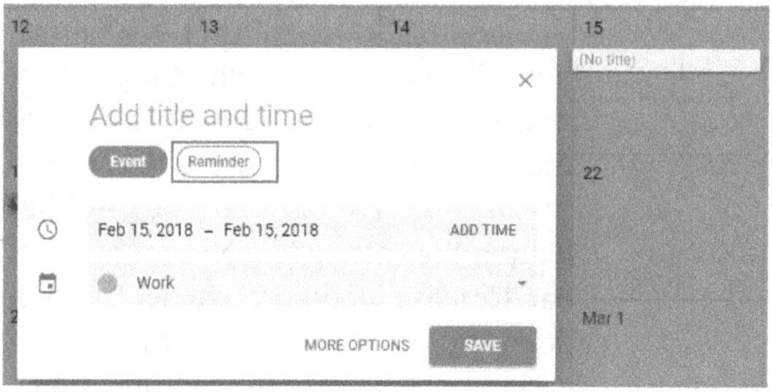

Press the "in addition" to the symbol on the Google Calendar application and get three choices. These incorporate the alternative to set an objective, make an update, and make an occasion. None of those choices is offered when you click a similar symbol on the PC, yet one is accessible. You will not see it when you press the logo, yet on the off chance that you click an unfilled spot in your calendar, the smaller than usual structure that Google offers permits you to make the two occasions and updates.

Snap that Reminder catch, and you'll get a structure that welcomes you to enter a title. Change the beginning date, demonstrate whether you need the suggestion to rehash and whether you need the idea to take up the entire day or whether you need it to trigger a warning at a specific time.

There are two contrasts between making an update and making an occasion.

Initial, an update shows up on your schedule. It's a little symbol that has a finger with a bit of string tied around it. Second, on the off possibility that you don't erase the update or imprint it as "done" on your schedule, it will at present show up the following day.

While you can make an update on your PC, it's substantially more helpful to make one on your cell phone. Press the "in addition to" symbol and afterward the Reminder alternative. This offers a rundown of mechanized updates. These updates incorporate booking a café by creating a call, sending an email, returning products, and dropping a reservation. Each offers a computerized list.

In principle, you ought to choose to make an update with only a couple of taps while never expecting to contact the console.

However, it merits recollecting that update in a schedule is to take back to mind something you've overlooked and done it in time.

Step by step instructions to set a Goal in Google Calendar

We've spared defining an objective till the finish of this area since it's so slick. All the highlights we've seen up to this point have been straightforward, and they've requested work from you.

You have to enter your occasion subtleties and set your updates. Without a doubt, Google can take nuances from your Gmail. In any case, some other organization, despite, everything needs to place those subtleties in the message, or you have to do it when you make your booking.

You can just set an objective on the application. Snap the in addition to the logo in the corner and pick the primary choice. Google will, at that, point offer a rundown of various objectives that you should accomplish and that request time. They incorporate exercise, fabricating an aptitude, such as learning a language, and meeting companions, saving time for yourself, and arranging your life.

Pick one, and Google will offer a rundown of choices. You can enter your custom objective. Decide to become familiar with ability. For instance, and Google will ask whether you need to gain proficiency with a language, figure out how to code, practice an instrument, or make artistry. Pick one of them, and Google will suggest another rundown, for example, a rundown of dialects; at that point, ask how regularly you need to rehearse, to what extent, and what time of day.

Google won't ask you which time you need to conjugate Spanish action words or practice the violin. It will ask you whether you need to do it toward the beginning of the day, evening, evening, or whenever.

If something arises and can't make the Time that Google has discovered, your schedule will naturally search for another time and reschedule. That can occur when you simultaneously enter the second occasion as the objective or on the off chance that you hit the Defer button when you get the notice.

You can likewise alter the objective by tapping the altered symbol. If you choose to finish a meeting early, you can bring it up on the schedule and hit the did it button. When you erase an appointment, you can choose between deleting only that solitary meeting or every single after meeting (and quit booking).

Computer-based intelligence Enabled

It's an exceptionally flawless component, yet what's too cunning about it is that it urges you to utilize your schedule—likewise, the schedule plans. The part uses a type of computerized reasoning to comprehend your timetable more readily. First, it looks through your schedule information to discover a period that suits you, expelling why you don't have the opportunity to work out or practice your Spanish action words. The more you utilize your schedule, the better the odds. Google will offer you a genuinely accessible period.

As you press "Concede" or alter the meeting to move it to another time, Google will better comprehend your way of life and change as needs are.

Step by step instructions to add an Event with a Key Press

Click the Q key, and Google Calendar will introduce the occasion smaller than the expected structure, permitting you to enter an occasion for the current day. It's quick and straightforward as long as you need to include an occasion that day.

Chapter 7: Other Features of Google

Google is a web internet searcher. It utilizes an exclusive calculation intended to recover and arrange query items to give the most significant and reliable wellsprings of information conceivable.

Google's expresses strategies to "sort out the world's data and make it generally available and helpful." It is the top internet searcher on the planet, a place that has produced analysis and worries about the force it needs to impact online data progression.

Google is prevailing to such an extent that the expression "Google" can likewise be utilized as an action word, so when somebody looks for something on Google, they may state they "Googled" it.

Google started as a hunting venture by Larry Page and Sergey Brin when they were Ph.D. understudies at Stanford University.

The internet searcher calculation they created was remarkable because it positioned pages' dependent on their substance, however on what number of different site pages connected back to them.

Page and Brin established that connects to a page were an indication of its online position, and Google's calculation in this way returned increasingly valuable outcomes, moving Google to turn into the most-utilized web search tool.

Google's calculation was protected and named PageRank. The ebb and flow search innovation depend on a portion of these standards; however, it has developed to a lot more factors impacting everything.

Although the Google organization has since spread out to give numerous different items past inquiry, the web crawler is as yet Google's most well-known help.

Staying aware of Google can destroy you because the organization consistently has something new to offer. Not all things work; however, Google tries continuously. Here are recent highlights that are turning out now for Google's applications and gadgets.

7.1 Google Forms-Free Online Surveys for Personal Use

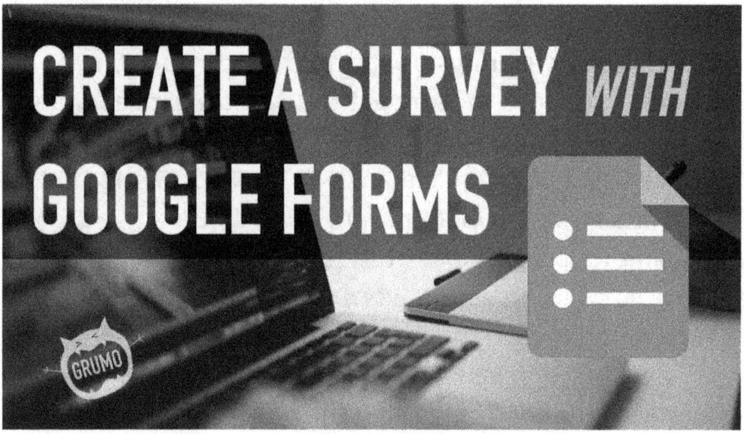

A Google Form is an extraordinary method to assemble data identified with gatherings or meetings. Andy Wolber discloses how to make it work for you.

Google Forms give a quick method to do an online review, with reactions gathered in an online spreadsheet. Make your review and welcome respondents by email.

Individuals answer your inquiries from practically any internet browser - including versatile cell phone and tablet programs. Every reaction in a separate line of a spreadsheet, with each question, appeared in a segment. What's more, Google Forms are free.

Structures

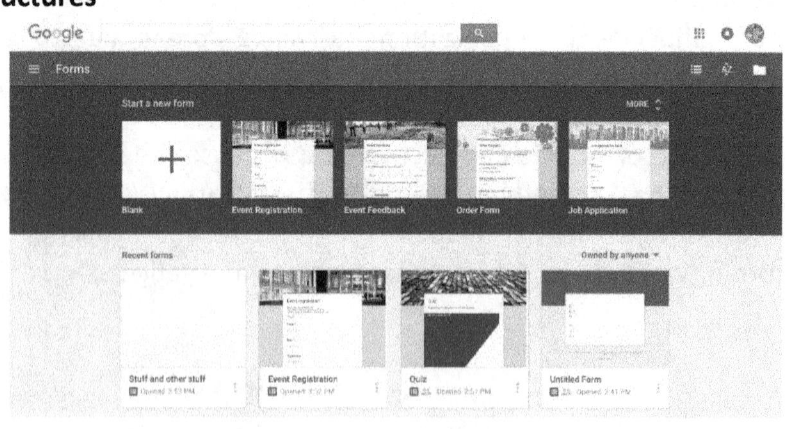

A Google Form is an extraordinary method to accumulate data identified with gatherings or meetings, for instance, before a group, gather the names and contact data for participants. On the day of an audience, study individuals to smooth out your lunch request. After the gathering, utilize a review to get criticism on meeting meetings and assemble development proposals.

In any case, Google Forms isn't directly for each circumstance. As of October 2012, Forms needs "skip rationale" found in some online overview devices. "Skip rationale" lets you construct an "on the off chance that -" succession: on the off chance that an individual reacts "yes," at that point pose inquiry and, in any case, raise inquiry B. On the off chance that you need skip rationale, THEN a Google Form isn't the correct device.

You can make a Google Form rapidly: Google discharged a "single tick" Chrome Web Store application to create a Google Form on October 23, 2013. The discharge corresponded with the dispatch of a few single tick Chrome Web Store applications to make Docs, Sheets, and Slides. Chrome program clients can introduce these applications from their separate connections in the Web Store. (In case you're a Chrome OS client, you can substantially hold up a piece. The links ought to show up as a significant aspect of a framework update.)

Google Forms in the Chrome Web Store

Make a basic overview structure

To begin, we should expect you have four things: a Google account with Google Drive empowered, the Chrome program, and the Google "a single tick" Forms web application introduced. Follow the connections to get every one of these three things, if necessary.

1. Snap-on the Forms web application symbol

The Forms symbol will be recorded nearby your other Chrome web applications, which show up when you include another tab.

Google Forms web application symbol

2. A single tick

The "a single tick" Forms web application opens another program tab, loaded up with a clear Form.

New Google Form page

3. Overview arrangement

Give your overview a title, alongside an illustrative sentence or two.
Three checkbox alternatives show at the head of the overview:
Permit clients to alter reactions
Require sign-in to see this structure
Consequently, gather respondent's client name

4. Include and alter questions

Next, include your inquiries. Each question has a Question Title and Help Text field. The Help Text field can be utilized to clarify a positioning framework (e.g., "Utilize 5 to demonstrate the best, one the most noticeably terrible.")

Each question has a checkbox alternative to "Make this a necessary inquiry." Utilize this only if the data is fundamental. For instance, you may require an individual's name on a lunch menu overview.

At the point when you move the cursor over an inquiry, altering controls show up. Snap the pencil symbol to alter.

Google Forms offers seven distinct inquiry types:

- ✓ Text, for short answers;
- ✓ Section text, for article-length reactions;
- ✓ Numerous decision, where one response from many might be chosen;
- ✓ Checkboxes, where innumerable things might be selected;
- ✓ Look over a rundown (valuable for segment classification questions, for instance);
- ✓ Scale, for positioning stuff from 0 to 10; and
- ✓ Network, for giving a reaction from 1 to 5.
- ✓ On the off possibility that your study is unusually long, include Section Headers or Page Breaks between questions. Supplement these things by tapping on the "+Add Item" menu in the upper left at the head of the structure.
- ✓ Separation long studies into areas or pages

5. Alter the Survey Completion Confirmation

Alter the content, respondents will see after finishing the education. To do this, click on the "More activities" drop-down menu found in the upper right corner; at that point, select "alter affirmation." Make sure to thank individuals for their reactions.

Review finishing affirmation

6. Convey the overview

Snap "email this structure" to convey the overview.

Email the connection to the review

Then again, you can convey a connection to the study on Google+.

Offer a review on Google+

7. View reactions

Review reactions assemble in a spreadsheet spared to your Google Drive. Open the spreadsheet to see the responses.

View reactions in your Google Drive spreadsheet

8. Alter the review later

Should you have to alter the Google Form then, open the spreadsheet from your Google Drive. Snap-on the "Structure" menu thing and pick "Alter Form." This will help you to return the first screen, which is used to do the review.

- ✓ Alter your Form later
- ✓ More uses for Google Forms

Google Forms can likewise be inserted. This implies you can utilize a Google Form on your site. A site guest could enter their name and data, which would go straightforwardly into the spreadsheet.

Or on the other hand, utilize a structure to lead a study after a Google+ Hangout or occasion, since a Google Form can be shared on Google+. Offer the review with the general population or any of your Google+ circles. Google Forms makes online studies essential.

7.2 Google Photos

Propelled in 2015, Google Photos is a device that can store photographs, recordings, and screen captures taken by your telephone.

It's a strong media reinforcement available to you. Furthermore, because it's a cloud-based device, it can let loose space on your telephone. Also, it takes a shot at both Android and iOS gadgets.

Here are a couple of more things to think about how Google Photos functions:

How accomplished Google Photos work?

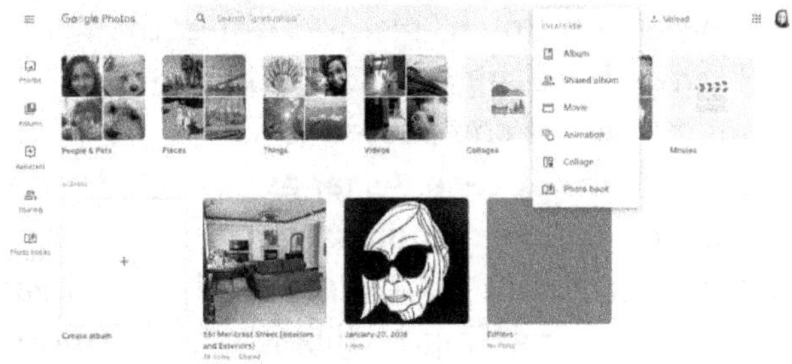

Google Photos clients can transfer new photographs, see, alter, spare, and make original recordings, liveliness, and arrangements, collections, and photographs books. You can likewise download everything, which means your cloud-based reinforcement would itself be able to be effortlessly sponsored up onto your PC or external hard drive.

For the individuals who don't have a Google gadget (like the Pixel telephone), you can select to naturally reinforce and sync your photographs and recordings as you take them. If you have an Android gadget, you can constrain reinforcement information use, so you don't come up short on information transferring things out of sight.

You can likewise set your Google Drive to keep a duplicate of your photographs and recordings by heading off to your drive's settings, turning on "Make a Google Photos Folder," and clicking save. As pictures are added to your record, they will be arranged into classifications.

You can spare and offer all your photographs and recordings on Google Photos.

Without much of a stretch, you can offer photographs and collections utilizing the offer element, regardless of whether they have pictures in them. Furthermore, if you have the "reinforcement and sync" include turned on, you can recover your records from the waste for as long as 60 days after hitting erase. Or on the other hand, you can generally file photographs to move them, yet have them stay accessible inside your record.

It has the free, boundless capacity — with a couple of warnings

Google Photos accompanies free, limitless capacity — yet that is just if you select to spare "top-notch" pictures rather than unique quality pictures, which may be a higher goal. That implies those more essential documents will be compacted to save space, except if your record's settings state in any case. As far as possible for photographs is 16MP, while recordings are compressed to 1080p.

You can permit auto-pressure for future transfers by heading off to your settings and choosing "high caliber." Furthermore, you can apply that change to past photographs by clicking "recuperate capacity," which is additionally situated inside settings.

For the individuals who want to go with unique document measures, it's free up to 15GB, and that incorporates everything from Photos to Gmail to everything else in the drive. From that point forward, you could overhaul through the Google One membership plan, beginning at $1.99 every month for 100GB.

It includes an AI-fueled colleague

Google Photos gives clients a ton of auto-produced additional items. For instance, it can make photograph book assortments, gathering pictures dependent on factors like the date, individuals, and the spots included. Clients are additionally given a choice to print and boat those books (for a charge obviously.)

Likewise, the Assistant will take photographs that were caught in quick progression and transform them into GIFs (alluded to as "activities").

At the same time, individual pictures can be spared as movement photographs — which means they record videos of a couple of moments when you've made an effort. These may likewise be known as Live Photos to iPhone clients.

It has other savvy highlights

The strong hunt alternative is a significant draw for the stage. It lets you look for normal subjects, similar to "canines" or "seashore" to limit your choices, which is particularly helpful because you haven't yet arranged your photos into collections.

It additionally gives you a choice to recognize various individuals in your photographs by physically putting a name to the face. From that point forward, pictures with those individuals are naturally arranged so you can later scan images that highlight explicit people. Tap the inquiry bar and snap the bolt close to the photograph air pockets to begin giving countenances friendly personalities inside your Photos.

In a comparable vein, you can likewise set it to make "live collections," which naturally populate with photographs of loved ones.

For those looking to reinforce their physical photograph prints, you can rapidly 'examine' those who have them transferred by taking a quick pic utilizing your telephone or different Photos-accommodating gadget. What's more, for the individuals who photo paper reports, Google Photos additionally lets you feature wanted segments of text, and even harvest out foundations to make it simpler to do things like transfer and cost a receipt from a work trip.

Google Photos is a ground-breaking and adaptable instrument that requires little exertion to use to its fullest. Also, given the way that it gives free, boundless capacity without relinquishing a lot on the photograph and video quality, it tends to be a healthy alternative for sponsorship up your media documents.

7.3 Google Keep-Notes and Lists

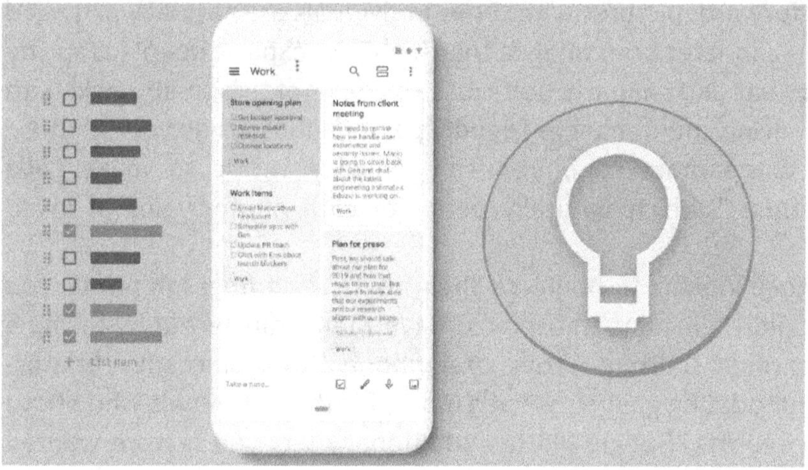

How about we talk about Google Keep. Do you recollect Google Keep? It should change in taking and arranging notes in 2013, yet it's confronted with a ton of rivalry.

A lot of profitability and hierarchical applications will assist you with shepherding your life over different gadgets. Evernote might be a PCMag Editors' Choice for note-taking applications. Yet, Keep has its advantages as a free, moderate device that improves the way toward sharing thoughts over different gadgets.

For instance, you can write down notes in Keep on your Android or iOS gadget while in travel, and get it later on your PC. Or then again, on the other hand, when you're going to take off to an arrangement, include information (like locations or bearings) on the web application so you can get to them out and about. Likewise, you can keep on the head of errands with daily agendas that can be added to or confirmed from various screens.

So if you haven't been utilizing Keep or had no clue it even existed, there are many reasons you should check out it. Peruse on to show signs of improvement feeling of what Google Keep offers you, and how you can all the more likely sort out your notes.

Effectively Copy to Google Docs

Probably the best advantage of "Keep" is its consistent incorporation with the whole Google environment. That implies, on the off possibility that you depend intensely on Gmail, Google Drive, or Google Docs, without much of a stretch, offer things in Keep between stages, from inside the Keep application or through a Google program that supports Keep.

In case you're in the application, you should simply tap a thing, select the three-spot menu, and pick Copy to Google Docs. A warning will reveal to you that the note is being spared; at that, point another notice will show up with a connection to a Google Doc that contains your Google Keep information.

Import things from Keep by tapping on the Keep symbol on the right side of the screen. This will open a side menu loaded with every one of your notes and pictures, which can be added to messages, Drive organizers, or existing reports. Either utilize the thing's three-spot menu or drag it into place.

Share and Collaborate with Others

Things in your Keep application can be shared legitimately with different clients without experiencing the standard offer menu you may see in various projects. Select a note or picture you wish to share and pick the individual symbol. You will have the choice to include a client's email address or their name from your contacts.

This transforms you both into teammates. Presently at whatever point anybody makes changes to a note, alters will consequently be noticeable to all individuals with whom it is shared; however, the first organizer can renounce access whenever.

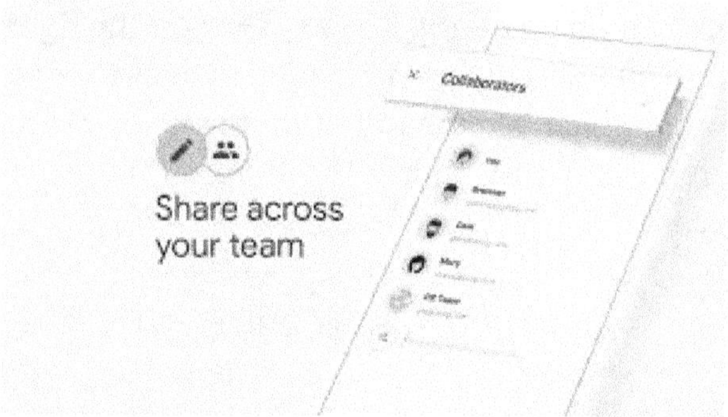

The Keep Widget: Always On, Always Live

Add a gadget to your telephone's home screen for speedy and straightforward access to your notes. Contingent upon the size of the device you pick, late notes can be seen directly on the home screen without opening the application.

Include the Android gadget by long-pushing on any vacant space on the telephone's home screen, tapping the Widget button, at that point, choosing Keep. On iOS, swipe directly from the home screen into Today View, look to the base, and tap Edit. Discover the Google Keep gadget and tap the, besides, to fasten to include it.

Interpret Text from Images

Keep on the web can interpret a text from pictures. Snap-on a transferred picture; at that point, click the three-speck menu and select Grab picture text. All content in the image will, at that point, be changed over into accessible and editable content.

It's ideal for digitizing data on business cards, indications of intrigue, and bits of paper. You can do likewise with transcribed notes, yet your mileage may change contingent upon your handwriting's nature.

Keep Is Your Stenographer

Ever had a splendid thought yet didn't record it promptly, and afterward, when you, at last, have a second, you locate that whatever you had as a primary concern is presently gone? Is it fair to say that you are a columnist needing an application that can translate interviews?

With the Google Keep application, you can direct a note into your gadget, and the chronicle will be deciphered into an accessible, editable note.

Set Reminders

Make a spring up update in Keep, and it will appear over your Google account. Begin making a note like you typically would and click the ringer symbol.

Set an update for a specific date/time or in any event when you arrive at a particular area. You will get a notice in your program or on your telephone.

Of course, Keep furnishes you with specific update times for quick access, yet you can transform them. Open the Settings menu, and you will have the option to change the default time for Morning, Afternoon, and Evening.

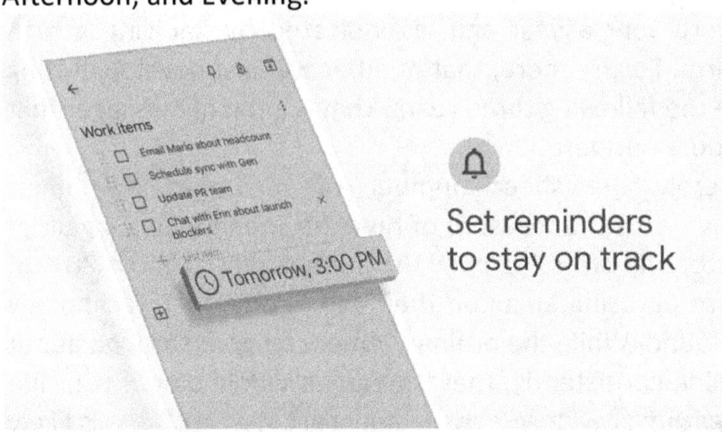

Channel Search

In case you're utilizing Keep consistently, its workspace will get topped off decently fast. Be that as it might, this being a Google item, the application's hunt smarts are hearty.
Tap the hunt bar at the head of the screen, which will show search classes—channel by updates, records, pictures, drawings, or connections. The application likewise bolsters shading coding—red for necessary food item records and blue for business-related plans for the day, for instance—so you can look by tone.

7.4 Easy and Secure Emailing with Gmail

Summer, as a rule, implies an excursion from your Gmail inbox. In any case, all your new messages won't get replied all alone (well, really, they may — yet I'll get to that later). More than 281 billion messages were sent a year ago, as indicated by Radicati, a tech promoting firm. Furthermore, that number will just develop, hitting 330 billion in the following three years. That is a ton of messages that will require our consideration.
It's not merely the sheer number of messages that feels overpowering — it's the measure of time we spend taking a gander at, reacting to, and stressing over those messages. Almost 80% of Americans are perusing email on their cell phone, MIT Technology and Review found. While the ordinary American goes through about 24 hours online consistently, that is nearly a whole day of your life every week gazing at your screens — and a great deal of that is likely spent in your Gmail inbox.

Fortunately, there are approaches to ace your inbox before it aces you. Here are 10 Gmail tips and deceives to assist you with overseeing your email.

This is the only method You Should Sign Your Emails

Let Smart Compose assist you with reacting all the more rapidly

Gmail's Smart Compose highlight completes your sentences for you. When you start composing an email, Gmail's human-made brainpower calculation will describe what you're attempting to state. By squeezing the "tab" key, the proposal will consequently populate the email. It resembles we're completing one another's —

To turn on the Smart Compose, go to Select General Settings; at that, point flips the "Keen Compose" button on. By all the while, empowering, "Personalization," Google's AI will tailor its arrangement proposals to your inclinations and propensities. You can even give input to Smart Compose with the goal that this component can get familiar with your inclinations and style. To do this, go to the "More Choice" button at the base of your email toolbar close to the Trash icon and select "Savvy Compose Feedback."

Calendar and Email to send later

Is it accountable for sending dismissal messages at 8 p.m. in any case, needing to return home to watch The Bachelorette finale? Reporting a significant advancement one week from now yet heading on an excursion with "no Wi-Fi?" With Gmail's planning highlight, you can choose when precisely an email gets sent. By tapping the little upward bolt close to "Send," and selecting a period and date, you can keep steady over cutoff times while as yet carrying on with your life. At the point you're done with your email, click the sliding bolt at the left base of your new email that is close to the "Send" button. You will be provoked with "Calendar Send." Click this choice and pick a date and time to send the email. When this is chosen, click "Timetable Send" The email will send without anyone else without you putting down your glass of wine.

Cut (trackpad) corners with console accessible routes

Gmail is crammed with alternate console ways that can make it far simpler to deal with your inbox. Watch your email form screen unexpectedly show up when you press the letter "C" on your console, or consequently, visit your drafts by clicking B+D. Gmail has many adjustable accessible routes that can make your life simpler.

Go to → Settings → Advanced, and empower Keyboard Shortcuts. Presently there ought to be a tab for alternate console ways in the settings window where you can see and modify your choices. You'll have to ensure that console accessible routes are additionally turned on in Settings → General → Keyboard Shortcuts.

To see a full rundown of more Gmail alternatives and accessible routes (counting an entire bundle of choices gathered by work), hold down Shift +/. A sheet will spring up with a registry of available routes.

A couple of final top choice Gmail console easy routes:

Move +!: Report as spam (messages you don't care for will *poof* from your inbox)

Move + #: Delete (read previously)

R: Reply (rapidly react, additionally keeps you from the humiliating "answer all")

U: Mark as new (to return to later, except if you have the nap hack empowered)

C: Compose a new email

A: Reply all (once more, don't mistake this for "r")

E: Archive a message

Squeezing G + (I, D, S, or T) takes you to a wide range of inboxes, featured messages, or drafts, contingent upon which letter you press.

Un-send an email

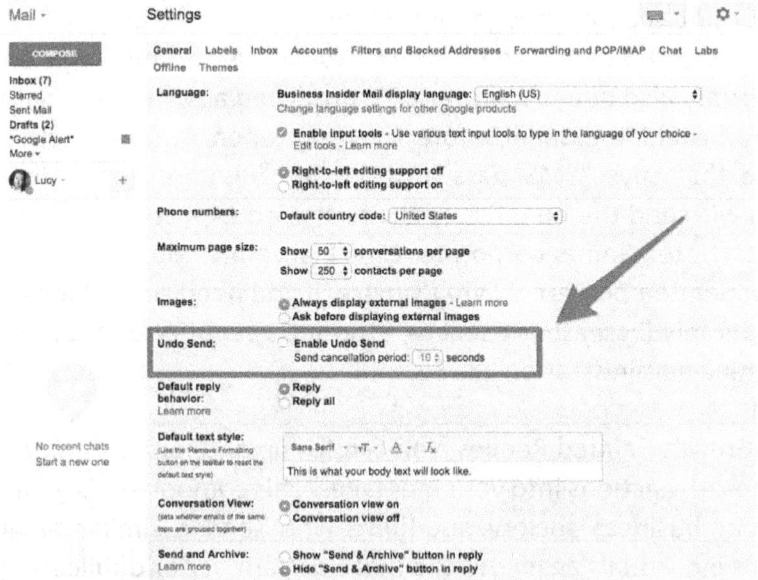

The fleeting frenzy set in when you state "Dear Kylie" rather than "Dear Kendall" on that work email is presently and everlastingly formally taken care of. Gmail now has the choice to review a sent message for as long as 30 seconds after you've sent it.

To set this up, go to the Settings symbol in the upper right-hand corner of your Gmail landing page, pick Settings → General, and switch on "fix send." You can choose to what extent you have before deciding to get back to your email from the dull web gap vanishes. Anxious Nellies can settle on the 30-subsequent choice, while the Masochistic Marges can choose five seconds.

This email will fall to pieces in 3, 2, 1.

Sending humiliating photographs of your canine in a tutu or classified organization data is consistently somewhat unsafe — so check out Gmail's fall to pieces. Like the Snapchat of messages, these messages just remain in the beneficiary's inbox for whatever length of time that you need them to. The email can't be sent, duplicated, stuck, downloaded, or printed, and you can even repudiate access from your record before times done.

After you've formed your email, click the little clock with a lock symbol on the base toolbar, and select the beneficiary and period.

That is not secure enough, you state? This new element likewise gives you a choice to the secret key to ensure the message, so the beneficiary also needs to enter a PC produced a secret key that they get by instant message before they can open it. Simply click the choice that says "SMS password" under "Require Passcode" and Gmail will send the beneficiary the password expected to get to the email. (Note: Some corporate Gmail accounts do not have this component empowered. What's more, if you need something that is considerably increasingly secure, attempt a security-disapproved of informing administration like Signal.)

Can it

With Gmail's Canned Replies, you can set up and rapidly import pre-composed reactions into your messages. This component is generally for your business society out there who send a similar email to various individuals again. It's the more current, lazier duplicate/glue, yet without the tension of inadvertently sticking an inappropriate name in your welcome. It even imports titles and any connections that you spared with the format email. By marking these canned reactions, you'll have the option to rapidly and successfully discover what you need.

To turn on Canned Replies, go to Settings symbol → Settings → General → empower Canned Responses (Templates).

After composing the underlying email, click the "More Options" symbol close to the Trash symbol in your Gmail toolbar, and select "Canned Responses." From here, select "Spare Draft as Template," and afterward, "Spare draft as a new layout." From here, it will request that you name your format — suppose I'm calling mine "Systems administration Template," and I would now be able to send this email at whatever point I have to. Simply open another email, select More Options → Canned Responses, and your layout will show up. At the point when you press on it, the new email will be populated with the spared format. Presto! Less composing, increasingly canned reactions.

Put your Gmail on rest

Getting an upsetting email after work hours can indeed discourage your party time or family time. Actuate Gmail's "nap" include when you need a break from your inbox, and messages will return at your picked time.

To nap an email, float over the message in your fundamental Gmail screen, and snap the clock symbol to the extreme right. You can nap the email for a day, seven days, a month, hell, you can nap for a year. The email will return in your inbox when you're prepared to react. Likewise, there's an assigned mark for these napped messages on the left half of your inbox just on the off possibility that you have to discover them sooner.

If that is insufficient for you to make sure to react to Grandma Jane's email, take a stab at clicking and hauling the email from your Gmail inbox directly to your undertakings tab on the right hand board of your screen. The email update will show up there, with a connection legitimately underneath it that takes you directly to the message being referred to. Coordinating these messages into your schedule can be a successful method to make sure to react.

The individual right hand, you didn't have any acquaintance with you required. Rather than scrambling through your Gmail inbox to discover which door you're flying out of or where you're meeting your mother for informal breakfast, utilize the installment and membership highlight to see and deal with your flights, supper reservations, memberships, and that's only the tip of the iceberg. It resembles out of nowhere getting an individual partner that you don't need to pay. This Gmail highlight looks your inbox for any flight, inn, show, occasion, or eatery reservations you've made and perfectly gathers them in once place. It even monitors past reservations and memberships that have just lapsed.

Go to the hover in the upper right-hand corner of your Gmail screen with your underlying or individual photograph. Snap Google Accounts → Payment and Subscriptions. Select which choice you need to see, regardless of whether it's memberships, reservations, or buys you've made, to view and track them.

Put it on your tab

Gmail's tabs update resembles a free close to the home coordinator, isolating your inbox between numerous tabs, including Social messages (like Facebook, Twitter, and Instagram), Updates (Newsletters, and so on on.), Finance, and Promos. The magnificence of this element is that your cerebrum doesn't need to continually change undertakings from news to work to Mom's new labeled Facebook photographs and back to work once more. Instead, pick which inbox mark you need to manage, and go forward and overcome those new messages. Your essential inbox will contain all the most critical messages to react to, while the different mailboxes take to a higher degree a secondary lounge.

Go to the Settings symbol → Configure Inbox and select which tabs you need to channel messages coming into your Gmail inbox. You can pick upwards of five unique channels.

Never break the chain

You need to repeat an affiliate in the Gmail email chain, practically type "+ [their name]" in the email section, and pick their email address. Presently, this email will naturally circle them into the discussion. You could likewise type in their email into the location field; however, along these lines are the only is the sort of feeling more relaxed.

Google Apps: Conclusion

All organizations need to cover their everyday exercises in office organization with a solitary arrangement of office instruments. Having the option to hide these are the primary advantages of utilizing Google Apps (G Suite). With G Suite, Google gives organizations a cloud answer for their everyday work. It has numerous applications that cooperate to cover the entirety of the daily exercises in office organization. The charging of administrations is client dependent on a membership model, from fundamental capacities to increasingly extra highlights.

Google G Suite segments incorporate interchanges on applications like Gmail or Google Hangouts and arranging board applications like Google Calendar, cooperation, and distributed storage applications like Google Drive or Google Sites, and requests for Office utilize like Google Sheets, Google Docs, or Google Slides.

The best advantage of utilizing Google applications (G Suite) is that organizations needn't bother with their framework to send requests. The applications can be used through an online association from any gadget and area.

Past supplanting capacities gave by another programming; Google Apps offers particular highlights intended to change and improve office working.

a) Collaboration: Features like report sharing, concurrent altering, shared schedules, and talk makes bunch work more straightforward, and urge office individuals to turn out to be increasingly mindful of every others' work.

b) Searching: Documents and messages in Google Apps are intended to be looked at as opposed to arranged by the client. This implies clients can invest less energy arranging documents and don't need to know and recall a specific arrangement of association to discover what they are searching for. As shown by the LSNC Findability Project, moving to a framework where about all office information is accessible through Google Search Appliance (GSA) can help workplaces altogether increment their adequacy.

c) Integration: Google Apps are intended to connect, and are all the more impressive in the mix.

Google client information is put away by Google on its server farms. As indicated by Google, I just chose representatives to approach the data. The applications are affirmed to different protection and security measures. Furthermore, Google partakes in the Privacy Shield Agreement.

All together for cloud administrations to agree to European information insurance prerequisites, EU clients can utilize Google to conclude their own EU model agreement provisos and information preparing additional items. Applications like Gmail have worked in spam blockers and infection scanners. Google Drive transferred information is encoded. Dissimilar to Google's free application contributions, clients' data isn't checked and assessed for a limited time. Thus it is demonstrated that google applications give the best of the highlights in it, which are prescribed to each client for routine utilization, and giving them a short, exhaustive, and a supportive viewpoint to progressively safe perusing and routine utilization.

If you enjoyed this book, let me know your thoughts by leaving an Amazon review.

I would be so glad to hear your thoughts!

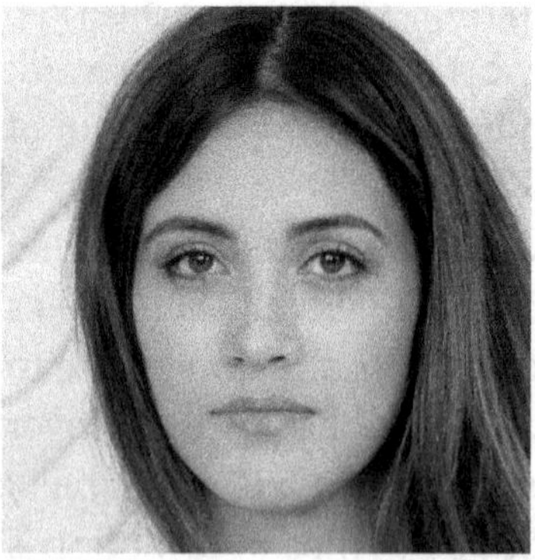

Thank you so much!

-Emily

Teaching with Zoom: Introduction

Zoom is software available on multiple platforms such as Windows, Android, Mac, and iOS devices. It is the brainchild of Eric Yuan. This software is a videotelephony software even though there are other applications in the market. Still, this particular software takes precedence over others as it is smoother for Online meetings with multiple participants, and this is what made Zoom the primary platform for online education in this COVID-19 pandemic. The availability of this software on different platforms makes it easier for students to get access to online education.

Zoom is not only used by teachers but also by people of different professions as it makes the discussions easier over long distances. Whether one participant is at home, other in-office, and third, in the field, all three participants can easily hold a meeting to discuss any particular project over Zoom.

Zoom basic is completely free for users to utilize for day to day usage. Still, for different business models, there are also different subscriptions available that come with additional features and enables the user to host a conference call with multiple participants. The duration of the video conference call exceeds the 40-minute mark. Basic Zoom only allows the user a time limit of 40 minutes per call. But on the basic package, users have access to an unlimited number of video calls, but their duration or time limit cannot exceed 40 minutes. This time limit was scrapped due to ongoing global pandemic and due to this platform being utilized by educational institutes. The pandemic led to an exponential growth of Zoom, mostly due to educational institutes using it worldwide.

Educational institutes adopted Zoom due to its ease of use, made possible by a user-friendly graphical user interface (GUI). These features make Zoom stand out from its competitor in the video telephony market.

Some of these features are whiteboard that allows the professors to draw or write something on the screen, shared with attendees or students to be precise. The whiteboard acts like a literal whiteboard that is used by teachers in class during teaching. Another feature that led to the boom of Zoom usage was the ability to share the lecture screen. This feature allowed the host or teacher to share their computer screen with students, just like in-class lectures. You can share the PowerPoint slides and other notes on the screen and simultaneously allowing the host or teacher to monitor the video feed of students if they are paying attention or not. Another feature that is convenient for both teachers and students alike is of raise hand, this allows the students to raise their hands, and this will prompt the professor that attendee has some questions rather than disrupt the flow of lectures by abruptly asking a question. That student who raised his or her hand, the video feed belonging to them will blink in professor's screens, thus letting him know about the students' query.

Zoom as the software does not require premium hardware but good internet access is a must. It will run even on minimum requirements for PC desktop or on any budget laptop with an inbuilt microphone or webcam. But a dedicated microphone is at least recommended for the host so that even if there is noise around them, they can adequately deliver their message to students.

Assignments are a major part of the learning curve, and Zoom ensures students can easily submit their assignments through the file-sharing feature of Zoom rather than the hassle of submitting them through a separate email. This also allows the students to carry on with their presentations on Zoom. The host or professor can even divide the ongoing class into small groups for students to hold discussions. This allows the students to work in groups rather than tackling any problem individually.

It is strongly recommended for both the host and attendees that before they join the video call, conference, or online classroom, they should take ten minutes and check through the equipment such as a microphone, webcam, and internet connection to ensure smooth working of Zoom. If the equipment is giving an error or an internet connection problem, the problem can be solved quickly. Still, it is better to tackle the problems before the virtual lecture rather than facing them during the lecture, as it will be a waste of time for both the host and the attendees.

Before getting started, I'd love to share some information about me. I am a 26-year public high school American teacher. I hold a Bachelor's Degrees in History, and my passion is technology applied to teaching. I have always used Google tools since 2000, and now write books about teaching online in order to explain to other teacher how to use those tools for an effective learning.

Thank you for choosing this book, please leave a short review on Amazon, if you enjoy it. I would really love to hear your thoughts!

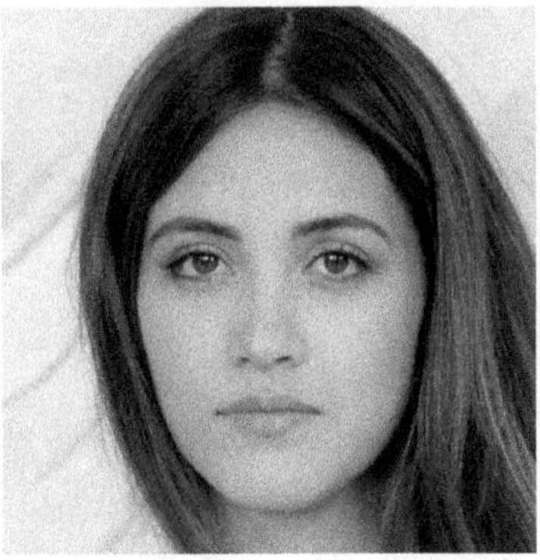

Thank you so much!
-Emily

Chapter 1: Introduction to Zoom - An Effective Tool

The value of language or communication is highly essential in our lives as it is a medium of thought and contact. English is both a regional and an international oral medium of connection. It and many other languages have led to the exchange of feelings and effects which have contributed significantly to any state's socio-economic and political growth. We live in a world where technology is pervasive. Even the pedagogy of teaching methods has undergone a sea-change due to the pervasive presence of technology. The term "Virtual distance learning" has become the buzz word in the field of education. Even in the business field, as the world becomes smaller and smaller, meetings are held on a computer screen where there are participants worldwide. So it is important to infuse technology into the field of education and business management as it serves the needs of the contemporary learners and those in managing departments.

Today the classroom atmosphere is completely different from the conventional classroom. Learning's technical aspect is rising all the time. More and more classes take place online – but instead of being merely a replacement for classroom lessons, they may be mixed in with a classroom approach. It also provides a more stimulating and inspiring experience for students.

Zoom's online platform has helped introduce various advances into businesses, foreign interaction, and language teaching with the widespread use of Computer systems, practices, and tools.

Assisted Language Learning has allowed many teachers worldwide to enhance their teaching skills for better learning opportunities for their students.

Luckily, on the one hand, more and more high schools and, on the other, households have computers and Internet access to allow technology-assisted learning.

There are usually two distinct groups of teachers who are involved in experimenting with online teaching:

• Those who are looking for more collaborative or customized online elements to supplement their classroom teaching.

• Those who advocate the use of distance learning for students who are unable to attend classes.

Zoom is a useful tool to connect in a situation where more and more of us have to stay home. The online distance learning platforms change the world in which we live and how we learn to live. One of the latest, initial conference room approaches focused on software is the Zoom system.

Zoom is a cloud-based application that offers meetings and webinars and share content and video conferencing. It helps teachers, for example, getting their students together to get things done in a frictionless environment. With a fast, secure cloud platform for audio and video conferencing, collaboration, webinars, and chats across desktops, mobile devices, room systems, and telephones. Zoom is the pioneer in modern enterprise video communication.

The features of the Zoom allow teachers to assess and explore the four competencies through rich experiences with students. Teachers can record their lessons on the locally or Cloud – students are also able to record and turn off and on recording several times as they want during a lecture.

Zoom motivates teachers to annotate their shared images, thereby making lessons more interactive.

Teachers can record lessons and review them again to assess the strengths and limitations of students, and by watching recorded lessons, and these learners can self-assess their abilities. Students can watch the studies documented in a series to see their progress over time. Therefore, this allows the teachers to evaluate the progress of students by showing the lesson reported to another teacher, whom they trust, and seeking positive feedback.

Teachers should encourage active questioning by students to evaluate student learning during lessons and after watching them. As well, educators should make students reflect on lectures via recording and sharing a video. Zoom gives teachers different ways of expressing the material of their lessons. The sharing of screens by Zoom will provide teachers with an excellent opportunity to improve the intercultural skills of many students by sharing engaging resources such as videos and posts, and presentations. Throughout the field of education, online distance learning has become a sensation throughout, and today it meets the needs of modern-day learners. Infusing innovations in classroom learning has added stimulation and increased the engagement of learners within the classroom. Learning from afar has a large presence in almost every region. Language teaching is one of those areas where technology has taken over and enhanced the learning methods.

The attributes of an online distance learning course come to mind as to the following. They are:

- To promote access to tools for the course. Give teachers and students greater comfort and versatility on time.

- It can be personalized that various teachers can meet the skills and learning goals of each student by offering various online tools to particular students so that they can focus on them at their own time.

Since the advent of the internet and the world becoming a global village in recent decades, the influence and importance of education in the world have grown tremendously. If teachers teach as they taught before, then in the current global scenario, the necessary goals of learning might not be achieved.

There will probably be increased dynamism in the area of computer-based educational applications and teaching techniques. For the future, maybe most universities will benefit from the equipment and services available for online distance learning. Online distance learning is, therefore, an opportunity within the information society for lifelong learning.

1.1 History of Zoom App

Early Years

It came into being in April 2011 by Eric Yuan, former vice president of Cisco Webex. He left Cisco with 40 engineers, and with their assistance, he started a new company, called Saasbee, Inc. initially, since the video telephony market was saturated, so the company was having difficulty attracting investors. In June 2011, WebEx CEO Subrah Iyar, venture capitalists Matt Ocko and Bill Tai raised $3 million for funding.

The company changed its name from Saasbee to Zoom in May 2012, inspired by the children's book Zoom City. Zoom released a beta version in September 2012, which was capable of hosting conferences of up to 15 participants in the picture. The firm signed Stanford University as its first customer.

The service was released in January 2013 after Qualcomm Ventures, WebEx creator Subrah Iyar, and General Counsel Dan Scheinman raised a $6 million Series around for the fund. Zoom released version 1.0 of the software, which allows the maximum number of participants to be 25 per session. Zoom had 400,000 users by the end of the first month and had 1 million users by May 2013.

Growth of Zoom

In mid-2013, Zoom formed partnerships with software vendors operating with B2B, like Redbooth, and also developed a program called Works with Zoom. It led to the formation of partnerships with Vaddio, Logitech, and InFocus. In the 4th quarter of 2013, the firm raised more than $6 million from Waze, Facebook, and established investors in Series B. It had about more than 2.5 million users at the time. Zoom was seeing more than 9 million users by mid of 2014.

The business raised about $30 million from investors, like Horizons Ventures, Emergence Capital, Qualcomm Ventures, in Series C funding in February 2015. After its creation, Zoom had more than 35 million users, with more than 60000 organizations subscribed, and a staggering total of about 1 billion minutes of the video telephone. The company merged the applications with Salesforce, Slack, and Skype throughout 2015 and 2016. With October 2015 version (latest at that time) 2.5, Zoom increased the number of entrants enabled for business customers per conference to 50 and then later to whooping 1,000.

The company managed to raise 100 million USD in funding in January 2017 to a valuation of 1 billion USD, making it, unicorn. In April of 2017, a telehealth product by Zoom was launched that allowed doctors to host patient consultations remotely.

Zoom integrated itself with Polycom's conferencing systems, allowing the use of features like multiple screens, mobile meetings, and screen sharing (wireless), and integration of calendar with Google Calendar, Microsoft Outlook, and iCal. In September 2017, Zoom held its first user conference, Zoomtopia. Zoom announced at the conference collaboration with Meta to facilitate the integration of Augmented Reality, Facebook integration with Workplace and Slack, and initial steps towards a speech recognition platform for artificial intelligence.

IPO and Beyond

The firm became a public company with an initial public offering in April 2019. The share price rose over 70 percent on the first day of trading after pricing at more than US$ 30 per share. At the end of its first trading day, the company was valued at 16 billion US$. Dropbox had spent $5 million in Zoom before IPO.

Throughout the COVID-19 pandemic, Zoom's use for remote work, distance education, and online social connections increased exponentially. Thousands of educational institutions moved to the Zoom to conduct online classes. In several countries, the organization provided its services to K–12 schools for free. In 2020, Zoom had reached 2.22 million users in February 2020 — more users than it received in 2019. The Zoom app was downloaded more than 2 million times in one day in March 2020. Average users of Zoom increased from around 10 million in December 2019 to over 300 million regular attendees in April 2020. This led to a rising stock price in the company in early 2020 and a general fall in the stock market. Zoom stock boomed from less than $70 per share to $150 per share at the end of March. The company was estimated at more than $67 billion by June 2020.

Zoom revealed in May 2020 that it had purchased a company that specializes in end-to-end encryption, Key base.

Zoom launched its first hardware as a service offering in July 2020, bundling its video conferencing program with third-party hardware from Neat, Yealink, Poly, and DTEN, and running on the network service. This will continue with the offerings of Zoom Mobile and Zoom Rooms, with both services accessible to US consumers who can buy devices from Zoom at a fixed monthly rate. In July 2020, the company revealed Zoom at home, a range of home-use items tailored for home-workers. The first model with Zoom software and DTEN hardware is called Zoom for Home-DTEN ME. It is a 27" screen with eight microphones and three wide-angle cameras, with a preloaded Zoom program onto the unit.

1.2 Zoom App's Uses

Zoom is a platform for video telephony created by Eric Yuan. It facilitates a video chatting that can allow close to 100 devices, with a time limit of 40 minutes (removed due to pandemic) for free user accounts. Users can opt to upgrade by subscribing to their plans, premium subscription allowing 1000 people simultaneously, with no time limit.

Since the pandemic COVID-19, Zoom's use for distance education, online social networking, and remote work has increased considerably. Zoom is being used by universities, government departments, and banks around the globe. Zoom formed a collaboration to make a virtual club with Formula One. Fans starting with the Grand Prix (Hungarian) in July 2020, can go behind the scenes and participate in interactive activities through Zoom.

Play by written Richard Nelson, this plays over Zoom, where the main characters meet online via Facebook during the COVID-19 pandemic.

Directed and written by Nelson, the play was presented as a benefit show by Public Theater, with it being premiered on YouTube at the end of April 2020. A live reading of the 2009 play by Kristoffer Diaz, The Elaborate Entrance of Chad Deity over Zoom, broadcasted from August 2020 on Play-PerView.

Zoom is an application that has multiple uses for teachers, students, and business professionals.

1. **For Teachers**

Teachers can use Zoom for online education as they can use it to:

- **Time their Training Sessions**

They can arrange meetings with the Zoom in different ways. By default, in Canvas course, Zoom is allowed and will be the easiest way for students to find the meetings. In Canvas course, teachers can schedule a Zoom Meeting and pick repeated meetings where necessary so that the URL stays the same over the course. If a teacher intends to use Canvas than meetings of the course occur inside the platform of Canvas course

Cloud recordings are made available automatically via the course platform on Canva. The course meetings can be isolated from other ongoing meetings. Canvas scheduled meetings also appear in Canvas Calendar as activities for the class members.

- **Students Prepare Roles**

If you, as a teacher, deputize for someone else to handle aspects of online space, the experience of classroom management will be a lot less stressful. Through default, you can automatically select your TAs and all other teaching staff as substitute hosts for your meetings, and you can also choose co-hosts during your meeting.

Try asking one student or TA to assist their partners with technical issues. This way, a teacher can teach and offer additional skills such as digital data handling to the students.

- **Foster Sense of Culture**

Once everybody displays their faces through their webcam, a sense of existence is enhanced. Students should turn the video on a key component of engagement because if you can see them, it becomes easier to communicate with class, students are likely to be attentive if they feel monitored. Coach students to turn to the view of the Gallery (this is a view of "Brady Bunch" where everybody is simultaneously visible to one another).

Tips for Pupils

Mute mics in case you do not participate.

Speak in a conversational tone - you would not need to raise your voice.

Eye-catch the camera (class and camera are the same)

Ensure the source of light is in front, not behind you.

2. **For Students**

The Zoom menu contains multiple features that can be used during class meetings at any time. We can find the menu in PCs, Macs, and even by hovering over the Zoom window at the bottom. You can reach the menu in the Zoom app by clicking the button at the bottom of the screen.

- Invite: If your professor/meeting host offers such permissions, encourage you to bring more people into the class or meeting.
- Mute: The microphone is quiet and silent.
- Share Screen: Allows the sharing of a range of windows and applications. Participants can share their desktop views and different windows currently open on their device, write on a digital whiteboard, and even display a screen directly.
- Chat: Works like Messenger on Facebook but without extra features like stickers. Students may send messages to everybody, just to the professor/meeting host or to a specific individual.
- Upload: You can record and save as much of the meeting as you want if the host allows it.
- Leave Meeting: Tap this to get some off-screen time when you are ready to chill out.

Some guidelines for the student to follow while on meeting with their teacher are as follow:

- If a student cannot use photos, upload your face to your Zoom Account with a nice profile picture. Provide something for your classmates to look at as you speak.
- Keep your head high within the frame of the photo. It conveys confidence.
- Have Professional wear.
- Having a simple video is like taking a good selfie — everything is about contrast. Lighten your face brighter than the backdrop to make your visibility easier.
- Simply be yourself. Physically turn, and render expression of the lips.
- Microphones pick up any ambient noise, so keep the microphone silenced until it is time to talk.
- Note that other things like eating, shuffling papers, drinking, etc. are highly distracting while the camera is on.

3. **For Professionals**

Zoom lets you record your online conference calls as videos, a useful function that helps you to share the meeting with people who may have missed it or replay what has been said. It can even be used by teachers to record lectures in advance for the class. When recording, you must choose whether to use the option local or Cloud. Local means that you store the video file yourself, whether on your device locally or in another storage space. With Cloud, which is only for paying members, Zoom saves the video for you in its cloud storage. One advantage of the cloud option is that, once it is ready, people can stream the video through a web browser.

While making a video from a conference call, adjusting a few settings in advance allows a significant difference in the end output. Some calls, for example, maybe broadcast-style, where only the host appears on the computer. In this case, set the Zoom to capture only the host's audio and video. Some calls can be in the style of a group meeting, in which case you want everyone to record.

1.3 Zoom App's Subscription and Pricing Plans

To facilitate education through Zoom with the spread of the COVID-19 pandemic, Zoom immediately eliminates the 40-minute time limit on free Basic accounts for Coronavirus-affected primary and secondary schools. Teachers can Sign in to see if they have already approved your account. If not, they can click on the "Request Bid" to request an addition to their grade.

Overall, Zoom has various subscription plans, including Basic, which is free. The plans and features are mentioned below:

1. **Basic**

For: Personal Meeting

Cost: Free

Limit: Hosts 100 participants

Features:

- 40 min time limit for group meetings
- Unlimited one on one meeting
- Ticket Support
- Unlimited number of meetings

2. **Pro**

For: Small Teams

Cost: $14.99/Mo/host

Limit: Purchase up to 9 hosts/account

Feature:

- Basic features are included in it
- 100 participants included
- Assign scheduler
- Skype for Business (Lync) interoperability

- Custom Personal Meeting ID
- Duration of Meeting is limited to 24 hours
- REST API
- User management
- Admin feature controls
- 1GB of M4A or MP4 cloud recording

3. **Business**

For: Small and Medium-sized Businesses

Cost: $19.99 /Mo/host

Limit: Starts at ten hosts for $199.9/Mo

Features:

- All Basic features
- All-Pro features
- Single sign-on
- Company branding
- 300 participants Included
- Custom emails
- Admin dashboard
- Vanity URL
- On-premise deployment
- Managed domains
- Dedicated phone support
- LTI integration
- Transcripts for Cloud Recording

4. **Enterprise**

For: Large Enterprises

Cost: $19.99 /mo/host

Limit: Starts at 100 hosts for $1,999/mo

Features:

- All Business features +
- Enterprise, 500 participants included
- Bundle discounts on Zoom Rooms and Webinars.
- Enterprise Plus 1,000 participants included
- Dedicated Customer Success Manager
- Cloud Storage (Unlimited)
- Reviews for Executive Business

5. **Zoom Phone**

Cost: Starting at $10/Mo/user

Feature:

A single voice and video, fax, meeting, voicemail, and conferencing software! Users can receive and make PSTN calls over mobile Wi-Fi connections or cellular data. The app is native to iOS, Windows, Android, and macOS.

Chapter 2: Getting Started with Zoom

Zoom combines quick online meetings, cloud video teleconference, and easy-to-use community messaging in one single platform for ease of the user. The solution of the single platform offered by Zoom to these tasks gives the best experience in audio, video, and screen sharing covering multiple platforms.

2.1 Equipment Needed to Use Zoom for Effective Learning Smoothly

Before downloading the application, it is necessary to familiarize oneself with its system requirements to ensure its smooth workability without any hiccups. System requirements of Zoom vary over a great detail due to its availability over a large spectrum of platforms covering all major and popular ones ranging from Windows, MACs, androids, and iOS devices, to even those used by field professionals such as IT experts including Mint, OracleLinux, Archlinux, Ubuntu, Fedora, and CentOS, etc.

System Requirements

The basic requirements to use Zoom application on any system includes:

An internet connection, either link-wired or wireless broadband (mobile-based such as 3G and 4G)

Camera or HD camera-built-in (laptops) or webcam plug-in via USB

Speakers and a microphone-built-in or portable Bluetooth plug-in or USB

HD monitor and video-capture camcorder

Zoom's bandwidth will be tailored for the optimal experience, depending on the network of participants. It can automatically switch to environments with 3G, Wired, or Wi-Fi. Since the Internet is the basic requirement to use it, the recommended speed and Preferred Meeting Bandwidth and Webinars by Zoom for various type of calls are as follows:

Audio calling in 1:1

1. High-quality video 600kbps (up and down)
2. 1.2 Mbps for HD 720p video (up and down)
3. It needs 1.8 Mbps (up and down) to receive HD 1080p video
4. It takes 1.8 Mbps (up and down) to send HD 1080p video

For video calls in the group

1. Videos of high-quality 800kbps/1.0Mbps (up and down)
2. To display gallery and or recording with 720p HD: 1.5Mbps (up and down)
3. 2.5mbps (up / down) for receiving 1080p HD video
4. 3.0 Mbps (up / down) to send 1080p HD video
5. for sharing screens (no thumbnails): 50-75kbps
6. video thumbnail screen sharing: 50-150kbps
7. VoIP audio: 60–80kbps
8. Mobile Zoom: 60-100kbps

Webinar Attendee (Students) Bandwidth (Recommended)

For one on one video calling: 600kbps (down) for high definition video and 1.2 Mbps for videos of HD quality

Only to share screen (no thumbnail for video): 50-75kbps

For video thumbnail screen sharing: 50-150kbps (down)

VoIP audio: 60–80kbps

After getting to know basic system requirements and internet requirements, it is time for equipment that needs to be used by teachers and students for online classes on Zoom.

- **PC/Laptop**

PC/laptop is used in almost every household today. It is the basic requirement for conducting and taking online classes because the Zoom application will be downloaded in it. Mobile phones, as popularly termed as "smartphones," can also be used to download Zoom, but it is not recommended for a healthy learning environment. However, if there is the unavailability of desktops or laptops, mobile phones can be used for online learning through Zoom.

A teacher can easily sit in front of a PC/Laptop and conduct the online session and even use a whiteboard for writing and explaining the topics to students. If a teacher wants to present the lecture by writing then either, they can conduct the lesson in front of a whiteboard or use the inbuilt function of a whiteboard. Still, the practice is needed to draw something with the computer mouse, so it is recommended to buy some cheap graphics tablet for better use of whiteboard function.

- **Headset**

A good headset can cancel noise and deliver quality sound. It is a recommended tool for all, either students or teachers but especially the students. By this, they can mostly ignore surrounding noises and focus only on the ongoing lecture.

Microphone

A microphone is an equipment of utmost importance, especially for teachers as without it, it is not possible to deliver the lecture or record it for the students. If students do not have a microphone, they can still type the question in the chatbox, but the whole online lecture cannot be delivered in the chatbox. A good quality microphone can cancel the surrounding noises and deliver the sound with clarity that is easy to understand for the students or attendees.

For PC or desktops, a microphone is an individual peripheral device you need to buy. Still, if a person is using a Laptop, then it is very likely that it comes with a microphone pre-built it in them along with a webcam for video (almost all the laptops today in the market have built-in webcam and microphone).

Mobile devices are already equipped with a camera and microphone since the primary function is communication. All the other features are luxury and intend to make it a palmtop computer.

2.2 Steps for Downloading and Installing Zoom

In the current situation, in most sectors, people have started to work from home, so there is a need for remote conferencing technology, and it has never been more relevant than today. Services such as Zoom, which provides online meetings and video calls, are more important than ever in the present day scenario to help keep companies working smoothly when physical offices are closed down due to the pandemic. Fortunately, downloading Zoom on the PC is a quick process. After installing the application, the user needs to sign up for a free account. Then, he can easily use the Zoom application for the desired purposes.

- **Downloading on PC/Laptop**

Downloading Zoom on a PC or Laptop is an easy process. The user just needs to follow the following instructions:

1. Open the internet browser of your machine.
2. After opening the browser, go to the Zoom.us website.
3. Scroll down to the bottom of the website, and in the footer of the web page, click "Download."
4. Tap "Download" on the Download Center page under the "Zoom Client for Meetings."
5. Then the Zoom app starts downloading. To begin the installation process, you can then click on the.exe file.

The installation process begins by clicking on the .exe file.

When installed on your system, you will need to log into your Zoom account, set up via the Zoom website, if it does not have one already. Once you've set up the account, the user can use Zoom to meet all their video calls and online requirements as per their need.

To sum up, a person simply needs to go to their website and download the Zoom client from the server.

After downloading Zoom, it is installed on the platform, and in the case of iOS devices and windows, it is done as follow:

- Download and Install on Windows

It is effortless to install Zoom once the file is downloaded. Simply click on the downloaded file, and a pop up will show, click run on it, and show where you want to install the application. By default, it will install it in the "C" folder and will install the Zoom client on Windows.

- Download and Install on iOS

1. Tap on the Apple App Store icon on your iOS device.
2. Press on Search at the bottom right of the screen.
3. Enter Zoom in the search text box.

4. Select ZOOM Cloud Meetings from the app choices presented, and then tap on the download button.
5. The install process will start.
6. Once installed, tap Open.
7. In the Zoom app, tap Sign In.

- Downloading on Smartphone

1. Tap on the Google Play Store icon on your android device.
2. Tap on Search at the top right of the screen.
3. Type Zoom in the search text box and select ZOOM Cloud Meetings from the available app choices, and then tap on the Install button.
4. The install process will start.
5. Tap Open once downloaded.
6. In the Zoom app, tap Sign In.

2.3 Making an Account or Signing Up

After installing the Zoom app, it is time for signing up or creating an account on Zoom if the user does not have an existing one. Registering for a Zoom account is simple-whether the user wants to do on their mobile device or a computer.

If the person is planning to use the Zoom app regularly, particularly with large universities and businesses moving to remote or isolated work because of the COVID-19 pandemic, it is better first to download the Zoom file and then to sign up.

To make a profile on Zoom, you will need to access your email address. When a person is signing up, the Zoom app will pop-up in the default browser. You can join the meetings on Zoom without having an account. However, it is better to create one to track appointments while working remotely.

The method of signing up for Zoom on iOS, Android and/or iPad in the mobile app looks and feels the same.

Below are instructions to make Zoom account on a smartphone:

1. Tap to open the app after you download it from the App Store or Google Store. On the Welcome tab, press "Sign Up." The other choices are "Sign in" (For user already having an account) or the option "Join a Conference/Meeting" (if the user receives a text or email having the conference ID).

2. Press the "Sign in" button. Sign in to your IOS or Android App.

3. Enter the email address user wants for the account and the user's first name and last name.

4. Click the "I agree to the terms of service" option.

5. Click the top-right corner to "Sign Up." Type your information in.

6. A screen showing a message will appear telling the user that Zoom has sent the confirmation email to the address provided by the user. To search your Inbox, press "OK" to shut the pop-up and open the email app.

Tap the "OK" button.

7. Press the email message in the user’s Inbox to open. Scroll and click the button 'Activate Account' in blue. On your Laptop or phone, that will open the window.

Activating your Zoom account.

8. Start by the first step that is checking the account's information then selecting a password. Type in your first name and last name again. Type password, and retype to validate the password provided.

If the user's password is not following the criteria of Zoom, instructions, it will pop up on the screen. The password, for example, must contain a minimum of one letter and number, and it should be eight characters long, at least.

Choose a name.

9. The very next step prompts the user to invite co-workers to a conference. You can complete this move if you are in a rush, but if you are merely setting up the account to use, choose to skip instead.

Press Skip

10. The next step now urges the user to initiate a meeting. Tap "Return to My Account" to skip this part again.

Please go to the user account.

11. Type the email address you have provided and the password.

12. Enable the option "Stay signed in" and press the blue "Log in" toggle to go to the user's account. When you have completed these measures, users can go to the version of the app they downloaded. (Many browsers might even prompt the user to open Zoom at the top of the page).

Type in your login info

13. Tap this time, the option of "Sign In" in place of the option "Sign Up."

Sign In

14. Enter the password and email address.

15. To complete the process, press the blue button for "Sign In."

Press the "Sign in" button.

The user has Set up their Zoom account successfully now, and they are now signed in on their device.

Signing up for a Zoom account is similar to mobile phones and browsers. However, completing the necessary steps is easier on the browser.

When using the Zoom via your browser, installing the app might be helpful, so you can use it whenever you like if you are planning to use Zoom regularly for job-related calls.

Below are instructions on how to make a Zoom account for computer and **sign in:**

1. Tap on your Mac or PC to open the Zoom program.
2. Click the "Sign In" button.
3. Click the "Sign Up" button.

4. This opens the Zoom website automatically on your default browser.
5. Type your email.
6. Select the "Sign Up" button in blue.

To sign up, enter your email.

Instructions via email.

7. Open your Inbox and find your email to activate.
8. Click the "Activate Account" button in blue.

Turn your account on.

9. Now your browser's Zoom signup page will open. The screen will prompt the user to enter their first name and last name as well as password.

Type in your password and name.

10. This time the second move will prompt you to add your colleagues. To proceed to the final step, click on "Skip this step."

Choose to start or skip a conference.

11. The final move prompts you to start a test meeting. Click "Return to My Account" instead. The account will already have you signed in.

Please go to your account.

12. If you wish to use the service there, reopen the Zoom app on your desktop. Tap again on "Sign Up."

13. Type your password and your email address. Check the option for "Keep me signed in" the button will follow it “sign-in” click it to complete the process of login, only if the user intends to use this application.

To complete the operation, log in.

Now you are logged in to your brand new account.

2.4 Different Features and their Functionality

The tale of Zoom started in 2011 when the video conferencing market was competitive, as companies were looking for a more efficient way to convey messages in person. The Zoom has become a revolution in that same market where several businesses offer an innovative approach to the complex communication problems with an expensive solution of video techniques of the modern-day.

Zoom showed that present-day companies could interact just as easily through video as they could through the medium of audio and talk – and it is possible to do so without the bugs of many previous solutions. The "Zoom Meetings" was the portfolio's main product, offering an impressive mix of audio and HD video, also items like call transcripts and smart apps.

The organization has now launched its free tier, so the solution provided by Zoom is even more eye-catching as the members of a team can communicate without charging anything. Through online training sessions and webinars, to modern-day art of calls and even video messaging, you can now use Zoom for anything.

Study Zoom Meetings: Features

Zoom offers everything a person needs to keep amazing video conferencing at all price ranges. The quality of the video is outstanding, and the audio quality is crystal clear. People can share several screens and annotate projects using whiteboard functions. Also, Zoom lets you attach to any device – including your Smartphone.

Zoom Meetings' most extravagant features include:

- Easy use due to WebRTC technology.
- Enable all reliable security solutions.

- Support for 1,000 participants in the workshops and 49 workshops.
- Recording built-in and transcripts.
- Photo HD and calls to audio.
- Securely meet the requirements that are dependent on user permissions.
- Streamlined Google Calendar systems.
- Built-in Screen Sharing Tools.
- Unit talk and private messaging for all parties.
- Join any computer from anywhere.
- Some extra features such as chat, phone access, and webinars.

Home Screen:

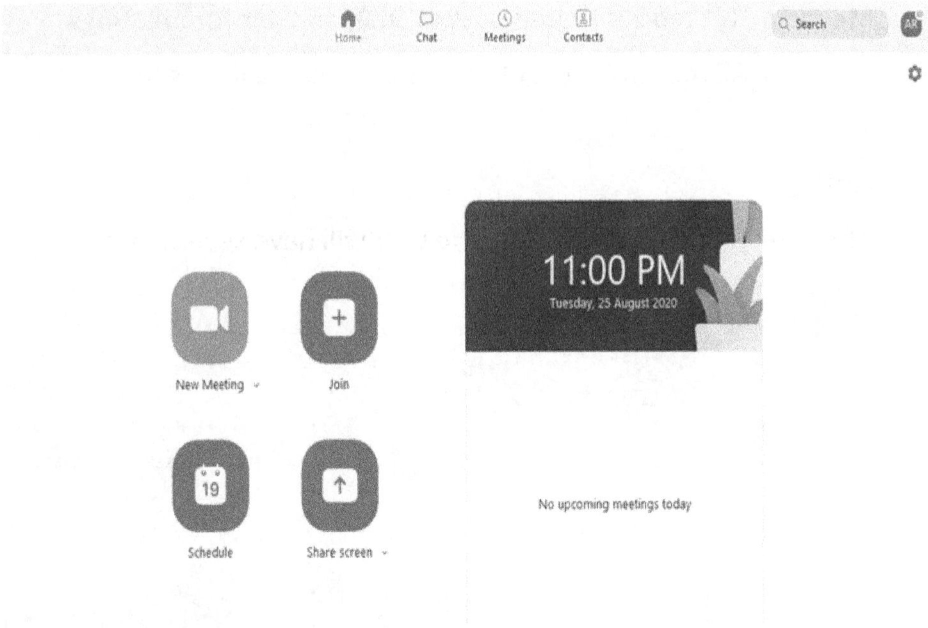

In-home screen, the options at the top of the ribbon are as follow:

Home: Home screen has further options such as new meetings, join, screen share, and schedule. These are the four big square icons in the middle of the screen.

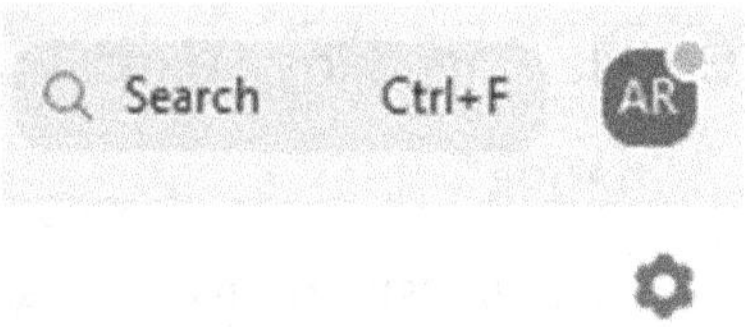

At the top right, there is a search bar, and next to it is an account option from where the user can sign out. Just below the account option, there is the setting icon.

Chat: If the user wants to chat with someone, this is the tab user will go to; it is right next to the home tab.

Meeting: This tab is situated next to chat, and it is for meetings.

Contacts: All the contacts of the user are located in this tab.

Settings:

After pressing the setting icon, the user will have several options.

They include:

General:

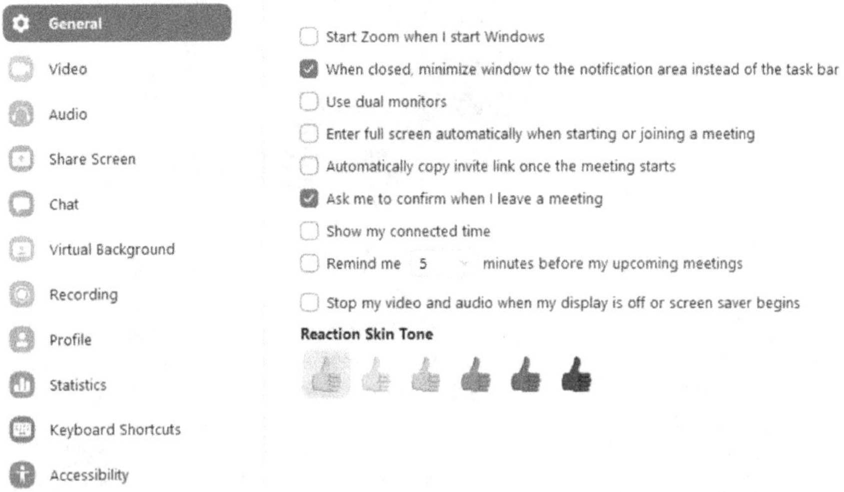

If the user presses the setting icon, the above menu will pop up on the screen. The first option will be general, which includes various other options like using dual monitors, showing the connected time, asking to confirm when leaving a meeting, etc.

Video:

The next option after general is a video tab, and here the options include displaying the participants' names. To touch up the appearances, turning off video when joining the meeting, and many more.

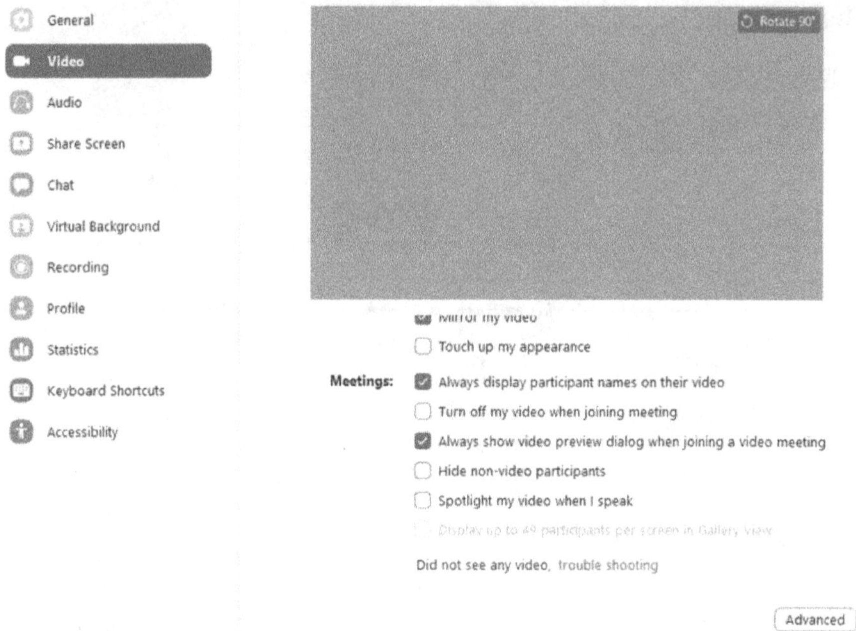

Audio:

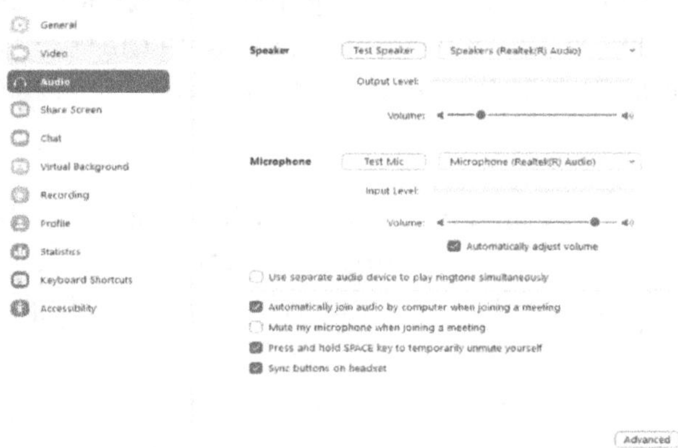

The audio panel in setting deals with the audio-related settings such as speaker-test and microphone test.

Share Screen:

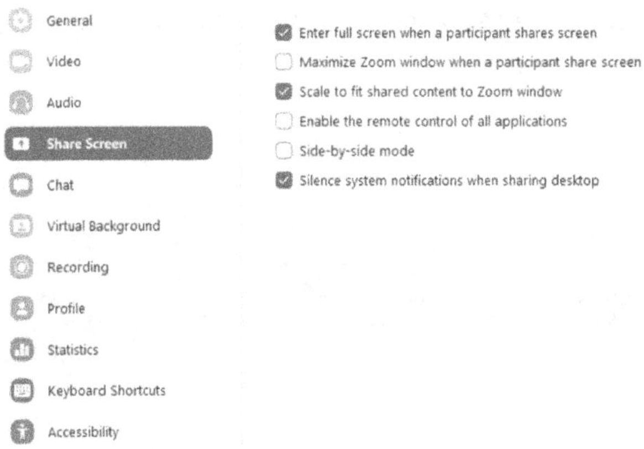

This settings panel deals with the share screen to proceed into an advanced option. For the share screen setting, click on the "Advanced" button at the bottom right. This panel enables the user to switch on or off notification silencing when sharing desktop and in side-by-side mode etc.

Chat:

In this panel, the user can block someone and manage previously blocked users, and set themes for his/her Zoom app, such as dark mode (which is comparatively easier on eyes). Status can also be placed in this panel

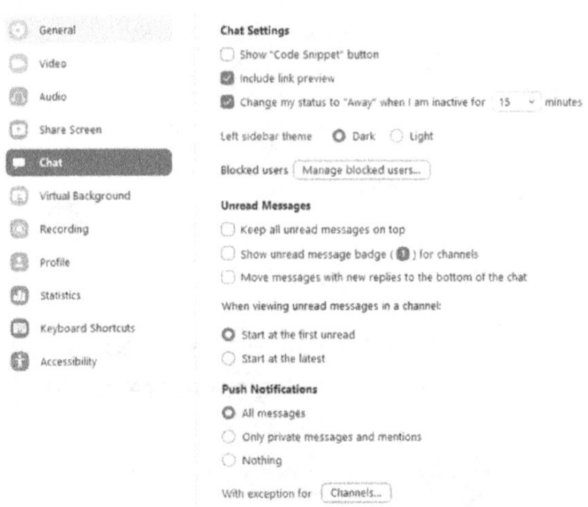

Virtual Background:

In this tab, users can set virtual backgrounds for meetings; it can be anything like any scenery to even videos.

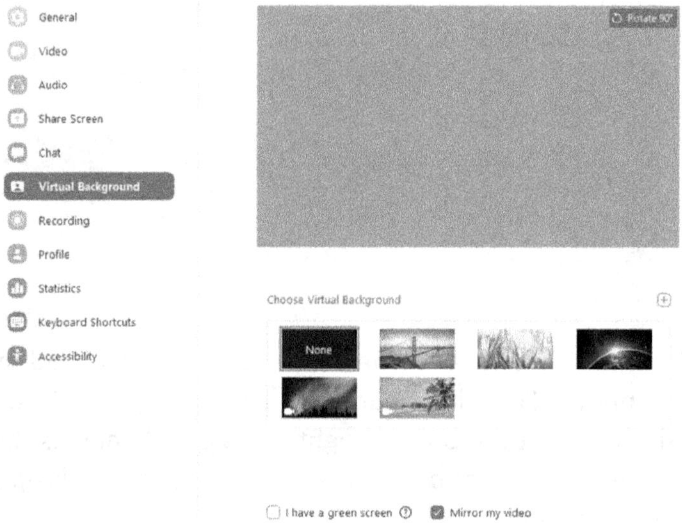

Recording:

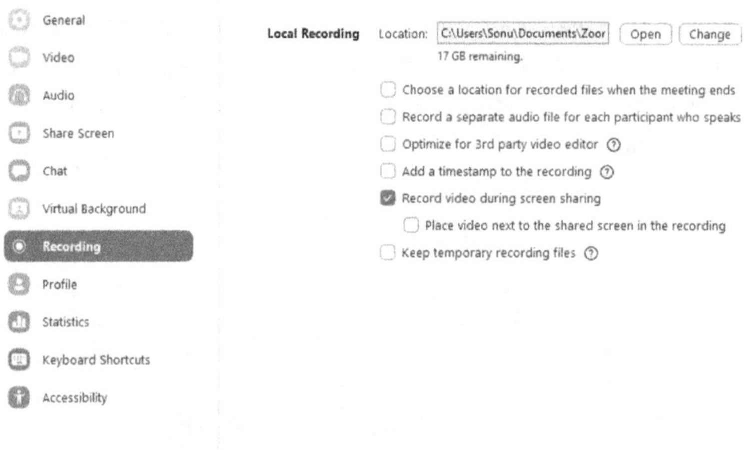

This setting deals with where to save the video for local recording and whether the user wants to save a separate audio file.

Profile:

Below the recording option, there is a profile tab, where the user can view his/her profile.

Statistics:

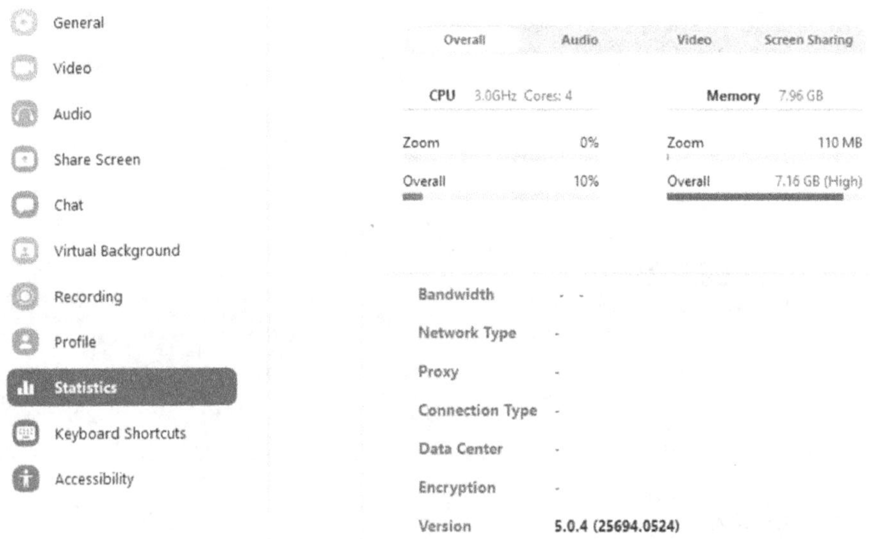

This tab deals with statistics like the version of Zoom installed on PC, etc. It also tells about the specs of PC.

Keyboard Shortcuts:

This tab deals with all the shortcut keys, whether to enable them or change them.

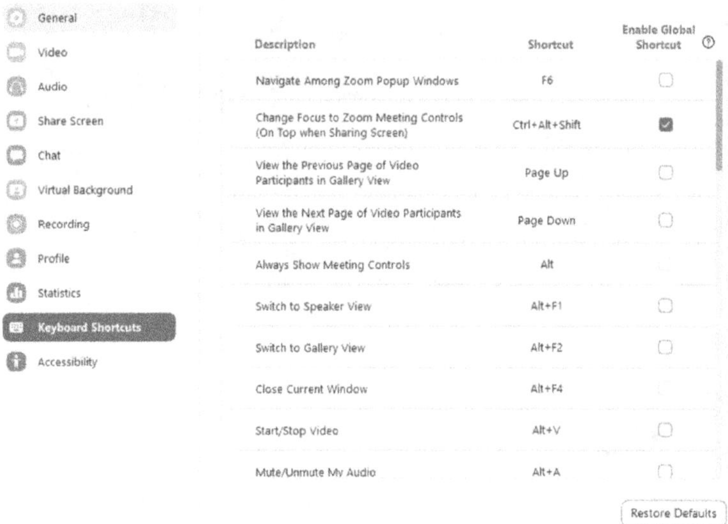

Accessibility:

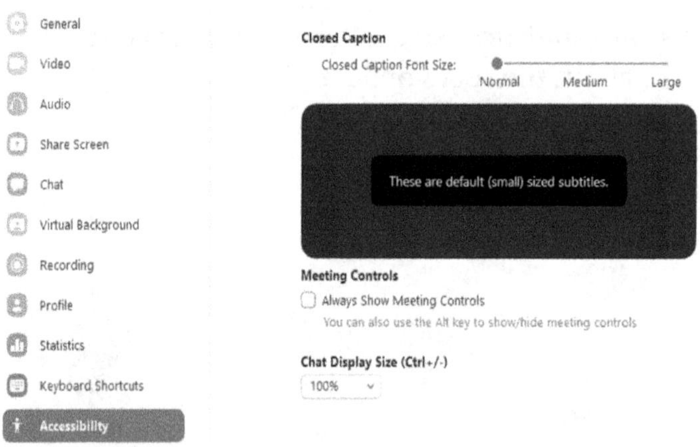

This option deals with the display of chat as in font size and display size, etc. It also deals with meeting controls.

Zoom Toolbar Features

When Zoom is enabled, a new window will open for a meeting session to start. At the bottom of that screen, there is a toolbar. You will need to allow Zoom to use the microphone and camera on your device, or you can connect through your phone if that feature is available.

During the session, you can change your camera and microphone settings by clicking on the microphone and video icons at the bottom left corner.

The toolbar for the Zoom program has the following buttons across the bottom of the screen:

- Invite: to invite people to the meeting.
- Manage Participants: Manage the participants (Rename, Mute) at the conference.
- Share Screen: share your laptop or computer screen or some other app with the participants.
- Chat: open chat box to communicate with all or individual participants.
- Record: record session of the meeting.

Chapter 3: Setting Up and Conducting Virtual Classes

Teachers around the world were forced to transfer their whole classroom online due to coronavirus or COVID-19 pandemic. Schools worldwide shut down their physical entrance, and they opened virtual gateways to assist students in completing their studies. All students and educators had to change – at a breakneck pace. What many learn in their hurry to advance the online system of education is that adding 'internet' before the word 'classroom' is not the only distinction between a digital and a traditional classroom. It works exceptionally great in one setting, and it cannot work well in the other; people tend to find it out by experience.

Teachers still want to be involved in their online classes, but they certainly do not want all of their waking hours trying to navigate this contemporary digital world. In reality, according to a survey conducted in 2017, less than 9 percent of the academics prefer the "fully online environment." Instructors may worry in a simulated setting that they will have absolutely no control over students or their learning environment. Technological failures can undoubtedly take place. Yet virtual classrooms do have advantages — a minimum of it is the opportunity to stay in the course in a global pandemic.

So to conduct a virtual classroom, it is necessary first to set it up, not just to meet learning needs but also to promote student engagement and involvement in such a critical time when it is most needed. Those are abilities that will be in use as the world slowly but surely returns to the 'new' culture, present and shortly.

Setting up Virtual Classroom

Some educational institutes and teachers have tried digital educational devices such as flipped classes or even interactive textbooks with online instructions. These were just experimental phases on behalf of some institutes and teachers. Still, in a matter of weeks, the pandemic forced universities and colleges to move infrastructure of classes online — and that might lead to overwhelming educators and students.

Luckily, many educational institutions now deliver online academic courses and at least have some of the most relevant resources in place so that teachers would not need to reinvent the whole process on a trial and error basis. Nonetheless, adapting the current lesson plans to the online world and teaching methodologies is not something anyone can do overnight.

Firstly, to start hosting your virtual classroom, the classroom would require a Content Delivery Network (CDN) or a video provider (online) to gain access to the delivered lectures. Much higher education institutions have in place something known as a learning management system, aka LMS, that provides at bare minimum functionality a teacher will need. Also, it is possible but not enough in itself to provide students with good quality and captivating learning experience.

Students typically log in a portal to attend the class, with live video or audio streaming. They can also ask questions with the right resources, seek input, attend student forums, transcripts of lectures, access assignments, quizzes and surveys, and written exams.

Much like life lessons, a virtual class allows attendees to communicate with each other and with the teacher.

While for everyone involved, there can be a learning curve, it is important to note that an online classroom is also, in the end, a classroom. The primary goal is the same: improving awareness of subject matter and engaging with students.

Next, to set up a virtual classroom— The user will be using software and hardware instead of mortar and brick as the focus is on the word "Virtual." This would be made simpler by advancements in eLearning systems, but those who are not familiar with technology and are not confident in front of the camera should take small steps while building up their comfort level.

The user should also search to see if their educational institutes have a learning management system capable of hosting video tutorials, online chats, and assignments inputs. Most likely, LMS of many institutes does not support any such features). You might need to look in some instances at other solutions to go across the limits of LMS.

Your online courses will then be broadcast on a content distribution network. Teachers can share them on social media platforms, but a specifically tailored platform for education allows them to organize digital classes and measure learning. Here, the emphasis is Zoom as an online education platform. For example, few dedicated eLearning platforms will allow you to take the attendance and track the numbers and participation of viewers, which is especially useful in a digital class — so teachers know if any student left the stream. For certain instances, you may choose to create your lectures that are accessible on request, which includes the capabilities of on-demand videos, or VOD.

Bear in mind that the Livestream replaces the person to person lecture, so quality must be high if not the same — not only the material but also the streaming.

Grainy footage that cuts is not only frustrating for students, but it also becomes difficult to keep focus irrespective of content quality. According to one such survey by Top Hat conducted due to pandemic, most students did not enjoy the experience of remote learning. More than 65% of students felt that online instruction was worse than classic education, 25% have experienced navigating difficulty while utilizing online tools, and 21% face difficulty accessing digital learning material.

3.1 Popularity of Virtual Learning Mode in Recent Years

Most digital platforms for learning provides free basic access to their platform in response to substantial demand, such as BYJU'S, a Bangalore-based digital tutoring firm, came into being in 2011. Tencent classroom, have been extensively used since February after a quarter out of billion students were instructed by the Chinese government to continue with their studies via an online platform. This culminated in one of the largest "digital revolution" in education history, with more than .7 million or 81 percent of entire K-12 students, attended their classes through the Wuhan Tencent Online Class.

Many businesses are improving their capacities to provide teachers and students with a place where everything is covered.

A collaboration suite Lark, which is Singapore-based, was initially created by ByteDance, was an internal resource for its internal exponential growth. It began offering unlimited video conference time to teachers and students, capabilities of auto-translation, project work in real-time co-editing, and scheduling of smart calendar, among other features offered by them.

Lark has been ramping up global cloud engineering and infrastructure capabilities to maintain stable connectivity. Alibaba's distance learning service and DingTalk faced a completely similar influx. The company taped Alibaba Cloud, was forced to deploy approximately one hundred thousand cloud servers in a time frame of just over two hours to enable large-scale remote work – setting a record for capacity expansion.

Many school districts developed specific alliances, such as PBS SoCal / KCET and The Los Angeles Unified School District, to provide local educational programming, with various networks based on ages, number of multimedia options, etc. The media organizations like the BBC also support interactive learning. On April 20, Bitesize Daily released a curriculum that offers 14 weeks of learning for children around the UK, with some celebrities also help teach some course work.

There is proof that learning online can be more useful in various ways for those who already have access to the appropriate technology.

Some research indicates that, on average, when studying online, students retain 25-60% more content compared to only 8-10% in a classroom. It is also due to the students learning online faster; e-learning takes 40-60 percent reduced time to learn than in a typical classroom environment as students can study at their speed, go back and re-read, skipping, or speeding through concepts as they want. Online learning's effectiveness differs among age groups.

The general opinion about children, particularly younger ones, that there is a need for a maintained environment, as children are easily distracted.

To get the full value of virtual learning, a concerted effort for this framework must be put in place. Also, to go further beyond just simply replicating another physical class / reading through video technologies, by using a variety of interactive resources and communication methods that encourage the traits of personalization, inclusion, and knowledge, according to Tencent's Senior Executive Vice President.

According to BYJU's, making learning enjoyable and successful through technology is crucial because studies have shed light on how children use their senses extensively to learn. It has been observed over a period that intelligent game integration has shown higher engagement and increased motivation for learning, especially among younger students, thus enabling them to love learning. Students should adjust them into present obligations and commitments, and they can interact with learning materials and digital content at whatever time is feasible for them. Perhaps better, they do not have to go anywhere to school and simply log in from their workplace or home to the digital campus.

There is a second explanation of why learning online became so accepted: it is cheaper. Price is a prohibitive factor in why many individual students do not enroll in courses that do not catch their eye. This is a major concern for businesses who want to enable their staff to receive enhanced training, but budget constraints hinder training courses and conferences. For a small budget, online courses are the solution. A great quantity of students is opting for digital learning courses. This is due to cost and convenience. Those serious about improving their existing understanding, new skills as well as valid certificates only enroll in those courses that are popular.

Here are a few reasons as to why digital learning is effective than simply enrolling in the classic training course:

1. **The students learn much more online than in a conventional classroom.**

IBM has researched that in virtual learning courses that use digital content, students learn up to five times more than conventional courses. This is due to online courses offering students control on their learning, and they can function at their respective pace. Students usually work much faster than otherwise, and they take in more details. They are pushed quicker through contents, of course, in which they are relaxed but slower in those they need to spend.

2. **Online learning always requires a smaller investment of time.**

Regardless of the time commitment it would take, most students put off in enrolling in a conventional course. It usually includes time to commute between school and home, plus the waiting period for students and tutors. A study by Brandon Hall on eLearning inside companies found that this learning method usually takes 40-60 percent less time for workers than learning through a conventional classroom environment. It is important to remember that eLearning choices typically permit students to divide the amount of time they spend in their course in whatever way it works best. Students do not have to commit huge amounts of time on their course. It will work out fine, even setting half an hour per day from their daily routine.

3. **With online learning, the retention rates of education are higher.**

Most of the conventional offline courses struggle to keep students through the course.

The American Research Institute found that that is not the case with eLearning. Virtual courses have now raised retention rates of students from a mere 25% to a staggering 60%.

This has been proposed that more interactive content of multimedia, more flexibility over how it incorporates into the material of course, and less probability clashing of classes all contribute to the growth.

4. **The Greener Choice is eLearning.**

Virtual learning is the most convenient choice for students and also safer for the environment. The Open University in Britain has found that online courses are equal to an average of above 80 percent less electricity and 85 percent less CO2 emitted per student as conventional courses cause more CO2 emission in individuals. This makes online learning and digital content an even more productive form of education. Promoting and participating in this form of learning will help the individuals and companies do their part for the environment and stay committed to their respective goals.

5. **More regular appraisals can reduce distractions.**

Some of the best things about online courses are that assessment can become something of an ongoing operation. This is a piece of positive news for students as interspersing digital content and learning materials will boost student interaction with daily short tests. In reality, Harvard research found that using these brief, daily tests half distracted students, tripled note-taking, and improved overall content retention. It should also be remembered that the students are also human. Sometimes, due to depression and anxiety, they often choose suicide so tutors can keep track of problematic students without them knowing it will be an online lecture. Improved monitoring of students ensures that tutors will step in as soon as students need assistance.

3.2 Scheduling a Class

Teachers can conveniently arrange a meeting for each of their class sessions by conducting online classes in Zoom, and they have their Zoom rooms. This subchapter will lead them through the scheduling process and the start of class sessions in Zoom.

Each Zoom user at their respective educational institute has its dedicated meeting space. (If their institute has approached Zoom or bought the subscription for the institute), and the ability to set up a customized URL for their personal space that is easy to remember. They will use their meeting room to hold the meetings they schedule and for sessions not planned.

To build a meeting place

Click Personal Meeting Room in the toolbar over the top of the page to go to the settings for the user's personal meeting place or room. Your room settings will load. Scroll to the bottom of the page to initiate the process required to change user settings, and press Edit this meeting.

Options for the "Edit Meeting" will load. The user can change settings they need to modify depending on their class needs.

Select Profile in Navigation menu on the left side of the page to edit the personalized path to your meeting place.

Look up "listing" for the user's link in the profile options. To edit the link, click "Customize" situated on the right side of the user's URL, and type what the user wants for their custom link. (Personal URL suggestions is to use the user's educational institute's username or anything easy for other people to remember).

Now that the user is done updating their custom URL, press Save Changes will save the respective changes to the system.

Scheduling any Meeting

The user will need to sign in to Zoom for the process to start arranging a meeting.

Once a user is signed in, they will be taken to Zoom's Meetings screen. To start a new meeting, click the Schedule of a New Meeting on the upper left of the page.

The schedule will show a Meeting option. Users can fill the required information for their meeting here, such as topics of the meeting, a description of the meeting, and change in another setting as needed.

Teachers will want to arrange a weekly meeting to hold class sessions online. After they have set the time and date for the first meeting, the user should also check the checkbox for recurrence options for meeting in the Recurring Session. For example, they can set the recurrence to Weekly for such a class that meets on Tuesdays and Fridays, and the user should use checkboxes for Tuesday and Friday.

Once the settings have been adjusted as needed, press on the Save button to save the meeting. You will be taken to the Detailed page of the meeting. You can find the link for the meeting on this very page.

This link may be shared with students as needed. Also, teachers can share out additional information for the Zoom session. Teachers may want the link to be added to their Canvas course and send it to their students by email.

Startup any meeting from the desktop application Zoom

Note: Screenshots have been taken on PC; the interface on the macOS device should be identical. The Zoom graphical user interface (GUI) can also look subtly different from the screenshots, depending on the iteration of Zoom you are using.

To start any conference using the Zoom desktop program, sign in your account via the Zoom first, if necessary.

In the end:

Open the app to Zoom in.

The dialogue box for the Cloud Meetings opens, and click Sign In.

Tap Sign in with SSO.

In the text box "Type user's company domain," type the name of the organization whatever it is, and press Continue.

Type your username ID and password on the log in panel and press Sign in.

You will be prompted to open your window by clicking on the Zoom Meetings.

The dialogue box "Pro Account" appears by clicking on the Meetings icon.

The list of the meetings that the user arranged will show up:

To pick the meeting the user wishes to launch, click on the meeting list on the left panel of the Zoom window. The specifics of the meeting will show up on the right side of the frame.

Press on the Start button to enable the online meeting.

Zoom's new window will open, and the meeting will begin.

3.3 Inviting Students

Inviting others while in a meeting

1. Sign in on PC, Zoom Desktop application.
2. Users will get the option to either join or start a meeting.
3. Click on Participants icon in-meeting controls.

4. Tap on Invite that is shown at the bottom of the participant's panel.
5. Select any of the invite options available:

Email

1. Press the Email icon.
2. Select your email provider:

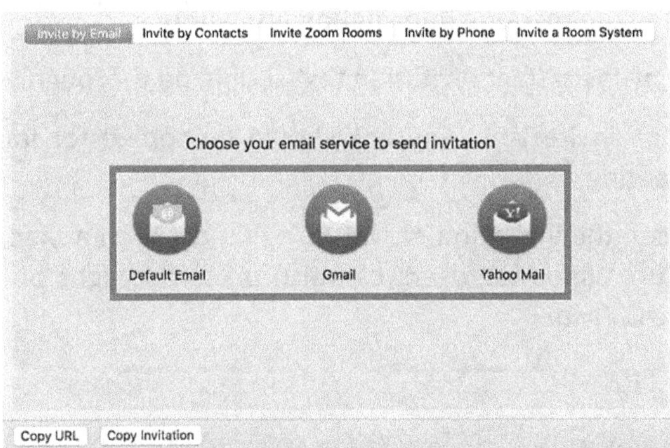

- The Default Email: Using the user's default email to invite others.
- Yahoo mail or Gmail: Invite others using the Yahoo or Gmail website. Users will be shown a message to sign in into their respective accounts.

- Do note that a new email automatically will be created with the information about the meeting in the email body.

3. Add recipients and send the email to recipients.

Contacts

1. Click the next tab, which is the Contacts tab.
2. Select search for a contact or name of the person from the window shown on screen.
3. Click on the name of the individual user you want to invite. Multiple contacts can be selected. Once it is done, their name(s) will be highlighted in color blue and will appear at the list, situated at the top of the window.
4. On the bottom right corner, click Invite.

Invitation text or URL

Click on Copy Invitation or Copy link to invite if the user wants to send their immediate meeting information elsewhere.

- Copy Invitation: invitation text should be thoroughly copied.
- Copy Invite Link: The link should be copied for joining the meeting.
- Paste the invitation or URL using Cmd + V on a Mac or Ctrl + V on Windows. Users can also press the right button and press Paste.

Inviting other users to any scheduled meeting

It is also entirely possible to invite others and schedule meetings before even starting the actual meeting.

The Desktop client

1. Sign in to Zoom Desktop Application /Client.
2. Then schedule a meeting.
3. Click on the Meetings icon.

4. Select a meeting that others should be invited to. Then press Copy Invitation.

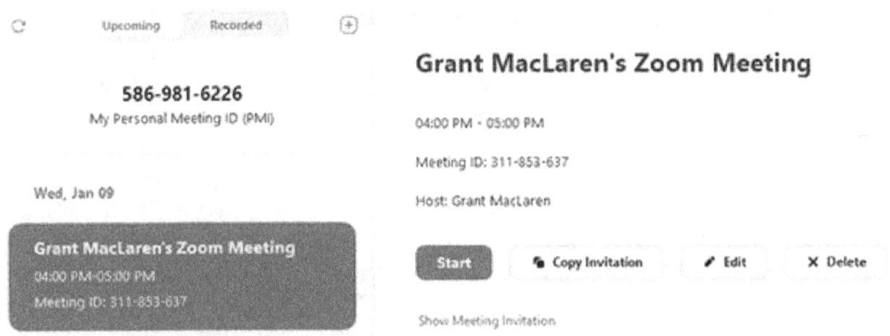

A meeting invitation is going to be copied, and then the user can send that information through an email to anyone so that they join the meeting.

Web portal

1. First, Sign-in in the web portal of Zoom.
2. Select the navigation menu, press on, meeting icon.
3. Press on the option of "topic of the meeting."

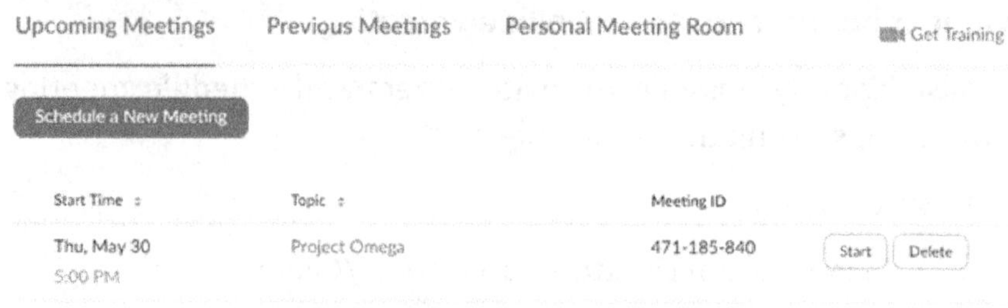

4. Next to the icon of the time, there is an option to add things or tasks to the calendar.

- If the user clicks on Yahoo Calendar or Google Calendar, the calendar event will be created automatically in the email service chosen by the user.
- If the user selects Outlook Calendar, a.ICS file will be generated to import to their Outlook calendar.

5. The user is also able to manually replicate the information about the meeting by pressing the Copy Invitation icon.

- If the user clicks "Copy Invitation," a new window will pop up with the invitation text for the meeting.
- Click on Copy for Meeting Invitation.
- The user can replicate the invitation and can send it through email.

3.4 Delivering a Lesson Over Zoom

Before moving on to delivering lectures on Zoom, practice it beforehand. Some simple instructions when delivering the lectures as a teacher are as follows: Check video and audio that they are working. Make sure your face has a light, and the source of light is not behind you. Also, make sure that the screen is free from distractions. Users should practice looking at their webcam when they are presenting and not the computer screen. Use screen sharing feature of Zoom.

Review controls on your host and settings for the meeting. Determine if you should have other hosts, mute attendees' microphones (recommended for sizeable meetings or can be done for students and they can ask a question via chat box), or record the session to use at later stages.

User as a teacher should make slides or discuss the questions which are accessible through Canvas, etc. Do this in advance so that if screen sharing does not work, students can easily access the important content. Anticipate possible obstacles, including the risk that students do not have perfect communications and not listen and watch anything. Use the feature of screen sharing to display your slides or screen while you are talking, e.g., slides on PowerPoint are being discussed in the lecture, so screen shares those and continue to elaborate them.

Present a schedule from the beginning of the lecture to let students know exactly what they will gain from the online lecture. Narrate the content you are visually showing on the screen. Just like you would read content out aloud in the class, only, in this case, students can completely see the important text, read screen content that the user shares on the screen.

Post questions that need to be discussed on the slides, so students suffering from a poor Internet connection, frequent disconnections, or who fail to hear audio can see these. Use the chat tool for communication with the students regularly during meetings. Speak at the start of the lecture (session) to address technical problems if the teacher has access to a TA willing to help the class with the instruction and with technical assistance, which can also respond to the students in the chatbox with troubleshooting tips. Also, monitor the chat to find queries of students and areas of concern or uncertainty for the students. Assign TA to monitor the chat for larger groups, and ensure you deal with relevant questions and feedback. Particularly in smaller lectures, it might be worth asking some students to assume some important roles like "chat monitors" for voice if questions arise that are overlooked by the teacher(host).

As a teacher, try to engage in conversation with the students. You can do this by discontinuing a lecture to ask questions from the students and encourage them to comment or answer to find out whether they are paying their undivided attention in the class or not. "Call on" the students to clarify with a text statement or a question.

To make the classroom interactions more exciting and involve the students in active learning, the teachers should use collaboration tools.

Use the Zoom polling tool to gather feedback from students, and then exchange results with students both online and in-person. Use of breakout rooms for helping students converse in smaller classes, much as in a broader class setting, they would do breakout classes. As the coach, when it is time to regroup, the user can visit different breakout rooms, relay messages to different rooms to end the sessions.

Consider asking students to work together as a group, to make collaborative Google Doc as a broad group or split groups.

Call on the students to cooperate through Zoom as they can hold study sessions on it in groups. Students, including professors, can use the Zoom to present in the synchronous meeting in real-time or to film presentations on a video to share through Zoom by using the screen-sharing feature.

3.5 Setting up an Assignment or Discussion Board

Instructors can set up an Assignment or Discussion Board in all courses, allowing students to add or upload a file. Sadly, large recording files may take up too much room in the Canvas course, or the submission region of the student's Canvas file.

Canvas has an exceptional resource for Zoom recordings that will ensure that students can keep their quota of files to a minimum. The feature is known as the Media Record / Upload method. It will allow students to upload 500 MB files to Canvas without limiting either the course or the students.

Setting up an Assignment or Discussion board post with these resources and letting them know the correct way to apply is particularly important for the teacher.

Do not test the "File Uploads" box when setting up your assignment as the students will take up much of the course room. Alternatively, you can allow the "Record / Upload Files" feature to prevent large files for your task.

If the user copies Assignments from previous classes, they will also need to change them. Configure your Canvas Assignment according to the screenshot below to ensure proper submission of a Zoom image.

3.6 Recording a Zoom Class

It can be incredibly profitable to schedule, prepare, and deliver a digital course, but it also requires much input in energy and time. Teachers include their course material; it is highly customized, but recording all this in videos is a very strenuous and time-consuming task for online content creators, even for veterans.

To show your audience that you are serious in assisting them, you'll need to make a professional course video, and this turns out to be tricky if they have to learn about technology. The only positive news there is; is that there is a device that can be used by anyone to help them: Zoom in.

Zoom, as a company, has something called "Freemium." It ensures that the user is as long as you can use other elements of Zoom and not spend a cent as long as the user goes with less than 40 minutes' rule. Other aspects of the software are paid options, such as webinars.

Phase 1-Sign up.

Proceed to the Zoom website on the browser and click on the blue icon at the top right, which says to Sign Up, It is Free. Some restrictions are in place, but meetings under 40 minutes are free.

Phase 2-Scheduling a meeting.

The user needs first to Sign in and pick the Dashboard meeting schedule.

Write down the name of the user's video on the next page, and press Save at the bottom panel of the page.

Do not worry about other available options, as the user will start by setting up the tools necessary for recording the video and start shooting it.

Click Start the Session. If you do not have a Zoom application on the desktop already, the user should download it.

If you are not ready, do not worry as when users click 'File,' nothing will be registered.

Phase 3-Setting up User's Documentation and Equipment.

Users will see the control panel next for their meeting.

Users can start the set up by preparing their microphone and enabling their camera by pressing the 'Start Video' button (if you have it).

> Make sure user is prepared with their notes and other documentation that they wanted to share on their video before they hit record.

Consider turning off computers, alerts, and everything not needed as that will cause annoying background noise.

Phase 4-Begin Recording the Video.

The user's camera and microphone are ready and in place, and now it is time to screen-share the video through your computer.

Click the Sharing icon situated on the control panel, pick the folder user wants to be on their video. Customize the paper to fit inside the boundary of the outline, which is green in color. Notice that at the bottom panel of the screen, the control panel is minimized for when it is needed.

Calm your nerves down by taking a few breaths, and when the user feels ready, they can start by clicking the button for the record.

Take ample time and do not rush through. Stop if you need input, and use already prepared notes.

Once you have your document registered, go to the control panel situated at the screen's bottom, and select the option for more and Recording Start.

On completion, go to the menu of the control panel, pick End Meeting, or the option to finish the meeting for all.

Phase 5-Save the Picture

Zoom can entirety convert the whole meeting into a recording, and the user will be shown the Zoom screen folder (desktop folder) where users can see that their recording is saved for them in both Audio and MP4 files.

Phase 6-Edit the Video (optional)

If they are kept short and with a clear picture, then editing the videos is not necessary. Many people make entire videos in one go without facing any problems whatsoever. When the user finds it essential that they need editing or remove parts of their images, though, the user will require other tools that are outside of the Zoom platform. Most free video software programs, such as HitFilm Express, VSDC, iMovie, or VideoPad, can easily get the editing done.

The option of the automatic recording provided by Zoom enables the user to start cloud recording or local recording automatically at the start of the meeting.

Whether host joins, mobile devices, telephone dial-ups, or Automatic computer, cloud-recording will start regardless of the option selected by the host to join the scheduled meeting, given that enough space for cloud recording is available. The local recording option will be automatically available to use when the user (acting as host with administrative right) joins through the desktop application of Zoom.

Turning ON, Automatic Recording

To start the feature known as, Automatic Recording for organization and its member:

1. Sign as an administrator into a web portal of Zoom; it allows the user to edit the Account settings, and then click on the Account Settings.
2. Go to the Recording tab and check that Settings for Automatic Recording is enabled.

- In case of it being disabled, press on the Status toggle to activate it. A verification dialogue will likely be displayed; select the Turn On option to confirm the change.

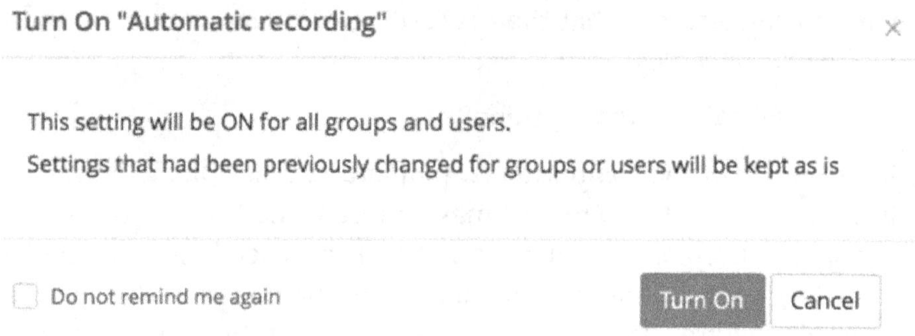

3. Select an option to record in the cloud or record on the local computer and press Save.

4. The setting for Automatic Recording can be made compulsory for all the available users in the account, press on the lock icon, then again press Lock to accept the setting so they can be saved.

Note: Owners and Account Admins can disable the feature of Cloud recording downloads through the Account Settings page.

To Activate the Feature of Automatic Recording for any Specific Group

1. As an administrator, sign in to the web portal of Zoom, it grants administrative rights for editing User group, press on Group Management to proceed.

2. Go to the name of a particular group, and then press on the Settings tab.
3. Go to the Recording tab to verify that the setting for Automatic Recording is enabled.

- Suppose it is disabled, press the “status toggle” to turn it on. If verification dialogue pops up, select the option of Turn On; you can save such a change.

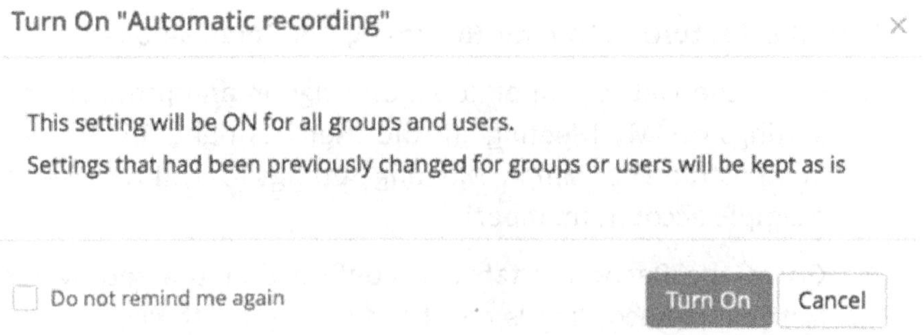

4. Select options to record on the local computer or Record in the cloud and then click to Save.

5. The user can make the Automatic Recording setting compulsory for all the members in the group, first press the lock icon, and then press Lock to confirm and save the setting.

To Start this Feature Automatic Recording, for Personal Use

1. Go to the web portal of Zoom and sign in and press on the settings of “My Meeting” (if the user has rights of account administrator) or simply Meeting Settings (only if the user is a simple account member).
2. Go to the Recording tab and confirm that the setting for Automatic Recording is on. If the setting is off, click on the Status toggle for enabling it.

Note: If Status toggle shows up greyed out, then it is locked, either at the Account level or group, then Zoom administrator needs to change the settings.

3. Select options to record and save on a local computer, or Record in the cloud and Save, to change the settings.

Note: If the user has turned on or enabled automatic recording in their Meeting Settings, that will be set and saved for any number of meetings that the user's schedule is going forward too. It is not going to apply to all the existing meetings or their ID of Personal Meeting. Users will have to activate it for such meetings individually.

Setting the Automatic Recording, Individual Meeting

If the user does not wish to enable the feature for all meetings of automatic recording, they can disable it for the individual meetings. They can also enable it for a personal meeting, and this setting on at the group, user level, or account level is not needed.

To Control Setting of Automatic Recordings, Specific Meeting

1. Select My meeting.
2. Press Schedule a (Zoom) Meeting or simply select the topic for meeting from the list available for Upcoming Meetings, then press on Edit Meeting option.

The user should note that they can select their PMI by pressing on the tab.

3. Under the Meeting Options, press on the record meeting automatically.
4. Click Save.

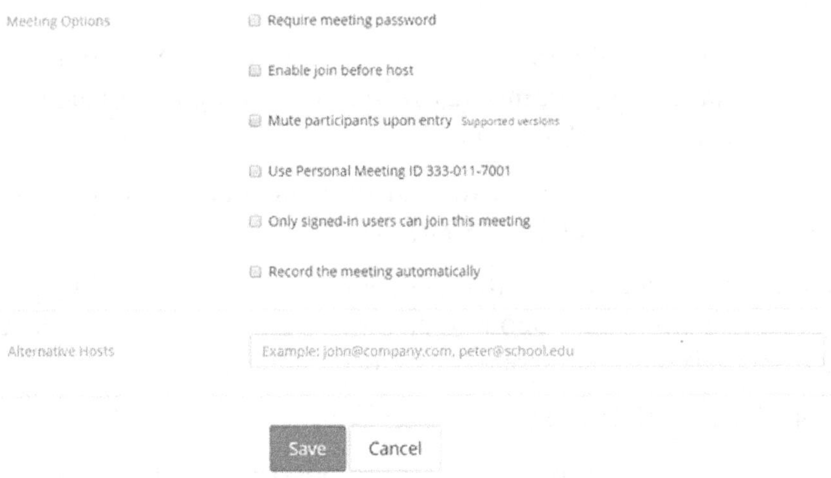

3.7 Virtual Instructions

Virtual Instruction is a course taught online or face-to-face, such as Blackboard and other course management systems. Digital learning requires the delivery of class materials to students in digital form.

The Virtual Background function allows the user to display an image or video during a Zoom Meeting as your backdrop. With a uniform lighting and green screen, this feature works best to allow Zoom to detect the difference between user and their surroundings. Users can add images or videos of their own as a virtual backdrop. They can also use a Zoom Room with Virtual History.

Zoom suggests using a solid background color, ideally green, to achieve the best virtual background effect. Better quality cameras result in a better backdrop to the interactive session.

Using Light and Standard Lighting Techniques

Do not wear a dress that is of the same color as the virtual context. View at the context.

There are no size limitations when adding your virtual backgrounds, but before uploading, Zoom suggests that users crop the image that suits their camera's aspect ratio.

If the user's camera is set to a ratio of 16:9, the picture will fit better with 1920 by 1080 pixels or 1280 by 720 pixels.

Use a background picture with a minimum resolution of 1280 by 720 pixels, if you are unsure about your camera aspect ratio. Use those sites for royalty-free photos: Pexels, Unsplash, Pixabay.

Enabling a Virtual Context

Note: Users must sign out of the Zoom Desktop Client and sign in again to be influenced by Virtual Backgrounds.

Accounting

To allow all users in the account to have Virtual Background feature:

1. Sign in as an administrator to the web portal with the permission to change account settings.
2. Click Account Management and then Account Settings in the navigation menu.
3. Navigate to the Virtual Background option (under the Advanced section of in Meeting) in the Meeting tab, and verify that setting is enabled.

Note: If the setting is deactivated, press the allow toggle. Select Turn On to check the adjustment when a verification dialogue appears.

4. (Optional) Click on the lock icon to make this setting automatic for all the users of your account, and then press Lock to confirm the setting.
5. (Optional) Click Manage virtual background to upload user-friendly, default background images.

Note: To display the background photos you are uploading; users must have client/app version 5.1.1 or greater.

3.8 Using Different Zoom App Features for Teaching

Zoom comes preloaded with many useful features that help in a virtual classroom, and they are accommodating for both teachers and students. Some of the features are as follow:

The view of the gallery and the speaker

Zoom provides its user with two options: the gallery view and the speaker's view. The user can switch between these two distinct modes by pressing on the top right of the toggle. Speaker view, it is a default option that displays a broad picture of the speakers that are active when the user starts a meeting. The view of the gallery shows all participants of the same size. It is suggested to use the gallery while teaching to track your students better during real-time while teaching.

Avoiding noise in the background

Make sure everyone remains quiet. Students will mute themselves, the same way as the user mutes himself, but as acting as a host, the user has the power to mute all the participants as well.

If a student forgets to mute himself or is very young and cannot be trusted with controls, the user can silence him in gallery mode by hovering its pointer over the student's video feed. Here the user will see a blue button for mute. Also, the user can unmute the students.

Hand lift

Zoom gives the students a way to lift their hands digitally. To expand the panel of participants, students can press the 'Participants' button. There is a button called "raise hand" at the bottom panel of this screen. Students may use that option to get the attention of the teacher when muted; this function works surprisingly well for large parts. If the user places pointer on their feed in the gallery mode, the user will see the option to lower a student's hand.

Remove one student

The hold function acts similarly to a virtual timeout, which should be used simply as a measure of last resort. This will throw the student off the meeting before you want to grant them success to join the meeting again. Those students will have a view of the blank screen showing the message "waiting for the host (user) to let you back in." Users can view the option for a hold by placing the pointer over the name of the student on the option Manage Participants and by pressing the "more" icon.

Disallow students to change the name

Zoom highly suggests using setting to avoid learners or students from editing their respective Zoom titles. Users can click on the "More" drop-down menu from the Manage Participants screen and by unchecking the setting "Allow Participants (students) to rename (editing of titles) themselves" to disallow students to change their names in the meeting.

Please note this update is stored in the Zoom desktop app, so the user would not need to update it every time you visit.

Functions of Zoom for Practical Instruction

Chatting email

You can use the chatbox, which is accessed from the last panel of the computer screen, to send chat messages during class. Users can monitor how the attendees use this feature by selecting whom to chat with while the lecture is ongoing from the dropdown menu "More." Another feature there present is of the group, by default. You can opt to restrict learners to talk with the host, only you. Or, the user can select the option of "No-one" to disable chat entirely. There is no one on one student chat option available, so the user does not have to fret over private messages between students while teaching the online class.

Annotating

Zoom also lets you annotate when sharing a computer. It helps the user to make the class more engaging, as the user can draw arrows directly on PowerPoint, highlight difficult words in posts, and other helpful things for the students to follow the material along. You will see the option of annotation at the top panel of the screen while sharing the screen. It also gives students access to the same tools for annotation.

Clicking on the "More" dropdown situated on top of the screen will allow the user to adjust the setting for annotations. It will require the user to:

Disable / Enable Students Annotation: It can be helpful when students are distractingly using annotation devices.

Show / Hide Annotator Names: When you have several learners annotated on the shared computer screen, the user can swing over an annotation to view which student has generated it.

Breakout Spaces

Zoom provides teachers with a way to split students into multiple video rooms independent of one another, for discussion about the activities or other work in the group.

Among all the Zoom features, two features are most important, namely whiteboard and Screen Sharing.

- **Using Whiteboard**

The most useful tool for teachers is Whiteboard, as it acts as a board for teachers to write and draw something for students. If many illustrations are involved, then it is better that teachers also use any cheap graphic tablet with it as it makes it easier to write and draw on the Whiteboard.

1. Click the Sharing Screen button in the menu bar while you are at an active Zoom Meeting.

2. Press on the Whiteboard, and tap share.

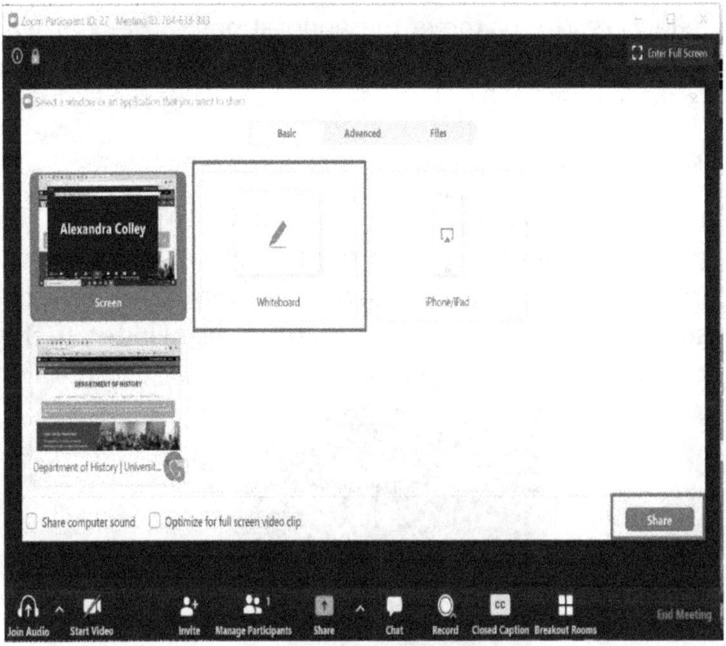

4. At the bottom of the page on the right side are situated page controls, use them to switch between multiple pages, and to create pages.

5. To annotation tools, use the toolbar. Clicking on Whiteboard will cause the taskbar to disappear. Tap on the Whiteboard again to put it back up.

- Select: resize, or move the annotations if the user wants to select many annotations at an instance, press and drag the pointer to display the selection area.
- Text: to Insert the text.
- Draw: arrows, shapes, and Insert lines. To highlight the area of a whiteboard or shared screen, select the following circle or square icon; it is for inserting a semi-transparent circle or square. It will function even like a highlighter if the user changes the color to yellow for format.

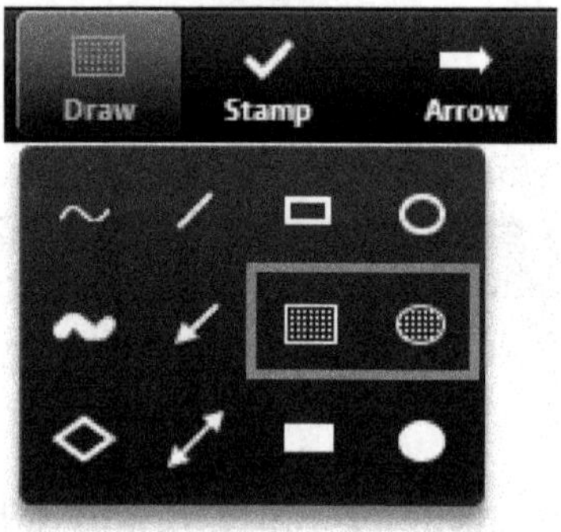

- Stamp: Insert the predefined icons such as star or checkmark.
- Spotlight / Arrow: Press the Spotlight icon to select the two available options for switching the user's cursor into an arrow or spotlight.
  - Spotlight: It shows all participants your mouse cursor when the user's mouse is inside the shared region. You are using this to direct students on the screen to different parts, like an electronic laser pointer.
  - Arrow: To show an arrow in place of Mouse, the cursor id displays a simple arrow. Press to place an arrow that will reveal your name. Every corresponding click would remove the arrow that was put before. You may use this particular feature to draw students' attention to your annotations.

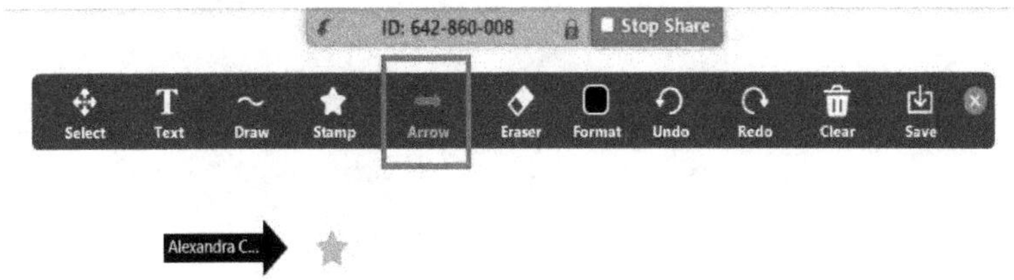

- Eraser: To erase different parts of the user's annotation, press and drag the erase icon.
- Format: To change the options available for annotations tools such as line width, font, and color.
- Clear: All annotations will be deleted. The user can select to delete students' annotations or their annotations. To delete simply one annotation, use your pointer to select it and simply use the eraser tool or press delete on the keyboard.
- Save: It will save all the annotations shown on the present screen as a screenshot. This screenshot is sent to the local (PC storage) recording location.

5. When the user is done, simply press Stop Share.

  - **Screen Sharing**

Perhaps Zoom is the most useful teaching tool. Screen sharing lets learners see what is on their display. It could include a PowerPoint slideshow, a website, a video, or something entirely different on a computer that would prove useful to the class.

Zoom also provides an interactive whiteboard as a screen-sharing tool, which can be very useful for multiple groups. To show your screen, click on the green button at the bottom of your Zoom window and select the option you wish to share. Please note: if you are interested in sharing a video with students, check the "Use Computer Audio Checkbox" at the bottom left of the window screen. Otherwise, the recording will be registered as background noise on your side and will not be sent to class.

Chapter 4: Guide for Students to Use Zoom Effectively

For students to use Zoom effectively, there are some guidelines and especially some etiquettes since they are still students, whether they are studying online or in the classic physical class. Some of the etiquettes that students must follow in the digital class are as follows:

Proper clothing is necessary

Students should realize that their professors and colleagues will SEE them even though they might be at home alone. Students can attend the meeting in pajamas or trouser, but they should be looking presentable because they have to appear in front of their teachers. Put some clean shirt on. Have a brush run through the hair, clean the teeth and look presentable and even put body spray even if teachers cannot detect you in the online class, but it is an excellent habit and common hygiene.

Be conscious of the surroundings

Your teacher and classmates will see what is BEHIND too. Ensure there is nothing the background that can detract you as a student from the digital class (unkempt bed, laundry pile, etc.). Although attending class from their messy bedroom is not always the best option, it entirely possible that the place is such that the user may be able to find some quiet time and peace away from family members or roommates. If such is the issue, the user may use a Virtual Backdrop to mask what they do not want their peers to see.

Mute is necessary

When logging into the virtual online classroom, make sure to mute the student's microphone (bottom left corner).

It would help minimize background noise capable of disrupting anyone.

Always raise the hand and wait for the professor

If students wish to chat, they should either lift their hands physically or use the "Raise Hand" icon in the middle at the bottom of their screen. If the teacher has called you, unmute and start speaking or ask your question. When students have finished asking the question, show that you are done using some phrase something along the lines of "thank you " or "that's it," and then stop using the microphone by muting it.

Better to remain quiet than to say anything not useful

The feature of Zoom Chat is a convenient tool for commenting and asking important questions without even interrupting the host or speaker but always be mindful that comments in chat are public for the group and also registered in the session minutes. As almost all the users most likely have learned back in the kindergarten in their first-ever classic physical classroom that "If you have nothing good to say, then they should remain silent. Suppose they do not have anything important to say, they should maintain the decorum of the classroom.

4.1 Check Equipment before Joining a Class

If the user has not allowed machine audio to enter the setting automatically, you can test your speaker and microphone before they enter a meeting or conference:

Select Test Microphone and Speaker after the user enters a group.

The conference shows a pop-up window to test the speakers. If the ringtone is not heard, use the drop-down button, or press No to switch speakers before hearing the ringtone. To begin the microphone test, similarly, press the icon of yes.

If you are not listening to an audio replay, use the drop-down menu or press No to turn microphones, but if you hear the replay, press Yes.

Select Machine Audio to Join.

Click Join Machine Audio to access the microphone and speakers selected for the testing.

Check Audio Setup

Navigate to your audio settings in Zoom application before or after a meeting to test your audio:

During a conference

Sign in to your Zoom account.

Tap on the image of your profile, then tap on Settings.

Tap the audio tab.

To test your microphone or speaker, press the tab test mic or test speaker.

At a Meeting

When you are already in a conference, you can access your audio settings and test your audio.

Click the arrow next to Unmute/mute in the controls of the meeting.

Tap Options to Audio. This opens up your audio controls.

Test the Spokesperson.

To play a test tone, press the Test speaker command.

If you cannot hear it, pick another speaker from the menu, or change the volume.

User's Microphone Test

In the Microphone area, when Zoom picks up the audio, you will see the green Input Level bar rise.

To test the microphone, press the Test Button.

Your recording will start on your audio. When you are done, press recording, and it will playback. From the menu, you can pick another microphone or change the level of input.

Check adjustments for the microphone settings automatically if you want Zoom to change the input volume automatically.

Troubleshooting Microphone

If the user works on macOS 10.14 and has problems regarding the microphone, the user needs to check system permissions to check whether Zoom has been granted access to use the microphone in the operation system.

If the user is on the famed and most widespread OS of them all, the Windows 10, and cannot reach the microphone, use the Windows search box to navigate to privacy settings for your microphone. Turn on the Allow applications to access your microphone toggle, and allow it the Zoom access.

4.2 Using Chat Options to Ask Questions

Another approach is by using the chat feature to ask questions or make comments. Click the "Chat" button to open the chat window to send a Chat message.

You may use the drop-down menu in the chat window to select whether to give the message to everyone or the instructor.

Recall being respectful and professional this way when asking questions or making remarks. Anyone, host or participant, can save the chat at any time as a text file, so do not type something that you later regret on.

The chat feature helps webinar attendees, hosts, co-hosts, and panelists to connect over the webinar's length.

Participants can communicate with anyone in the meeting, but only the host can modify the settings.

As a webinar attendant, you can chat with other guests, panelists (including the moderator), depending on what webinar moderator chat permissions are enabled. Learn about all monitoring guests.

Click or tap chat in your controls at the foot of the page.

The Chat window will appear when you click on chat. If you are not on the full screen, it will be on the top. If you are in the full screen, a preview that you can pass around your computer will pop up.

Type your message and press Submit it to Join.

By clicking on the drop-down next to To, you can also pick who you want to send it.

The User will receive a notification at the bottom of his screen when they get a chat message if the chat window is not open at that time.

If the host has Attendee chat disabled, messages sent by the host and other panelists will still be viewable.

4.3 Delivering Assignments through File Sharing

Students can easily deliver assignments they get from their online classes through a file-sharing feature present in the Zoom. It makes it possible for teachers to handout questions and assignments to students in online classes, so that they can easily practice and apply what is being taught in the online virtual classroom. They can share the file by following the given procedure:

Enable file transfer in-meeting

- First, go to the account and log in.
- To allow the transfer of files to all members of your organization in-meeting:
- Log in as an administrator to the web portal of Zoom with the right to change the account settings.
- Press on the Account Management and then Account Settings in the navigation menu.

- Use the Meeting tab to navigate to the File Transfer option and verify that the setting. Allow the settings so that the students can share and deliver the assigned files.
- If the setting is turned off, press the Allow Status toggle. Select Turn On to check the adjustment when a verification dialogue appears.

This step is completely optional; press on the lock icon to make the setting compulsory for all the users of your account, and then press Lock for confirming the setting.

For the group

- To allow the transfer of the in-meeting file for all the members of a particular group:
- First, Log in as an administrator to the Zoom application's web portal to edit classes.
- Click on User Management, then Community Management in the Navigation menu.
- Click on the group name, and then click on the Settings tab.
- Use the Settings tab to navigate to the feature of File Transfer and check its option to verify that setting is allowed.
- If the setting is turned off, press the Allow Status toggle. Select Turn On to check the adjustment when a verification dialogue appears.

Users should note that if the option is greyed out or cannot be clicked, it is locked at the level of the account and needs changing at such a stage to allow that option to be used.

This step is completely discretionary; press on the lock icon to make such settings compulsory for all the users in the community or the group, and then press the Lock icon to confirm the setting.

For the User

To allow the transfer of the in-meeting file for your use:

- Log in to the web portal for the Zoom.
- Press Settings.
- Use the Meeting tab to navigate to the File Transfer option and verify the setting is allowed.
- If the setting is disabled, press the Allow Status toggle. Select Turn On to check the adjustment when a verification dialogue appears.

Users can detect if the options are greyed out, then either the Account or Community level has been locked, and they need to contact their Zoom administrator.

It is possible to restrict the types of files which can be exchanged.

For security purposes, the file extensions/file types that can be exchanged through file transfer may be restricted by the account owner or an account admin.

Log in as an administrator to the Zoom web portal with the luxury of changing account settings.

- Click Account Management in the Navigation menu then IM Management.
- Tap the Settings tab for IM.
- Navigate to Option for File Transfer.
- Enable Allow specified types of files only.
- Enter the approved file types/extensions, with each extension separated by a comma.
- Press Save.

No file transfer through in-meetings

- Press on the Chat icon during a Zoom Conference.
- Pick More, and pick the Share file option to submit a file in the meeting.

If the file is successfully submitted, then a sign will be shown, which means it is uploaded. When a file is submitted, the participants will see a note, and the option to download the file will be given. They will be able to access the file until Download is selected.

4.4 Record Presentations Using Zoom

User can easily share their screencasts or presentations using the Zoom application. Users may share or send the cloud-recording connection to their Canvas task.

At first, the user needs to build a Zoom account even to use Zoom.

When they have their account, they will certainly be "planning a meeting." Think of the meeting in this case as their show, or screencast, but for students, it will be their virtual classroom where they will send their presentation.

Next, the user will "start the meeting." Again, they just open the application to record your presentation.

Students will want to share their computer screens to display their presentation slides after opening the Zoom program. In the foot of the page is a "Share" tab. At last, they will follow the cloud recording instructions to record their presentation for their class. This will allow the user to retrieve a shareable link to their presentation.

4.5 Schedule Meeting for Group Discussion

It is important to schedule the meetings first as spontaneously everyone cannot be available for the meetings or group discussions. So meetings must be prepared beforehand so everyone, including teachers and students, can create the time or free time from their schedule to make it possible for them to attend the online classes, making it possible for the group discussions.

How to schedule Zoom Meetings with someone else?

1. Download Applications for Zoom Client and Outlook Plugin:

• ITS tagged PC: Zoom installs via Software Center.

• ITS-Tagged Mac: Zoom installs via Self Service.

• Non-tagged device: Install, Zoom via their web site.

2. Make sure that you have usual delegate access to the Outlook calendar for the other person to schedule the conference.

3. Make sure you are in Zoom with Schedule Privilege (delegate access). The individual you want to meet or hold the meeting with.

Users will need to schedule a meeting to delegate their Privilege Schedule. They will log in to their Zoom account.

Press on the "Meeting Settings" in their Zoom account, and then scroll down to the section.

Select the "Privilege plan," and then press Add to add your name.

The privileges go right here in Zoom.

4. Open a calendar of that person in Outlook.

a. Timing a new meeting.

b. After timing, press the "Meeting Schedule" button at the top of the window.

* Note * If the user clicks on the Meeting Schedule button and they are not in the meeting of that person.

Invite, you are going to send it out as yourself.

The choices on the invite appear this way:

The meeting it creates will look like this

As a member, the name at the top of the invitation will change the user's name to whoever it is.

Chapter 5: Tips and Tricks to Use Zoom App

Zoom is a platform that has several uses and functions. There are tips and tricks necessary to make it easier for users to utilize correctly.

5.1 Additional Tips for Teachers and Students

Some tips for professors and students to make lecture easy are as follow:

1. The button for the mute

The teacher can easily become agitated when students ignore their lectures, and this situation is far worse in digital classrooms as even if students do not speak. Still, background noise can easily disturb the whole lesson or lecture. So to avoid such problems mute button is there to facilitate teachers and professors so that they can efficiently conduct their class without any disturbance from the students or unwanted background noise from their side. With this mute button or whole feature group, chatter can be silenced at once.

Users can silence participants individually using the option on their video profile or silence them as a group using the "Participants" button at the bottom of the screen in your Zoom toolbar. It is a perfect way to ensure that individual students can talk with others without interference and to maintain the decorum of the class.

2. Making Notes

When viewing your computer, hover your cursor over the top of the screen, and drop down a toolbar. Click "Annotate," and a new menu bar appears. This helps you to highlight, stamp, or write to your shared computer.

3. Disabling "Contributions" for participants

Some students, for fun, like to add annotations to the screen of their teacher, such as smiley faces (or the name of their teacher surrounded by heart-shaped stamps). By the end of their online lesson, the screen is filled with wild annotations while they exchange their screens and unmoving themselves. While encouraging students to share their work and annotate is sometimes astonishing, it is better to verify when and where this occurs.

Muting- Pick the "Mute All" option in "Manage Participants." You will be asked to let the participants unmute. Make sure you deselect this option.

Annotation — Choose the "More" button on the right while sharing a computer. Toggle the option "Allow Attendee Annotation" on and off in the dropdown menu.

Screen Sharing — Disable screen sharing for the attendee via the menu option "Screen Share." Choose "Advanced Sharing Options," and pick "Only Host" from the options for screen sharing.

Turning Videos Off / On — If there are students who are trying to distract the class in the video chat, the choices on your video profile can be used to turn off their videos. If their video is switched off, the user can ask them to restart it too.

4. Tone while coming in and going out

Not everybody has a stable internet connection and, when attendees or students wi-fi cuts out, they will start to disappear during the online lecture. It will also probably take them a very long time to get back into the class, and most of the time, the host or professor will fail to notice their presence since they are gone. Toggling the Enter / Exit chime will let you know when someone leaves to welcome them back to ASAP.

5. Calls during training, and invites to submit

Professors, when starting the online lecture, should always post the invitation link to the channel chat meeting. Usually, it seems to be overlooked by most students, but savvier students can use this connection to hop back into a meeting without any involvement from the professors.

Students should not answer telephone calls during the online lecture. If someone attends a call, they will move somewhere else or log out of the lecture creating huge problems for themselves and their teachers. Instruct your students not to call but instead to send their professor a message.

6. Shortcuts keys

Reduce the mouse faffing time and use a few keyboard shortcuts by allowing them in the menu of the settings.

5.2 Troubleshooting Common Problems

Some common Zoom problems and detail on how they can be fixed:

Audio or Webcam does not function.

Nothing is frustrating than getting a Zoom call running on your monitor with completely no or little audio. If the user's web camera does not show up or it is selected, it still does not work on the Zoom; then the user should try out some of the commonly employed tips.

Just before the user enters a call, Zoom provides two choices that the user can review on the screen that shows a message to the user to get a Zoom meeting ID: Do Not Link to Audio and also Turn Off the video.

If the user wants to enter into a call with automatically activated video and audio, leave those choices unchecked.

If the user web camera does not turn on, the first thing they need is to verify that all webcam related programs that employ webcam are locked. Zoom cannot use the camera or webcam if the user has already provided it in another program.

User can test their video and audio in Zoom by clicking the link for testing meetings provided in Zoom if their camera or audio still isn't working. You can enter the test call on the Zoom application once opened, and follow instructions shown on screen.

The user can also pick their webcam by pressing Start Video (the screen could show Stop Video only if they are in-call) if they have entered the webcam (or just double-check their webcam in the main Zoom app). They can then press the arrow icon next to the video camera button and select the "Same as Device" (or user can see Integrated Monitor) or, more precisely, called webcam from the list if the screen is blank.

Screen video setting

Also, the user may want to download again and reinstall the Zoom application.

The issue may not be due to the Zoom application at all, at times. If the user is on a computer running macOS or Windows 10, the webcam can be blocked. This can be fixed by testing their App permissions to ensure that their web browser or Zoom app can use their camera. You may also verify this configuration directly on the web by restarting their call and making sure they have clicked Allow when asked about the connection to the microphone and camera.

You can check on Windows to see if their webcam is blocked by searching for the webcam in the search box located in the taskbar of the desktop and selecting from the menu the apps that can access your camera.

Scroll down, and the user will see a list of applications enabling them to use their webcam. They will need to make sure that the toggle for Allow Desktop Apps to access their camera is moved to non-Microsoft Store applications. The user may also check for the microphone in the same way, and select Microphone Privacy Settings to do the same.

On macOS, in Device Settings, they will need to select Protection and Privacy, press the lock and enter the password to make adjustments. From the sidebar, users can then push the camera, and check their web browser and Zoom. They will also need to ensure that the microphone box is also tested.

Few laptops also have a physical webcam switch, which has to be activated to make the webcam work properly. Double-check if you have one, that the users are in the correct orientation.

Echoes while calling

Another common issue with Zoom during a meeting is the audio echo. If, during the user's meeting, they tend to hear audio feedback or echo, then there are few potential explanations for the problems.

First and foremost, someone could simultaneously have both machines and telephone audio enabled. In this situation, the user needs to ask them to quit one manually in place of the other. By pressing the up arrow next to the microphone icon and selecting Leave Machine Audio, they would either have to leave the audio or hang up the phone call during the ongoing Session.

Another reason may be that users with telephone or computer speakers can be situated nearby. Finally, there may be several machines in the same conference room with active audio.

You will have to ask the two people who are too close to each other to step apart to overcome one of these other problems. Or simply ask the attendee or student to leave the audio conference on their computer, or mute audio.

Problems with freezing or lagging in Zoom during meetings

Usually, lagging and freezing suggest the issue with the user's internet connection. Try switching to another place with a more secure connection while on a mobile device to see whether this helps.

For a good video chat, you should also strive for good Internet speed. In a team environment, when talking to several people, you want to strive for a download speed of 1Mbps and upload speed of approx. 800kbps. Users can always take a fast internet speed test to verify your current speeds.

By also adjusting their Zoom settings, they can be able to boost the video quality. Disabling HD options, for example, or the Touch Up My Appearance setting, can decrease the amount of bandwidth their video link takes (and the overhead on the hardware of your system), which will help in mitigating lagging issues.

Problems with screen sharing

Sharing your screen is a vital part of many Zoom calls, and is as simple and easy as clicking the bottom of the window on the Share Screen icon.

If the user intends to share their screen during a call, they might need to review a few settings first. Make sure they have a good internet link and are linked to the call. Sharing the computer takes up substantial bandwidth.

Trying a Share Screen meeting first in Zoom, too, is a smart idea. They can do this by unchecking the Start with Video box under the Home section, and then clicking on the down arrow next to the New Meeting option.

Then, their meeting will start with audio conferencing only, freeing up a specific bandwidth, not automatically turning on their video.

If the user is already on a call and needs to share their phone, try turning off their video by pressing on the Stop Video button and then selecting the Sharing Phone green button.

Remote control issues when sharing screens

The person watching the screen will request remote control while sharing the screen to help the user fix their issues or clarify a process more clearly — under View Options is a method to request remote control while sharing the screen. If you want to allow remote control, but it does not work properly, there are a range of potential problems to consider:

The sharer does not consent to the request: A message will appear on their screen, and they will have to select Allow screens to be shared.

The sharer stops the process: Theoretically, by clicking on their mouse, the remote control can be stopped. In practice, people always do something before the user can do something that ends the remote control session. Often advise people to leave their machines alone when the remote control is being initiated.

It is also entirely possible that they may be on the wrong device: For example, iPad and Android devices currently do not allow remote control to be requested or provided.

Zoom Problems of email messages

Another popular issue is not being able to get emails from Zoom. This will include emails to alert and trigger. It typically takes 30 minutes to arrive and can take longer, but if it does not arrive, the user needs to make sure their email is correctly configured.

This is generally not anything on the user's end, so they will need to ask their IT department to whitelist the IP addresses of Zoom's account. User can also search their spam account if they are using a personal email service or a Gmail.

Problems of crashing with Zoom

If Zoom crashes and closes itself completely, the first step of a user should be to check the Zoom Service Status and down detect to see if their area has a regional Zoom problem. Often problems with servers or Zoom doing network maintenance can mean the service will go down for a while, and then the user will have to wait for it to come back up again.

If it does not look regional, it is then recommended that the user try Zoom's web version instead of the app. As long as the user's internet connection is appropriate, the web version appears to be a little more stable; the app has problems.

At last, take a peek at the peripheral settings. Often the audio versus video settings will cause Zoom to get very confused. For example, if you are trying to use your webcam link as an audio source, it will always crash as a consequence. Ensure that video connections are routed to your webcam and that your audio is routed to connected speakers where appropriate.

Zoom bombing

Zoom bombing is the growing fad of entering and disturbing a private meeting with everything from porn to blaring music — and even the courtrooms are not exempt. If a user has been Zoom-bombed in the past, there is one solution that is amazingly successful in preventing it from happening again: a passcode requirement.

The host who creates the meeting and sends out invites may require participants to enter a passcode to join the meeting, meaning outsiders have trouble finding ways to drop in.

In reality, as of the 2020 May update, the default is set to require a password, so all users will need to do is change the Zoom to start using this feature.

If the user is concerned about hacking in more complicated ways, then Zoom has even got that covered. In June 2020, Zoom revealed it would add end-to-end encryption to all meetings and not just paid premium versions to help secure content and avoid more advanced Zoom-bombing versions even while the user is using a free account.

Teaching with Zoom: Conclusion

The purpose of this book is to facilitate the teachers and students by assisting them in how to use Zoom applications for online education as physical classes cannot be conducted due to the global pandemic.

This book deals with the history of Zoom, and the brain behind this project is Eric Yuan. This platform is primarily dedicated to video calling as it allows multiple people in one conference, thus giving a sense of meeting room. This particular application is available on multiple platforms. It has different packages depending on the user needs and demands—also, the subscription cost for the application increases as the limit of participants in one call.

The basic equipment needed to use Zoom is to have a webcam, microphone, and computer with internet access. This platform is available on smartphones, but as this book is for teachers and students, so smartphones are not an excellent tool to study with. This book acts as a guide on how to download Zoom on different platforms and make an account on it. Different features of Zoom are also discussed in various chapters of the book.

Chapter 3 deals with arranging Zoom classes and how teachers can send an invitation to their students to the classroom so that they do not end up compromising their education.

Chapter 4 deals with the basic etiquettes that the students need to follow when attending online lectures.

It also discusses how they can check their equipment before attending the lecture and how the assignments can be shared using the file-sharing feature of Zoom to revise what they learned.

Even students can create presentations on Zoom and deliver them by sharing their PowerPoint presentations through screen sharing option.

The last chapter deals with troubleshooting and common problems while using Zoom and tips and tricks for students and their professors to make this application even easier to use. It has student and business-friendly features.

If you enjoyed this book, please let me know your thoughts by leaving an Amazon review.

I would really love to hear your thoughts!

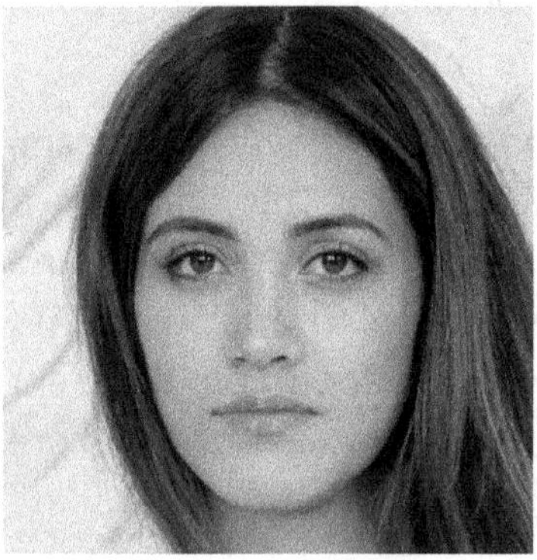

Thank you so much!
-Emily

CPSIA information can be obtained
at www.ICGtesting.com
Printed in the USA
LVHW050330261120
672644LV00012B/497

9 781801 250443